STRESS MANAGEMENT
for Health Care Professionals

Steven H. Appelbaum, Ph.D.

Associate Professor of Management
Faculty of Commerce and Administration
Concordia University
Montreal, Canada

AN ASPEN PUBLICATION®
Aspen Systems Corporation
Rockville, Maryland
Royal Tunbridge Wells

1981

Library of Congress Cataloging in Publication Data

Appelbaum, Steven H.
Stress management for health care professionals.

Includes bibliographies and index.

1. Health facilities—Administration—Psy-
chological aspects. 2. Health services administrators
—Job stress. 3. Medical personnel—Job stress.
4. Organizational behavior. 5. Health facilities—
Personnel management.   I. Title [DNLM: 1. Stress,
Psychological. WM 172 A646s]
RA965.3.A66   362.1'068'1   80-25213
ISBN: 0-89443-332-6

Library of Congress Catalog Card Number: 80-25213
ISBN: 0-89443-332-6

Printed in the United States of America

*For Barbara
and . . . Jill, Wendy, Geoffrey*

Table of Contents

Preface

The author was conducting a workshop on the management of stress for nurses and hospital administrators when it became clear that there were definite factors leading to this problem and definite symptoms experienced by those caught in the middle between patient and administrative demands. What they experienced was stress. They described it as being painful.

The participants and this facilitator "groped" for definable factors and symptoms in the quest to find a solution for managing this complex phenomenon. The results of this experience quickly led to the writing of an article titled "Managerial-Organizational Stress: Identification of Factors and Symptoms" that appeared in the Spring 1980 edition of *Health Care Management Review*. At that point, Michael Brown, a most insightful editor of Aspen Systems Corporation, Publishing Division, read the article and encouraged the author to expand it to a full-length book to be directed to health care managers and professionals seeking relief and solutions for stress experienced in their organizations. This is the result of that stimulus.

It became more evident as numerous sources were examined that many organizational and personal factors contributed to stress on the job. A managerial-behavioral approach was developed to actually "manage" this problem, which initially had appeared to be unmanageable. A tentative solution was to examine the management systems selected by the administrators of health care systems and determine their effectiveness and impact. The elimination or reversal of dysfunctional systems is *the* starting point in encouraging and assisting any health care organization to adapt to change and resolve conflict. The message appeared to be:

> If a managerial process is creating a stressful situation for the individuals in the system, then this event must be

eliminated or reversed in order to actualize the mission of achieving objectives and fulfilling needs. Stress can be managed. Every achievement of a health care manager is the achievement of a professional manager. Every failure in not identifying and implementing more effective alternatives for dysfunctional processes is a failure of a manager. People, not forces or facts, manage. Understanding the factors and sources of managerial stress is the key step in the reduction of this force.

This book deals with the following factors and sources of stress in the health care environment:

The Managerial Paradigm
Psychoanalytic View of Stress
The Health Care Manager
Occupational Stress
Coronary Disease
Nursing
Impact on the Health Care Professional
Effect on the Family
Coping with Stress
The Troubled Employee
Participation and Enrichment
Quality of Work Life
The Management of Conflict
Management by Objectives
The Management of Time

The book is in three parts, with theory and practice interwoven within each chapter. Each chapter begins with highlights of its contents under the umbrella of "Considerations for the Health Care Manager." The first part of the book examines the impact of stress on the health care manager and its physiological, psychological, and sociological factors. The focus of this part is on the managers, their role, their family, and potential problems created by dysfunctional, counterproductive stress.

The second section is intended to assist professionals seeking relief and offers solutions for stress experienced in their organizations. The section emphasizes the management of stress and deals with coping, participative management, managing time, and managing by objectives. These solutions are applicable in health care systems in need of managerial-behavioral models.

The third part presents six case studies and incidents that illuminate the impact and net effect of stress in health care organizations. The cases extract concepts and ideas from the preceding 12 chapters, serve to stimulate new insights, and form a blueprint for future applications.

The author wishes to acknowledge the assistance given in this undertaking: by Paul A. Scholfield, executive director of The Graduate Hospital in Philadelphia, for permitting me to practice my craft and to use the hospital as an experiential laboratory for the fermentation of the concept and actualization of the project leading to the development of this book, by Ms. Susan Regan of Concordia University, Montreal, for managing the typing and production of this stressful project, and by Ms. Sandy Pritchard of Concordia University, who contributed an acute editorial focus.

Finally, it is hoped that health care managers and graduate students of this discipline can adopt in their own organizations the insights and findings accumulated from the many personal and research sources included in this book to reduce situations that are counterproductive and dysfunctional. Managing is both science and art, and a synthesis such as is presented here is the component needed to unravel the complex fabric in the quest to achieve goals and fulfill needs.

Steven H. Appelbaum, Ph.D.
December 1980

Part I

The Impact
of Stress

Chapter 1

Management of Stress in Health Care Organizations

CONSIDERATIONS FOR THE HEALTH CARE MANAGER

1. Maintenance of an organization is an activity in existence, while managing is a process characterized as being alive and progressing.
2. The management of stress in a health care organization can be examined psychologically-physiologically and managerially-organizationally.
3. Psychological-physiological stress factors are:
   - coronary disease
   - occupational stress
   - stress on the health care manager
   - coping
   - stress on the family
   - nursing
4. Managerial-organizational stress factors are:
   - health care management
   - occupational medicine
   - the troubled employee
   - managing conflict
   - managing time
   - management by objectives
5. Managing stress can be attacked by reversing dysfunctional processes that prove to be on a collision course and also by eliminating identified stressors.

6. The scarcity of resources creates anxiety for the health care manager who must decide upon allocations, professional issues, and survival decisions.

7. Wear and tear on the individual under stress and caught in the organizational bind not only may involve progressive damage to the system but also, in extreme forms, may result in the actual breakdown and disintegration of the individual and organization.

8. The patterns of upward mobility at any cost lead to neurotic systems often too advanced to manage the unresolved conflicts. This activity must be controlled in order to reduce the stressors.

Managers have been conditioned to believe they can manage just about any operation seemingly rational and measurable. The attraction of a professional manager for a complex, dynamic organization is similar to the quest of the youth reaching for the brass ring at the far side of the merry-go-round. When the ring seems so close, the reach just misses. However, the attractiveness is just as serious the next time around.

Managing stress is like managing work—it is an illusion. Contemporary elixirs often suggested include relaxation, meditation, nutritional habits, vigorous exercise, finishing unfinished business, assertiveness, time management, and total self-management.

The solutions are limited since stress is one of the organizational components along with motivation, planning, decision making, communications, and so on. To manage stress is not to eliminate it but to identify the dynamics creating unresolved conflicts within the organization for all members (Appelbaum, 1980, p. 7).

Health care environments are most complex yet fascinating organizations to attempt to reach for the "brass ring." Experience tells this author that most problems are not technical but behavioral. Administrators who have been trained professionally possess the tools needed to maintain their organizations, but that is not what managing is all about. *Maintenance is existence while managing is living and progressing.* The functions of a health care manager—namely, planning, organizing, staffing, directing, coordinating, reporting, budgeting, etc. (Wren, 1972, p. 235), cannot be attempted until other factors are anticipated and managed. These other factors serve to block the arteries of the managerial systems of health care organizations because they impact directly upon the administrators and related personnel responsible and accountable for achieving the critical objectives of these institutions while attempting to fulfill the psychological and physiological needs of the human resources employed within these dynamic, anxiety-producing systems. These factors, which appear in varied sizes and degrees of stress will be examined thoroughly here.

THE MANAGERIAL PARADIGM

Management of stress in a health care organization is a multifaceted and multidisciplinary task. Two broad-based systems impact on the total functioning of the organization (Figure 1-1).

These differentiated yet integrated systems are composed of 12 components that, when fully examined, yield an infinite combination of elements needed to anticipate and ultimately manage stress in a health care system. This is the task for health care managers: to manage stress with a greater intensity than they devote to the many caretaking activities that are necessary, yet redundant. If stress is not managed, the basic administrative functions will assume a minor, clerical role during the disintegration of the system.

The 12 components are equally divided between the two systems. They are explored throughout this book, with recommended actions for professionals provided. The psychological and physiological stress

Figure 1-1 The Two Systems of Stress

factors to be examined are presented in Figure 1-2, the managerial and organizational factors in Figure 1-3. The discussion of each component covers the many implications for managerial action as well as incidents and case studies for comparison contrasting.

MANAGERS MANAGE EVERYTHING ELSE BUT . . .

The management of organizational stress in the health care organization is an enormous project but it is essential and achievable. The creation of stress is accomplished by encouraging the use and adaptation of managerial systems that have limited credibility and unproved track records. Unfortunately, managers of health care systems perpetuate organizational theories and techniques that they were exposed to earlier in their own career indoctrination and socialization. Since those methods and philosophies were considered acceptable to their earlier mentors and professors, they continue to be stressed even when it appears the result is unfeasible, counterproductive, and stress producing.

Figure 1-2 The Psychological and Physiological Factors

Figure 1-3 The Managerial and Organizational Factors

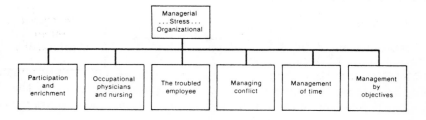

A tentative solution in dealing with stress is to examine the management systems employed by the administration of the health care organization and determine their effectiveness and impact. The reversal of dysfunctional management-organizational systems is the starting point in developing these institutions to the point where they become more organic in adapting to change and in resolving conflict. If a management technique is creating a stressful situation for individuals, then this must either be stopped or be reversed in order to actualize the mission of achieving objectives and fulfilling needs. The key to managing stress in a health care system is either to identify the stressor and eliminate it or to reverse the process completely until the stress is reduced to a level considered manageable.

A fundamental problem in need of solution in health care systems is rarely dealt with or confronted: how much change can human beings accept, absorb, and assimilate, and at what rate can they take it. Can they keep up with the ever-increasing rate of technological change, or is there some point at which the human organism goes to pieces? Can they leave the static ways and static guidelines that have dominated all of their history and adopt the new processes, the continual changes that must occur if they are to survive (Rogers, 1973, p. 122)?

This is a double-edged sword for health care managers. They have a difficult time juggling the fiscal-physical-human resources of the system since a major fear is to remain static in a turbulent environment. It is equally disastrous to inject unregulated change processes into the system on the premise that dynamic organisms are the survivors while mechanistic systems are doomed to fail. Most managers are not entirely comfortable with the dynamic nature of their industry that also forces emulation by the system for which they are partially responsible.

The complexities of this interactive connection between the environment and organization may be described as a system: A system may be defined as "a purposive collection of interacting entities." It consists of a set of elements that are related to each other in such a way that the actions of one element affect the states of, and initiate or modify activity in, other elements of the system. The first step in describing a system is to establish its boundaries—the principles by which it can be decided whether or not some particular entity is an element of the system. A system is said to be bounded by the relationship of its entities to a purpose, function, or sphere of activity: If the element is relevant to the attainment of the system's objectives, it is an element of the system (LaPatra, 1975, p. 9).

The health care manager is faced with many conflict-laden uncertainties in these systems. Activities may spill over into areas unrelated to the organization; many political, economic, social, legal, cultural, and similar constraints may impede operations and frustrate the best planned efforts. For example, the strong economic pressure to control rising health care costs influences the roles of many health care professionals as well as affects the boundaries between groups. More problems may arise as traditional lines of authority and task assignments become obscure as perceived personnel shortages are met. The linkage between managing health care and the resulting stress is becoming more of a problem since delivering the service and organizational survival are complex tasks that often are on a collision course.

DELIVERING THE SERVICE: HEALTH

Health care managers often are caught in the middle of cross-currents since they must promote the concept of health as their service and manage the professionals and organizational resources needed to deliver this service: Health is a state of complete physical, mental, and social well-being and is not merely the absence of disease or infirmity. This definition was adopted in 1946 in the original constitution of the World Health Organization (WHO). It draws heavily on the conception given voice a few years earlier by the great historian of medicine, Henry Sigerist: "Health is . . . not simply the absence of disease: it is something positive, a joyful attitude toward life, and a cheerful acceptance of the responsibilities that life puts upon the individual" (Sigerist, 1941, p. 100). The WHO definition represents, without doubt, the most concerted effort to develop an explicit consensus regarding the meaning of the word health, and yet, as will be seen, by no means has it been accepted universally as a proper description. It does serve as a foundation for understanding the technical, human, and managerial missions of health care systems. The fact that modern societies, however organized, devote such great resources to health attests to its social importance. Since resources are limited, choices must be made. Health care at some point must be weighed against other social preferences and commitments (Mechanic, 1972, pp. 3-4). In other words, the real world inevitably must stop short of attaining the ideal of health for all people, however it may be defined. Attention can be devoted to considering the ways in which humans go about the business of protecting and improving their health without concluding what such efforts might entail. The scarcity of health care resources creates further anxieties and stress for the managers of these systems, who must arrive at decisions concerning allocation, management, professionalism, and survival.

A paradox faces those who work to deliver health services: at a time when medical knowledge and clinical capability are at an all-time high, so also is dissatisfaction with health care. The dissatisfaction is not expressed merely by a few malcontents. It is real and widespread, and it comes from all quarters: government, consumers, the providers of care, and those who pay for care as third parties (Longest, 1976, p. 1). The problems that fall within management's domain can create stress that affects the performance of the institution both in delivering its service of health care and in its organizational survival.

Stress is considered one of society's most urgent problems. Stress arises when there is a deviation from optimum conditions that the individual cannot correct easily, resulting in an imbalance between demand and capacity. For serious stress to occur, the individual must view as serious the consequences of failure to have demands met. Such a formulation of stress demands that social and environmental conditions, as well as native endowment, training, and bodily conditions, be examined. In short, anything that affects demand or capacity has the potential to produce (or to alleviate) stress.

The "Inverted -U" hypothesis states that performance improves with increasing arousal up to a point, when it declines as arousal becomes more than optimal. The individual must establish a cutoff point so that everything below it will be considered random "noise" and everything above it will be considered a signal worthy of attention. It has been hypothesized that stress causes the cutoff point to be lowered, thus increasing the number of signals correctly identified, but also increasing the frequency of false positives (Welford, 1973).

These stressful events requiring behavioral adjustment by health care managers often raise blood pressure by the conditioned "fight-or-flight" response in which increases occur via metabolism, heart rate, blood pressure, breathing, hyperventilation, and muscle response. While the fight-or-flight syndrome still is an essential ingredient for survival, the stresses of contemporary organizational life create a heightened problem for those experiencing this situation. Those who are under constant stress and who resort to the fight-or-flight response have a greater chance of developing chronic hypertension, anxiety, gastrointestinal disorders, ulcers, colitis, and coronary heart disease that force them to retire prematurely from active organizational life before fully realizing their potential and career.

The United States Clearinghouse for Mental Health Information reported that the productive capacity of American industry had decreased $17 billion annually through 1978 because of stress-induced mental dysfunctions. Other studies estimate even greater losses (at least $60 billion) arising from stress-induced physical illnesses (Adams, 1978, p. 1). An added statistic: the National Institutes of Health reports that in 1976, 500 million valium tablets were consumed in the U.S. These data would indicate that individuals are located in systems highlighted by the interconnection of a stress level, health, satisfaction, personal growth, and productivity (Figure 1-4).

Stress then actually can be described as an internal reaction to an environmental event. The stress response, however, is a nonspecific psychological and physical series of events triggered by disruption to an individual's level of equilibrium. If this response is triggered often over long periods of time, there will develop a likelihood that latent physical and psychological disease will occur. Wear and tear on the system not only may involve progressive damage to the system but also, in extreme form, may result in the actual breakdown and disintegration of the system. All individuals have their own level of stress tolerance; when this level is exceeded, they "break down" physically and/or psychologically, and further exposure to the stress may lead to disintegration and death (Rahe & Lind, 1971).

One of the early lessons to be learned by the health care manager is that complex problems that ultimately create stress usually must be solved in parts. One essential part of the health service delivery problem is effective management of those who work to deliver those services. Pressures are being exerted on all managers for more health services at lower costs. Health professionals often are placed in a management position and held responsible for how effectively they manage their system and for its efficiency. Managers have a common problem: they lack the specific management training and development so necessary for controlling conflict and reducing dysfunctional stress which often characterize health care organizations functioning at less than national levels.

Figure 1-4 Organizational Stress System

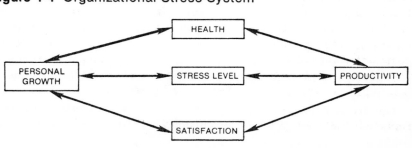

NEUROTIC ORGANIZATIONAL SYSTEMS

Health care organizations often create a climate in which stress is one of the component underpinnings along with decision making, leadership, communications, motivation, planning, and so on. Heightened competition in the organization may well be a planned management strategy to increase productivity since "to the winner go the spoils." This creates internal competition since the manager who is excessively competitive against his own standards is more likely to have physiological difficulties. Individuals often may turn their anger on themselves, in which case they become their own worst enemies by repeatedly getting into difficulties, accidents, or (in extreme instances) turn their anger inward. When competition is perceived and practiced extrinsically, a limited reward system manifests apparent and hidden systems of intergroup conflict (Appelbaum, 1975, p. 15). The root of the problem lies in corporate emphasis. Instead of instigating competitive situations, management should emphasize departmental contributions (Appelbaum, 1977, p. 40).

One of the most common situations producing fear, stress, and anxiety for the health care manager is "change," which usually means some disruption of the status quo and of relationships. Even a change for the better is perceived as a loss in which something has to be given up for a new replacement or system. For example, when historically highly controlled organizations must become more decentralized, when previously authoritarian managers are asked to become more democratic, when dependent employees are required to become more aggressive, they not only have lost support, gratifications, and goals, they also must cope with new requirements for which they may be unprepared or unsuited (Levinson, 1976, p. 49).

This situation of loss as well as new demands operates simultaneously by forcing the individual caught in the middle to adapt quickly. But, both demands psychologically affect the individual via physiological or mental exhaustion. As an example, from the moment individuals receive their primary promotions they are caught in the middle since they always will be responsible for subordinates and accountable to superiors. This ambivalent situation creates anger within the individual occupying the key managerial position under fire. There appear to be few outlets for this emotion that are organizationally acceptable; therefore, the repression of anger is an important factor in almost all emotional illness. To put it another way, when circuits are overloaded, a fuse is likely to blow; when the body is overloaded with emergency demands, something eventually has to give. Overload in most systems leads to breakdown, whether single biological cells or managers in organizations are involved (Miller, 1960, p. 116).

The scarcity of resources accompanied by the need to contain costs creates other problems for the health care manager that can only begin to be resolved in an organic, organizational climate. Well-designed managerial systems and interventions are essential in turning around counterproductive and maladaptive organizations. The competitive battleground of the health care institution must be neutralized since this climate produces stress and permanent damage to the system. Organizational research has focused on this dilemma; even animal research has found that when male rats were paired to combat each other, approximately 80 percent of the defeated ones ultimately died although their wounds were not severe enough to warrant death. The British psychoanalyst, Elliott Jacques, also contends that a peak in the death rate between ages 35 and 40 is attributable to the shock that follows the realization that an individual's life and career are on a descending path (Jacques, 1973, p. 154). This often creates a period of depression that increases the individual's vulnerability to stress-induced illnesses.

Medical studies support the relationship between depression and illness. This critical age (mid thirties) is when upwardly mobile health care managers must confront the fact that their fantasies and reality are incongruent since both internal pressures for achievement are so intense that the pain of defeat is devastating. The essence of the problem is that the managers are underutilized but qualified to contribute, and their position undercuts the actualization of the value. At best, to continue to develop, these managers now must either change their job, stagnate and accept it, seek external interests, or change career. These are pessimistic alternatives for individuals trying to cope with and balance their world, life, and organizational bind (Appelbaum, 1977, p. 41).

This dilemma creates further stress for the individual caught in the middle. The creation of stress symptoms thus is not a simple matter. To be retained in a situation of unbalance between level of work and capacity, with or without excessive financial reward, requires a combination of an individual's unconsciously working toward a breakdown and a stress-inducing opportunity to collude unconsciously with a manager (Jacques, 1973, p. 154). Managers face this stressor at the perceived peak of their careers.

COMPLEX STRUCTURES

The organizational structure of the typical general hospital differs substantially from the bureaucratic model of many other large-scale organizations. This difference results from the unusual relationship between the formal authority represented by the administrative hierarchy and the authority of knowledge possessed by health professionals in the hospital. The hospital might be a much less complex institution if it did fit the typical pyramid. However, this is not the case. The medical staff does not fit into this pyramid. Only those persons who work for the hospital (i.e., have their salaries paid by the hospital) typically fit into the pyramid. The medical staff consists of physicians and professionals who have been authorized by the governing board to admit and attend patients in the hospital. They generally are not paid by the hospital but by their patients, meaning that they do not usually fit into the hospital's formal organizational pyramid. Most physicians relish the independent nature of this relationship; the organizational pattern therefore is literally a dual pyramid (Longest, 1976, pp. 8-9).

The complex pattern becomes evident when it is considered that hardly anyone in the organization has only one immediate superior (a highly desirable attribute of bureaucratic organizations). In fact, employees such as nurses must take orders from their own head nurse—who is a member of the administrative hierarchy—from the medical chiefs of their respective services, and, in regard to patients, from every individual physician on the medical staff. It is not uncommon for these orders to be contradictory, since each group of participants interprets the means for meeting objectives in terms of its own value systems and requirements.

The hospital is a very complex social system with substantial conflicts among the participants—patients, physicians, trustees, administrative staff, and paramedical personnel (Longest, 1976, p. 10).

The conflict experienced within this network can be quite stress inducing for health care managers. Perhaps no single organizational problem facing these organizations is more important than that of developing a more effective working relationship among the hospital, medical staff, and administration. An active management process and intervention is required to turn around these conflicts in order to accomplish effectiveness, efficiency, and satisfaction.

In examining how to cope with stress or any organizational activity, the concept of management is brought to the front as a process intended to achieve organizational goals while fulfilling the needs of its members. Drucker states that management is a task and a discipline. He adds:

> But management is also people. Every achievement of management is the achievement of a manager. Every failure is a failure of a manager. People manage rather than forces or facts. The vision, dedication, and integrity of managers determine whether there is management or mismanagement (Drucker, 1977, p. 11).

The management of stress in the health care system actually must begin with an understanding of the dynamics and counterproductive effects of induced organizational stress. The pattern of upward mobility at any cost leads to neurotic systems often too advanced to manage the unresolved conflicts. Understanding the factors and sources of managerial pressure is only the first step in stress reduction (Cooper & Marshall, 1976). The basic responsibility for maintaining organizational and individual health is a reflection of the relationship between both parties. The solutions are somewhat limited since stress is a component dynamic of organizational functioning. However, as stated several times in this chapter, if a managerial process is creating a stressful situation, that activity must be either stopped or reversed in order to actualize the mission of the health care system for achieving goals and satisfying needs.

The management of a health care organization can best be understood by examining the complex requirements and structure within which the professional must manage. A psychoanalytic perspective can help to unravel the fabric and expose the weave to determine the pattern necessary to yield satisfaction and effectiveness. The individual manager is a complex player in the organizational game, as most individual personalities are. The next chapter examines this perspective.

BIBLIOGRAPHY

Adams, J.D. Improving stress management. *Social Change: Ideas and Applications,* National Training Laboratory Institute, 1978, *8*(4), 1-11.

Appelbaum, S.H. An experiential case study of organizational suboptimization and problem solving. *Akron Business and Economic Review,* Fall 1975, *6*(3), 13-16.

————. The middle-manager: An examination of aspirations and pessimism. *The Personnel Administrator,* January 1977, *22*(1), 39-44.

————. Managerial-organizational stress: Identification of factors and systems. *Health Care Management Review,* 1980, *5*(1), 7-16.

Cooper, C.L., & Marshall, J. Occupational sources of stress: A review of the literature on coronary heart disease and mental ill health. *Journal of Occupational Psychology,* 1976, *49,* 11-28.

Drucker, P.F. *An introductory view of management.* New York: Harper & Row, 1977, 11.

Jacques, E. *Work, creativity and social justice.* New York: International Universities Press, 1973, 154.

LaPatra, J.W. *Health care delivery systems.* Springfield, Ill.: Charles C. Thomas Publishing, 1975, p. 9.

Levinson, H. *Psychological man.* Cambridge, Mass.: The Levinson Institute, 1976, 49.

Longest, B.B., Jr. *Management practices for the health professional.* Reston, Va.: Reston Publishing Inc., 1976, pp. 8-9.

Mechanic, D. *Public expectations and health care.* New York: John Wiley & Sons, 1972, 3-4.

Miller, J.G. Information input overload and psychopathology. *American Journal of Psychiatry,* 1960, *8,* 116.

Rahe, R.H., & Lind, E. Psychosocial factors and sudden cardiac death: A pilot study. *Journal of Psychosomatic Research,* January 1971, *15*(1), 14–24.

Rogers, C.R. Interpersonal relationships: USA 2000. In J.S. Jun & W.B. Storm (Eds.), *Tomorrow's organizations: Challenges and strategies.* Glenville, Ill.: Scott Foresman and Co., 1973, 122.

Sigerist, H.E. *Medicine and human welfare.* New Haven, Conn.: Yale University Press, 1941, 100.

Welford, A.T. Stress and performance. *Ergonomics,* September 1973, *16,* 12, 567-580.

Wren, D.C. *The evolution of management thought.* New York: Ronald Press, 1972, 235.

Chapter 2

A Psychoanalytic View of Stress in Management

CONSIDERATIONS FOR THE HEALTH CARE MANAGER

1. While management theories are intended to help executives cope with organizational uncertainties (creating stress), they often are contradictory, suggesting a polarized version of participative management and at the same time advocating punitive measures in order to obtain subordinate compliance.

2. The use of leaderless groups often is suggested when managers cannot fulfill role responsibilities and goals need to be achieved.

3. Anxiety occurs when there is a conflict in the value system of individuals who feel they must compromise their principles— or else. While anxiety physiologically protects the individual in need of a defense, it manifests emotional and physical reactions that are damaging. Anxiety is experienced by upwardly mobile managers most concerned with success.

4. When managers cannot function with increasing responsibilities, they often adopt a crisis style that is subjective and stressful. They feel isolated and become hostile toward, and at the same time dependent

upon, peers and supervisors. Dependence increases stress.

5. Managers who attempt to balance their needs for achievement with their imperfections are more capable of being ruthless and using excessive power to achieve goals.

6. The job of the ego is to balance the forces from the id, the superego, and the environment. The ego sets up a unique system of defense mechanisms to protect the individual from anxiety and maintain equilibrium.

7. Problems occur when individuals have been trained to contain the drives that they were conditioned to believe are not acceptable. The expression of aggression directly to people in authority positions sets off a chain of responses that demands control. This repression often is turned inward against this individual. The result: stress and emotional/physical disruption.

8. Problems of high aspiration, high ego ideal, and low self-esteem start early in life but are transferred to organizational situations. When defense mechanisms no longer protect the managers, they may self-destruct and attempt suicide. They often direct their aggressions at subordinates, which is a way of avoiding an attack on the target of their anger—themselves.

9. A manager who suspects a subordinate is depressed should *not* suggest time to be taken off. This only allows the troubled employee more time to deal with the depression and impose self-punishment in isolation.

10. Managers who may appear to be neurotic may also be undergoing physiological changes that may be affecting their overall physical and organizational performance. Some examples are extreme rigidity in thinking, reactionary behavior, much worry

on the job, escape behavior from the job, nondelegation of duties, and suspicion.

11. Some individuals are abrasive and create stress for managers who must deal with them. Some recommendations are:

    • limit their frequency of communications
    • give them feedback about their progress
    • legitimize their positions

Executives in health care organizations and other related systems work under stress. This happens to be a fact of organizational life. Some degree of stress is essential to life since without any stress the organic functioning of individuals may begin to disintegrate. But when stress becomes excessive and uncontrolled, it can contribute to psychological and emotional disease for individuals and their families, and even premature death. In one study, the annual cost of executive stress in the United States was estimated at $10 billion to $20 billion—a figure higher than the gross revenue of any one of all but the three top industrial corporations on the *Fortune 500* list (Greenwood, 1977, p. 41).

Contemporary managers definitely are subject to personal and organizational stressors. Stress arising in the family environment also would affect the individual, thus creating additional vulnerability that, in turn, could produce symptoms that might not be controllable at the time. The individual's personality, performance, and attitude following a poor performance appraisal or the announcement of restructuring or reorganization within the institution would represent situations illuminating personal vulnerabilities. These situations, which may reflect upon managers' weaknesses, will expose them to psychological threats affecting their health and life and make them most vulnerable to stressors.

Of course, the managers can take steps to reduce their personal vulnerability, using a wide variety of means that are receiving widespread attention in the literature of stress. Various meditative techniques, deep breathing, biofeedback, and many unique theories are being espoused daily. But do these panaceas actually accomplish what is being attempted in this problem area? The basic principles of management, to which most potential supervisors are exposed, are intended to help them cope with the uncertainties of their positions but also may serve as sources of managerial stress at the same time as they are considered to be analgesic compounds for solving organizational stressful situations.

Certain management theories are contradictory. The principles often suggest the popularized version of participative management and at the same time advocate punitive measures in order to obtain compliance from individual subordinates. Managers who have some exposure to and training in management science are encouraged to use a "humanistic approach" or experience an unsolvable bind that serves as a source of stress for them. The manager is caught in the middle in interfacing with and mediating the demands of supervisors and subordinates, with each having their own "hidden agendas." The manager has a status and success orientation and is motivated to be oriented toward upward mobility.

Managers must be willing to take risks to achieve these goals, but the risks frequently are the source of stress since it is known that the outcomes are uncertain and difficult to control. The result of this dilemma usually is anxiety, followed closely by stress. Many successful managers are "workaholics" or "type A" behavior patterns which is discussed in Chapter 4 on occupational stress.

ABDICATION OF RESPONSIBILITY

When the pressures mount, managers have the option of assuming an absentee role and abdicating their responsibilities—a contradiction of the management practices of hierarchical control and Henri Fayol's principle of unity of command, which states that for any action whatsoever an employee should receive orders from one superior only (Wren, 1972, p. 219). All members of a management network are interdependent. Each manager is trying to achieve team productivity goals for which all members generally are responsible and at the same time is pressured with an individual contribution that ultimately leads to achievement of results and upward mobility. If the manager abdicates these responsibilities, additional stressors are placed on the work group, which now must collectively pick up the pieces that have not been completed. In addition, the group members have the added pressure to fulfill their individual missions that have a results orientation.

Managers often find it difficult to view their roles and responsibilities as leaders who are less than strong. This occurs because the concept of leadership is a confusing and questionable commodity. To support this point, the use of the leaderless group has now been encouraged as a new phenomenon in management strategy. Routine decisions are made by individuals, important decisions are made by consensus, and the dilution of the leadership role is apparent in this structure where participative management actually connotes majority rule as a safe way to abdicate the responsibilities and conflicts inherent in the leadership position.

Membership is a critical decision. The team must be able to purge itself of dysfunctional members—those who cause trouble or refuse to become productive. This is an important role, and it is difficult for a team to survive very long without it. Experience has shown that membership control may be used vindictively, and consensus teams generally are quite responsible in using the membership control process (Greenwood, 1977, p. 49). This process actually puts the manager in the middle. The conflict exists between seeking out those valued rewards and at the same time being anxiety ridden regarding the risks involved in attempting to be successful. This results in a constant state of anxiety for the manager who is at the core of the turbulence.

Most authorities who examine anxiety and related issues agree that a basic cause is a conflict in value systems. Most organizations do not offer well-integrated patterns of values and give out mixed messages to their managers. Psychoanalytically, Freud felt that anxiety was something displeasurable to be felt by the individual. He felt it came as an individual response to either a felt or real danger. It involved various intensities of unpleasant feelings and effects including anguish, terror, panic, apprehension, and a sense of gloom. It also could be felt by an individual experiencing embarrassment or confusion in certain situations.

Common to all of these was an uncomfortable, sense of some vague, unpleasant event impending. Therefore, anxiety was associated with unanticipated and unexpected events to come and produced concern for the future. It often has been accompanied by an increase in excitation. The function of anxiety is to give a signal to individuals of an impending danger so that they may act or react in relation to that danger. The signal function of anxiety serves as an alarm mechanism. If the alarm goes off and the individuals hear it, they can mobilize their resources. By fight, flight, and adaptation, they are able, upon heeding the alarm, to restore themselves to normalcy. Thus, anxiety performs the normative function of protecting and enhancing the individual's welfare (Jennings, 1965, p. 40). It is a component of the managers' role that often protects as well as debilitates them.

The individual experiencing anxiety may have accompanying spastic colon, diarrhea, perspiration, tremors, abdominal pain, sensations, vomiting, changes in muscular reactions, increased heart and pulse rate, and increased respiration. If these symptoms and the anxiety manifest themselves for a long period, then stress, if felt continuously, may become quite chronic, resulting in physical damage to organs or vulnerable tissue.

ANXIETY

Anxiety often is experienced by managers who are most concerned with success. The intensity of the success ethic is strongest among middle managers. The quest for success through achievement and all of the symbolisms that go with this such as money, prestige, and power creates a conflict situation in which individuals compete against each other. If an individual succeeds and does a good job, therefore, something or someone else must fail, resulting in a condition of anxiety with stress acting as a mediating factor. Individuals who are extremely oriented to upward mobility suffer severe anxiety, depression, low sociability, and at times may feel suicidal when their careers become blocked. Individuals who have high ambitions but who are moving up the organizational ladder at a limited pace may become fantasy-oriented as a defense mechanism and, as a result, may begin to jump from one job to another as a way of dealing with their feelings of inadequacy.

The upwardly mobile were found more likely to be more neurotic than those who remained in the same class as their fathers had. The downwardly mobile, on the other hand, were more likely to incur various forms of psychosis. The upwardly mobile were more apt to be neurotic, experience restlessness, and anxiety, were troubled with sleep, had hands that felt damp or trembled often, and so on. Anxiousness and expectation without direction or objective formed their predominant emotional pattern. The downwardly mobile were more prone to probable psychosis, alcoholism, depression, rigidity, and suspiciousness (Jennings, 1965, p. 55).

Executives as a group basically represent middle-class value systems with associated anxiety as a byproduct. A study of more than 200 managers by Jennings found that executives showed marked defensiveness, strong control, relative lack of insight into themselves and their emotions, and considerable use of denial and repression mechanisms. These traits are connected in the following way:

The typical executive is very ambitious for personal growth and achievement and values competition very highly. The individual gives a moral equivalent to being ruthless with colleagues by equating the results achieved with corporate goal achievement. This belief in competition serves to justify any acts the executive might regard as unfair or immoral. In reality, the function of competition as a spur to organizational growth is really a facade behind which lies a guilt-bearing competitive drive. Such executives are ruthless in the drive to succeed, but to avoid the middle-class stigma of ruthlessness, they keep themselves under a tight rein.

These executives tend to deny their ruthless tendencies by repressing them onto the rubric of strength of character or of company loyalty. While insisting that there is no wish to hurt anyone, the individuals at the same time will point with a certain satisfaction to other people who are really tough (Jennings, p. 56). It is interesting that if executives do not hit a home run every time they come to bat, they feel a strong threat of failure or disappointment with their success and their lack of achievement. This brings out a certain degree of negative motivation and illuminates the inadequacy of their roles and values. They then become more neurotic, which creates crisis, anxiety, and stress for themselves, subordinates, and peers.

The executives basically are involved with a psychological mobility pattern in which they always are moving up the organization in a continual process of coming and going. At each level, the person must disengage from a prior role and now move into a new role and then disengage again. Toffler referred to this in *Future Shock* as the condition of the organizational "modular man" (Toffler, 1970, p. 97). This situation creates role anxiety and role conflict because the commitment the individual made at one level is now in transition with all the trappings of uncertainty facing the manager. What happens is that when the executive leaves one organization and moves to another, or changes one job within the organization, the person experiences certain relationships with authority figures that are necessary for success. The mobile executive becomes very attached to these authority figures and to disengage from them creates certain internal conflicts. With peers, the manager is able to make and sever emotional ties and can risk maintaining aloofness toward them. The mobility of the middle manager with regard to peers is no problem, but when the executive disengages from an individual who serves as a model and authority figure, certain feelings of anxiety may begin to manifest themselves.

Managers have a difficult time in separating from one organization and job while connecting with another one. The problem is that they feel abnormal anxiety because they now are put in the same position as they occupied when they had to experience separation from their parents and family, and this brings out more feelings of inadequacy. These feelings of inadequacy have been important to managers who have tried to repress them and overcompensate for them throughout their careers. The very nature of the work may have as its goal the need to prove how adequate these individuals actually are. Because the mobile executive has a need to achieve larger and larger administrative challenges, arrestment of this upward mobility is interpreted as a threat to the opportunity to realize the potentialities of the manager. Anxieties or feelings of inadequacy or incapability are caused by a halt in mobility. Executives who face separation from the central administrative tasks of the firm, and junior executives who incur arrested movement toward the central tasks, feel the essential elements of career crisis.

A career crisis is a crisis of self. Invariably it involves a narrowing of awareness to include problems of authority, organizational goals and performance, and self (Jennings, 1965, p. 69).

CRISES IN MANAGING

It becomes more apparent that managers who assume increasing administrative responsibilities and commensurate difficulties are better candidates for career crisis. They feel their crises at a much more intense rate. What then occurs is that as events become cumulative, the stressors become multiplied at a higher level.

Some managers have the insight to anticipate stress because of the nature and scope of their administrative responsibilities. But this insightful anticipation becomes stressful in itself because of many uncertainties. Executives react to this anticipation by adopting a crisis style and, rather than dealing objectively with the factors leading to this anxiety and crisis, they react in a subjective, anxiety-heightened style.

The crisis itself may be the most extreme condition they must encounter that also possesses some clues as to the method needed to deal with and eventually cope with the crisis. Unfortunately, they do not deal as well with this item at their level as they do with their programmed activities.

Guilt and Shame

One factor leading to their crisis is the level of isolation that these managers experience within their administrative structure. Feelings of guilt and shame provoke feelings of isolation. Guilt represents inner directives that make the individual feel isolated from this important group. Shame represents external directives that make the executive isolated. Feelings of shame imply the acceptance of the validity of the executive group's distinct ways of organizing its activities (Jennings, 1965, p. 101).

When managers experience acute feelings of guilt and shame, self-damage results, with the impending incapacity to be productive and effective. These individuals basically will become quite hostile or even more dependent upon peers, subordinates, and supervisors. This dependency renders the managers helpless, with more feelings of inadequacy and guilt for assuming a position they may not be equipped or worthy to handle. Managers in a career crisis may have different perceptions of the productivity demands on them due to their feelings of anxiety. They may often overreact to the present danger, and in many cases they abort via abdication (previously discussed) of their responsibilities because of the high level of anxiety they are experiencing. When this happens they become quite alienated from themselves and become separated emotionally from their peers in the organization.

Many of these managers gain a great deal of surface stability and nurturance from being involved with the organization on a day-to-day basis. The organization also brings about a false sense of reality for these individuals. But managerial isolation is so pervasive that it may even extend beyond the scope of managers' jobs to encompass their personal lives where other problems are festering within the network of their own families. This career and personal crisis usually is the first step managers experience on the way to becoming more neurotic.

The Concept of Reality

Managers can become very inhibited and restrained, and their concept of reality because of this crisis becomes quite distorted. Reality becomes only a concept that must be supported by hard facts. Then they begin to explore and select new methods of functioning and behaving that are quite different from the patterns they used when they were "moving and shaking" the organization effectively. This career crisis dispels a myth for managers who at one time felt they were solidly anchored in their organization. They now begin to question their status and security, and come to feel threatened. This is a danger signal to the executives. What often happens is that their defense mechanisms are brought into play so they can protect themselves and, it is hoped, not be alienated from the organization and themselves. Attacking other people in these conflicting situations becomes a common pattern of coping behavior for these managers.

One of the problems in dealing with these crises is that the problems never are clearly identified in manageable units by the individuals involved because of their heightened anxiety. Many of them already have been severely damaged, as evidenced by emotional and physiological stress symptoms. It is important to remember also that stress has an effect on individuals' perceptions and is instrumental in bringing about the damage caused by defective and overworked coping mechanisms. Executives often will panic, become desperate, and will not seek out professional help in the manner that would be expected as a result of their organizational, analytical, and problem-solving skills. There does not appear to be a moderate-to-high correlation between personal and professional diagnostic problem-solving capacities. It is unique that managers are very quick to diagnose and recommend the intervening facilitators needed to solve problems in organizational-oriented types of situations. In personal stressful situations involving these behaviors and their problems, the executives are unable to do this as efficiently. It appears that willingness and ability are two very different factors.

The guilt and shame the managers feel prevent them from seeking help from third parties. When the situation becomes critical, this usually indicates a multiple problem exists. The first concern would be a problem of authority, the second would focus within the organization, and the third would be the managers' concept of themselves. When managers' self-image is threatened, their total equilibrium is in question. Generally, they will react to this state by feeling very inadequate, insecure, and incapable of performing what they have always done automatically. They begin to feel humiliated and isolated because they will not make any sacrifices nor can they make any decisions. As they feel more helpless, they may become more aggressive, destructive, and problem laden because they place a high value on their abilities and skills and become more highly critical of their own performance than their own supervisors would be. An added problem occurs when these anxiety-ridden managers must deal with these conflicts with their own supervisors as authority figures.

AUTHORITY MODELS

Typical managers actually view authority figures as controlling and helpful rather than destructive and prohibiting. These executives have the ability to attract the attention of the older, better-trained employees and to learn from them for a considerable advantage. This notion of authority seems to be common to society, particularly to the middle classes. While the trust pattern seems certainly true for many persons, particularly executives, others have a distinct mistrust pattern toward superior authorities (Jennings, 1965, p. 123). One of the missions on which many of these managers embark is to seek out their own identities. This search for identity often is restricted, particularly when the individuals feel threatened and their mobility is thwarted. When this happens, the managers must continue to fulfill this need for upward mobility and now must actively seek out the human resources in the organization that they deem to be most productive. The complication is that they are doing this at the same time their resources are restricted. These managers are achievement oriented and must feel they are in control.

It is interesting to philosophize and hypothesize as to how these career crises multiply so quickly in individuals who have been selected for their leadership positions because they appear to be emotionally and cognitively equipped to succeed on the job. Maslow (1954), the architect of the hierarchy of needs, had some ideas concerning this dilemma. He felt these managers always were attempting to balance their high achievement needs with their imperfections. In doing so, they are capable of being ruthless and not reluctant to use a great deal of power to achieve personal objectives. In addition to being oriented to upward mobility, they were not concerned with other individuals' feelings and opinions while functioning in an impersonal environment devoid of humanistic support of subordinates and peers.

However, they are not free from their guilt, their anxiety, their isolation, and their conflict. Within this turmoil, these crisis situations bring out managers' unconscious fears of authority. In childhood, managers, because of their own feelings of helplessness, may have viewed parents in a highly negative way because of the parental power and authority. The executives may have reacted acutely to parents' use of their power differentials in punishing and corrective efforts. But because hatred of parents is an act against the conscience, these managers as children may have repressed their negative feelings and thus may have created strong feelings and desires to be like them in their adult lives. Lurking behind this positive identification may be the hostility that never was allowed to work itself out. Managers always have some feelings of restriction in the presence of superiors.

Confronting Feelings of Worthlessness

Occasionally, these anxieties break out (Jennings, p. 145). These conflicts and anxieties do erupt in response to individuals' objectives that are being blocked. What happens is that these individuals are most fearful confronting these feelings of worthlessness that have been there historically and that have created current neurotic patterns. They develop unrealistic estimates of unrealistic goals that must be achieved, and they place unreasonable demands upon themselves.

The danger of having these feelings of worthlessness and inadequacy revealed is tantamount to suffering a catastrophic defeat in their jobs. The closer they come to understanding their inadequacies and failures, the more aggressive they become in driving for success. In their neurotic state of existence, these achievement-oriented drives are developed from historic feelings of internal weakness. They also attempt to avoid these feelings of inadequacy and helplessness that are tremendously painful to swallow.

Managers who are experiencing these crises are attempting to maintain a certain life style that projects what they would hope others think of their own personalities and adequacies. The career crises they experience indicate they constantly are trying to cope and identify with managerial problems that reappear and must be resolved throughout their corporate and organizational careers. This in turn helps them develop managerial styles that may be congruent with their general life styles. The necessary connections would be their own concept of self and how this self relates to their managerial roles and their own roles as members of their families. Basically, their whole life becomes enmeshed in their managerial style, which directly affects their jobs and indirectly affects their personal lives, creating further crisis and conflict if both are not in harmony.

Over a long period of time, individuals' jobs occupy a major portion of their lives, and this does become ingrained in the managers' total experience. Managers who are extremely achievement oriented want to enjoy the accomplishments of their performance, which they feel was extremely well done. They also look at the ambivalence of long-term commitments and upward mobility. These individuals actually commit themselves emotionally to the job of becoming a highly professional manager and administrator, and those who seem to make it to the top have been the individuals who have had the strongest identification with the role of manager.

But there is a conflict inherent in this commitment. These managers do identify closely with their work role. The problems begin when they attempt to disengage from the job and return to their private lives. They cannot disassociate freely from the commitments and conflicts that have manifested themselves for the basic part of their day because their linkages and achievement-oriented goals and ambitions are firmly anchored to the job. Their domestic commitments create further conflicts with their own careers because they identify managerially with their organizations at an unconscious level and struggle with the demands of family at an overt level without really understanding the ambivalence. They do not realize how much their total lives pivot around their managerial roles, and identification with these roles actually is an absorption of their own personality.

The threat of any separation from their managerial positions will bring out further anxieties that affect their total concept of self. Managers who form basic relationships with their managerial roles will face crises that are unique. They are motivated to perform well not by the satisfaction of administrative achievement but by the satisfaction of the secondary rewards of money, power, prestige, and status. These secondary rewards have become primary. When this is the case, separation from the immediate administrative situation may not be intolerable if those secondary rewards are not threatened (Jennings, 1965, p. 175).

Internal Controls

These executives who do achieve generally do not enjoy the plateaus situated between hierarchical achievements. They never are satisfied with themselves, their successes, and what they accomplish on the job. Each new success sets up a new objective pattern for higher goals and the achievement drive increases geometrically to become uncontrollable. They never relax and enjoy any satisfaction. The rocky road to the top is a journey into self-insight and development. Operating within the demands and expectations of their authority and corporate objectives and policies calls for strong internal controls. Individuals with a high need to achieve, to get things done their way, need these internal controls that keep a check on impulsive performance. In the course of their careers, the internal controls usually are strengthened adequately to fulfill the achievement drive. When they are not sufficiently strengthened, difficulties will ensue (Jennings, p. 206).

When the upward mobility goals of these executives become thwarted at the same time their achievement drive is at an optimum peak, career crises may result. These crises are not incubated solely within the organization but actually are manifested within the individual based on the concept of self. These crises become painful, humiliating experiences in which individuals destroy themselves emotionally and/or physically in certain cases. This occurs when they may decide that an individual who has given them the greatest degree of pain should be done away with. They handle such decisions by self-destructing on the job, retiring early, or even inflicting a great deal of pain as a result of their anxiety. Their manipulative skills, often in the form of proved successful managerial performance that had been considered most effective in the past, now may be used against them to reduce the efficiency of their organizations.

This complex, self-destructive process has a direct effect upon their careers and an indirect effect upon their organizations, since these behaviors are counterproductive and very dysfunctional. Why does all of this happen at the peak of managers' careers and how do individuals become so disenchanted with their own performance? This phenomenon can be examined psychoanalytically.

PSYCHOANALYTIC ANALYSIS OF THE MANAGER

Executives, managers, supervisors, physicians, nursing supervisors, and, to a certain extent, all employees frequently deal with their own and others' emotional problems on the job. Individuals who do not achieve their personal blueprints start experiencing feelings that have been repressed for long periods and do not understand how to cope with these feelings of inadequacy and helplessness. These problems all have similar factors:

1. They are painful for individuals who are experiencing them and for those who must deal with such persons.
2. They are destructive to the managers and to the organization.
3. The basis for the problems usually are so complex that they cannot be broken down into a clearly identified problem-solving nature.
4. It is uncommon for the individuals responsible for dealing with these problems on the job to know what they can do about them.

There usually is a multiple series of management efforts that are accompanied by feelings of failure, anger, and guilt on the part of those who must make the decisions with regard to what must be done to identify and solve these situations. These emotional problems and disturbances experienced by managers have multiple ramifications upon others in the organizational network who must deal with them.

There is a way of understanding the nature of this conflict and, in doing so, some psychoanalytic concepts can be examined. According to Freud, there are two constantly operating psychological drives within the individual's personality. One is a constructive drive and the other a destructive drive. The constructive drive, sometimes referred to as the libido, is the source of feelings of love, creativity, and psychological growth. The destructive drive gives rise to feelings of anger and hostility toward others. The major psychological test for every human being is to fuse these drives so that the constructive drive tempers, guides, and controls the destructive drive and so that the energy from both sources thus may be used in the individual's own self-interest and that of society (Levinson, 1963, p. 29).

Individuals learn from their early childhood that the only way to obtain affection from their parents is by positive performance. If high performance is essential, then the price of affection may be great. This is accompanied by a feeling of anger toward the parents. These objects of affection become very difficult to live with, but the child must repress these angry feelings. While not being overtly aware of these angers, the individual pushes these feelings down to an unconscious level, but the feelings still are there. The individual's id, being the unconscious, now has no concept of time and since this action is contradictory and not really logical, these angers arise when the individual is not prepared to deal with these feelings at a much later date and time in life.

When the child develops a conscience, the individual becomes self-governing. The person thus has developed a superego that is based on the internalization of the values of the culture in which the individual lives that is transmitted through educators, parents, and other contacts. The superego also focuses upon rules, regulations, and prohibitions and has associated with it an ego ideal that is the manner in which individuals would like to be seen at their best. This dilemma produces a great deal of frustration later because people attempt to achieve this psychological state, which is most difficult to do. The superego serves as a governor and a self-critical device to control some of people's conflicts. This superego generally is acquired from the culture in which the individual lives and is reinforced by external value systems. Individuals actually must look upon themselves to see how their image relates to the superego. One way of performing this self-evaluation is to look at the difference between individuals' ego ideals and how they actually perceive themselves at that point in time. The result is self-esteem.

When individuals' self-esteem is enhanced, the critical nature of their superego can be somewhat diffused and some of the aggressions neutralized. Self-esteem, when attacked by others, is a very vulnerable component of individuals' personalities. When this attack becomes an onslaught, individuals feel quite guilty and attempt to overcompensate for violations of the superego by some form of atonement.

The superego actually is a built-in governor and an agent that maintains homeostasis within the personality of the individuals. If, however, values and rules that the children are taught are inconsistent, the superego also will be inconsistent throughout adulthood. If there are too many or unrealistically strict rules, the superego becomes a harsh test, either constricting too narrowly the way persons can behave or burdening them excessively with feelings of guilt and demanding constant atonement. But even without punishment for strict rules, a tyrannical superego can develop if performance is the basis for obtaining love and there are unrealistic expectations of extremely high performance. Unless they constantly are doing what they feel they ought to do, individuals feel uncomfortable, not knowing what they ought to be doing or why they feel uncomfortable if they are not doing it (Levinson, 1963, p. 33).

The need for esteem and status is essential for managers who seek love and affection. Everyone wants to be held in esteem and to be viewed affectionately. Few individuals can survive without giving and receiving love, although these emotions generally are disguised even from the individuals' own cognition. These needs focus upon the constructive forces and are concrete indications that other individuals hold them in esteem. However, the environment of the organization also may bring about aggression, anger, exploitation, and competition. Every individual has to deal with realities of this climate. What often happens is that the individuals are frustrated in the achievement of their personal goals and in the development of satisfying relationships with other people. Therefore, some of the basic needs for status and affection are afforded only temporarily.

The ego is the mechanism required to balance out and serve as the "manager" of the personality. Freud used the term ego to describe this phenomenon. The ego actually is a way of describing the organized executive functions of the personality that impact directly upon self-control and reality testing for the individual. The ego includes such mental functions as recall, perception, judgment, attention, and conceptual or abstract thinking that are the aspects of the personality that enable the individual to receive, organize, interpret. and act upon stimuli or psychological-physiological data.

The ego develops normally except in individuals who are mentally retarded. When the ego can balance out the id and superego, this is called psychological maturity. When it cannot do so, it can be stated that an individual does not have enough ego strength and has not matured. The ego is stimulated by reality issues such as the short-range and long-range ramifications of the individual's behavior. The ego has the job of initially balancing the forces from the id, the superego, and the environment.

The next task of the ego is to mediate and synchronize these forces into a system that operates relatively smoothly. This activity requires the assistance of two psychological states to make its task possible: some anxiety to serve as an alarm system to alert the ego to possible dangers to its equilibrium, and defense mechanisms that can be called into play, triggered by the alarm system. These will help the ego either to fend off the possible threats or to counteract them (Levinson, 1963, p. 35).

DEFENSES

Anxiety can be a positive vehicle in certain instances. Generally, however, it is viewed as a very heightened and uncomfortable state. It is a feeling of tension or uneasiness, but there is a more complex rationale that operates spontaneously and unconsciously for the individual when the ego experiences some danger. There is no state of peaceful emotional stability just as there never is a pure, positive environmental climate in which the individual reaches psychological equilibrium. Therefore, the ego sets up a unique system of defense mechanisms in order to protect the individual and maintain equilibrium. These defense mechanisms are:

1. **Identification:** a process of behaving like somebody else, in which an individual may identify with the supervisor with whom the person has a relationship in the organization.
2. **Repression:** a process in which the individual is pushing down drives that are quite threatening.
3. **Sublimation:** a process of refining basic drives and directing them into acceptable channels.

4. **Denial:** a form of repression in which the individual denies the reality of the situation because the ego has a difficult time accepting what has happened to it.
5. **Rationalization:** a temporary device that everyone uses in an attempt to justify a painful event in which a loss was experienced.
6. **Projection:** a method of attributing one's own feelings to someone else and identifying the individual who is the target as thinking in a similar manner.
7. **Idealization:** a method of putting the halo effect around another individual and therefore being unable to see the person's negative characteristics.
8. **Reaction formation:** a process of acting in an antithetical (oppositive) position in order to avoid the threat of giving in to the impulses. Some individuals become extremely fearful of their own aggressive impulses and deal with this by behaving in an extremely passive, meek manner, which is a "check and balance" against their feelings of aggression. This is one way to neutralize the id.
9. **Substitution:** a process often referred to as displacement, in which an individual, through the ego, is unable to direct those feelings to the appropriate target and therefore aims them at a safer substitute target. This occurs when a manager has a difficult time in confronting a supervisor, and comes home in the evening and inappropriately "dumps" frustrations upon the family, an action that cannot be done at work.
10. **Compensation:** a method and process of developing individual skills to compensate for those deficiencies and assuming those activities considered essential for achievement in attempting to overcome failures.

This defensive process usually comes into existence when the individual's ego is threatened and anxiety begins to trigger the mechanisms needed to block the threat. What often occurs is stress for the individual, who now performs personally and professionally at a less than optimal level. If there are too many emergencies for the individual to handle, the circuits become overloaded. As a result, the manager must use these mechanisms repeatedly, which ultimately will distort the person's perception of personal and organizational reality, which in turn creates more stress. Individuals can rationalize occasionally, but if they do so as a coping mechanism on a constant basis, they will experience other problems of dealing with fantasy and not with reality.

By and large, self-fulfillment has to do with the ego's capacity to function as effectively as it can. When emotional conflicts can be diminished and when the need for defensiveness can be decreased, the energy that ordinarily maintained those defenses is freed for more useful activity. In a sense, the effect is to remove some of the brakes from the psychological wheels. The individual then can relate to other people more reasonably and can communicate more clearly. A psychological blossoming-out can occur. When such balancing fails to take place, the ego is overwhelmed for the time being (Levinson, 1963, p. 38).

Some of these problems occur when individuals have been conditioned and trained to contain their drives and have learned throughout their development that it is not acceptable to express their aggression directly to people who are in authority positions. Such individuals have aggressive impulses but also have strong superegos, experience guilt about feeling this way, and invest a great deal of energy to repress these feelings. This energy becomes an investment in protection and a loss for productivity. This may occur when a supervisor criticizes individuals for being too aggressive. This sets off a stimulus in which the persons repress other feelings without being aware of them. The persons are so controlled that they cannot deal with the normal feelings of what every individual experiences.

With this great need to control the demands of the superego, the individuals now are put in a much more explosive, dangerous situation since it is necessary to present a defense against perceived external threats and at the same time to control these troublesome inner feelings. One problem is to control the anger within themselves. There is the option of turning the anger onto themselves or dumping it on other people as well. The result is a great deal of anxiety, stress, and often psychosomatic disability. Such individuals experience trauma and actually begin to "stew in their own juices." By not dealing with feelings of anger and aggression, the resolution also is avoided.

This guilt makes the managers feel inadequate and they turn their hostility (as discussed previously) onto the objects that have created this feeling of inadequacy—themselves. This may be acted out via a self-destructive act such as losing their job, or sabotaging their own performance or that of others, thus giving a clear message. The managers have another alternative that entails becoming acutely depressed by not dealing with the situation, which has become intrapsychically explosive. Depression is an indication of being angry with oneself because people avoid dealing with their anger toward others.

This is a direct confrontation of the superego and the ego. This state creates a sense of invalidism.

The very fact that people do not radically alter their patterns of behavior makes it possible to detect signs of emotional stress. Given certain characteristic modes of adaption in the form of personality traits, once people experience emotional stress, they are likely to initially make greater use of the mechanisms that worked best before. One of the first signs of stress is that individuals seem to be conspicuously more like they always have been. If they ordinarily are introverts, they may become withdrawn under stress. If this first line of defense does not work too well, or if the stress is too severe, inefficient functioning may begin to appear in the form of vague fears, an inability to concentrate, compulsions to do certain things, increasing inability, and declining work performance. The results of physiological defensive efforts will emerge. There may be problems with sleep, additional tension, and the inability to hold down food. If the individuals' defense mechanisms cannot contain their anxiety, there may be sharp changes in personality in which the persons no longer behave in the previous manner. A neat person may become very sloppy, or an efficient individual may become dependent upon drugs or alcohol.

Between 1960 and 1970, 13 percent of all new jobs in the United States were in the area of health care (Fein, 1976, p. 656). The problems of these professionals seriously interfered with the care of patients. It is easy to see how severe malfunctioning—for example, drug abuse and alcoholism—can be injurious to the patient. But even with less severe problems, the quality of health care will diminish when providers are distressed. These changes in personality indicate a more severe illness that usually may require hospitalization for the anxiety and the stress. These behavior changes are clear indicators that the ego no longer is able to maintain control and balance between the id and the superego. A severe imbalance could even lead to self-destructive behavior (suicide).

SUICIDE

If all the defense mechanisms discussed previously fail to work, individuals then may move into areas of self-destruction that may be used by managers experiencing severe stress. Managers are men and women of high aspiration. As a rule they are ambitious, seek power, prestige, and money, and nearly always are competing intensely with other managers. They have extremely high ego ideals that revolve around power. They have deep-seated unconscious pressures requiring attainment while their conscious goals are merely the tip of the iceberg. Persons who have such high levels of aspiration frequently are nagged by the feeling of being a long way from achieving their goals. No matter what they achieve, it never seems to be enough. As a result, they always view themselves as inadequate. Everyone tries constantly to narrow the gap between ego ideal and self-image. The failures of persons with irrational and unreachable high self-demands usually lower their self-image and thereby increase their anger at themselves. They experience self-directed anger as depression. While depression is widespread and usually is amenable to treatment, in its extreme form, as has been seen, it often leads to suicide. The problems of high aspiration, high ego ideal and low self-image start very early in life and contain significant components of irrationality (Levinson, 1975, p. 119).

When individuals pray to the shrine of achievement and scholastic professional goal accomplishment, then the probability that failure could occur becomes an even more significant threat to their self-esteem. When they reach mid-career, for example, many ambitious managers may feel that all the years of intense competition have not been worthwhile and that they now are carrying around the heavy weight of fear of failure as opposed to fear of success. While they have been striving to become high achievers, they also have been vulnerable to their self-image, which is moving in the opposite direction from their ego ideals.

This variance certainly illuminates the void that increases as the self-concept and planned goals do not automatically actualize. The managers become angry and extremely critical of their own performance, while feeling inadequate, depressed, and guilty. These feelings may lead eventually to the need to self-destruct that actually is the prime object of failure in the first place. These managers, who are tremendously demanding of their own performance and potential—which may be limited—often fail to cope with situations that are pressure packed and may see limited alternatives as a way out. If they do not become involved in a therapeutic relationship intended to help them to understand and deal with these factors, they may develop psychosomatic disorders and, as a final act of self-destruction, attack themselves or, in the extreme form, commit suicide.

In an effort to avoid the attack upon "self," some managers attack and sabotage their organizations quite unconsciously. They make stupid mistakes, provoke and discharge competent people, reorganize without reason, or go off on what prove to be tangents of diversification. Some try to overcontrol their organization with rigid systems that allow them to "whip people into line" and punish those who don't "shape up." They may become involved in some forms of self-directed aggression that occur with greater intensity in persons who are very conscientious and who have overidentified with their profession, business, occupation, or major life interest. The more these persons circumscribe their sources of ego gratification and organize their lives around one activity, the more vulnerable they are. Defeat or loss in that area can be cataclysmic (Levinson, 1975, p. 121).

It is difficult dealing with managers who may be suicidal, but there may be a factor or two that needs to be considered. Any manager who may suspect that a subordinate or peer is suffering from depression should not urge this individual to take time off and correct the problem via self-insight or a rest break. Troubled individuals then will have a greater degree of freedom to deal with their depression and punish themselves in isolation. Individuals whose depression does not require institutionalization need to be involved in an environment in which these problems can be worked on, get nourishment and support from supervisors and peers, and be involved with others through reality testing. Individuals who are depressed should be treated professionally and not be given "free therapy" by supervisors, peers, and subordinates who have jointly determined that these persons' problems are not very serious and that they probably will get over it as soon as individual insights are experienced at their level of consciousness.

This type of thinking is dangerous and generally will result in the individual's fulfilling the prophecy of doing away with the object of anger (themselves) by suicide. It is interesting to note that suicide, which is the most drastic reaction to stress, appears more prevalent in health care (medicine) than in the general population. Some even go so far as to say that suicide is an occupational hazard for all health professionals (Rose & Rosow, 1973, pp. 800-805). While suicide is the most extreme form of destructive behavior, the most pervasive occurs within the neurotic chasms of the organization.

MANAGERIAL NEUROSIS

Neurotic managers can function in an effective manner in an organization. On the surface they appear to be quite normal because some of the manifestations of their behavior are congruent with the mission of the organization. Generally they are extremely ambitious and unusually competitive. They can produce both quantitatively and qualitatively and are totally devoted to their jobs. This attracts the attention of top management, which moves these individuals on to higher responsibilities. These people are workaholics, are willing to travel, and often devote their life to the job. Involvement over the weekend and lack of family life appear to be no problem in their quest for achievement. They frequently are persons who are basically insecure and frustrated but who appear on the surface to be very dynamic and self-confident.

This conflict of internal turmoil and external facade is a source of anxiety and stress for these managers. They have a strong need to deny these characteristics and will initiate a campaign against individuals who they feel are in competition with them by demonstrating rivalry, resentment, and even overt hatred in an extremely aggressive manner. When they are promoted to demanding positions, their own deficiencies become apparent and they feel threatened since their inadequacies may be exposed, thus creating more pressure that illuminates their limitations and weakness. To compensate for this anxious state of affairs, they work even harder at their jobs, thus plunging deeper into their own anxieties.

This managerial neurosis is an extreme problem for many organizations because executives who demonstrate some of these patterns usually do not have these inadequacies and limitations recognized by top management until after they have been placed in positions where they are highly visible and in control. The idea of placing these individuals in top positions creates the need to assess their performance, but an individual who is particularly well qualified to manage an operation under one set of circumstances may not be qualified to do so under other conditions. The major and inescapable characteristic of the top executive's role is its excruciating demands in terms of time and continuous mental and physical pressure (McMurry, 1973, p. 290).

As managers progress in an upward spiral, they find that there are rigid structures, segmented operations, and stratification with which they must deal. Each level has its own social structure, its own mores, its own folkways and loyalties. Rivalries begin to develop at one level and move to other levels. These factors keep managers in a constant state of turmoil. A safe way for executives to ensure that they may be considered for promotion is to carefully avoid as many responsibilities as they safely can throughout their careers. This has to be handled delicately because the managers' concerns are that if they assume a great deal of responsibility they will have a higher probability of failure because of their feelings of being basically inadequate. If a problem does occur, they personally cannot be charged with the responsibility for it and, as a result, the more neurotic they become, the more isolated they become as well.

These managers know they must accomplish and achieve the primary objectives of the organization by working through people and at the same time are concerned with maintaining only a minimum of communication. They work in an atmosphere where many subordinates and peers have their own problems and hostilities. This results in the withholding of data from their supervisors or the distortion of communications that are essential for managers who are involved in and must be totally aware of all processes. These additional pressures create more anxiety for the managers, and the accompanying frustrations have a tremendous effect upon such individuals, whether they are neurotic or perfectly adjusted. Just what the effect is upon the managers varies with the nature of the pressures and their own personality, motivation, and ability to cope. It is no wonder that individuals have neurotic tendencies and sooner or later show an inability to cope with the responsibilities of a major management position, i.e., an inability to make decisions demanded of them (McMurry, p. 293).

Executives who are well equipped to handle management jobs usually are emotionally mature and have high emotional and physiological energy levels. The extent of individuals' emotional maturity depends upon their early training, background, and experiences and how their talent capabilities have been developed. The most important qualities are self-reliance, the ability to receive as well as to give, to deal with other people, to develop self-discipline, to be intrinsically motivated, and to be a long-range thinker. Neurotic executives do not possess these essential qualities and often create a negative environment by resorting to an authoritarian, autocratic style that is terribly frustrating for subordinates. The subordinates at that point, realizing they cannot control this counterproductive environment, basically give up on the job. As a rule, they become very passive and dependent or will even psychologically sabotage the operation and, to use popular "transactional analysis" terminology, become obedient children for their supervisors, who play the role of overbearing parents.

Most of these managers attempt to mask their inadequacies by avoiding the painful reality that they are not superhumans, are not totally self-reliant, and are not as capable as they feel they should be. They spend a tremendous amount of energy and time attempting to camouflage their deficiencies and to present an unrealistic profile for others who they hope will view them in a much more positive way than they view themselves. Another difficulty is that the subordinates depend upon these super "managers" and seem to seek out these leaders as strong parent figures for their own selfish reasons. This creates additional pressures, and managers may become extremely demanding, arbitrary, and inconsiderate and therefore exercise more controls over subordinates as a defense, hoping the employees will not depend upon them for the strength they actually do not possess.

These managers who are extremely dependent and passive also can be conformists. What they will do is introject the norms of the department or group within the organization that seems to be in control at that time, thereby ensuring the support of the membership at both subordinate and supervisory levels. It is most interesting that with all the pressures and stress, high-ranking managerial positions are very appealing to individuals who possess this personality profile. This is one of the dangers and problems to be found in organizations since these managers' expectations are not realistic. They give little thought to the prerequisites, trade-offs, and stress associated with the position and instead think of the power and glamour the position seems to project. It is common to discover that managers who are improperly placed in positions and who actually should not be managers or executives demonstrate this neurotic pattern.

One way of determining whether individuals have a congruent mix with their positions is to carefully review past performance up to the date that they are being considered for moves into managerial positions. In general, they must at least have demonstrated on previous assignments:

1. the ability to accept heavy responsibility without undue anxiety
2. the capacity to make sound judgments under pressure without panic or undue aggressiveness
3. an active, creative, dynamic orientation toward the job environment; that is, must not merely have adapted passively to it, but have shaped and molded it to meet their needs

Yet today, nearly all promotions to top management positions are based on such obvious factors as the amount and type of the individuals' education and technical training, the level of their intelligence, and length and character of their experience (McMurry, p. 303).

Managers who are experiencing this neurotic pattern also may be undergoing certain physiological changes that may have affected their overall cerebral functioning. One condition that contributes to the development of this managerial neurosis is the physiological deterioration of the prefrontal lobes of the brain and even of the entire cerebral cortex. Some individuals gradually deteriorate at midcareer, while others begin to deteriorate in their late thirties. Some of the most common causes of this prefrontal lobe and cortical deterioration are diabetes, arteriosclerosis, high blood pressure, physical accidents, and histological changes through senility. This usually is characterized by a reduction in learning, memory, judgment, and self-control. There also appears to be some pronounced rigidity in thinking and decision making and the tendency to become more reactionary while recalling events from the past. An individual who is affected in this way tends to regress to childhood patterns and behavior such as dependence, incapacity to accept responsibility, and other immature symptoms.

There are other organizational situations that may indicate individuals may be suffering from a managerial type of neurosis. Managers who are deteriorating have been found to have a difficult time relaxing, have outbursts of temper, worry a great deal of the time, and are not in control of their position. They are not able to make even programmed decisions and they usually are involved in seeking out individuals as scapegoats on whom they can dump their frustrations. They may become involved in fantasy thinking in the quest to escape the reality of decision making. These individuals are basically fearful of most events with which they are not even remotely familiar and they will try to eliminate any subordinates who do not support their troubled behavior pattern by firing, demoting, or transferring them. They have a difficult time in dealing with most people, accepting personal responsibility, and cooperating with peers. They may become suspicious of other managers and peers with whom they are working and ultimately develop emotionally defensive attitudes toward anyone who questions their policies.

These managers become hypercritical and have a tendency to replace individuals who question their decisions with other subordinates who appear to support them. In many organizations, this group is not very difficult to find. In the more tragic cases, neurotic managers stay on the job indefinitely and find it essential to develop "flight behavior" in which they avoid all the responsibilities of the job and take a great deal of time off. This may occur in the form of attending many professional seminars in which they abdicate their decision-making role to others by their absence or become heavily involved in alcohol and drugs, preventing them from performing effectively. This is basically a mechanism for self-destruction in which the individuals turn their aggressions on themselves. As a result of this conflict, the managers at this same time may be prone to hypertension, arteriosclerosis, ulcers, colitis, and other problems that become very dysfunctional. These conditions quite often are stress induced.

One of the major issues to address at this juncture is the identification of this troubled individual within the organization. It is clear that the reduction of stress and altering the nature of the work is a primary step. The person may be transferred from a pressure-packed line position to a staff position or moved to a status position as an internal consultant where the pressure and stressors are kept at a minimum. The organization can involve this distressed individual in counseling sessions where the employer assumes responsibility for the situation and is truly concerned with the manager's welfare. Any sessions with outside counselors or external therapeutic interventions must be maintained confidentially and must be kept between the manager in turmoil and the counselor selected since trust is a major issue in the reduction of stress for the neurotic executive. This issue is addressed in Chapter 8 on the troubled employee.

THE ABRASIVE MANAGER

Unfortunately, organizations reward and support individuals who are overly aggressive and even abrasive based upon a results-oriented reward system. The abrasive manager occupies an interesting role as a stress agent in such an organization. These individuals often occupy solid managerial positions and usually are considered to be bright. They are perfectionists, need to be always accurate, and push themselves extremely hard. They usually will achieve what they had planned in an excellent manner. They want to do the job themselves and find it difficult to work in groups. This is a problem when they are in managerial positions since it is difficult for them to delegate. They are analytical and are capable of cutting clearly through muddled issues to the core of the problem, but with their need for high achievement, they become impatient with those who cannot move as quickly as they can on this level. Their ability to analyze problems usually is not matched by others in the organization. Their intense rivalry leads them to undercut others, which also increases the general tension level in the organization. When they are involved with groups, they tend to dominate and treat any differences of opinion as challenges that must be argued and resolved only in their favor.

They are quite domineering and are difficult to deal with from a supervisory position as well. They feel they are so completely competent that they may challenge their supervisor's competence and authority. They move both intellectually and physically very quickly and their range of interests is vast. Their ideas are quite insightful and their supervisor may have to reject their inputs because these individuals always are directed in the path of trying to take control of the department. Their supervisor may feel that it is very difficult to contain these individuals and, as a result, will attempt to do so by keeping them in lesser positions that are antithetical and demotivating to their own needs and desires.

If they become controlled by their supervisor, abrasive managers feel they have been rejected and their efforts have not been worthwhile. At this point, they may become extremely angry, and it is difficult to keep this stressful situation in check. The abrasive individuals now may begin to see other people in the organization as devices for their self-fulfillment. They also perceive other persons as extensions of themselves rather than as true individuals who have their own unique needs and who should be treated in a humanistic way. These abrasive individuals are in need of self-control because this appears to be one of the methods for keeping them in control. These individuals will overorganize their jobs and attempt to deal with imperfections in others by controlling them in an extremely tight managerial style. Abrasive personalities who are not controlled produce a very uncomfortable situation and create tremendous stress. To compensate for this, they develop very rigid postures in which they refuse to compromise. In fact, for these managers, making a compromise is the same as giving in to lower standards. They therefore have low capacity for the necessary give-and-take of organizational political systems (Levinson, 1978, p. 89).

Anna Freud contributed some insights with regard to the abrasive personality and aggression: If individuals' ultimate aspiration is ego ideal and perfection, then they always will fall short of it, and by astronomical distances. If their self-image already is low, the distance between where they perceive themselves to be and the omnipotence they want to attain will increase constantly as the feeling of failure continues. Therefore, they must push themselves even harder—all the time. Others who are or may be viewed as competitors threaten these individuals' self-image even further; if these others win, the individuals lose by their own definition. Their intense need to be perfect then becomes translated into intense rivalry.

If persons always are pushing themselves toward impossible aspirations and never are able to achieve them, there are two consequences for these emotions:

1. The greater the gap between their ego ideal and self-image, the greater will be both their guilt and anger with themselves for not achieving the dream.

2. The angrier persons are with themselves, the more likely they are to attack themselves or drive themselves to narrow the gap between their ideal and their present self-image.

Only in narrowing the gap can they reduce their feelings of anger, depression, and inadequacy. However, as the unconscious drive for perfection is irrational, no degree of conscious effort can possibly achieve the ideal nor decrease the self-punishment such persons bring down on themselves for not achieving it. The anger and self-hatred are never-ending, therefore, and build up to the point where they spill over in the form of hostile attacks on peers and subordinates, such as treating them with contempt and condescension. These feelings may spill over onto spouses, children, and even pets. In fact, abrasive persons' needs for self-punishment may be so great that they may take great, albeit neurotic, pleasure in provoking others who subsequently will reject them—that is, punish them. In effect, they act as if they were their own parents, punishing themselves as well as others. They become good haters (Levinson, 1978, p. 89).

SOME REMEDIES

The concern appears to be how to deal with abrasive employees. The fact that abrasive managers and their personalities have as their foundation vulnerable self-image, need for affection, and a need not to become angry can be understood. One way of dealing with these individuals is to limit the frequency of communication with them. When discussions do occur, it may be best for the superior not to inform them of their abrasive behavior but to describe to them what the executive perceives is happening and to react unemotionally to them. The superior may want to ask these subordinates how they feel their behavior affects the people involved or may even want to indicate to them that top officials understand their need to achieve and are in favor of their achievement.

If the abrasive persons do not accept these inputs in a very positive way, it would be best for the superior not to counterattack and develop a secondary hostile environment. Executives may tell the abrasive persons that they are not interested in perpetuating an unresolvable conflict. Managers, in their quest to defuse the situations, have found it helpful to discuss with their abrasive subordinates legitimate achievements of which these people certainly can be proud. These abrasive individuals need frequent feedback from supervisors as they move up in the organization.

Feedback seems to be a process that keeps their anxiety level at a minimum. These are very achievement-oriented individuals who feel anxious a great deal of the time and also feel they are not succeeding as well as they should. When they feel this pressure, the conflict and frustration makes them appear even more abrasive. When this method of informing the individuals of their behavior fails, then it is time for management to inform the abrasive persons of the net effect that their behavior has upon others in the organization. The next procedure is to legitimize this position organizationally in order to reduce the stress by having these individuals cease and desist from behaving in this manner. Most managers do not deal well with performance appraisal or constructive criticism such as this recommendation entails. It may be very essential to neutralize the abrasive personalities who also may be very valuable to the organization and individuals that it is desirable to retain for a long period of time. Levinson has postulated 13 questions that individuals may want to ask themselves to determine whether they have an abrasive personality. These indices may be an insightful beginning for managers trying to cope with this type of problem:

1. Are you condescendingly critical? When you talk of others in the organization, do you speak of straightening them out or whipping them into shape?
2. Do you need to be in full control? Does almost everything need to be cleared with you?
3. In meetings, do your comments take a disproportionate amount of time?
4. Are you quick to rise to the attack, to challenge?
5. Do you have a need to debate? Do discussions quickly become arguments?
6. Are people reluctant to discuss things with you? When someone does, are their statements inane?
7. Are you preoccupied with acquiring symbols of status and power?
8. Do you weasel out of responsibilities?
9. Are you reluctant to let others have the same privileges or perquisites as yourself?
10. When you talk about your activities, do you use the word "I" disproportionately?
11. Do your subordinates admire you because you are so strong and capable, or because in your organization they feel so strong and capable—and supported?

12. To your amazement, do people speak of you as cold and distant when you really want them to like you?

13. Do you regard yourself as more competent than your peers? Than the boss? Does your behavior let them know that? (Levinson, 1978, p. 94)?

If an individual is in fact abrasive, the antithetical reaction to these questions would be the first step in attempting to neutralize the net effects of this attitude that have negative connotations for subordinates, peers, and supervisors. In the long run, the organization has a difficult time of functioning and coping in a healthy way with varied individuals occupying important positions who are extremely abrasive. This situation creates further anxiety and stress for those who are attempting to operate in a positive, productive climate.

This chapter has examined the effect and impact of anxiety, crises, authority figures, defense mechanisms, neurotic systems; and aggressive-abrasive styles that activate stress in organizational members and climates. Health care managers experience these events and still must function within the constraints of the complex roles they occupy. The intricacies of the roles, as well as integrated structural-individual components, are explored in the next chapter.

BIBLIOGRAPHY

Fein, R. Health manpower: Some economic considerations. *Journal of Dental Education*, 1976, *40*, 655-661.

Greenwood, J.W. Management stressors. In *Reducing occupational stress: Proceedings of the National Institute for Occupational Safety and Health*, White Plains, N.Y., May 1977, pp. 41-51.

Jennings, E.E. *The executive in crisis.* New York: McGraw-Hill Book Co., 1965, 40, 55, 56, 69, 101, 145, 175, 206.

Levinson, H. What killed Bob Lyons? *Harvard Business Review,* January-February 1963, *41*(1), 26-42.

_____. On executive suicide. *Harvard Business Review,* July-August 1975, *53*(4), 118-122.

_____. Reprinted by permission of the *Harvard Business Review.* Excerpt from "The Abrasive Personality" by Harry Levinson (May-June 1978). Copyright © 1978 by the President and Fellows of Harvard College; all rights reserved.

Maslow, A. *Motivation and personality.* New York: Harper & Row, 1954.

McMurry, R.N. The executive neurosis. In R.L. Noland (Ed.), *Industrial mental health and employee counseling.* New York: Behavioral Publications, 1973, 282-316.

Rose, K.D., & Rosow, I. Physicians who kill themselves. *Archives of General Psychiatry,* 1973, *29,* 800-805.

Toffler, A. *Future shock.* New York: Bantam Books, 1970, 97.

Wren, A.D. *The evolution of management thought.* New York: Ronald Press, 1972, 219.

Chapter 3

Roles and Stress of the Health Care Manager

CONSIDERATIONS FOR THE HEALTH CARE MANAGER

1. The role of chief executive officers of health care organizations is undergoing substantial change and these individuals now are more broadly engaged in policy level activities and external representation of the institution.
2. The most time-consuming roles for the health care manager are those of leader, entrepreneur, and monitor.
3. The most important managerial roles for these managers are those of entrepreneur, leader, and monitor.
4. Goals and policies rarely are clarified for personnel to follow, which creates ambiguity and conflict.
5. There is a need to separate official and operative goals for all committed to these goals. When the goals remain vague, this is a message to all subordinates that the objective is tight control and not the supposed quality of health care services being offered.
6. The goals of the following interest groups are likely to shape the health care organizational mission to comply with whomever is in control:

- trustees   • administration
- medical staff

However, the lowest conflict system is that of multiple leadership.

7. Hospitals are characterized by an advisory bureaucratic model based upon administrative authority but where the physicians retain decision-making power in professional domains.

8. A negative relationship exists between experience and satisfaction with promotion for administrators. Fewer promotions are available as administrators achieve more experience.

9. Stress increases for administrators (but not professionals) if they have low involvement in decision making and goal setting.

10. Where authority relationships are dominant, alienation is experienced by subordinates who perceive satisfaction to be nonexistent. This situation illuminates the need for extrinsic rewards to be offered to subordinates who now want to be compensated for this less than humanistic treatment.

11. Contemporary health care managers are functioning as power brokers, balancing and manipulating authority, information flow, and managerial processes in the quest to enhance their position in the power hierarchy of their organizations.

Recent studies have indicated that the role of the hospital chief executive officer is undergoing substantial change and that even more change can be expected. Hospital administrators appear to be broadly engaged in policy level activities and in external representation of the organization (Forrest, Johnson, & Mosher, 1977, p. 400). It is important to develop a managerial role description, and Henry Mintzberg of McGill University has performed this task admirably in his text, *The Nature of Managerial Work* (1973). However, it is essential to note that a role is a pattern of behavior associated with a distinctive social position and often is subject to conflicting pressures (Broom & Selznick, 1968, p. 18). This is the plight of the health care manager.

MANAGERIAL ROLES

The manager is the person in charge of a formal organization or one of its subunits. The individual is vested with formal authority over the organizational unit, which leads to the person's two basic purposes:

1. The manager must ensure that the organization produces its specific goods or services efficiently. The executive must design, and maintain the stability of, its basic operations, and must adapt it in a controlled way to its changing environment.
2. The manager must ensure that the organization serves the ends of the persons who control it (the "influencers"). The executive must interpret their particular preferences and combine these to produce statements of organizational preference that can guide its decision making.

Because of the role's formal authority, the manager must serve two other basic purposes as well: act as the key communication link between the organization and its environment, and assume responsibility for the operation of the organization's status system.

There are ten working roles for the health care manager. These basic purposes are made operational through ten interrelated roles, performed by all managers. These fall into three groupings: three interpersonal roles, which derive from the manager's authority and status; three informational roles, which derive from the interpersonal roles and the access they provide to information; and four decisional roles, which derive from the manager's authority and information (Mintzberg, 1973, pp. 166-167).

Interpersonal Roles

1. *The Figurehead Role:* The chief executive is a symbol required by the status of office to carry out a variety of social, legal, and ceremonial duties in which the individual represents the organization.
2. *The Leader Role:* The chief executive has interpersonal relationships with subordinates and as the manager hires, trains and

motivates them, the leader must essentially bring their needs in accord with those of the organization.

3. *The Liaison Role:* The chief executive has interpersonal relationships with people outside the organization and spends a considerable amount of time developing a network of high-status contacts in which information and favors are traded for mutual benefit and through which the chief executive exerts community leadership.

Informational Roles

1. *The Monitor Role:* The chief executive continually seeks and receives information about the organization in order to understand changing situations and the organization's environment.

2. *The Disseminator Role:* The chief executive shares some of the environmental information with subordinates.

3. *The Spokesman Role:* The chief executive informs outsiders about the progress, problems, and activities of the organization.

Decisional Roles

1. *The Entrepreneur Role:* The chief executive takes the responsibility for bringing about changes in the organization, looking for problems and opportunities, and then initiating projects to deal with them.

2. *The Disturbance-Handler Role:* The chief executive takes charge when the organization faces a major disturbance or crisis and deals with the resulting problems.

3. *The Resource Allocator Role:* The chief executive decides who will get what in the organization; establishes priorities, designs the organization, and authorizes all important decisions.

4. *The Negotiator Role:* The chief executive takes charge whenever the organization must enter into crucial negotiations with other parties; this manager's presence is required because this individual has the information and the authority to make the decisions that difficult negotiations require (Forrest, Johnson, & Mosher, 1977, p. 396).

EMPHASIZING ROLES THAT FIT THE SITUATION

Although required to perform all of the basic managerial roles, most executives must give special attention to certain roles in certain situations. A variety of factors determine what roles particular managers must emphasize. These factors include, among others, the industry, the size of the organization, the level in the hierarchy, the function supervised, the situation of the moment, and the manager's experience.

The job itself, as well as the environment, may suggest some obvious needs. Managers of governmental organizations may have to spend extra time on liaison and spokesperson roles to satisfy outside pressure groups, production managers may need to concentrate on the disturbance-handler role to maintain the workflow, managers of competitive organizations may be required to emphasize the entrepreneur role in order to keep ahead of the competition. Clearly, managers must study the needs of the job and tailor their work accordingly.

The choice of which roles to emphasize must also reflect the current situation. The manager's job is a dynamic one, requiring continual adjustment to meet the needs of the moment. In every managerial job there is a time to concentrate on change and a time to seek stability, a time to stress leadership and a time to build a data base, a time to handle disturbances and a time to replenish resources.

This situation suggests certain patterns. In beginning a new job, managers are likely to find a lack of the external contacts and the information necessary to make and implement effective decisions. Clearly, managers must devote considerable time at the start of a new job to developing liaison contacts, to building their own information channels, to collecting information about the new organization and its environment. Later, when they feel more secure in this knowledge, they may shift emphasis gradually to the entrepreneur role in an attempt to mold the organization to their own wishes.

The need to balance stability and change also may influence managers' attention to roles. Managers may find it effective under certain circumstances to alternate periods of extensive change with those of consolidation of change, rather than to adopt a pattern of slow, steady change. In other words, the managers emphasize the entrepreneur role for a period, making what they consider the necessary changes all at one time. Thus the organization undergoes all the disruption at once. When no more change can be tolerated, the managers then consolidate the gains and bring back stability, emphasizing the leader and disturbance-handler roles. Later, when all is normal, a new cycle can start (Mintzberg, 1973, pp. 182-183).

A study by Forrest, Johnson, & Mosher of the role of the chief executive of a health care organization used the Mintzberg managerial role description questionnaire to classify health care managers via a profile. The most time-consuming roles were those of leader, entrepreneur, and monitor. Interestingly, while being the most time-consuming, these three were selected from the categories of interpersonal roles, informational roles, and decisional roles.

The three most important managerial roles for the chief executive officer of the hospital were those of entrepreneur, leader, and monitor. These also were extracted from the categories of interpersonal, informational, and decisional roles. Health care managers must focus upon effective interpersonal relationships with their subordinates and must bring their needs into accord with those of the organization. The managers also must continually seek out and receive information about their organization in order to understand changing situations intraorganizationally and interorganizationally. Finally, the health care administrator is an entrepreneur and takes the responsibility for bringing about changes in the organization and looking for opportunities.

These contemporary managerial roles may be in conflict with the traditional role of the health care manager; however, those managers today are engaged in conflict, and as such do experience great degrees of strain and stress. They must be able to achieve a balance between the environment and the human resources since the incongruency between them creates stress and makes individuals quite vulnerable to situations that should be managed. In health care organizations, managerial strategies are considered to be significant mediators in the quest to identify and reduce the stress that affects all members of the organization.

STRUCTURE: ANALYSIS OF GOALS AND STYLES

To understand fully the organization and behavior of the membership, an analysis of goals in complex health care institutions is a starting point. Most administrators would agree readily that their organization's goals are clear and taken for granted, and therefore this is not the place to begin since all is OK. However, experiences accumulated from working in the health care environment indicate that goals and policies are not taken for granted or universalized, and managers are left with "procedures du jour." There is a great need to differentiate between the types of goals in use in the health care environment and to determine which goals are essential for effective operation. Conflict occurs when goals are not put into effect and when systems laden with role ambiguity are fully operative within the structure of the goal environment.

Managers should develop traditional goal models to define the success of an organization as a complete or partially complete actualization of its mission. The key point is the degree to which the organization is goal oriented and not how it achieves its goals. It is very important to determine the institution's basic goals and communicate them to all administrators who need such clarification.

There are two basic types of goals in organizations—official and operative. Official goals signify the general purpose of the organization as put forth in official statements of what it is attempting to accomplish. However, this type of analysis is inadequate since goals generally are stated purposefully in vague terms to provide executives with the prerogatives and control to change the goals arbitrarily. This keeps management in a one-upsmanship position. The other important goals are the operative ones that designate the end result and indicate what the institution actually is attempting to do. These are the "means" to the official goals, but since these goals have been stated in a vague manner, the means become the "ends" in themselves. This creates further conflict and of course leads to stresses for the in-· dividuals involved in attempting to carry out the missions.

These operative goals are related to group interests and are not actually connected to the official goals. For example, how hospitals use interns and residents as "cheap labor" actually may subvert the official goal, which is medical education. It may further the official goal in the long run by providing high quality of patient care. These goals must be stated accurately so that every member of the organization understands what the initial step is in their achievement. Unfortunately, this idealistic view is not shared universally.

These goals can be examined in basic terms if something is known about the tasks of the institution and the characteristics of the controlling elite. The tasks of the health care organization are:

1. to obtain inputs
2. to obtain legitimization
3. to regulate necessary skills
4. to coordinate the activity of members
5. to depend upon technology, development stage, and the nature of work

The characteristics of the controlling group impact upon the operative goals that it will shape, reflecting the imperatives of the particular task area that is most critical, the group members' background characteristics, and the unofficial uses to which they put the organization for their own ends (Perrow, 1969, p. 371). An example of this occurs when a hospital is in financial difficulty and puts heavy emphasis on fund raising. This critical emphasis permits the administrative personnel to dominate and to shift control from medical staff to administration for as long as the problem is active and the mission clearly focused.

This goal analysis can be used in examining a voluntary organization such as a hospital. The purpose is to analyze how each authority structure shapes or even limits the type of operative goals that have been designed to determine what the ends are and what the organization actually is attempting to do. The goals of the following groups are likely to shape or limit the type of goals that will dominate (Perrow, p. 375):

Trustee Domination: This is based upon trustees' obtaining capital and legitimization, meeting community needs, involvement with the community, controlling appointments of physicians, and using the hospital to further their personal philanthropic objectives. They will make sure the administrator's power is controlled tightly as they shape the operative goals by developing their own priorities and standards.

Medical Staff Domination: The medical staff controls the hospital by the use of technical skills. It designs the bureaucratic structure for the medical requirements and medical-based rewards. Physicians are in power to handle both line and staff operations. Operative goals always are medically defined. Physicians use the hospital resources for private paying patients and not for community needs, and they use charismatic authority to have medical personnel achieve individual personal goals.

Administrative Domination: The administrators implement both internal and external coordination. Their importance is due to the new interdependence of health services. They can buffer power struggles between trustees and medical staff. It is important to determine whether the administrator is trained in medicine or in business—the focus of power will depend upon that orientation.

Multiple Leadership: In this situation, all three groups—trustees, medical staff, and administrators—share power and fulfill their own interests. It also is a division of labor that determines the goals and the power to achieve those aims in a multiple fashion. It symbolizes a situation in which all three groups are involved, which protects their interests and reconciles their individual goals to this multiple leadership type. This system seldom creates a conflict situation in which confrontation and showdowns are prevalent. Greater emphasis is placed upon cooperation, and the organization can prosper even with ambiguous goals through this system of forced interrelationships. It was found that under this system the hospital prospered and led its region in progressive innovations and responsible medical-social policies despite some subversion of the official goals of patient care, teaching, research, and preventive medicine. The organization could tolerate considerable ambiguity of goals and achievements as long as standards remained high in most areas, occupancy was sufficient to operate with a minimum deficit, and a favorable public image was maintained.

Contemporary practices have moved from this approach studied in 1969 to one that is more adaptive, systems oriented, and interrelated (a contingency view) (Kast & Rosenzweig, 1979, p. 120).

CONTINGENCY THEORY: THE BEST STYLE?

The contingency theory of management indicates that no one style really is correct for every organization or situation. The appropriate style of management depends upon the task and the environment of the organization. In the same organization, management policies and procedures may vary from department to department and from individual to individual. This probably is much more apparent in health care organizations because of the variations between professional and nonprofessional employees and between administrative staff and medical staff. There are more precisely described entrance requirements, distinct roles, and status symbols in health care organizations than in most corporations where ambiguities can add to confusion and mixed messages.

To cope with problems confronting the health care sector of society, organizations in this field have attempted to adopt structural forms that have proved effective in the industrial and governmental segments of society. However, hospitals are characterized by many lines of authority, various sources of power, and complicated lines of communication. The hospital is characterized by an "advisory bureaucratic" model based on administrative authority in the administrative realm, but where doctors retain the power to make decisions regarding matters in which they have professional expertise. As a result of these advisory bureaucratic organizational structures, changes have occurred in the role requirements of health care occupations (Welsch, LaVan, & Erickson, 1979, pp. 1-2). The role of manager also takes into consideration the characteristics of management as a profession. The characteristics of a profession within an occupation are:

1. Professionals have a degree of knowledge concerning their specialty that evolved through a long training period; the knowledge could not be acquired by anyone outside of their occupation.
2. Professionals have an authority that their clients lack and that the clients will surrender to the professionals, who judge and evaluate the quality of the service they provide.
3. Professionals are both socially and behaviorally responsible and appear to be more altruistic.
4. Professionals exert tighter self-controls rather than being controlled externally.
5. Professionals are recognized by the community as being in an occupation that is a profession; this entails a distinctive professional culture.

Health care professionals have increased quantitatively in recent years and there has been a trend to enter this field as an occupation and not as an administrative discipline. This is not to say that their occupation does not have an administrative framework or some functions where performance is evaluated by external occupational groups to which the workers belong. But these employees still possess authority and control over their work.

A study by Welsch, LaVan, & Erickson (1979) looked at the organizational climate of a hospital and the relationship of this climate to job satisfaction for health care professionals (nurses and administrators). The linkages between the climate and job satisfaction were similar for both administrators and nurses. This illustrated the point that different occupations were affected equally by negative climate dimensions.

A recent study among registered nurses found that role stress increased with the degree of professional training, with baccalaureate nurses experiencing the most. The results indicated that the type of anticipatory socialization called nursing education did not influence the activities performed by general duty nurses. Role stress was negatively correlated with job satisfaction, and on-the-job tenure did not mitigate the impact of an anticipatory socialization on role stress (Welsch, LaVan, & Erickson, 1979, p. 6).

Another interesting point was that professionals who were highly experienced appeared to be less satisfied with supervision, and the more experienced administrators were equally dissatisfied with a scarcity of promotional opportunities. A negative relationship seemed to exist between experience and satisfaction with promotion for those administrators. This is illustrated by the fact that fewer promotions are available as administrators gain more experience. A strong positive relationship does exist between work-related stress for professionals and the number of years of their experience. This factor, however, was not important to administrators who were not under similar pressures and experiencing the same stress. Women in administration in health care seemed to be less satisfied with salaries and promotional opportunities. This factor is supported in other industrial studies.

The number of years health care administrators have invested with their present hospital and their satisfaction with salary also are not related positively. There is a negative relationship between the years spent with their present employer, satisfaction with the supervision received, and the type of work. It may be explained that promotions for professionals are based upon their skills with their clients and not upon their supervisory abilities. If managers and administrators in health care organizations are evaluated only on an administrative and technical basis, and not with regard to their human resource skills, this establishes the underpinnings of a conflict situation that will result only in stress for those in the system. The results of the previous studies indicate this incongruency.

STRESS AND ORGANIZATIONAL STYLE

In looking at the impact of goal setting on the organizational climate, the Welsch, LaVan and Erickson study indicated both the lack of involvement in decision making and low participation in goal setting were associated with a higher level of stress for the administrators involved but not for the professionals. Lack of accurate communications and of supervisors' knowledge of problems faced by subordinates both were associated with stress among the professionals, but not among the administrators. Strong relationships were found between a directional flow of communication and job satisfaction. Apparently professionals react more positively (are more satisfied) when the information flow is in all directions (up, down, and with peers). Administrators may accept a more centralized, bureaucratic model of communication that flows mostly downward, and they are not disturbed by lack of all-directional communications. This suggests the more traditional structural models may be appropriate for administrative personnel, whereas a more flexible, open, and free-flowing informational climate may be necessary for professionals. Varying needs in informational requirements with respect to the specific task to be performed may account for differences between the groups (Welsch, LaVan, & Erickson, p. 13).

It appears that professionals and administrators differ on orientation toward work. Various professions may attract particular personality types, some of whom are affiliation oriented, achievement oriented, and even power oriented. The administrator's personality may be unique when compared with the personalities of professional groups. The management of health care organizations must deal with the heterogeneity of the administrators and professionals with managerial actions and organizational processes that are uniquely different. Demographic differences between employees and administrators have differing impacts on stress, autonomy, job satisfaction, and goal achievement. These organizational issues are linked directly to the health care professional and the administrator in this dynamic environment, and the resolution of these differences in a symbiotic relationship may be essential for a smooth-running organization.

NINE SOCIAL-PSYCHOLOGICAL INTEGRATION STUDIES

In viewing the health care institution as an integrated system, it is essential to look at the psychological and sociological factors and dynamics affecting the organization, membership, and system. It is important to examine the organization's impact upon the individual participant in the administrative structure. Also to be explored is the net effect of the individual's impact upon the organization and upon the macrosystem that may be impervious to any change. This factor is essential in examining the individual's tolerance level and anxiety with regard to the level of stress experienced that may be the result of this integration. The often complex roles and conflicts of these managers need to be examined. Fortunately, a good deal of research has been completed to illuminate some of the intricacies.

Health care organizations are sets of integrated units with varying value systems. There are multiple subsystems within the hospital that may include the board of directors, the administration, the medical staff, and other elements. These multiple groups, each with a different value system, can be problems at times. The following nine research summaries address these integrated components and problems.

Research Summary A: Organizational Change

Hospitals deviating from the typical model of bureaucracy become an exceptional study in organizational dynamics. This can be illustrated by a case study of organizational change conducted over a ten-year period in a small general hospital. The author distinguished three stages of organizational change:

1. At the beginning, this hospital was in a state of equilibrium based largely on a system of personal relationships and cliques and on status patterns that had developed informally in an ad hoc fashion. This situation deviated considerably from a bureaucratic form, and physicians practicing in the hospital then found it difficult to carry out dominant roles unless they could accommodate to the strong in-group clique situation.

2. The institution's governing authority intervened, however, with the intention of changing the organization to a form closer to the typical hospital. This, of course, disturbed the existing equilibrium, and for two years a condition persisted with staff personnel unwilling to comply with the new directives. This increased intraorganizational tensions, with opposing cliques intensifying mutual antagonisms, thereby reducing staff morale and the effectiveness of patient care.

3. In the third and last phase, a newly appointed medical director gradually broke up the cliques and the earlier informal, personalized authority structure. A structure in accordance with the bureaucratic pattern considered appropriate for hospitals was substituted. The earlier dominance by the nursing hierarchy gave place to a more conventional system dominated by physicians (Georgopoulos, 1975, p. 172).

Research Summary B: Goals and Effectiveness

Another study focusing on the social and psychological integration of the health care system examined the relationship between psychiatric staff consensus on organizational goals and hospital effectiveness, and the conditions giving rise to such a consensus. The investigators believed that generally there was no complete consensus on organizational goals, and that there were different degrees of consensus within and between various staff groups. They posited that the different degrees of consensus were related to occupational training and experience, the organizational structure, and the communication network. The authors concluded that the staff members might be directing their energies in diverse directions at the expense of concerted effort. To the extent that it did exist, agreement on goals between staff groups appeared to be influenced by similarity of purpose and by physical proximity in work relationships (Georgopoulos, p. 174).

Research Summary C: Etzioni Theory

Questionnaire data were collected from 423 clinical staff members at two western psychiatric hospitals to study member compliance patterns and their relation to clinical and administrative staff perceptions of organizational goals. Etzioni's three types of organizational power (coercive, remunerative, and normative) and corresponding types of involvement (alienative, calculative, and moral) provided the theoretical framework of the research and were tested. The result was only partial confirmation of the theory (Etzioni, 1961, pp. 61-62).

A direct relationship was found between use of coercive power by administrators and alienated involvement by the staff in both hospitals. In addition, in one hospital there was an association between normative power and calculative involvement. Overall, the findings were accounted for by differences in the relative size of staff complements in the two facilities, but not by the composition of individual work units or by staff tenure. While there was no relationship between compliance patterns and staff perception or endorsement of organizational goals, staff involvement patterns were correlated with goal perceptions (Georgopoulos, p. 178).

A consideration of this type of organizational behavior and relationships characterized by increasing anxiety and stress leads to the problem of alienation that is experienced by individual administrators and/or professionals. They report feelings of powerlessness to control their own activities. Alienation is more intense in health care organizations where authority relationships limit the reciprocal influence of subordinate staff. Where there is great status variance between supervisors and their subordinates or where authority is exercised in less than humanistic ways, the result is limited achievement and dissatisfaction by professional staff members. Extrinsic work rewards occupy more significance than intrinsic rewards in this climate. In addition, staff members work in isolation and lack social relationships for support. This pattern in itself is significant in examining the level of stress experienced in these organizations since an absence of social support is both apparent and badly needed.

Research Summary D: Conflict Resolution

In researching role conflict and conflict resolution, questionnaires were collected from 90 nurses in eight outpatient departments in Boston hospitals. Data on nursing performance were obtained through observation. Using these same research sites, studies were conducted examining interpersonal relations in the outpatient departments with interview and questionnaire data from 90 nurses. Relationships among nurses and between them and physicians, nursing supervisors, and patients were considered.

The actual responses of nurses concerning various situations were compared to the responses the same nurses thought would be made by a physician, supervisor, patient, or another nurse in an identical situation. The data indicated that administrative duties received high priority. This partially accounted for the fact that these outpatient department nurses had less contact with patients than would be considered desirable. Moreover, in their contacts with patients, these nurses focused on aspects of care that, if not performed, would inconvenience the department considerably (Georgopoulos, p. 278).

Research Summary E: Alienation Among Nurses

Professionals continually attempt to balance intraorganizational conflicts that can lead to crisis and additional stress if not identified and resolved. Another study examined the organizational consequences of alienation and focused upon the nursing staff of a large psychiatric hospital. Alienation was shown to be more intense on units where authority relations limited the reciprocal influence of subordinate staff. This was reflected in situations in which there was great positional disparity between superiors and their subordinates, where authority was exercised in a preemptory fashion, and where authority figures were physically inaccessible. Lack of career advancement opportunities also was related to alienation. Limited achievement and the dissatisfaction of some staff members with extrinsic work rewards were alienative conditions. Finally, staff members working in isolation and without outside social ties to fellow workers were found to be more subject to intense alienation (Georgopoulos, p. 278).

Research Summary F: Occupations and Structure

A study analyzed the professionalization of 11 occupations in relation to variations in the organizational structures in which the performance of occupational functions occurred. Three organizational structures were examined:

1. autonomous professional organizations such as medical clinics
2. heteronomous organizations in which professionals were subordinated to externally based structures such as social work agencies
3. the professional department of a large organization

Of 338 professionals interviewed, 34 were nurses at a university health center or general hospital. The nurses were classified as participating in a heteronomous organization, subject to administration policy and the practices of the medical staff as well as to their own professional code. The various occupations, including nursing, were categorized using six bureaucratic scales and five professionalism scales.

In contrast to some of the other groups, nurses emerged as strongly professionalized in terms of belief in service to the public and a sense of calling. Other findings indicated that autonomous organizations were less bureaucratic than the others. Generally, moreover, there was an adverse relationship between professionalization and bureaucratization. The relationship of head nurse leadership style to staff cohesiveness was studied. Leadership style was measured with questionnaire data from 25 head nurses, and four typologies of style were used analytically: autocratic, benevolent autocratic, democratic, and laissez faire (Hall, 1968, pp. 92-104). Another questionnaire completed by 130 staff nurses provided data about job satisfaction and group cohesiveness. The proposition that under democratic head nurses the work group would be more cohesive was not supported by the data. However, staff cohesiveness and satisfaction were related to each other.

Research Summary G: Leadership Effectiveness

In the same area, another study tested a contingency model of leadership effectiveness in a field experiment with 86 nursing students in a large midwestern hospital. There was no support for the contention that leaders with different styles differed in their number of responses to individuals in their respective groups. Further, there were no significant differences among leaders of different types concerning the way in which they responded qualitatively to different members of their group. Relationship-oriented leadership was related positively to group effectiveness, however, regardless of whether the tasks were structured or unstructured. Task-oriented leaders interacted more with the members of their group and were more supportive, while relationship-oriented leaders were more directive of their groups—a finding opposite to the typical pattern of results obtained in many industrial studies (Georgopoulos, 1975, p. 282).

One fact that appeared to be significant is that these managers all were under stress and also heavily involved with responsibility. Responsibility can bring substantial rewards, public esteem, and financial remuneration. However, while responsibility may lead to positive outcomes for the manager, the risks of failing are great and the avoidance of failure may not be available to the individual who must accept the responsibility for the administrative task. Persons who have a high fear of failure generally are at excessive risk in jobs involving heavy responsibility.

Research Summary H: Responsibility Stress

Responsibility in the form of being accountable for people and their futures is a role that creates strain and stress for managers. Some physiological studies on this problem found that diastolic blood pressure was a coronary risk factor related to one of the responsibility measures. It was associated positively with the amount of time the managers said they spent in exercising responsibility for others' futures, but not other aspects of responsibility. Furthermore, this was true only of persons in the upper third in any of the four dimensions of the Type A personality. Cholesterol level was associated with the self-report of time spent exercising responsibility for others' futures, but only in those high on the first two Type A personality dimensions.

The conscientious person is encouraged to take on responsibility for people and their futures, is rewarded for it with increased status and income, and pays the price of increased risk of myocardial infarction. This is a rather tenuous chain, and the relationships are not strong, but they certainly suggest that the matter should be studied further (Cobb, 1974, p. 64).

Research Summary I: Mortality Incidence

A study of anesthesiologists and general practitioners reported they had two to three times as much coronary heart disease as dermatologists and pathologists. Without comparing the data concerning mortality, these differences may be misleading. It is interesting that the dermatologists and pathologists do not have as direct a relationship with the patient as the anesthesiologist and the general practitioner and therefore are not responsible for the patients' lives.

This is similar to the bind experienced by the manager who assumes the responsibility for individuals' careers. To support this, a British study of physicians indicated that mortality from myocardial infarctions was about twice as high in general practitioners between the ages of 40 and 60 as there was in other members of the medical profession of comparable ages (Morris, et al., 1952, p. 503). The incidence of stress and coronary diseases was further supported by this study.

These research summaries focused upon hospital organization and intraorganizational relations, and social-behavioral, and administrative-management processes. These empirical studies can be adapted by health care managers attempting to clarify their own roles and reduce the stress experienced in the structure of their organization. Other concerns that are equally important include power, political impact, and organizational control.

RESPONSIBILITY AND POWER

The gap between responsibility and authority may lead hospital executives to assume an administrative style that becomes a life of leverages—of using tonal qualities, facial expressions, and body language to buttress their skills in carefully controlling information, agendas, and timing. They basically need skills of persuasion in one-on-one situations, but they also need to appreciate how these conversations fit into an overall plan to solve multifaceted, complex problems.

The chief executive of a health care organization actually is a power broker who must balance authority and responsibility while probing for new information, anticipating organizational behavior, focusing attention on major problems, collecting information, and solving these problems within the organization and its complex network of processes. These health care administrators are referred to as power brokers and, increasingly, the hospital administrator is being renamed president and is serving on the governing board as a full-fledged member. But there are basic differences between the corporation executive and the hospital administrator (Johnson, 1978, p. 70).

The core of chief executive officers' (c.e.o.) influence rests in having an information base that is wider and deeper than any other individuals in the organization. Their success with their administrative style depends on their being psychologically sensitive and having a system of values that is respected by those with whom they have contacts. While they may be tough and authoritarian in certain instances, they also have to practice multiple leadership styles in order to avoid some of the conflicts that have been proved to be dysfunctional and counterproductive and that have been explored in previous organizational studies in this chapter.

A great need for health care executives to serve as power brokers is due to the positioning of the medical staff in the organizational structure of a typical hospital. New administrators quickly learn that physicians may talk quite openly in the privacy of the c.e.o.'s office but that this is no indication of their willingness to say the same things in an open forum, even if the group is composed entirely of physicians (Johnson, p. 71). By virtue of their role in the hospital, c.e.o.s become recipients of a great deal of information. Over the period of a decade, this enhances their position as power brokers, but in a way that might not be expected. Early in their administrative careers they have come to understand their role as being helpful and sensitive when confronted with events and to forget them as quickly as possible after they have been resolved.

Physicians, trustees, and community leaders who experience serious personal or family problems come to appreciate that executives can be trusted to be discreet and never use such knowledge for their own benefit. This tends to build a strong reservoir of support and goodwill for their administrative decisions (Johnson, p. 72). Chief executive officers in the future must be more flexible persons. They probably will be more limited in their ability to make decisions and to act on their own. More emphasis will be placed on management team activities, and the administration will be more involved in coordinating and overseeing the activities of a divergent staff. Thus, an understanding of the behavioral sciences, human relations, and motivation, as well as the ability to maximize the efforts of others will be crucial (Forrest, Johnson, & Mosher, p. 438).

To some individuals, power brokers are manipulators who employ this approach because they lack a solid foundation in management. To those who have tried to cope with a considerable gap between responsibility and authority, this capacity represents a difference between failure and success. The chief executive of the health care organization is put in the position where manipulation and management often become intertwined and it is difficult to balance out the conflicts and stressors needed to maintain the hospital in equilibrium as a fully functioning organization. The clarification of an often muddled role is a beginning in managing counterproductive stress that may result in psychological and/or physiological problems. These issues are components of the profession and are dealt with in the next chapter, on occupational stress.

BIBLIOGRAPHY

Broom, L. & Selznick, P. *Sociology*. New York: Harper & Row, 1968, 18.

Cobb, S. Role responsibility: The differentiation of a concept. In A. McLean (Ed.), *Occupational stress*. Springfield, Ill.: Charles C. Thomas Publisher, 1974, 62-29.

Etzioni, A. A basis for comparative analysis of complex organizations. In A. Etzioni (Ed.), *A sociological reader on complex organizations,* 2nd ed. New York: Holt, Rinehart and Winston, Inc., 1969, 61-62.

Forrest, C.R., Johnson, A.C., & Mosher, J. The changing role of the hospital administrator. *Proceedings of the Academy of Management,* Kansas City, Mo., August 1976, pp. 434-438.

_____. A profile of the health organization chief executive officer. *Proceedings of the Academy of Management,* Orlando, Fla., August 1977, pp. 396-400.

Georgopoulos, B.S. *Hospital organization research: Review and source book.* Philadelphia: W.B. Saunders Co., 1975.

Hall, R.H. Professionalism and bureaucratization. *American Sociological Review,* 1968, *33,* 92-104.

Johnson, R.L. The power broker—Prototype of the hospital chief executive. *Health Care Management Review,* Fall 1978, *2*(4), 62-73.

Kast, F.E., & Rosenzweig, J.E. *Organization and management: A systems and contingency approach.* New York: McGraw-Hill Book Co., 1979, 120.

Mintzberg, H. A new look at the chief executive's job. *Organizational Dynamics,* Winter 1973, *1*(3), 20-30.

_____. *The nature of managerial work.* New York: Harper & Row, 1973, 166-167.

Morris, J.N., Heady, J.A., & Barley, R.G. Coronary heart disease in medical practitioners. *British Medical Journal,* 1952, *1,* 503.

Perrow, C. The analysis of goals in complex organizations. In J.A. Litterer (Ed.), *Organizations, Vol. II, Systems, Control and Adaptation.* New York: John Wiley & Sons, 1969, 369-378.

Welsch, H.P., LaVan, H., & Erickson, L.G.W. Comparative analysis of health care professionals and administrators' responses concerning climate, autonomy and job satisfaction. *Academy of Management* meeting, Atlanta, August 1979, p. 24. (Paper)

Chapter 4

Occupational Stress and Coronary Disease

CONSIDERATIONS FOR THE HEALTH CARE MANAGER

1. The work environment seems to be the hub of conflicting forces and particularly a source of stress, which is the nonspecific response of the body to any demand.
2. Hans Selye has identified the stages of stress and its effect upon the body: the alarm reaction, the stage of resistance, and the stage of exhaustion where physiological damage is prevalent.
3. A certain amount of stress is necessary to keep an individual keenly perceptive and in touch with external environmental stimuli that are essential for general adaptation.
4. When normal stress reactions are prolonged, a psychosomatic disorder generally will develop. Psychosomatic symptoms occur when an individual is forced to choose between two equally unacceptable alternatives and cannot express the dilemma openly.
5. When individuals ignore the symptoms of stress, they are training themselves to assume a greater load of stress. In this sense, coping becomes disastrous.
6. Research has supported the fact that organizational stressors can induce

changes in the physiological-psychological makeup of some individuals. These changes can be contributors to coronary heart disease.

7. Some organizational stressors are role ambiguity, role conflict, role overload, relationships, absence of feedback, demotion, demands from several managers, lack of involvement in decisions, lack of cohesiveness, underutilization or overutilization, and inequity of rewards. These result in low job performance, absenteeism, turnover, dissatisfaction, and finally to physiological problems—a coronary.

8. Stress results from an improper fit between person and environment when the climate is incongruous, with personality patterns leading to frustration.

9. The intensive Type A manager is competitive and restless and has a higher probability of developing coronary heart disease in the 35- to 40-year-old bracket. Organizational reward structures encourage and support Type As.

10. A congruent fit between an individual's perceived expectations and desired expectations for output results in higher job satisfaction and less risk and stress associated with coronary problems.

11. The role perception of supervisors is related to the amount of internal and interdepartmental stress. To increase employee compliance in the institution, it is important to achieve greater internal integration rather than introduce a human relations program to help expand worker identification.

12. Social supports via coworkers and supervisors are essential to keep stress at a modest level. Lack of support increases interpersonal tensions and reduces satisfaction, ultimately affecting the health of those involved. Even a single source of support can reduce stress levels.

Work occupies one of the significant components of our lives and is both exciting and satisfying when it is good, and painful and even harmful when it no longer is good. Therefore, the position and occupation of the health care manager can be stressful. This chapter examines relationships among occupational stress, coronary disease, the role of the health care professional, stress management, and the role of the organization as the arena where these factors interact and operate. In the quest to reduce occupational stress, it is necessary to be able to identify the stressors and diagnose the situation intraorganizationally and intrapsychically.

Continuing and chronic emotional stress is considered to be an important etiological factor in many emotional and physiological disorders. The work environment seems to be a hub of conflicting forces, particularly the health care organization that, being a unique and dynamic environment, serves as a source of stress as well. One way of examining occupational stress is not to set up a paradigm and structured definition but to demonstrate some of the connections between organizational and managerial events that occur and their results that ultimately have an effect upon the individual and the organization.

Stress and its impact on the individual in the health care organizational environment is a topic that must be addressed in considering the overall management of this problem. Hans Selye has been a pioneer in the study of stress and a great deal of what is currently being reviewed in medical, psychological, or health care literature can be attributed to his ongoing research regarding stress, distress, the stress of life, and the general adaptation syndrome. His work *Stress in Health and Disease* is a most extensive encyclopedic treatise of the literature on stress in medicine and life. It cites and evaluates about 7,500 references from pertinent texts and periodicals.

General health basically is maintained by a stable balance referred to as homeostasis. It is only when this balance is disrupted and in disequilibrium that disease may set in. A great number of studies of disease processes have shown that stress, more than any other factor, can determine whether there is the proper balance (equilibrium) in the life of the individual. Most individuals are born relatively healthy but if the harmful stresses resulting from improper perception, environmental conditions, or personal problems become overwhelming, they move from health to disease.

Today, stress diseases are on the increase in the form of cardiac problems, gastrointestinal disturbances, and mental disorders. Most of these appear to be stress induced and can often kill people in their thirties, forties, and early fifties. The tremendous advances in medical knowledge in recent years have not brought with them any significant improvement in the health of these individuals. Currently, the skills and knowledge demanded by any job, as indeed the goals of society, are developing or at least changing at such an unprecedented rate that the first objective must be to learn how to cope with the stress of adaptation to change. Stress is a response that has both positive and negative connotations. By definition, stress is the body's nonspecific response to any demand. In its medical sense, stress essentially is the rate of wear and tear in the body. In any event, wear and tear is only the result of many factors, and therefore, stress is defined as a nonspecific response of the body to any demand (Selye, 1978, p. 1).

One of the major characteristics of individuals is their ability to maintain internal constancy despite many changes in the environment. Walter Cannon, a Harvard physiologist, defined this power to maintain constancy as homeostasis, which can be translated as staying power. Cannon's classical research in 1939 demonstrated that higher animal species defended themselves against various types of aggression, insult, or injury by a fundamental response that he referred to as a fight-or-flight response (Cannon, p. 404).

THE WORK OF HANS SELYE

It appears that individuals are endowed with a highly developed nervous system. The stress response could well be initiated by emotional response. While the first mediator may not be identified, it is known that in individuals and other mammals the stressor eventually stimulates the hypothalamus, a complex bundle of nerve cells and fibers that act as a bridge between the brain and the intricate system (Selye, 1976). Selye felt messages then were relayed to the primary endocrine gland in this chain, which is the pituitary, and the result is a discharge of ACTH, which may be referred to as the adrenocorticotropic hormone from the pituitary, into the general circulation. Upon reaching the adrenal cortex, ACTH triggers a secretion of corticoids, mainly glucocorticoids, such as cortisol or corticosterone. These are stress hormones that supply a readily available source of energy for the adaptive reactions necessary to meet the demands made by the stressor agent. The corticoids also facilitate various other enzyme responses and suppress immune reactions such as inflammation, thereby helping the body to coexist with potential pathogens.

Stress is the body's nonspecific response to any demand, whether it is caused by or results in pleasant or unpleasant stimuli. It is essential to differentiate between the unpleasant or harmful variety called distress, which often connotes disease, and eustress, which often connotes euphoria. During both eustress and distress, the body undergoes virtually the same nonspecific responses to the various positive or negative stimuli acting upon it. However, eustress causes much less damage than distress. This factor unequivocally demonstrates that it is how an individual accepts stress that determines ultimately whether the person can adapt successfully to change. The general stress syndrome affects the whole body; a local stress syndrome influences several units within a part; but stress always manifests itself by a syndrome, a sum of changes, not by one change. An isolated effect upon any one unit in the body is either damage or stimulation to activity; in either case, it is specific and hence not stress (Selye, 1978, p. 75).

While it is necessary to examine what stress is and have it defined clearly, it also is essential to discuss what stress is not. Key factors to consider are:

1. Stress is not simply nervous tension.
2. Stress is not an emergency discharge of hormones from the adrenal medulla.
3. Stress is not everything that causes a secretion by the adrenal cortex of its hormones, the corticoids. ACTH, the adrenal stimulating pituitary hormones, can discharge corticoids without producing any evidence of stress as supportive evidence for this fact.
4. Stress is not always the nonspecific result of damage. Normal activity such as sports events or emotional feelings can produce considerable stress without causing any physiological damage.
5. Stress is not the same as a deviation from homeostasis, which is the steady state of the body and equilibrium sought out by any biological forms.
6. Stress is not anything that causes an alarm reaction. It is the stressor that does this, not stress itself.
7. Stress is not identical with the alarm reaction or the general adaptation syndrome as a whole.
8. Stress is not a nonspecific reaction since the pattern of the stress reaction is, in fact, very specific. It affects certain workings in a highly selective manner.
9. Stress is not a specific reaction. The stress response by definition is not specific since it can be produced by almost any agent.
10. Stress is not necessarily something that is negative. It all depends on how stress is used. The stress associated with a creative, successful working experience may be beneficial while

that of humiliation and failure may be detrimental.
11. Stress cannot and should not be avoided. It is part of an individual's existence.

When all these points are considered, it may be concluded that they are so complex that stress cannot be defined easily. Perhaps the concept itself is not that sufficiently clear to serve as an object for direct scientific analysis, but what may need some clarification is the difference between stress and stressors.

Stress is a common denominator for all adaptive reactions in the body and a stressor naturally is something that produces this stress. In view of what has been said already about the relativity of stress, it is evident that any one agent is more or less a stressor in proportion to the degree of its ability to produce stress—that is, nonspecific demands and changes. Initial exposure to a stressor produces the nonspecific response characterized by a triad of its adrenal enlargement, thymicolymphatic involution, and gastrointestinal ulcers. Selye's general adaptation syndrome now becomes operative through its three stages.

This first stage, often referred to as alarm reaction, represents a generalized "call to arms" of the body's defensive forces. In other words, the body is preparing for the fight-or-flight syndrome discussed previously in this chapter by Cannon. The second phase—the stage of resistance—is an important level, followed by the final stage of exhaustion. The body becomes adaptive to the challenge and even begins to resist it. The length of this stage of resistance is dependent, of course, upon the body's innate adaptation energy and upon the intensity of the stressor that determines the chemical changes that are to be experienced. These chemical changes are the opposite of those observed during an alarm reaction. However, just as any machine wears out even if it has been maintained properly, so do living organisms that sooner or later become the victim of this constant wear and tear. The acquired adaptation is lost if the individual is subjected to still greater exposure to the stressor. The organism enters into the third and final stage—exhaustion—and then the organism actually dies. It has used up its resources of adaptation energy. This is the crux of concern here.

Every part of the body appears to be involved in a stress response, but the two great integrators of activity, the hormonal and the nervous system, are especially important. The facts known today lead to the belief that the anterior pituitary and the adrenal cortex play significant roles in coordinating the defense of these organisms during stress. This view has been somewhat distorted because the general adaptation syndrome has been studied primarily by endocrinologists and because other scientists concerned with the participation of the nervous system are handicapped by the greater complexity of the required techniques.

It is not necessary for all three stages of the general adaptation syndrome to develop before it can be spoken of as a total system. Only the most severe stress leads rapidly and directly to the stage of exhaustion and death. Most of the physical and mental exertion, infection, and other stressors that act upon the body during a limited period produce changes corresponding only to the first and second stages: at first they may upset the alarm, but then the body becomes adjusted to that.

In the course of a normal life, everyone goes through the first two stages at many different times. Otherwise, they never can become adapted to perform all the activities and place all the demands which are humanity's lot (Selye, 1978, p. 79). In the general adaptation syndrome, the alarm reaction develops and corticoid activity rises sharply. During the stages of resistance it falls to a level only slightly above normal and finally in the stage of exhaustion it rises again to the maximum level reached during the alarm reaction. These are facts that can be verified by actual determination of corticoids in the blood or by studying bodily changes that are characteristic of increased corticoid activity.

All of these signs are pronounced during the alarm reaction and the stage of exhaustion. If a biological organism is attacked continually by a stressor, the local adaptive responses can be developed sufficiently to cope with the situation. However, if irritation continues over a long period of time, the directly affected cells within the organism eventually break down from fatigue, wear and tear, or exhaustion since the adaptation energy has been exhausted. During the stage of exhaustion, the reactions for or against the wear and tear have led to the disintegration of the most appropriate channel of defense. Another reaction then must extend to other organic areas within the organism.

In essence, the adaptive hormones of the pituitary-adrenal system appear to be most necessary for survival whenever large fissure regions are under stress. By the maintenance of life during the alarm reaction, the body gains the time necessary for the development of specific local adaptive phenomena in the region directly affected. During the subsequent stage of resistance, this region can cope with the stress test without the help of adaptive hormones. Finally, they help with the acquisition of adaptation by alternative channels and thereby prolong survival, but only until even the auxiliary mechanisms are worn out. After this occurs, there is a further thin line of defense, and death usually follows the breakdown of defense.

No illness is exclusively a disease of adaptation. Considerable evidence has been accumulated in favor of the view that stress, and particularly the adaptive hormones produced during stress, exerts an essential regulating influence on the development of numerous psychosomatic and psychological problems. Most everyone for years has tried to resist the stresses caused by preoccupations, frustration, physical fatigue, tension, overwork, cigarette smoking, excessive consumption of alcohol, chronic infection, and innumerable other agents that demand constant adaptation. However, there comes the day when a normal well-balanced individual begins to show signs of increased blood pressure, or suffers a heart attack, or notices the symptoms of gastrointestinal disorders.

Diseases of adaptation are maladies caused principally by errors in the body's general adaptation process. It should not be assumed that stress diseases are inevitable. They will not occur when all the regulatory processes are properly checked and balanced. They will not develop when adaptation is facilitated by improved perception and interpretation. Thus, adaptation need not necessarily result in disease, for the toll it brings ultimately depends upon how everyone sees the world as composed of individuals who must react to it.

Among the derailments of the general adaptation syndrome that may cause disease, perhaps the most important is an absolute excess, deficiency, or disequilibrium in the amount of adaptive hormones—for example, corticoid, ACTH, and growth hormones produced during stress. Unfortunately, if stress is induced chronically, the defensive response of the organism also lowers its resistance since fewer antibodies are produced and an inflammatory response dwindles. In actual cases this diminished resistance makes people hypersensitive. But how do individuals know they are under stress before they suffer the damage previously described as diseases of adaptation such as nervous breakdowns, gastrointestinal disorders, and coronary problems?

A certain amount of stress is necessary to keep an individual keenly perceptive and in touch with external environmental stimuli that are necessary for a person's general adaptation to the environment and the everyday problems to be solved. A certain amount of stress also is necessary for general everyday action and reaction. This is especially true of eustress, which in itself is enjoyable and makes life much more rewarding. On the other hand, managers must be cognizant of the limits of what they can endure so that the stress does not become distress. As has been stated often, certain signals and reactions are common to stress as such and it does not matter whether an individual is initially healthy or unhealthy.

All of these are signals that eventually lead to the diseases that must be avoided as much as possible. Among the most generally used and reliable methods for diagnosing stress are to be found in the blood levels of adrenalines, corticoids, ACTH, and decrease in blood eosinophils. It also is necessary to examine the elevation in certain blood lipid substances such as cholesterol and fatty acids, which are comparatively simple to estimate although they do require laboratory tests. Increases in glucagon, insulin, and prolactin not only are more difficult to determine but are not completely reliable indicators of stress reactions. The measurement of the electrical activity of the brain by the electroencephalogram (EEG) may yield some valid indications of irregular activity but also requires specialized machinery and specific reasons for using this type of test. An elevation in blood pressure can be determined even without medical training if individuals happen to be trained in the use of relatively simple apparatus. Unless hypertension is constant and severe, it has little diagnostic significance since daily blood pressure variations can depend upon many fluctuations associated with normal responses to ordinary life events. It is important to know these indicators and tests that can be used to measure the impact and event of stress upon the individual.

The following symptoms of stress are adequate indices since more dangerous distress can develop further unless these initial symptoms are dealt with in the early stages of stress (Selye, 1978, p. 177):

1. general irritability, hyperexcitation, or depression, usually associated with unusual aggressiveness or passive indolence, depending upon the personality style
2. pounding of the heart and indicators of high blood pressure often due to stress
3. dryness of the throat and mouth
4. impulsive behavior or emotional instability
5. the overpowering urge to cry or run and hide
6. the inability to concentrate, flight of thoughts, and general disorientation
7. feelings of unreality, weakness, or dizziness
8. predilection that becomes fatigue, and loss of the joie de vivre
9. floating anxiety—that is to say, people are afraid although they do not know exactly what they are afraid of

10. emotional tension and alertness, feelings of being keyed up
11. trembling and nervous tics
12. a tendency to be easily startled by small sounds
13. high-pitched nervous laughter
14. stuttering and other speech difficulties that frequently are stress induced
15. bruxism or grinding of the teeth
16. insomnia, which usually is a consequence of being keyed up
17. hypermobility—often called hyperkinesia—an increased tendency to move without any reason or an inability to take a physically relaxed attitude
18. sweating that becomes evident only under considerable stress by inspection of the skin
19. frequent need to urinate, chronic diarrhea, indigestion, queasiness in the stomach and sometimes even vomiting that are all signs of disturbed gastrointestinal functions that may lead eventually to severe diseases of adaptation such as ulcerative colitis, peptic ulcer, spastic colon, and other maladies
20. migraine headaches
21. premenstrual tension or missed menstrual cycle
22. pain in the back or neck
23. excessive loss of appetite
24. increased smoking
25. increased use of legally prescribed drugs such as amphetamines and tranquilizers
26. alcohol and drug addiction—like the phenomenon of overeating, increased and excessive consumption of alcohol and the use of various psychotrophic drugs is a common manifestation of exposure to stressors beyond individuals' natural endurance; in this case managers still are dealing with slight reactions that are considered to be deviations to which they resort, presumably to help them to forget the cause of the distress
27. nightmares
28. neurotic behavior
29. psychoses
30. accident proneness

It appears that for individuals, the most "distressful" stressors are those that are emotional. Naturally, truly physical demands on the body such as respiration, loss of blood, and fighting of infection can become of paramount importance. These are met far more commonly in normal everyday life than the emotional stimuli that managers face almost constantly. Besides, even somatic reactions affect individuals, largely because of the nervous responses such as pain, frustration, and fear that the reactions impose. This probably is because, among all individuals, humankind has the most complex brain and is the most dependent upon it. Thus, it is especially true that in life events, the stressor effects depend not so much upon what individuals do or what happens to them, but on the way they adjust to them. Humanity seems to be developing into well-conditioned escapists and the (fight-or-flight) reaction is fast becoming an enigmatic scientific curiosity. Bodies often are mobilized involuntarily for fight or flight, but the process seldom is carried through in physical terms, so individuals actually are stewing in their own juices. It should be clear that people are unable to unwind from these daily stressors that create the physiological damage.

Research has been conducted with various occupational groups to determine the net effect of stressors on their lives and individual reactions to them. These results are presented later in this chapter. The four most obvious lessons derived from Selye's research on stress were that:

1. Bodies can meet the most diverse aggression with the same adaptive defensive mechanism.
2. This mechanism can be dissected so as to identify its ingredient force in objectively measurable physical and chemical terms such as changes in the structure of organs or in the production of certain hormones.
3. This kind of information is needed to lay the scientific foundation for a new type of treatment, whose essence is to combat disease by strengthening the bodies' own defenses against stress. Once it has been learned that in given situations, an excess of a certain hormone is needed to maintain health, that hormone can be injected whenever the body is unable to manufacture enough of it. Conversely, once it is recognized that a disease is due to the exaggerated adaptive activity of some hormone-producing gland, the offending organ can be removed or an attempt made to block it effectively by drugs.
4. The body possesses a complex machinery of self-regulating checks and balances. These are remarkably effective in individuals' adjusting themselves to virtually anything that can

happen to them in life. However, this machinery often does not work perfectly. Sometimes body responses are too weak so that they do not offer adequate protection and at other times they are too strong so that people actually hurt themselves by their excessive reactions to stress (Selye, p. 402).

EMOTIONAL ASPECTS OF STRESS

Psychological and physical problems caused by stress have become the number one health problem within the last ten years. Common medical guesstimates indicate that approximately 75 percent of all diseases have their origins in stress. Stress-induced disorders have long since replaced infectious diseases as the most common problems of the postindustrial period. Certain setbacks such as financial difficulties, death in the family, violation of the law, or foreclosure of a loan are obvious sources of severe stress. But not all stress arises from negative events; positive occurrences such as a marriage, a promotion, obtaining some achievement, or a vacation can produce stress of some type. Most of the body's reaction to stress is normal and appropriate. If an individual needs a specific challenge, the body returns to a normal level of activity relatively quickly. But when the source of stress is not known, is ambiguous, or is from multidimensional sources at one occurrence, the individual's physical resources do not recover as rapidly.

Stress then becomes pathological when the body reacts as though it is threatened long after the actual threat is past. Blood pressure normally increases under stress, which is acceptable, but when it persists it becomes hypertension. Heartbeat rate accelerates under stress; if prolonged, this is diagnosed as tachycardia. In addition, an abnormal amount of blood begins to shift away from the stomach; if continued beyond the period of stress, this results in loss of appetite or even in an ulcer. When normal stress reactions are prolonged, a psychosomatic disorder generally will develop. The genesis of the stress disorder can be described as follows:

A person is confronted with a situation that is extremely difficult to resolve or avoid. The situation then becomes overwhelming and the person sees no escape. As a result, the individual makes an unconscious decision that provides a means of coping with this irresolvable situation. Often the choice actually is manifested in the development of symptoms. Once this course of action proves successful, the individual will repeat the same pattern in a generalized response to the stress. The response continues far beyond the point at which it was effective for dealing with stress, so that the individual finally suffers from a maneuver that originally was selected to bring relief. Since the decision that leads to the development of the disease in response to stress is made at an unconscious level, the person is not in a position to change the original decision that brought on the problem initially.

When an individual transforms stress from a psychological conflict to a physical symptom, the resulting disorder is classified as a psychosomatic disorder. These disorders persist in the absence of any organic changes. Psychosomatic symptoms often occur when a person must choose between two equally unacceptable alternatives and cannot openly express the dilemma. This often is called a double bind. By developing a psychosomatic symptom, people free themselves from having to deal with the stress of the double bind. Now, they become ill, friends and family change their demands on them accordingly, and the sickness brings relief from the pressure of the double bind, postponing or preventing a confrontation with the underlying conflict (Pelletier, 1977, p. 36).

The problem of psychosomatic disorders can be examined in the same way illness is viewed. Since the Middle Ages, Western philosophers have segmented individuals with regard to the separate aspects of body, mind, and spirit. These are thought of as parts rather than as an integrated whole. The split is apparent in the present division of the healing profession. Physicians treat physical ailments of the body while psychologists and psychiatrists attempt to heal the mind. One of the problems in dealing with stress is the professional insensitivity to it. The prevention of needless stress seems to be a major focal point for the new movement in holistic medicine.

For many people, prevention of stress means a major reevaluation of attitudes and habits that are taken for granted. Individuals' own attitudes with regard to relaxation often are extremely naive, since many people assume that the absence of obvious tension implies they are relaxed. An individual still can have both mental anxiety and physical symptoms of prolonged stress without any apparent discomfort. For these individuals, stress is so unremitting that they do not even recognize it any more—a lack of sensitivity that can be dangerous in the long run. Individuals ignore the clues of stress and behave as though they are anesthetized psychologicaly and physically. When people ignore the signs of stress, they are training themselves to take on a greater load rather than seeking means to alleviate it. In this sense, coping becomes disastrous.

Prevention actually begins when individuals identify the stresses and their sources. They must sensitize themselves to crucial bodily signals and take steps to reduce this stress. This is difficult without any input or guidance, but there are a number of therapies that can help and that will be examined later in this chapter. Some of the techniques, such as meditation, deep breathing, and biofeedback, are among the more popular treatments, and physicians are advising patients with disorders ranging from heart disease to ulcers to relax via these methods. One of the major problems is that these professionals cannot actually help the patients relax since they never have been trained in this aspect of holistic medicine. This is another example of the double bind experienced by both patient and physician. Multiple double bind situations that heighten stress will result in emotional damage and, in severe instances, in coronary disease.

CORONARY DISEASE AND STRESS

Each year in the United States, approximately a million people die from various forms of cardiovascular disease, about three quarters of them from heart attacks or coronary heart disease. This problem is of great magnitude because many organizations have a vested financial and personal interest in their personnel, particularly in those who are skilled in certain areas. The loss of these valuable resources due to coronary disease or the indolent state within which many are left are major organizational problems. It has not been easy for top management to accept the fact that for some individuals, organization-related stress can be a contributor to coronary and other diseases. In recent years, medical journals have devoted increased space to studies dealing with the relationship between life stress, organizational stress, and coronary heart disease. From these studies, one stream of thought tends to show up repeatedly: *organizational stressors can induce changes in the physiological-psychological makeup of some individuals.* Further, these changes can be contributors to coronary heart disease as well as to such other ailments as peptic ulcers, migraine headaches, asthma, sexual dysfunctions, and alcoholism (Ivancevich & Matteson, 1979, p. 104).

It is clear that certain aspects of stress are positive and result in productive consequences. However, the amount of organizational stress that is optimal or needed to contribute to high job performance is difficult to determine. Some organizational stressors such as a demotion, losing a job, or receiving conflicting demands from more than one manager have negative consequences for most individuals. On the other hand, some stressors—such as being passed over for promotion or not being involved in a decision—produce no negative or harmful stress reactions in certain individuals. There are even some stressors that have positive consequences. Some of the organizational stressors are role ambiguity, role conflict, role overload, relationships with others, lack of cohesiveness, underutilizing an individual's ability, career progress (or lack of it), and inequity of rewards. These organizational factors do in fact create stress as well as do extraorganizational elements such as family situations, common economic conditions, and the quality of life.

What these factors do is create physiological problems such as serum cholesterol, blood clotting, high blood pressure, and blood glucose. They also result in lower job performance, absenteeism, turnover, and dissatisfaction with the job. These factors do in fact lead to coronary heart disease, a diagnosis supported by foundation studies presented shortly. About the best any manager can do about subordinates' extraorganizational stress is to be aware of their potential significance, be alert to their presence, and show compassion, interest, and understanding. Attempting to intrude on such stress-filled situations as marital problems or child-rearing practices is definitely not recommended. Well-meaning managers who attempt to play amateur psychiatrists may find that the only thing they have accomplished is elevating their own stress level (Ivancevich & Matteson, p. 107).

It has been hypothesized that a correlation exists between occupational stress and coronary heart disease. This was the starting point for a study carried out by Dr. Lennart Levi in collaboration with Dr. Lars Carlson and Dr. Lars Fuller (McLean, 1974, p. 4). It was based upon several investigations indicating that chronic exposure to emotional stress leads to increased plasma, concentration of cholesterol, and a very low density of lipoproteins. A chronically elevated blood lipoprotein content combined with a direct cardiotoxic effect of the adrenal hormones has in turn been considered capable of contributing to the degenerative changes in the myocardial tissue (McLean, 174, p. 4). The study indicated that increased plasma triglyceride levels, which are in response to an increase in the sympathoadrenomedullary activity, are induced by work situations that may bring stress for even a short period. These stressor reactions can be physiological, with psychosomatic reactions such as ulcer, cardiac disease, and high blood pressure. The stress also may impair the individual's performance, create anxiety and rigidity, and reduce decision-making skills. In some cases, performance is not affected but when people are experiencing distress, as postulated by Selye, their performance can even improve. Under situations of stress, it is known that perception is affected and disrupted and that an individual will be less likely to be able to tolerate any ambiguity and will be exploring coping behaviors immediately.

Individuals in the organization attempt to cope with stress in a passive manner by working harder and longer or by attempting to alter some of these environmental circumstances. Individuals also cope with stress by overloading their information network, producing excessive and conflicting input that results in further stress. Work overload can increase the smoking and cholesterol levels that affect cardiovascular disease.

It has been found that quantitative and qualitative overload had a direct relationship to feelings of threats to a job. Individuals who felt threatened became much more vocal, smoked a great deal more, and increased their anxiety and sensitivity to stress. Objective and subjective overload had a direct link to increased heart rate and cholesterol. There also was a link between role ambiguity in the situation and stress. Researchers defined such ambiguity as a state in which people had inadequate information to perform their roles in an organization. Drawing largely from Robert Kahn's 1974 research (McLean, 1974, p. 8), they observed that major findings showed that men who suffered from role ambiguity experienced lower job satisfaction and high job-related tension. They went on to conclude from their own work that, with regard to role ambiguity, it was significantly related to low job satisfaction and to feelings of job-related threats to managers' mental and physical well-being.

French and Caplan (cited in McLean, 1974, p. 8) showed in several studies that the various forms of workload produced at least nine different kinds of psychological and physiological strain. Four of these (job dissatisfaction, elevated cholesterol, elevated heart rate, and smoking) are risk factors in heart disease. They concluded that it was reasonable to predict that cutting down on work overload would reduce heart disease.

It has been found that administrators have a higher probability of developing coronary disease because they experience different types of organizational stress that are linked to risk factors in the disease. When individuals feel supported and not threatened in their work group, they are under less stress and, as a result, under less risk of developing these physiological problems. It has been noted that certain attempts to decrease stress by increasing participation at work should be accompanied by a supportive environment and supportive supervision that will yield a much more cohesive effort. This supportiveness will reduce physiological strain and psychological strain by increasing effectiveness of participation. Participation in trivial decision making has little effect, but if it is a valid attempt, it certainly can produce significant success.

Stress is experienced by individuals who do not always know or understand what they are feeling and are unaware of why they are feeling the way they do. This is experienced by subordinates involved in relationships with their managers. Anger is an example. The more important an individual such as Manager (M) is to Top Administrator (A), the more vulnerable A is to M's behavior and the earlier A may become angry with M. How individuals handle these feelings of anger is often confusing and conflicting. They may have feelings of both positive and negative emotion toward the same person, but in a subordinate-supervisory relationship the repression of anger becomes a method of operation. This process is threatening and becomes stressful.

Stress may be viewed as a threatening event since threats are important to balancing people's levels of equilibrium. There usually is a fear and threat of losing control with an individual with whom the manager works closely, or there is a threat to the individual's superego. When a subordinate is angry with a manager, the employee may want to cause the superior harm that creates feelings of guilt about these desires. Individuals may feel threatened as a result of some perceived personal physical harm that may develop during these encounters. Stress then escalates via a combination of factors that are related to the job and have an impact upon the individuals by disrupting their psychological and physiological equilibrium.

Studies at the Institute for Social Research at the University of Michigan hypothesized that when individuals did not have a proper person-environment fit, job stress resulted (Margolis & Kroes, 1974, p. 15). To put it another way, when the climate was incongruous with the individual's personality style, stress was the result of this poor fit. When the individuals' needs were frustrated and their abilities were not matched with responsibilities, stress was likely to occur.

When stress occurs on the job, the individual usually experiences anxiety, anger, tension, and a feeling of rigidity. These are short-term feelings and do not become problems unless they are not dealt with and are allowed to fester. As previously discussed, when stress continues to mount, individuals may become chronically depressed, fatigued, and alienated and may react physically to the occupational situation. As the stressor continues, the chances are good that the individual may experience transient clinical-physiological changes. Levels of catecholamines, blood lipids, blood pressure, gut motility, and other physiological variables change significantly under psychological stress and serve to indicate in an objective way that the individual is under stress.

Another measure of stress is physical health status. Such consequences of job stress as gastrointestinal disorders, coronary heart disease, asthmatic attacks, and other psychosomatic disorders all are established as consequences of psychological stress. A final measure of job-related stress is work performance decrement. Laboratory research and some field research for years has been demonstrating severe decreases in productivity and increases in error rates as a function of psychological stress associated with tests (Margolis & Kroes, 1974, p. 16). The effect of the occupational stress upon a worker is dependent upon the quality, intensity, and frequency of the stress agent or agents and the susceptibility of the worker, as determined by past experiences, defense mechanisms, etc. Factors in general that promote a feeling of well-being among workers include the following:

1. recognition of the individuals' needs
2. their feeling they are part of the decision process
3. approval from the supervisor
4. tangible evidence of success
5. security measures
6. open house opportunities
7. increased educational benefits

The general factors under occupational stress that can have a negative effect upon work performance may be classified as:

1. boredom
2. ambiguity
3. role conflict
4. lack of rewards
5. loss of control of the workers and organization in terms of their objectives
6. reduced feedback (work overload or underload) and interpersonal conflict (Greiff, 1974, p. 93).

The effect of occupational stress is experienced not only by the administrators in the health care system but also by the medical staff. It is interesting to note that physicians have lower mortality rates for infectious diseases, cancer, and accidents but a higher incidence of coronary heart disease, diabetes, strokes, and suicide than the general population. Doctors are more likely to die of heart disease than other professionals. American physicians are more prone to heart disease than medical practitioners in England and Denmark, suggesting that the professional role must be evaluated in its cultural context (King, 1970, pp. 257-281). Even the health care professional is not immune to the hazards of this malady that they often encounter in treating patients.

OTHER STUDIES: CORONARY DISEASE AND STRESS

There are data to support the significance of stress as a factor in coronary heart disease. Thiel studied 50 patients with myocardial infarctions and 50 aged-matched, healthy nonpatient controls. The patients with myocardial infarction showed significantly higher anxiety and depression than the controls, particularly more feelings of nervousness, sleep disturbances, and shortness of breath (Thiel, Parker & Bruce, 1973, pp. 43-57). Similar studies reported that sudden coronary deaths frequently were preceded by a period of depression leading to an abrupt change to a state of arousal. The arousal was marked by increased work, anxiety, or anger (Greene, Goldstein, & Moss, 1972, pp. 725-731). Myocardial infarction followed shortly upon the reactive arousal. It also is known that recent clinical studies suggest that either newly evidenced anxiety and depression or exacerbated chronic anxiety and depression may heighten the probability of the onset of coronary heart disease, and particularly of angina pectoris (Hurst, Jenkins, & Rose, 1979, p. 19).

Life change events also affect individuals. Rahe and Lind (Rahe, 1979, pp. 2-10) obtained a list of 57 individuals who had experienced sudden cardiac deaths in Stockholm, Sweden, during a three-month period in 1968. A total of 39 next-of-kin participated in the study and completed a *Schedule of Recent Experiences* on the deceased. The investigators found a statistically significant increase in the total life change units for the sudden death patients in the year before death compared to the preceding two years. The final six months before death showed the highest level of life change units. These findings held true for patients who did and did not have prior coronary heart disease histories.

It appears that systematic emotional arousal engendered by events relevant to the individual or in which the individual is involved may constitute the more important aspects of psychological stress in the early phases of coronary heart disease. It may well turn out to be the case that psychological stress is a catalyst for other risk factors rather than a true participant in the coronary heart disease process. On the other hand, chronic and repeated exposure to stress may have direct physiological consequences—a role in the etiology of heart disease (Hurst, Jenkins, & Rose, 1979, p. 21).

A study by AT&T indicated that excessive overtime such as hours exceeding 70 per week was clearly associated with incidents of myocardial infarction (Theorell, 1977, p. 86). Conflicts with supervisors also have been associated with increased risks in other studies. It was hypothesized in some of the research that individuals who had been exposed to extra work, responsibility problems, conflicts, or threat of unemployment would run an elevated risk of developing myocardial infarction. A two-year follow-up to this study indicated that 37 percent of the myocardial infarction group had reported a work problem in the preceding year (Theorell, 1977, p. 87).

A study in an Oxford, England, automobile factory indicated that staff workers with executive responsibility had the highest incidence of heart disease, almost three times higher than the community. The study compared major coronary risk factors for 30 staff men between the ages of 40 and 59 who were selected randomly. The staff men had a mean diastolic blood pressure significantly higher than any other individual in this organization, even on the production line. The differences were not attributed to obesity, as the relative weights of all the individuals involved were nearly the same, as were the mean values of the plasma cholesterol. It could be concluded that the staff personnel, in addition to their mostly sedentary jobs, had on the average a higher diastolic blood pressure. Fewer of them tackled heavy jobs around the house during their leisure time. Increased blood pressure and lack of physical activity are well known to contribute to coronary heart disease (Baxter, White, Barnes, & Cashman, 1978, p. 102). These factors all contribute to the syndrome or the coronary heart disease and are considered extreme problems for managers in either industrial or health care organizations who are attempting to balance stressors associated with the job while maintaining their physical well-being.

One of the problems involved with coronary heart disease is that more and more people are dying of this ailment at younger and younger ages. A cardiologist in a Massachusetts hospital commented several years before his own death that the sons of fathers he had treated for years were dying from coronary disease—that is, heart attack and strokes—at an average age of 14 years earlier than their fathers had died of their own attacks. These patients were developing these diseases at much younger ages than had their fathers. At the same time in many hospitals interns and residents now are treating individuals in their early thirties for coronary heart disease as a "matter of course." They no longer are surprised by seeing these diseases in such young people (Benson, 1979). Five or ten years ago, the sight of individuals in their early thirties with heart attacks would have been enough to have this information published immediately in medical journals as remarkable events. This may seem strange but is so common today that young physicians consider it the norm.

It is necessary to question what is causing the events leading to these premature heart attacks, which indeed are the major cause of death today. It also is essential to describe the physiological problems affecting individuals who are having coronary heart disease and even dying early in their careers. The underlying process leading to coronary heart disease is hardening of the arteries or arteriosclerosis. Certain risk factors and certain definable factors lead to an occlusion of the arteries through arteriosclerosis. Diet is one of these factors but, as time passes, it apparently is becoming less and less important in the development of arteriosclerosis. Put another way, to modify the amount of arteriosclerosis that is developing, there must be a very marked change in the diet—so marked that it will be virtually impossible to modify diets appropriately.

The most important feature in the development of arteriosclerosis appears to be high blood pressure. The higher the blood pressure, the more rapidly arteriosclerosis or hardening of the arteries develops. Conversely, the lower the blood pressure, the slower this development, and this is a direct relationship. With high blood pressure, more fats remain inside the arterial wall and plaque develops with the hardening occurring in the obstruction of the artery. It is at this juncture that some of these problems must be addressed because 95 percent of the cases of high blood pressure are due to unknown causes and physicians often dump these data into a general file called "Essential Hypertension."

In the last ten years or so, the concept that stressful life events require behavioral adjustment has proved to be related to increases in blood pressure. It is difficult to measure and quantify what is an individual's behavioral adjustment and what is a stressful event. Epidemiological studies have clarified some of these issues. As an example, in populations that were undergoing stressful circumstances requiring behavioral adjustment, people had higher blood pressures than those who were not under stress. Rural populations have lower blood pressure than urban populations. Tax accountants have their highest blood pressure around March and April—their busiest season. In Texas City, Texas, in 1948, an ammunition ship exploded with a force that knocked out windows 50 miles away. (The force was equivalent to that of the two atomic bombs dropped on Hiroshima and Nagasaki in 1945.) Texans within that 50-mile radius developed hypertension that lasted approximately six months before returning to normal. In many situations that are stressful and require behavioral adjustment, it can be demonstrated that high blood pressure results. This emergency reaction, which was discussed earlier, is characterized by a secretion of the hormones of the sympathetic nervous system—epinephrine and norepinephrine—that leads to an increased body metabolism and increased oxygen consumption. Emergency reactions also are anticipatory.

In another experiment to support the incidence of hypertension under stress, it was proved that if mice, rats, or other small animals were crowded together, they developed high blood pressure (Benson, 1979). Still another experiment demonstrated that if mice were put in a cage and a cat allowed to prowl around the cage, the mice—even though not overcrowded—ultimately developed hypertension. The stress resulting from the fight-flight syndrome is relatively clear in these cases.

A Czech scientist, Dr. John Brodt, attached instruments to medical students so he could measure the manifestations of the fight-or-flight response such as muscle blood flow, heart rate, blood pressure, and effects on the sympathetic nervous system. He had the students lie quietly while he took baseline measurements, and then directed them to perform a simple task. He told them he would give them a four-digit number, from which he wanted them to subtract a two-digit number, get the answer, then subtract another two-digit number as quickly as possible. He also said they should not be bothered by a metronome that would be clicking in the background, nor should they be affected by their fellow medical students who would be giving them encouragement on the sidelines. The encouragement took the form of statements such as: "I did much better than that," or "Come on, move it." After these stimulations were administered, the individuals experienced a full-blown fight-or-flight response within three seconds (Benson, 1979). The physiological manifestations were present and there was an increase in heart rate, blood pressure, and muscle blood flow, which rose several hundred percent as a result of these stimuli.

If this experience may be projected further, it is not difficult to see how individuals who are in stressful situations suffer physiological damage immediately. It can be hypothesized that the repeated stimulation of the fight-or-flight response ultimately can be translated into permanent high blood pressure. The link between increased hypertension and stress can be primary coronary heart disease and even a major heart attack that could lead to death or invalidism. This is costly to the health care system and a most traumatic experience for the staff personnel undergoing stress.

TYPE A BEHAVIOR

Two cardiologists, Friedman and Rosenman (1973) correlated the traits of hard-driving executives that they termed Type A and Type B personalities and produced a coronary profile. The Type A executive is intense, ambitious, competitive, restless, and has a sense of urgency. This type executive also has a higher probability of developing coronary heart disease or suffering a fatal coronary between the ages of 35 and 40. Type Bs are more relaxed and easy going, less hostile and less overly competitive, and might be described as more subdued. They are not necessarily free of stress, but rather confront challenges and external threats less frenetically. Unlike Type As, they show little evidence of multiphasic thinking, and thus are infrequently observed doing two things at once, such as reading while shaving, or memorizing flash cards while jogging. Vocational and avocational pursuits are managed in a more casual fashion. Type Bs seldom experience a frustrated sense of wasting time when not actively engaged in patently productive activities (Sparacino, 1979, p. 39).

Insofar as psychosocial factors cause coronary disease, it is likely that this occurs through their effects on the physiology of the cardiovascular system, on lipid metabolism, or on some combination of the two (Sparacino, 1979, p. 37). It is well established, in this regard, that stress generally induces transient elevations in blood pressure.

Over the last half century or so, it has been noted that numerous coronary patients are characterized by certain work-related behaviors that typically involve unmitigated striving and job involvement (Friedman, 1969). Sir William Osler's lectures on angina pectoris before the Royal College of Physicians of London in 1910 included particularly colorful observations. Of the 268 angina cases he personally encountered, 231 were men (Osler, 1910, pp. 696-700). Osler argued from a broad psychological perspective that: It is not the delicate neurotic person who is prone to angina, but the robust, the vigorous in mind and body, the keen and ambitious man, whose engine indicator is always at "full speed ahead" (Osler, p. 839).

In the last two decades, Friedman and Rosenman (1973) and their colleagues, working along the lines suggested by Osler and others, have described and studied more systematically the Type A or coronary-prone behavior pattern. In its extreme manifestations, this behavior pattern is described as representing a tightly woven array of habits, goals, characteristic modes of striving and achievement motivation, and personality traits. Persons displaying this pattern are overtly competitive, aggressive, or even hostile, exceedingly demanding of self and others, and chronically restless, impatient, and time conscious. These individuals seemingly are never truly content unless battling multiple deadlines, obstacles, and harassments. There never seem to be enough hours in the day for Type As to get everything done; their cluttered calendars serve as painful reminders of their incessant, compulsive striving. According to Friedman (1969), the Type A pattern refers to a characteristic action-emotion complex that is exhibited by individuals engaged in a relatively chronic struggle to obtain an unlimited number of poorly defined outcomes from their environment in the shortest period of time and, if necessary, against the opposing efforts of other factors or persons in this same environment.

The reward structures in business and industry facilitate the rise of Type As to higher status positions. It also is true that their competitive zeal and hard-driving qualities need not necessarily translate into vocational success. The attainment of high socioeconomic status is not, in this regard, analogous to a simple foot race with the prize awarded to the fastest (Type A) (Jenkins, 1975).

As a group, Type A subjects show a higher serum cholesterol, a higher serum fat, more diabetic-like traits or precursors, smoke more cigarettes, exercise less (because they can't find time to do so), are "overdriving" certain of their endocrine glands in a manner that can be expected to damage their coronary arteries, eat meals rich in cholesterol and animal fat, and suffer more from high blood pressure than Type B subjects (Friedman & Rosenman, 1973, p. 200).

It is interesting to note that health providers such as physicians and psychiatrists recently studied by Friedman were found to favor Type A orientations. This can be supported by the dual life they often live in their practice and academic appointments where "publish or perish" still is a stressful occupational reality. They actually experience a constant struggle.

If the executives' struggle becomes chronic, a chronic excess discharge of the various hormones also occurs. It is obvious, of course, that the Type A manager is engaged in a chronic, more or less continuous, minute-by-minute struggle. It was no surprise to find that most Type A subjects not only discharged more norepinephrine and epinephrine (the nerve hormones or catecholamines), but also "overdrive" their pituitary glands to secrete too much ACTH (the hormone that stimulates the adrenal glands to discharge cortisol and other hormones) and growth hormone. Most Type A subjects exhibit an excess of the pancreatic hormone insulin in their blood—a sign generally believed to indicate that something is seriously wrong with the disposition of fat and sugar in the body. As a result of these abnormal discharges of catecholamines from the nerve endings and hormones from the pituitary, adrenal, and pancreatic glands, most Type A subjects exhibit (1) an increased blood level of cholesterol and fat, (2) a marked lag in ridding their blood of the cholesterol added to it by the food ingested, (3) a prediabetic state, and (4) an increased tendency for the clotting elements of the blood (the platelets and fibrinogen) to precipitate out. In a sense, Type A subjects too often are exposing their arteries to "high voltage" chemicals even during the "low voltage" periods of their daily living (Friedman & Rosenman, 1973, p. 202).

Despite the distinction between Type A and Type B persons, the A-B variable was not intended to represent a typology but rather the endpoints of a normal distribution. Many persons demonstrate mixed aspects of Type A behavior, perhaps depending to some extent on differential social learning experiences and specific situational contingencies. Type Bs often display Type A characteristics (Glass, 1977).

Type As are achievement oriented. This point was examined in a research study of more than 4,000 employed men and women. Type As demonstrated higher educational attainment and occupational prestige. Thus hard-driving Type A individuals are somewhat more likely to attain higher levels of educational and vocational success (at least as typically defined in contemporary western societies) than their Type B peers (Shekelle, Schoenberger, & Stamler, 1976, pp. 381-394).

Another study showed that Type A behavior was as clinically significant as the classical risk factors, including blood pressure and smoking, and Type A subjects were approximately twice as likely to develop coronary heart disease (CHD) as Type B. A follow-up report eight and a half years later showed 11.2 percent of the men initially judged as Type A had developed CHD in contrast to 5 percent of those termed Type B. In addition, Type As were found more likely to suffer recurrent infarction (Jenkins, Zyzanski, & Rosenman, 1976, pp. 342-347).

Another research study reported that Type A coronary patients displayed a greater preference for working alone under pressure and were concerned with maintaining control over environmental stressors. Their motivation to actually confront stress alone may reflect their strong desire for control. In fact, however, such a preference for isolation while under duress may increase responsibility, pressure, and job demand. The researchers reported that subjects who showed a preference for working alone under stress also demonstrated greater cardiovascular reactivity. These studies represent an important contribution while further underlining the need for additional research examining the interaction of behavior patterns and stressful events (Dembroski & MacDougall, 1978, pp. 22-23). Organizations also need to consider the reward structure that actually encourages Type A behavior in managerial roles.

MANAGERIAL INVOLVEMENT

A major question to be addressed is: Do organizations have the social responsibility to reduce the stressors that ultimately result in coronary heart disease? Stressors such as role ambiguity, role conflict, role overload, underutilization of abilities, and poor working relationships appear to be potentially dangerous for individuals' health and for organizational effectiveness. Managers through clear communication, the establishment of unambiguous job demands, and properly planned divisions of labor can resist some of these job stressors. Discussions between subordinate and supervisor about the job, its range and depth, and its problems could reduce ambiguity and conflict. It is possible to change the overall climate of an organization by managerial action focusing on stressor reduction as a primary objective.

A chief contributor to this type of climate in a dynamic health care organization is the day-to-day practices and philosophy of its managers. Better managerial practices should include methods of early identification of stress-related problems so that employees who are under heavy pressure and stress can be helped. Managers can be used as an important resource for seeking help. Employees may be more likely to recognize their own stress problems and be more willing to ask for help (Ivancevich & Matteson, 1979, p. 111).

An important managerial action with some potential for reducing stress effects for some employees involves their increased participation in the decision-making process. Data have indicated that historically low involvement in decision making may be related to excessive job stress and to potential coronary disturbances. Health care institutions can reduce this stress by involving subordinates actively in important decisions. However, participation in insignificant decisions is likely to result in even more stress. Research has demonstrated that involving an individual in participatory decision making and then suddenly stopping this activity for a short period can create a negative, emotional, and physical reaction that could result in increased stress.

THE FIT: PERSON, ROLE, ENVIRONMENT

Connecting the individual to the job environment is essential to reducing some of the stressors previously described. One kind of fit between individual and job environment is the degrees to which the person's skills and abilities match the demands and requirements of the work. Another type of fit is the degree to which the person's needs are supplied in the job environment—for example, the extent to which the need to utilize the manager's best and highest ability is satisfied by the position. The basic assumption is that both forms of misfit will cause job dissatisfaction, depression, physiological strain, and other symptoms of poor mental health (French, 1974, p. 70).

Most administrators in health care organizations want less role ambiguity (as a source of stress) than they actually have. Those who have experienced conditions that have increased role ambiguity have experienced lower job satisfaction. When there is a good fit between the individual's perceived expectations and the desired organization's expectations for output, there appears to be a better fit between the manager and the environment, resulting in higher job satisfaction. When managers are being held heavily responsible for individuals, they experience some stress. However, there is increasing satisfaction when these managers have slightly more responsibility for subordinates than they expected originally. This is not an overload but apparently a congruent fit and one that results in a normative level of cholesterol as an index of low stress as measured by these individuals.

Managers in these organizations generally want more of a quantitative workload than they have, and it is these individuals who demonstrate higher job satisfaction and a better fit to their environment. When the fit of the individual to the environment is incongruent, the following stressors may be active: role ambiguity, subjective workload, lack of participation, responsibility for "things," responsibility for people, and underload. Most managers want less role ambiguity than they have since, as ambiguity increases, so does cholesterol, systolic blood pressure, and glucose. These physiological indicators are related to the nature of the fit between the individual and the environment.

The measure of good relationships with an immediate supervisor includes items such as:

1. the extent to which the manager listens to the subordinates' problems
2. the extent to which the manager has confidence in the subordinates and trusts them

3. the extent to which the subordinate can trust and have confidence in the manager

These measures, when reported in a positive manner, indicate a much more congruent fit between the working environment and the individual. Studies showed that managers who had poor relationships with their subordinates had demonstrated a significant positive correlation between role ambiguity and increased cortisol; but for managers who had a positive relationship, there was no such correlation. Diastolic blood pressure was related to workload only among those workers who had poor relationships with their immediate superiors. Serum glucose was related to workload only among managers who had poor relationships with their employees. Relations with subordinates had even stronger conditioning effects upon systolic blood pressure, on diastolic blood pressure, and on serum glucose. Thus, good relations with others, especially with subordinates, serve as buffers between the stress of quantitative workload and the physiological strains that may result (French, 1974, p. 77). The effect of job stress on individuals is eliminated by the buffering effect of good supportive supervisory relationships, positive peer relationships, and positive subordinate relationships. Some of the remedies for this lie in the relationship that managers develop with their employees.

EPIDEMIOLOGY

In studying occupational stress, managers always must be aware of the interplay between the physical work environment, physical task demand, and psychological reaction of the individual to these environmental factors. Administrators are concerned with the determinants of the state of health in the organization of the employees who play significant roles in affecting the efficiency and effectiveness of the institution. The epidemiological approach can help clarify the nature of stress and the working environment. This method of examining stress in the health care organization provides small but important segments of information about factors affecting occupational stress. For example, this method of study shows that among professional groups such as physicians and psychologists, women have higher suicidal rates than men, even though the reverse is true in the general population. Professionals with above-average suicide rates include dentists, psychiatrists, ophthalmologists, and anesthesiologists, while pediatricians, pathologists and surgeons tend to have low rates.

Another interesting contrast: optometrists' suicide rate is about one-tenth that of ophthalmologists (Kasl, 1978, p. 8).

These data are essential for health care administrators who are attempting to balance out the demands and needs of their institution while attempting to manage their human resources. This information is significant for them in identifying some of the stressors experienced by the various staff specialists and disciplines. Our current knowledge of epidemiological factors indicates that in health care organizations the following conditions are responsible for staff members' stress: job insecurity, excessive competition, inadequate and hazardous working conditions, unusual task requirements and demands, conflict in organizational careers such as job or disengagement, changes in task and task difficulty, and variation in organizational structure. These factors provide further data to consider on the connections between managerial systems and the net effect on the individual professional in the health care setting experiencing stress. Epidemiology has aided health care administrators particularly well with regard to the management of human resources via the job dissatisfaction variable, which is the absence of satisfaction. Interestingly, job satisfaction may be perceived as the absence of conflict.

JOB DISSATISFACTION

Dissatisfaction with certain aspects of work is associated with risk and coronary heart disease. There is even evidence to indicate that work satisfaction may be a contributing factor to an individual's not being affected by coronary heart disease. This is supported by studies indicating that an increase in angina pectoris was experienced by individual supervisors who reported problems with other supervisors and coworkers and who had greater risks for further coronary problems (Medalie, et al., 1973, pp. 583-594). The complexity of the possible relationships linking overload, excessive demands, and many responsibilities to cardiovascular health has been illustrated in studies conducted at the University of Michigan (French, 1974, pp. 70-79). One aspect of the complexity is that more finely differentiated variables lead to differential association:

1. Quantitative overload may be related primarily to coronary heart disease risk (smoking, cholesterol, heart rate) while qualitative overload may have primarily mental health consequences such as low self-esteem.

2. The amount of responsibility for other people and their work may be associated positively with blood pressure, while the amount of responsibility for "things" may be associated negatively.

Studies by the National Aeronautics and Space Administration indicated that the association between job stress (such as workload and role ambiguity) and physiological outcomes (blood pressure, serum glucose, and cortisol) were positive among men with poor interpersonal relationships (with coworkers, subordinates, and supervisors) and absent or negative among men with good interpersonal relations (Kasl, 1978, p. 21).

In addition to physiological problems among individuals under stress on the job, there are emotional problems related to increased stress. Poor mental health seems to be related to:

1. Conditions at work: exposure to health and safety hazards, unpleasant work conditions, necessity to work fast and expend a great deal of physical effort; excessive and inconvenient hours.

2. Work itself: lack of use of skills and ability; perception of job as uninteresting, repetitive work; role overload that was both qualitative and quantitative, involving a discrepancy between individuals' resources and the demands of the job.

3. Shift work: time-oriented body functions affected, leading to difficulty in role behavior (e.g., role of spouse or parent) if the role activities normally were performed during the time of day when the worker was on the shift.

4. Supervision: job demands that were unclear or conflicting (role ambiguity and role conflict); close supervision and absence of autonomy; lack of feedback from supervisor; reports of problems from supervisor.

5. The organization: working on the boundary of the institution.

6. Wages and promotion: inadequate income, perception of promotional opportunity as unfair or too slow.

In this study, the relationships generally were stronger for indices of life satisfaction, self-esteem, tension, and the like, and generally weaker for mental health indicators based on psychiatric symptom checklist (Kasl, 1978, p. 25).

There also were studies that looked at job enlargement and enrichment for their impact upon satisfaction experienced at work. The studies seemed to suggest and were in agreement that enlargement led to increased satisfaction on the job in which individuals used their skills and abilities and had the opportunity to learn new tasks. Perceptions of work as being meaningful and based upon a proper fit of responsibility and autonomy were found. It was suggested that absenteeism, turnover, and work performance could be affected and that these differences might explain how the benefits of job redesign were essential. (This topic is explored more fully in Chapter 9.) Managerial interventions do have an impact on how satisfaction can be enhanced and stress can be identified and controlled in the health care environment before it becomes dysfunctional and disruptive to the organization, its personnel, and its clients.

ROLE CONFLICT

It has been suggested earlier that role conflict is a contributing factor to stress and other problems affecting the organization. Individuals are put in compromising positions by having the simultaneous occurrence of two or more sets of pressures so that compliance with any one would make compliance with the other(s) more difficult, creating ambiguity and stress. Individuals whose institutions require them to engage in transactions across organizational boundaries are more apt to be involved in stressful situations in which incompatible demands are made upon them. These demands create tension and affect their health and ability to cope with environmental constraints.

The extent to which individuals experience tension and are involved in role conflict situations is dependent upon personality characteristics such as their rigidity and/or flexibility. These factors have an impact on the basic conflicts they will confront. The effects of role conflict generally are considered to be negative to persons subjected to this problem. They experience job-related tensions, lower work satisfaction, less confidence in their organization, and more conflict across organizational boundaries. While role conflict is related to poor interpersonal relationships, this inconsistency creates additional problems, such as a lower level of trust in the organization and the questioned validity of the communications that are being experienced by all members. Persons in positions involving problem solving—managers heavily responsible for subordinates and patients—rather than in routinized tasks would be more prone to be conflict ridden. The responses of individuals to role conflict generally are difficult to pattern. Under high conflict conditions, persons who tend to be anxiety prone experience the situation as more intense and react to it with greater tension than those who are not anxiety prone.

The personality dimension of flexibility-rigidity mediates still more strongly the relationship between role conflict and tension, with flexible individuals accounting for almost the entire effect of role conflict and the rigid ones reporting virtually no greater tension in the high conflict situation than in the low conflict one (Kahn, 1974, p. 55).

Most organizational conflict is situated in the hierarchy, and conflicts usually occur with individuals at higher levels in open conflict with those at lower levels. The hierarchical dimension creates role ambiguity that involves the discrepancy between the amount of information a person has and the amount required to perform the role adequately. Ambiguous communications create additional stressors and as the ambiguity increases, job-related tension and work dissatisfaction both grow. This results in low trust, lower self-confidence, and not a great deal of affection for coworkers. Ambiguity also is related to feelings of job-related threat and to problems with emotional and physical health.

It takes a great deal of redesign and planning to compensate for an ambiguous situation in a managerial system. A manager's thoughts, feelings, values, and behaviors are influenced by the authority and responsibility associated with the position or role, which is limited by expected behaviors on the executive's part as defined by subordinates. This role conflict leads to stress.

Stressful situations in organizations usually occur:

1. When an individual is confronted with conflicting demands from members of different managerial role sets. For example, when a manager's superordinate (a member of the occupational role set) requests attendance at an after-hours meeting at the office when the spouse (a member of either another job role set or a domestic role set) requests that the executive come home early to meet visitors they had invited for the evening.

2. When an individual is confronted with conflicting demands from within one of the role sets. For example, when a manager refuses to allow subordinates time off to attend a union meeting because of a belief that such activities should not take place on the institution's time.

3. When an individual is unclear about or rejects the expectations and behaviors appropriate to any one or more of the roles, which also may involve problems within and between the various role sets. These difficulties occur when managers and others move into new roles, e.g., through promotion and transfer, when they have their existing role modified in some way, e.g., as a result of

technological or organizational change (Gowler & Legge, 1975, p. 39).

These situations become stressful when a manager must select an alternative in a climate of conflict and/or ambiguity such as when this individual must enforce a decision or is not entirely clear about the system of reward and punishment that may be related to the decision that must be made. Through the mechanism of performance appraisal, the individual's role sets often are related to organizational success criteria and the manager knows where the net effect of cutting costs, higher productivity requirements, or quality standards actually will lead. These evaluations of managerial role playing often are related to the system of reward and status symbols. The relationships between the individual, the roles, and the success criteria of the organization contribute to the intensity and number of stressors experienced in the manager's domain and environment.

Managers often find themselves in stressful situations where both objectives and goals in the short run and long run are revised repeatedly unilaterally by top management and the means needed to achieve these goals are modified or changed arbitrarily. These situations are ambiguous and become quite stressful when individuals are unable to deal with demands made upon them while at the same time, they feel pressured that they should be able to deal effectively with those demands. Managers become anxiety ridden because of their inability to achieve tasks. This inability may not have any effect upon their own stability but may be based upon a neurotic organizational environment that changes the rules on almost a daily basis and creates unresolvable anxiety. This occurs in managerial situations when there are too many or too few demands that actually exacerbate the individual's feelings of frustration and anxiety.

Managers do not want to achieve solely to be rewarded by greater income and hierarchical positions but are personally and intrinsically interested in fulfilling the demands of their own potential and desires for self-achievement and self-actualization. When this does not occur, they experience the anxiety of a stressful situation. These managers are likely to feel anxious when they experience a lack of congruency between the need to achieve and their ability.

Stress was a subject of an investigation by Harold Oaklander and Edwin Fleishman (1964, pp. 520-532). Two familiar dimensions of leadership were examined: (1) consideration (behavior indicative of mutual trust, respect, warmth, and support) on the part of supervisor, and (2) initiating structure (ability of supervisors to define the roles of their subordinates and to structure their tasks in terms of achieving organizational goals). These two dimensions were related to measures of internal and interdepartmental stress in one government hospital and two voluntary general hospitals. Two questionnaires, one to measure leadership and the other to measure intradepartmental and interdepartmental stress were completed by 118 supervisors. Special attention was paid to the 44 nursing supervisors in the three hospitals. Results showed that role perception of supervisors was related to the amount of internal and interdepartmental stress; higher consideration was related to lower internal unit stress but in no instance was it related to stress between departments.

REMEDIES: ROLE ADAPTATION AND SOCIAL SUPPORT

One way of dealing with role conflict is to develop systems of role adaptation in which managers can adjust to the levels of adaptation and flexibility in the organization to reduce some of the conflict. Studies of this situation indicated that role adaptation was more likely when:

1. personnel understood each others' problems and needs
2. subordinates felt that supervisors understood their viewpoint about work
3. hospital rules, policies, and procedures were clear to staff
4. there was adequate communication among trustees, medical staff, and the administrator
5. there was minimum conflict between key hospital departments and divisions
6. staff did not feel under unreasonable pressure to perform
7. the hospital administrator was both aware of problems and effective in solving them
8. supervisors were viewed as having high technical competence
9. the hospital was relatively new
10. the proportion of professional nurses on staff with at least five years of service was relatively low
11. the ratio of registered to practical nurses was high

As a result of role adaptation, role conflict was reduced and role flexibility was increased. The role flexibility then increased when the following five conditions were administratively operative:

1. coordination between shifts was adequate

2. conflict between shifts was minimal
3. hospital problems were solved promptly
4. the proportion of professional nurses on staff with at least five years' service was high
5. role adaptation was neither very prevalent nor prompt

Role adaptation emerged from this research as a product of organizational integration and rationality, while role flexibility did not. The researchers concluded that to achieve the goal of employee compliance in hospitals, it would be more appropriate to make efforts toward attaining greater internal integration in the system that to introduce human relations programs or to try to effect employee identification with the institution (Georgopolis, 1975, p. 349). The studies indicated that role adaptation and role flexibility could be dealt with by health care administrators very cognizant of and sensitive to a proper balance of managerial systems and human resource interventions.

One organizational objective is to improve the emotional and physical health of personnel by reducing occupational stress and the impact of this stress on individuals. Occupational stress is a product of an interaction between the individual and the work environment. Reducing this stress involves modifying the design of the organization and/or the behavior of the individual. The idea of a social support as a mechanism for improving health and reducing occupational stress is significant. It is necessary to clarify what the concept of social support is. Social support actually is a buffer that affects the occupational stress on the individual's health. Supportive coworkers, as an example, are less likely to create interpersonal pressures or tensions. The experience of support satisfies important social or affiliative needs for most people and hence tends to make them feel more positively about themselves and their jobs. Thus, social support should reduce known occupational stresses such as role conflict and ambiguity, job dissatisfaction, and low occupational self-esteem. Available empirical evidence is quite consistent with this expectation.

In the absence of social support, physical and/or mental disorders should increase as occupational stress increases; as levels of social support rise, this relationship should diminish in strength, perhaps even disappearing under maximal social support. In multiple regression terms, the slope of the regression of disease on stress should be clearly positive when social support is absent or low but should diminish steadily as social support increases, perhaps declining to zero when support is high (House & Wells, 1977, p. 10).

Stress is perceived by individuals when they confront a situation in which their usual methods of behaving are not functioning properly and the consequences of not adapting to the situation become serious. These are situations where demands exceed their abilities and they are unable to fulfill the needs and values of others that are imposed, which create role conflicts. Once a situation is perceived as being stressful, alternate responses may be possible, some of which may modify the social conditions in the organization or the individual's perception of the condition so that the negative perception of stress can be reduced or eliminated.

Studies have found variables indicative of social support such as work group cohesion, personal trust, or the liking for managers associated with indicators of stress and/or health. For example, a study by Stanley Seashore found that as work group cohesiveness increased, anxiety over work-related matters decreased (Seashore & Barnowe, 1972, pp. 53-54). Findings of this type of research on coronary heart disease risk factors among administrators, engineers, and scientists, have indicated that among those who reported poor relations with their subordinates, such as low social support, there was a positive relationship between role ambiguity and high serum cortisol level, an indicator of physiological arousal tentatively linked to coronary heart disease (Caplan, Cobb, & French, 1975, pp. 211-219). Similarly, a positive relationship existed between perceived workload and serum glucose, blood pressure, and smoking among those having poor relations with their managers, coworkers and subordinates. In a related longitudinal study of the consequences of job loss and unemployment, perceived stress resulting from unemployment produced elevated cholesterol levels, increased incidents of illness and constant depression among men with low social support (House & Wells, 1977, p. 15). The data are worthy of consideration by health care managers grappling for a solution to this problem.

SOURCES OF SUPPORTS

There are various sources of social supports for subordinates such as managers, spouses, coworkers, and friends. These social supports were studied with regard to health outcomes and perceived occupational stress. The health outcomes were considered to be angina pectoris, ulcers, skin irritations, persistent cough, and neurotic symptoms. The perceived occupational stress was in the form of job dissatisfaction, reduced occupational self-esteem, overheavy workload, role conflict, too much responsibility, conflict between job demands, and a concern over the quality of one's work. It was found that when social supports were lowest, self-reported symptoms of ill health increased greatly and the effects of low support from family, supervisors, and friends were related directly to stressors (House & Wells, 1977, p. 16).

Enhancing social supports certainly should not be considered as a substitute for reducing occupational stress. Instead, social supports are potential means of alleviating that stress, and health care organizations have no right to expect managers, coworkers, family, friends, and relatives to serve as support systems for employees when the institution is remiss in alleviating the stressors. There is further evidence that positive increases in social support from supervisors directly reduce certain kinds of occupational stress such as role conflict and ultimately improve health if they are maintained at a low level. Increases of social support or closely related phenomena are likely to contribute toward a variety of individual and/or institutional goals besides reducing stress or improving health (e.g., higher morale, lower absenteeism, and perhaps enhanced organizational effectiveness) (House & Wells, 1977, p. 24).

It would appear that even a single source of support can assist the stress-health relationship significantly and can reduce certain levels of stress in the organization as well. The manager of a health care institution is especially significant for intervention purposes. The manager not only can provide some supports but also is important in influencing organizational channels while serving as a buffer in reducing occupational stress and its impact on employees' health.

Amelioration of the effects of occupational stress should utilize some combination of reducing individuals' exposure to the stress and increasing their resistance to it. Social support seems to be an excellent antidote. There is a relationship between these social supports, organizational stress, and job satisfaction.

Job satisfaction may be considered as involving well-defined tasks and roles and the absence of conflict. This is a climate in which positive mental health can prevail. Job dissatisfaction results from many factors, including overwork, role conflict, status inconsistency, job immaturity, and an atmosphere in which tension is generated in coronary-prone individuals. A research study (Brief & Aldag, 1976, pp. 468 - 472) found satisfaction to be related in a significantly positive way to supervisor supportive and instrumental behavior, and in a negative way to role clarity (Ford & Bagot, 1978, p. 35).

It is interesting to note in a tangential way that in the work structure and productivity of chronic schizophrenics employed in organizations, a personal or environmental support system is a necessity. Everyone requires such supports—"no man is an island, entire of itself," says the poet John Donne—but the schizophrenic needs it desperately. Therefore work becomes a powerful tool in the rehabilitation of these schizophrenics. Work environments and supportive systems are essential in this system (Black, 1977, p. 183). This prescription is a valid one under most normative health care settings and in human-environmental systems where occupational stress must be managed.

The next chapter addresses the critical topic of the impact of stress upon professional health care personnel in the attempt to deal with the serious hazards and maladies experienced by those who are responsible for delivering this service to the clients of the system.

BIBLIOGRAPHY

Baxter, P.J., White, W.G., Barnes, G.M., & Cashman, P.M.M. Ambulatory electrocardiography in air workers. *British Journal of Industrial Medicine,* 1978, *35,* 99-103.

Benson, H. The relaxation response: An innate capacity for dealing with stress. *Stress and Behavioral Medicine.* Gary E. Schwartz, (Ed.), Bureau of National Affairs, Biomonitoring Applications, Inc., New York, Tape Presentation, 1979.

Black, B.J. The potential productivity of the chronic schizophrenic. In *Reducing occupational stress: Proceedings of the National Institute for Occupational Safety and Health,* White Plains, N.Y., May 1977, pp. 181-185.

Brief, A., & Aldag, R. Correlates of role indices. *Journal of Applied Psychology,* 1976, *61,* 468-472.

Cannon, W.B., *Bodily changes in pain, hunger, fear and rage* (2nd ed.). Boston, Mass.: Charles T. Branford Co., 1953, 404.

Caplan, R.D., Cobb, S., & French, J.R.P., Jr. Relationship of cessation of smoking with the stress personality and social support. *Journal of Applied Psychology,* 1975, *6,* 211-219.

Dembroski, T.M., & MacDougall, J.M. Stress effects on affiliation preferences among subjects possessing the Type A coronary-prone behavior pattern. *Journal of Personality and Social Psychology,* 1978, *36,* 22-33.

Ford, D.L., & Bagot, D.S. Correlates of job stress and job satisfaction for minority professionals in organizations: An examination of personal and organizational factors. *Group and Organization Studies,* March 1978, *3*(1), 30-41.

Friedman, M. *Pathogenesis of coronary artery disease.* New York: McGraw-Hill, 1969.

Friedman, M., & Roseman, R.H. *Type A behavior and your heart.* New York: Fawcett Crest Publishing, 1973, 200-202.

French, J.R.P., Jr. Person fit role. In A. McLean (Ed.), *Occupational stress.* Springfield, Ill.: Charles C. Thomas, Publisher, 1974, 70-79.

Georgopoulos, B.S. *Hospital organization research: Review and source book.* Philadelphia: W.B. Saunders Co., 1975.

Glass, D.C. *Behavior patterns, stress, and coronary disease.* Hillsdale, N.J.: Erlbaum Publishing, 1977, 349.

Gowler, D., & Legge, K. Stress, success and legitimacy. In D. Gowler & K. Legge (Eds.), *Managerial stress.* New York: John Wiley & Sons, 1975, 34-51.

Greene, W., Goldstein, A., & Moss, A.J. Psychosocial aspects of sudden death *Archives of Internal Medicine,* 1972, *129,* 725-731.

Greiff, B.S. Work performance and occupational stress. In A. McLean (Ed.), *Occupational stress.* Springfield, Ill.: Charles C. Thomas Publisher, 1974, 91-93.

House, J.S., & Wells, J.A. Occupational stress, social support and health. In *Reducing occupational stress: Proceedings of the National Institute for Occupational Safety and Health,* White Plains, N.Y., May 1977, pp. 8-29.

Hurst, M.W., Jenkins, C.D., & Rose, R.M. The relation of psychological stress to onset of medical illness. In C.A. Garfield (Ed.), *Stress and survival: The emotional realities of life-threatening illness.* St. Louis: The C.V. Mosby Co., 1979, 17-23.

Ivancevich, J.M., & Matteson, M.T. Organizations and coronary heart disease: The stress connection. In J.L. Gibson, J.M. Ivancevich, and J.H. Donnelly, Jr. (Eds.), *Readings in organizations: Behavior, structure and processes.* Dallas: Business Publications, 1979, 103-113.

Jenkins, C.D. The coronary-prone personality. In W.D. Gentry & R.B. Williams (Eds.), *Psychological aspects of myocardial infarction and coronary care.* St. Louis: The C.V. Mosby Co., 1975.

Jenkins, C.D., Zyzanski, S.J., & Rosenman, R.H. Risk of new myocardial infarction in middle-aged men with manifest coronary heart disease. *Circulation,* 1976, *53,* 342-347.

Kahn, R.L. Conflict, ambiguity and overload: Three elements in job stress. In A. McLean (Ed.), *Occupational stress.* Springfield, Ill.: Charles C. Thomas Publisher, 1974, 47-61.

Kasl, S.V. Epidemiological contributions to the study of stress. In C.L. Cooper & R. Payne (Eds.), *Stress at work.* Chichester, England: John Wiley & Sons, 1978, 3-48.

King, H. Health in the medical and other learned professions. *Journal of Chronic Diseases,* 1970, *23,* 257-281.

Margolis, B.K., & Kroes, W.H. Occupational stress and strain. In A. McLean (Ed.), *Occupational stress.* Springfield, Ill.: Charles C. Thomas Publisher, 1974, 3-13.

McLean, A. Concepts of occupational stress, A review. In A. McLean (Ed.), *Occupational stress.* Springfield, Ill.: Charles C. Thomas Publisher, 1974, 3-13.

Medalie, J.H., Snyder, M., Groen, J.J., Neufled, H.N., Goldbourt, U., & Riss, E. Angina pectoris among 10,000 men. *American Journal of Medicine,* 1973, *55,* 583,594.

Oaklander, H., & Fleishman, E.A. Patterns of leadership related to organizational stress in hospital settings. *Administrative Science Quarterly,* 1964, *8*(4), 520-532.

Osler, W. The Lumleian lectures on angina pectoris. *Lancet,* 1910, *1,* 696-700, 839-844, 974-977.

Pelletier, K.R. Mind as healer, mind as slayer. *Psychology Today,* February 1977, *10*(9), 35-40, 82-83.

Rahe, R.H. Life change events and mental illness: An overview. *Journal of Human Stress,* September 1979, *5*(3), 2-10.

Seashore, S.E., & Barnowe, J.T. Collar color doesn't count. *Psychology Today, March 1972, 6*(3), 53-54, 80-82.

Selye, H. *Stress without distress.* Philadelphia, Pa.: J.B. Lippincott Co., 1974.

Selye, H. *Stress in health and disease.* Reading, Mass.: Butterworths, 1976.

Selye, H. *The stress of life.* New York: McGraw-Hill Book Co., 1978, 1, 75, 79, 177, 402.

Shekelle, R.B., Schoenberger, J.A., & Stamler, J. Correlates of the JAS Type A behavior pattern score. *Journal of Chronic Diseases,* 1976, *29,* 381-394.

Sparacino, J. The type A behavior pattern; A critical assessment. *Journal of Human Stress,* December 1979, *5*(4), 39.

Theorell, T. Workload, life changes and myocardial infarction. In *Reducing occupational stress: Proceedings of the National Institute for Occupational Safety and Health,* White Plains, N.Y., May 1977, 86-92.

Thiel, H.G., Parker, D., & Bruce, T.A. *Journal of Psychosomatic Research,* 1973, *17,* 43-57.

Chapter 5

The Impact of Stress on Nurses and Other Health Care Professionals

CONSIDERATIONS FOR THE HEALTH CARE MANAGER

1. Job previews and nurses' expectations need to be more realistic to produce greater job congruency and lower turnover rates.
2. Differences exist in expectations, not value systems, for new nursing personnel. This leads to a lower commitment and higher turnover when nurses find their expectations are not being met.
3. The following outcomes are important for both new and present nurses: pay, receiving cooperation, experiencing tension, autonomy, and opportunity to develop skills and abilities.
4. When nursing expectations and reality are incongruent, turnover is highest. There is a need for a psychological contract between the institution and nurse highlighting inducements and contributions.
5. When the nurse's capacity to solve problems and satisfy cognitive job requirements are impaired by burnout, job termination follows.
6. Organizational reward systems contribute to conflict between nurses, who identify with their profession, and supervisors, who

identify with the organization. Disproportionate power creates this stress.

7. A systems of socialization is needed to avoid burnout and cultural shock. This process helps to minimize employment changes.

8. Health care professionals who are responsible for patients with acute illness often are recipients of behaviors with which they have a difficulty coping.

9. Psychological stress, which often precipitates organic dysfunction, may bring about a regression in the patient's behavior.

10. Dying patients bring out feelings of guilt and shame in nurses and physicians, who thus experience increased stress.

11. The team approach in critical care settings decreases the possibility that one staff member will become overly burdened with this difficult task.

12. Preoperative teaching and admission teaching content in intensive care units should include the distressing features of delirium that patients may experience, to help nurses deal with such stress-producing problems.

13. Frustration through burnout results in personal stress and may lead the health care professional to increase the use of alcohol and drugs in an attempt to reduce tension.

14. Health care professionals need training in dealing with acute illness and death. Professionalism via detachment is rewarded too often when the emphasis should be on interpersonal relationships and emotional outlets. Burnout rates are lower for professionals who are encouraged to express and share their feelings with colleagues.

15. The process of anticipatory socialization has four phases:
    • skill and routine mastery   • moral outrage
    • social integration   • conflict resolution

16. Biculturalism is a method to resolve conflicts experienced by neophyte nurses by dealing with the value discrepancy that originally produced moral outrage and then rejection of the profession.
17. More flexible work schedules can help the professional reduce frustration and stress by providing a balanced work schedule of both intensive care and normative patients.
18. More emphasis should be placed on the social and psychological factors of health care by inservice education rather than by total immersion in the traditional mechanical-medical model.
19. Nurses and physicians are placed in a stressful double bind when treating colleagues. Conflicts over dependency-independence needs can be resolved by confronting these covert issues with the patient openly.
20. Most nursing educators are teaching because they disliked nursing practice and found it impossible to practice their profession the way they felt it should be. They transmit these values to their students, who thus arrive in the new work environment with a jaundiced view of the system.
21. Inservice education can be used to presocialize new personnel and reduce conflict before it becomes reality shock and rampant stress. Role transformation can help guide the neophyte from the sterile learning environment to the turbulent institution.

The role of the professional nurse is changing. Nurses are becoming more involved in planning and organizing health care activities and are also becoming more responsible for delivering total patient care services (Graves, 1971, pp. 491-494). In effect, the nurse's role is becoming one of managing patient care activities in general. In this new role, managerial responsibilities often include the supervision of other nursing and ancillary personnel, as well as the accomplishment of a wide range of organizational, patient care, and personal objectives (Dittrich, Lang, & White, 1979, p. 314). One may question whether the additional tasks of administration were presented to the prospective nursing candidate during initial education and training.

Nursing is an occupation in conflict, characterized by turnover and early burnout. It may very well be that prior to professional employment the candidates are not given the luxury of a realistic preview of what their job entails. This is a problem that leads to conflict and stress.

EMPLOYMENT PREVIEW: NURSING EXPECTATIONS

When job previews are realistic and nursing expectations are presented objectively to prospective condidates, lower turnover rates can be expected because expectations are connected more closely to the job and congruency is an anticipated result. If a new nursing staff member arrives with unrealistic expectations, greater pressure is exerted on the health care system to make congruency an issue since organizational commitment may be an unexpected price for the institution to pay. New staff members may have unrealistic expectations, but they do possess value systems similar to those of present members. They seek the same outcomes from their work as present staff but they do not have similar expectations. The differences in expectations and not in values seem to lead to a lower commitment and higher turnover among nurses when they find their expectations are not being met.

Nursing faces problems because of the phenomenon of reality shock among new employees since their expectations of performance-reward linkages are significantly higher than the reality under which existing nurses function. The greater the discrepancy between neophyte and present nurses in the perceived instrumentality, the lower the organizational commitment and the higher the turnover propensity. Finally, there are no basic differences between new and present nurses in the kinds of rewards and outcomes they value and desire (Seybolt & Ross, 1979, p. 2).

Several nursing outcomes were discussed with a sample of nurses as part of a study to determine what results were important to them. The outcomes with which they appeared concerned were:

1. pay
2. receiving help and cooperation from coworkers

3. experiencing pressure and tension on the job
4. autonomy, help, and recognition from immediate supervisors
5. the opportunity to develop skills and abilities
6. a sense of really helping patient and family
7. a stable work schedule
8. promotion
9. job security
10. an opportunity to learn new things
11. making independent decisions
12. responsibility

It was found that expectations of new nurse concerning performance-reward linkages were significantly more positive than those of present nurses. It might be added that these expectations therefore are highly unrealistic (Seybolt & Ross, p. 6). With this expectation and lack of fulfillment, problems leading to dissatisfaction, stress, and turnover must be dealt with initially.

In health care institutions where this shock is the most intense, the level of organizational commitment in staff nurses is the lowest and their turnover is the highest. Therefore, realistic job previews may be appropriate and necessary for nursing staff personnel. This process lowers the discrepancy between their initial expectations and those of current staff members. This may even lead to positive changes in turnover patterns. New nurses do not have perceived values regarding rewards strongly different from those of present nurses. Nursing staffs that seem to have the lowest variances between new and present employee expectations regarding the performance/reward connection can expect higher levels of commitment to the institution and lower turnover as a result of more congruency.

Exodus from nursing is another sign of career dissatisfaction. This is a common event in nursing, as are frequent job changes. It was found that among baccalaureate nurses, almost one-third left nursing practice in the two-year period following graduation. Another study reported that nearly half of graduate nurses either did not practice or failed to renew their licenses (Cartwright, 1979, p. 429). The implications in health care institutions are significant since they are interested in maintaining positive communication linkages between nursing staff and health care demands. If these professionals understand what is expected initially, a psychological contract may be drawn up, producing a clearer picture of expectations, organizational dynamics, and problems that can be incorporated into a blueprint for the nurse either to endorse personally or to reject initially prior to an extended stay in the institution.

NURSING MOBILITY

Nurses' mobility patterns should be explored since they do experience shock and burnout. It is difficult to accept the fact that nurses leave a profession for which they prepared so carefully and to which they demonstrated such an early commitment. Personnel who deliver direct medical or nursing care are vulnerable to the burnout syndrome in which their personal resources for coping with and managing stress are exhausted. Supervisory and administrative employees also become susceptible to burnout because of pressures to maintain an adequate support system for those who deliver direct health care services. Staff members experience the risk of burnout under the pressures imposed by standards for high quality medical care and an increasing demand for more humanistic approaches to nurse-patient interaction. It appears that nurses with baccalaureate or associate degrees or diplomas experience burnout more frequently than do licensed practical nurses, possibly because they have greater decision-making and leadership responsibilities (Patrick, 1979, p. 87).

BURNOUT: SOME SIGNS

When the expectations of the job of health care professionals vary greatly from the real world experiences of the institution, these professionals experience burnout. Some of the signs of this are:

- when nurses' capacity to solve problems and satisfy cognitive requirements of the work are impaired by burnout and they consider job termination
- when nurses begin to perceive patients, families, and clients from a negative, judgmental perspective and label them as problems or troublemakers
- when nurses feel the administration is not supporting them or understanding their job performance and these feelings are directed through anger toward the work environment, peers, and administrators
- when interpersonal contact between the emotionally exhausted

nurse and patient is affected adversely and the nurse experiences lower job satisfaction and self-esteem

- when perceptions of self-image begin to change drastically (negatively), accompanied by swings in emotional disposition
- when rigidity increases and the nurses' personal and social life changes via withdrawal and isolation
- when nurses have been trained to be aware of and sensitive to the needs of patients and then do not apply these skills
- when nurses increase self-imposed restrictions and experience stresses in their own lives such as marital and financial problems, parenting difficulties, social pressures, and other disruptive influences (Patrick, p. 88).

Unfulfilled expectations often produce conflict, which will increase when related reward systems are incongruous as well. A study by Benne and Bennis (1959, pp. 196-198) of 90 nurses in outpatient departments of seven hospitals reported varying reward systems between nurses and supervisors leading to tension among the nurses. Nurses bring with them into nursing schools an image that real nursing deals with the patient from a bedside perspective. This attitude and belief is one nurses hold onto very strongly. But in the work environment, nurses actually are required to carry out other duties that may be technical, organizational, administrative, and educational. Therefore, there is a great variation between the job the nurse expects to perform and the work actualities.

A health care system that is not aware of the risk of burnout for all employees will not implement the necessary supportive measures or maintain a consistent, appropriate degree of sensitivity to employees' needs. Nurses in leadership positions often experience isolation from other support personnel that may lead to more stress and a greater chance for problems. There also is a conflict between nurses and physicians, which creates a great deal of tension because of misperceptions on both sides.

Conflicts also occur involving professionalism as nurses have a great need to depend on behavioral sciences while physicians relate mostly to biological sciences and to areas of measurement. Nurses develop their professional relationships based upon communication skills while physicians employ a clinical, biological approach. This variance in orientation creates conflicts because physicians expect nurses should handle patients in the same manner as do the physicians. This creates problems for nurses, who feel they are being asked to compromise their values in order to satisfy physicians with whose basic style they may not agree in the first place.

Stressful situations are those in which individuals feel the greatest degree of pressure and inadequacy in dealing with painful and complex issues. Only by experiencing and sharing with other members of the health care profession and seeing how they deal with stressful issues can individuals gain a proper perspective on stress management. Burnout rates usually are lower for health care professionals who are able to express and share their feelings with colleagues. This provides a coping technique that appears to be effective. Executives can utilize this by applying the managerial device of assigning responsibilities and duties and varying the health care professionals' patient load so that they are not always dealing with high stress situations with dying patients. If these professionals spent some of their time with dying patients and other periods with individuals who have a positive prognosis, their stress will be reduced for them, their outlook much more positive, and their involvement more effective.

Health care professionals need some time off to decompartmentalize and put some distance between themselves and the situation that is creating the stress. Time off is essential; if possible, flexible work schedules could be used for managing a variety of job tasks. This is an effective way of improving sagging staff morale, reducing emotional stress, and lowering frustration levels. All health care professionals need free time to spend with their families or hobbies or on recreation; otherwise their mechanisms for dealing with their frustration and the ensuing risk of burnout will not be reduced if this activity cannot be legitimized by their health care institutions. This is not an exclusive nursing problem.

EMOTIONAL DYNAMICS

One way in which health care personnel maintain their psychological equilibrium and at the same time attempt to keep stress at a minimum is to maintain a psychological distance from patients. They often behave in ways that justify patients' complaints about the care they are receiving since they are too impersonal and fail to give adequate explanations concerning the nature of the patients' problems and other pertinent factors. There also are complaints that health care personnel lack personal respect for patients and deal with them as objects and not as individuals who have feelings and emotions. This behavior falls short of the professional-educational model that has been posed for health care professionals.

It may be very difficult for these physicians and nurses to recognize that they are operating in a mechanical manner. The failure of these professionals to understand and admit these feelings of vulnerability creates a block that seems to stand in the way of emotional coping. The professionals become so blocked that they cannot deal with either their own or their patients' feelings. When this occurs, the quality of health care declines. The uncertainty in medical and psychological research is compounded by the conflicting theories often espoused in this field.

Health care is emotionally demanding and physically draining and the feelings of frustration, exhaustion, and anxiety may lead professionals to negative attitudes toward the objects of treatment, whom they may see as their problem. When these professionals have a difficult time in dealing with patients and find that their contacts are creating stress, they usually reduce the contact or remove themselves emotionally and physically. This results in poor health care for patients and feelings of inadequacy and greater stress for professionals who cannot deal with this aspect of their career conflict. The emotional stress of caring for patients becomes more intensified as they become terminal.

When nurses and/or physicians begin to manifest negative feelings toward patients, they also feel guilty. They then become angry with the patients who they feel have created these feelings of guilt. This places an extra burden on the health care specialists and creates additional stress because death seems to be interpreted as failure by the professionals who are chartered to save lives. When they cannot achieve their objectives, failure creates anxiety. The health care professionals are trained to see death as a foe to be fought and beaten and the dying patient represents failure. If health care workers are to perform in an effective and professional manner, these stressful situations must be experienced by the health care worker with these patients.

These events often stimulate disruptive emotional feelings that many professionals attempt to deal with by detachment. Some health care professionals attain burnout early in their careers because they experience physical and emotional exhaustion and no longer are able to deal with empathy, respect, or positive feelings for patients. They become extremely critical of patients and of the profession and deal with individuals in a demeaning and derogatory manner. They view their patients as being worthy of their illness since the burnout changes certain of their perceptions and makes it extremely difficult for them to practice their role in a humanistic, helping, positive manner.

Burnout may be responsible for the growing number of malpractice suits. This increases the cost of insurance for physicians, who now become even angrier as a result of these additional constraints on their profession that affect their morale, performance, and even turnover. Some of them deal with this frustration by moving out of the profession and into administrative jobs—where they find greater frustration in dealing with other physicians and nurses who are experiencing the same burnout.

Moving out of the profession also may involve physicians who leave primary practice. In a study of this issue (Crawford & McCormack, 1971, p. 265) approximately 75 percent of the physicians surveyed were under 40 years old at the time of leaving their practice. Their practices were characterized by hard work and long hours. During a typical week, more than two-thirds worked longer than 60 hours, half conducted two or more evening office sessions, and a majority made more than ten house calls. Office hours on Saturday were reported almost unanimously, and 17 of the 73 conducted them on Sundays as well. Some 36 percent saw more than 40 patients daily. In addition, most respondents felt overburdened by an excessive number of telephone calls and unrealistic demands. They also had difficulty in regularly scheduling time for recreation or other personal activities.

By far their greatest complaint was the degree of overwork encountered. At least two-thirds of them gave this as the major reason for leaving. This, of course, included not only long hours but the physical and emotional strain of constantly feeling unable to get away. Although they felt they were filling a great need in the community and their practices contained a variety of other gratifications, this did not offset the problems they noted.

This burnout results in personal stress and often increases the use of drugs and alcohol by health care professionals who attempt to reduce their tension and alleviate some of the stress. Professionals respond to stress no differently from the patients who come to them experiencing anxiety and stress.

Physicians appear more prone to coronary heart disease (CHD) than other health providers. Pressures and stresses inherent in the work itself appear important in predicting CHD. Long hours, numerous patient contacts, many and changing demands on skills, and recurrent emergency calls appear salient factors, although how much each of these contributed to stress was not determined (Cartwright, 1979, p. 424). Physicians seem to deal with anxiety and stress with patients as they deal with their own frustrations. They begin to experience more emotional illness and become more detached and dehumanizing in dealing with patients. They reject the need to seek out personal psychiatric treatment since they feel their emotional stress cannot be resolved on the job and they continue to deal with this by displacing their frustrations at home and having more conflict in their own personal environment. These professionals react in a similar manner to managers who are experiencing stress by having problems with their families since they are losing control of their personal lives and certain components of their work.

Physicians and administrators also are affected by these serious issues. The uncertain outcomes of intensive care unit patients can bring about feelings of frustration and guilt in health care workers responsible for these individuals. These patients may be very demanding of their nurses and physicians and, in return, the health care personnel may be just as demanding of their patients. They may even avoid the patients as a way of putting some distance between their feelings of failure and the individuals' demands. As the physicians become less available to patients, more pressure is put on nurses, who therefore assume the additional role of answering technical questions for patients that they actually are unable to handle.

Administrators in intensive care units view their responsibilities as similar to other areas but they do not fully understand the complaints and feelings of nurses (experiencing burnout) who must staff these areas and who become emotionally distraught. The workload is quantitatively abundant and individuals need more flexibility to balance all tasks. With this increase in workload, mistakes become more frequent and may be quite serious for acute patients. Life dependency tasks create stressors for health care workers that often lead to crucial mistakes in judgment. When anxiety continues to increase, it affects efficiency and the effectiveness of individuals working in this area. These professionals, who are faced with the death of their patients, must protect themselves from anxiety, guilt, anger, and exhausted overcommitment. They have no visible means of escape except intellectual distancing—a turmoil that forces the nurse to "turn off." They now must find some way to unwind and reduce some of this anxiety and stress. Group loyalties also affect the pressures experienced by individuals in this environment.

Health care workers may not be feeling well personally but still must maintain their workload because any time a breakdown occurs in the staff reservoir, other members of the team are affected since they must pick up the overload and work more with the terminal individuals. The group norms must be maintained since it is essential for a cohesive link to be maintained among all the nurses. A solution may be to hold continuing group sessions devoted to exploring the work and the feelings and experiences individuals are undergoing. It would be important to bring to the surface the fear, the guilt, and uncertainties experienced so all involved can understand that these are normal feelings associated with the work and are held universally. It may be necessary for staff members to share creative techniques on specific problems. This occurs only when the members of a group are not fearful of rejection and assume their inputs have validity. An open climate is one that will support this process. It will be important to bring out into the open the fact that certain minor mistakes are inevitable. This frankness helps reduce some of the guilt and anxiety experienced by individuals who feel they have to be perfect and omnipotent. It is essential for these professionals to be able to express themselves emotionally as well as technically.

Emotions do have an impact on health care workers because a triangular network exists at all times among the professional, the patient, and certain issues related to patient care. When patients and their emotional needs begin to interact with the professionals, the issues and conflicts are brought into full view. Professionals must deal with their own feelings about death in order to cope effectively and comfortably with persons facing death. Without self-awareness, professionals in helping roles are vulnerable to a wide variety of unpleasant, negative manifestations of anxiety. This complex situation brings out feelings of anger, guilt, helplessness, frustration, and inadequacy.

It might be thought that the more experience caregivers have with dying persons, the more manageable their feelings and behaviors would become. However, a study (Pearlman, Stotsky, & Dominick, 1969, pp. 63-75) refuted this belief. In an examination of nursing personnel in a variety of institutions ranging from state hospitals to nursing homes, it was found that nurses who had more experience with dying persons were more likely to avoid the dying and felt more uneasy about discussing death. In fact, 77 percent reported "having difficulty" or avoided discussing matters related to death. Another study documented nurses' avoidance of terminal patients. It also was reported by Bugen that physicians were more concerned about death and more afraid of dying than were medical students and control groups. A number of observers have noted that, because of this high level of anxiety, physicians, like nurses, avoid patients once they begin to die (Bugen, 1979, p. 148). A starting point to understand this conflict is with the professional orientation and values of nurses and other health care professionals.

NURSES' PROFESSIONAL CONFLICTS

Theoretical dimensions of the professional-bureaucratic work organization problem can be examined by analyzing work tasks in a constantly changing technological society. Such an approach could lead to the development of organizational forms following function rather than structure. A review of some of the major research in this area indicates:

1. Professional-bureaucratic conflict is a relatively new phenomenon. It is an outgrowth of the combination of increased bureaucratization and professionalization, as well as the increased employment of professionals in organizations. This type of conflict situation can and does occur in a variety of settings and occupations.

2. Conflicting loyalties to the professional and bureaucratic systems of work organization lead to reality shock, a condition that is detrimental to the individual, to the profession, and to society.

3. The severity of professional-bureaucratic conflict, and resultant reality shock, is related to type of educational preparation, role configuration, disparity in reward systems, and structural features of the institution. With increased professionalism, there often is increased conflict. Organizational conflict is not necessarily detrimental; indeed it often is the source of innovation. The question is whether the bureaucratic structure is flexible enough to accommodate the conflict associated with the professional mode, (Kramer, 1974, p. 23).

Variations in the manner in which work in the health care institution is organized and how tasks are dealt with certainly affect the professional and bureaucratic value system of the institution. A professional system is used in nursing schools where work organizations actually employ bureaucratic models. This conflict and variance is attributable to differences in both the school culture and the work culture. This variation and shock is experienced by nurses when they enter health care institutions that emulate the organizational model. This personal incongruency does produce reality shock for nurses, which is a very uncomfortable experience and in time may cause them to leave their chosen profession because ultimately it may affect their health and effectiveness in the health care system. A lack of interpersonal competency on the part of nursing graduates also leads to reality shock and interferes with any corrections that could be made in the system.

Many values transmitted from nursing schools to student nurses often are accepted at face value without being tested by the students while they are in training. The students are quite vulnerable, and when they hold on to these values they create conflict for themselves because they actually are isolated from the "real world." When they continue to identify with these professional beliefs after they graduate, the result may be that they will have a difficult time putting them into practice. They may be fortunate and be exposed to the knowledge and behaviors of a reference group of highly adaptive nurses who will suggest to the students different strategies for when they begin to interact interpersonally in the work situations. A greater degree of congruence will decrease the net effect of this reality shock and help nurses adjust to new and different value systems that may bring about much more satisfying relationships and easier adjustments for them in their new careers.

SOURCES OF CONFLICT

It is essential to look at personal sources of conflict for nurses, beginning by examining nursing as a profession and looking at some of the characteristics of its practitioners. Kramer's research (1974, p. 96) concluded:

1   Nurses with high success aspirations were found attracted most often to groups supporting high bureaucratic structure, either high bureaucratic-low professional or high bureaucratic-high professional.

2   Married nurses with small children tended to identify strongly with low bureaucratic-low professional categories; they were most numerous in the low bureaucratic-high professional group.

3. Nurses with a high professional orientation appeared to have the highest dropout rate and the most job changes; a high bureaucratic orientation was associated with job transfers within the same organization.

4. Nurses with high bureaucratic-low professional orientation tended to be in administratively promoted positions more frequently than any of the other groups; the high bureaucratic-high professional nurses tended to be in unusual and clinically oriented positions more often than the others.

5. The high bureaucratic-low professional nurses appeared to experience the most job and nursing satisfaction; both the high

bureaucratic-high professional and the low bureaucratic-high professional groups experienced deprivation within the scope of what was expected of them. The latter also experienced much job dissatisfaction.

6. Nurses rated as highly successful consistently reported higher levels of self-actualization than their peers.

7. The low bureaucratic-high professional nurses were most likely to return to graduate school to prepare to be teachers or go into teaching without graduate preparation. High bureaucratic-high professional nurses also had a fairly high rate of return to school, but worked longer first. Reasons for their change included becoming clinical nurse specialists or nurse practitioners rather than teachers.

8. New graduates appeared less in high bureaucratic-high professional and low bureaucratic-high professional organizations. This may be because it takes a while to work out the conflict and compatible marriage between high bureaucratic-high professional role concepts and because many of the nurses with low bureaucratic-high professional role concepts leave nursing practice or go into teaching soon after graduation.

There obviously is a professional–bureaucratic conflict, and nurses do hold these conflicting value orientations at the same time. Nurses are encouraged to profess their loyalty to patients, to the organization that hires them, and to the profession. The problem occurs with regard to the priority they attach to these loyalties that constitute the specific role organization and create the potential conflicts. This conflict often is experienced in the form of deprivation because it is the variance between the ideal role concept that nurses envision and what actually is in operation in the work situation when they enter the organization. When they suffer role deprivation, it is a source of reality shock as well as of stress. When the stress continues, these professionals are personally vulnerable as they must continue to support their health care organizations and, at the same time, encounter patients with complex physical and emotional problems such as critical illness, delirium, catastrophic reactions, etc. These stressors impact strongly upon the professional who is quite human but has been conditioned to deny this reality, creating additional shock.

THE IMPACT OF STRESS

The following conditions have a direct effect upon the professional and personal adjustment of the health care worker. These patient-related problems are presented to demonstrate the impact of stress on these professionals.

Illness

Acute illness and critical care for patients are physiological stresses not only for the individual experiencing them but also for the health care professional involved. Physiological stress is a bit different from psychological stress since its origin is an organic base of psychological dysfunction. A study (Strain, 1978, p. 39) of organic precipitants of psychological dysfunction observed that 12.5 percent of patients in an acute care setting in the intensive care unit manifested delirium. Delirium of varying severity is present in every patient who is approaching or recovering from a coma, who is terminal, who has been given a general anesthesia, or who is drugged to the point of confusion. It is present in most patients with severe anemia, fever, peripheral circulatory collapse, cardiac arrest, congestive heart failure, respiratory failure, pulmonary insufficiency, hepatic or renal insufficiency, acidosis or alkalosis, electrolyte imbalance, or infection. It is present in those suffering from the effects of many different drugs and from the effects on the central nervous system of almost every disease that produces a disturbance and physiological homeostasis.

The evidence regarding patients' psychological deficits may be only their emotional reaction in discerning that they do not feel normal. The physical stresses that interfere with their cognitive functioning do alter orientation, moods, judgment, defenses, perception, consciousness level, and concentration. If their dysfunction is based upon a traumatic event that also is acute and does not give them sufficient time to develop adequate defenses, they will not be able to adapt to their psychological problems and may be vulnerable to catastrophic reaction.

Health care professionals responsible for these patients often are the recipients of behaviors with which they have difficulty coping. Patients who are critically ill do experience psychological reactions to these events that vary depending on the nature of the stress. Their method of coping and their previous experience with illness and physicians all comes into account. When there are psychological interventions intended to ease the stressors, patients will depend upon the physicians' and nurses' awareness of the psychological stress they are experiencing. The behavior also depends upon the physicians' and nurses' ability to establish relationships with the patients that will make use of the resources available to the patients in order to help them adapt to a new physical situation that may be of a critical nature.

A study by Strain and Grossman (Strain, 1978, p. 40) codified seven categories of psychological stress to which the acutely ill medical patient is vulnerable. These stresses take on heightened significance in intensive care unit patients. The categories include:

1. the basic threat to narcissistic integrity
2. fear of strangers
3. separation anxiety
4. fear of the loss of love and approval
5. fear of the loss of control of developmentally achieved functions (bowel and bladder), regulation and appropriate modulation of feeling states
6. fear of loss of, or injury to, body parts
7. reactivation of feelings of guilt and shame, and accompanying fears of retaliation for past transgressions

These psychological stresses parallel those experienced in the course of human development. For example, stranger anxiety emerges when an infant is about 6 months old; separation anxiety may appear from 6 to 30 months of age; fear of the loss of love and approval peaks between the ages of 2 and 4 and, concurrently, the toddler fears the loss of control of developmentally achieved functions, e.g., sphincter control or control of emotions. Fear of loss of, or injury to, body parts (castration anxiety) can be observed in children from 3 to 5; and after the age of 5, feelings of guilt and shame become increasingly prominent.

Today, behavioral scientists recognize that individuals' ability to cope with the normal vicissitudes of life, as well as to manage the overwhelming psychological stress evoked by acute illness that requires intensive care, depends on how well they adapted to these same stresses when they experienced them during their early development (Strain, 1978, p. 40). The quality and quantity of patients' suffering depends on the physician's attitude toward pain and its medication. Patients can deal with pain if the seven basic stresses just discussed are reduced. Psychological stress that precipitates any organic dysfunction may bring about a regression in the patient's behavior. This occurs if psychological stress is brought about by acute critical illness. The patient's defenses and relationships with others may become extremely infantile. The relationships may become less reality-oriented and the patient may begin to assume a passive-dependent role with the physician who no longer is needed.

Confusion

One problem health care professionals encounter in the intensive care unit is that the patient demonstrates certain behaviors that indicate confusion and disorientation. These behaviors are quite pathological and include delirium, catastrophic reactions, and euphoric responses. These reactions all create stressors in the nurses and personnel who are involved in the health care environment and, as a result, put additional pressure on them and the physicians.

Delirium

The symptoms of delirium have been described on a continuum ranging from slight clouding of consciousness to a full blown psychotic-like reaction to coma. Delirium is an acute organic brain syndrome characterized by progressive disorientation, first to time, then to place, and finally to person. Patients experience varying degrees of cognitive impairment. Illusions are common in the moderately delirious patient; hallucinations and delusions occur as delirium progresses. Hallucinations usually are visual and delusions often are paranoid in nature. Frightening dreams, which may be confused with hallucinations or illusions, sometimes are reported. Delirious patients may become agitated and combative or withdrawn and secretive. They often try to cover up and deny symptoms of delirium because they believe they are going crazy (Adams, Hanson, et al., 1978, p. 1504).

Many nurses must deal with executives who have been under stress and have been abusing alcohol who are referred to a hospital for treatment. The first stage is to get the patient into withdrawal. This normally occurs 36 hours or less after they have taken their last drink, but may not occur until as late as one week. Four progressive stages can be identified in the alcohol abstinence syndrome and they often become traumatizing to the nurse not equipped to handle them:

1. The patient becomes tremulous, acutely anxious, and has a short attention span. Signs of autonomic hyperactivity are present, including tachycardia, hypertension, perspiration, flushing, pupillary dilation, and increased temperature. The patient may be irritable and unable to sleep and have a poor appetite. Some patients have generalized convulsions as a presenting sign.

2. The patient begins to hallucinate. Hallucinations may be auditory, tactile, visual, or a combination of these. The

hallucinations usually are transient, but almost always are threatening in nature.

3. The patient becomes disoriented. Thinking is incoherent. The individual begins to have delusions, often paranoid in nature, that are not connected with hallucinations. The patient also is markedly agitated.
4. Generalized seizures, usually grand mal, begin. At this state, the syndrome can be appropriately labelled delirium tremens. Hallucinations continue, and the patient may participate actively in them.

The acute alcohol abstinence syndrome requires consideration of multiple treatment problems. For example:

1. Sedative-hypnotic and/or psychotropic agents are administered to alleviate the central nervous system irritability. Drugs in use include Vistaril, Valium, Librium and Chloralhydrate.
2. Maintenance of fluid and electrolyte balance is essential. The patient may be dehydrated due to vomiting, diarrhea, or malnutrition but more commonly is overhydrated. Magnesium and potassium levels may be low.
3. Blood glucose levels may vary widely and may fluctuate as the syndrome progresses. Hypertonic glucose administered intravenously can prevent hypoglycemia.
4. Seizures may be treated or prevented with Dilantin. Associated disorders such as infections, pancreatitis, gastritis, diarrhea, neuropathies, and traumatic injury may be suspected and ruled out or treated (Adams, Hanson, et al., p. 1505).

This type of patient and treatment is most stressful to the professional involved with the case, as are other issues in need of resolution at that particular time.

Catastrophic Reaction

A catastrophic reaction is a passive response to severe anxiety in which the patient reacts in a hyperalert manner and is quite immobile. There is no spontaneity and responses are limited to only a single word, with passive cooperation exhibited. These patients may be terribly frightened and have only partial memories of their medical and surgical experiences. This period ends after about five days and the patient may not remember what happened. These reactions raise anxiety for the individuals involved; they react by being very passive, since the anxiety is traumatic.

Euphoric Response

This response may be in the realm of massive denial of a serious illness, which is a cover-up for severe depression. These responses usually occur about two days after the individual has been admitted to the intensive care unit. The patients become extremely active, cooperate enthusiastically in their treatment, and are considered excellent subjects by their health care providers.

However, their activities may become antithetical to therapeutic processes and therefore they have to be controlled. These responders function as if nothing really has happened to them by denying the situation, and they may develop physiological complications such as hemorrhaging and high fever as a result of their hospitalization. Their activity levels, speech, memory, and interpersonal relationships may be affected and their reaction is to deny there are any such effects.

One way health care managers can deal with this is to provide preoperative teaching and admission teaching in all intensive care units, including the distressing features of delirium that patients may experience. Nurses may have some difficulty dealing with this because of a general reluctance in society to discuss "crazy" behavior. However, just by speaking of the possibility, nurses convey acceptance of the behavior, making it easier for the patients to discuss these experiences. Nurses should explain that many physical and environmental factors contribute to confusion, memory loss, hallucinations, fear of people in the environment, fearful dreams, and strange sensations, and should discuss the high frequency of such occurrences. Nurses should be reassuring that these states eventually pass and that patients may lessen the impact of the experiences by sharing their feelings, thoughts, or experiences with those they trust.

If the environment is kept simplified and well organized, many of the patients' stresses can be alleviated. Nurses certainly can have significant impact on the patient environment (Adams, Hanson, et al., 1978, p. 1511). It is important to note here that stress can be managed. One method of accomplishing this is to manage by diffusion of data that can be shared by health care workers. This has a multiple effect on the patients, the health care staff, and the institution with its dynamic climate.

SOCIALIZATION AND TRAINING

To deal with burnout and cultural shock, professionals need special training and preparation in interpersonal skills. However, they are not well equipped to deal with certain mechanical aspects of their job. They cannot develop a humanistic style of patient care just by verbalizing their commitment. The basic emphasis usually is on treating illnesses rather than interacting with individuals, which forces the professionals to deal with symptoms and not people. Hospital staff members often categorize patients by their medical problems, such as "the coronary in room 304." These specialists do not meet their patients until they are quite ill and deal with them as case-to-case individuals, not as a process in which the total human being is considered. In this way, health care professionals intellectualize but do not internalize their feelings, permitting the interpersonal interactions to become frozen.

Medical training also dehumanizes professionals by dealing with symptomatology and not with issues such as dependent patient behavior and other factors that affect the health care professional personally. Physicians have a difficult time dealing with their patients when the prognosis is not positive. They generally will tell their patients all too quickly that "I'm sure everything will work out OK." What they really do is tell the patients what they think the individuals want to hear, not the actual state of the case.

The philosophy appears to be "fail or succeed," since those who can deal with stress and pressure appear to survive effectively, and control and manage their careers. This philosophy is somewhat faulty because the implication is that professionals will be able to learn to cope with emotional stress. Those who do not learn to deal with stress will not be effective health care practitioners. This type of thinking is extremely illogical and primitive and continues to insulate the professionals from becoming involved with the total "being" of the patient.

Health care practitioners are trained to be professional and feel they must control all strong emotions, keeping them locked away for a long period of time Generally, the first contact with death that health care professionals have as students is a distressing, emotional experience that illuminates feelings of inadequacy and fright. They feel they should be cool and aloof. The need to control these feelings rigidly makes it worse for them because they feel failure and devastation while having no way of dealing with their emotional inadequacies. This creates more anxiety and greater stress, resulting in feelings of professional failure since they are not permitted to act like normal individuals who experience loss and, at the same time, empathy.

This lack of preparation and void in experiencing others' emotions and loss does not permit them to deal with the basic problem of how they must deal with their own feelings and emotions. Their detachment creates an insensitivity and makes the quest for objectivity and rationality paramount over any subjective area of their operation. Detachment appears to be a defense needed to cope with these issues since the students have not been prepared educationally to deal with death. Training in interpersonal relationships is essential for these professionals since it gives them coping mechanisms that they generally do not have or know how to employ.

The issue of socialization, the conflicts inherent in the job, and some of the problems they will encounter personally and professionally must be dealt with at this juncture to help health care providers who are hit constantly by these problems. Health care institutions must develop a formal program to cope with reality shock experienced by nurses who encounter stress in their first job. Socialization is the process in and by which the individual learns the ways, ideas, beliefs, values, patterns, and norms of a particular culture and adapts them as a part of the personality (Wolman, 1973, p. 350). The purpose is to avoid their leaving the nursing profession prematurely by giving them a coping mechanism that will allow them to become socialized earlier so they can make a significant contribution to their specialty. The purpose of socializing nurses to their occupations is to avoid or minimize employment changes and maintain the retention of effective professionals in hospitals. It has been found that nurses who have had a presocialization experience do not change jobs often and have lower turnover rates than those who have not been socialized.

If individuals are to perform effectively and deal rationally with the conflicts they experience in the current work value systems, it is essential that nurses experience these conflict situations initially so they begin to know how to deal with them and develop a compromise, decision-making pattern composed of professional and bureaucratic methods of organizing their work. Nurses who have experienced presocialization programs are better prepared to select personal preferred action choices, and they can select alternative compromised behaviors rather than having to choose one value system over another. When they are forced to perform in the latter manner, they feel as if they are caught in a bind in which they must make a decision between compromising their own value systems and adopting those of the institution that are often enigmatic and foreign to them. Based on these concepts and research, Marlene Kramer (1974) developed a program titled "Anticipatory Socialization." She delineated a basic process of socialization that was circular in nature, with many opportunities for exit and reentry in which all the phases overlapped, were not distinct, and were deliberative. In this process the neophyte is exposed to those stressors that result in burnout prior to the authentic experience via an experiential inservice educational method. This program and change process was affected by organizational and individual factors. The phases of this program encompassed:

Phase 1: Skill and Routine Mastery

This is a period of diffused generalized euphoria in which neophyte nurses begin the job and, in amazement, wonder how long the honeymoon will last. Shortly thereafter, some of the realities of their role begin to assert themselves both on and off the job and certain conflicts come into existence. On the job, neophytes usually are overwhelmed with the tremendous amount of material they must assimilate and begin experiencing feelings of inadequacy and lack of confidence. At this stage, the trainees' goals are basically congruent with those of the organization. Many nurses judge other nurses by their competency in performing diverse and complex technical skills. It is for this very reason that it is difficult to determine whether neophytes come to the employing organization with skill mastery as one of the items on their self-constructed test or whether they place it there shortly after their arrival because of the expectations of others in their environment.

The neophytes' next step is testing the actual environment within which they will function permanently via career choice. This process emerges from serious goal seeking in which they attempt to learn all of the routines, get themselves organized, and become skilled, competent nurses. Usually neophytes do not resist accomplishment of goals, and they usually receive considerable help and feedback on how they are progressing. Reality testing is no problem in this phase since the difficulties lie in other areas. There may be some shock and letdown when new nurses discover the extent of their skill incompetencies. With the mastery of some skills comes the recognition of all the many others that need to be attained. To compensate for this, neophytes must revamp their goals and make shifts in importance and perspective.

During this phase, the external feedback usually is positive since mastery is important to them. Reality shock may set in when they discover that skill and task accomplishment are seen by others as end results rather than means to an end. This often ruptures the rigid philosophy that they intellectualized during their tenures as students. Their educational goals are not shared as often by others in the work environment now that the neophytes have received positive feedback from others for their skills. They will not get any feedback, nor will they get direct negative reactions, when they start dealing with the social aspects of the job and share this with coworkers at the expense of the pedestrian technical tasks seemingly unimportant at the time.

Phase 2: Social Integration

During this phase it is likely that the new graduates are quite concerned with the image they present to others. Throughout this period of encountering and learning to work with others, they become very conscious of the basic assessments and evaluations they are making. They realize that others are continually evaluating them as well and they feel the need to manage the image they are projecting. Being new graduates allows them to maintain more juvenile, neophyte roles for the time being, but this is not tolerated for long since they soon become part of the organizational firing line. They now reach the point where they must decide between managing an impression of desirability or an impression of approachability.

In assuming the role of learners, they were highly approachable, which helped their social integration. When they abandon this role and begin to demonstrate their competence, they become highly desirable but not so approachable. High desirability and resulting low approachability block social integration (Kramer, 1974, p. 157). At this stage, nurses may advance into administrative positions because they may have been successful during the first two phases: demonstrating a mastery of skills and tasks and the ability to get along with others. Some settle down into a comfortable slot, do their job, and no longer test the system. It is highly unlikely for neophyte nurses with any degree of professional socialization to become fixed in this phase, which would become even more conflicting for them.

Phase 3: Moral Outrage

This phase is characterized by frustration, anger, and discomfort in which the nurses find that they are having a difficult time practicing the way they have been taught, and the hospital is operating in a much different fashion from anything they had encountered. They feel their professional-academic socialization experience did not prepare them for the realities of this situation, and the model under which they trained no longer is operative. At the time they are feeling this moral outrage, there is a change in perception and a distorted assessment of situations. They are experiencing turmoil that may last for a certain period in which they become most vulnerable. The nurses also become fatigued since their energy levels are being drained because of the emotion generated by their anger for the disruption of this situation. At this point they may even experience burnout or become quite apathetic while blaming the system for all of their problems. Those who do succeed in coping experience the job as something they must move through and something they will not allow to affect them emotionally.

Phase 4: Conflict Resolution

This phase is characterized by the nurses' methods of evaluation and choice. One method of resolving conflict is behavioral capitulation, in which the nurses solve the problem of conflicting value systems by holding tightly to the values they received in professional training but compromising their behavior. This method can be more or less of a "sellout" but the nurses will continue to verbalize the fact that they are maintaining their old values. This creates more conflict and increased stress. These individuals continue to hold on to their value systems but wait for the climate to change in the hospital so they can move back into a niche of congruency and comfort. However, it has been found that hospitals do not change their environments and climates, and therefore the nurses continue to wait for a situation that becomes more conflicting because it generally doesn't occur.

At this stage, the nurses no longer attempt to learn anything else on their job because they are identifying more strongly with patients through their professional commitment and realize that they cannot affect the bureaucratic structure within which they are trying to cope. Another way they can deal with conflict is to withdraw from nursing practice and turn to other professions or occupations. They can try to resolve their conflict by escape and avoidance and continuing to hold on to their original educational professional value systems. These methods of resolving conflicts often are disastrous. Basically, the role conflict becomes so great that the individuals retreat, even by enrolling in graduate schools for additional education and insulation. They may go so far as to become faculty members who now must preach the gospel of how nursing should be practiced and the values inherent in it.

Nurses resolve their conflict by dealing with value capitulation in which, after verbalizing their anger and their moral outrage, they become convinced that the work environment and its values really are more operational and, as a result of this new position, the patients really are getting a good deal after all. Therefore, the conflict ends because the tension has been reduced.

When nurses abdicate their professional school values and start identifying with the work values of the organization, they actually have become more connected to the work environment and are prepared to pay the price of belonging—which is actually the rejection of their professional values. This creates new conflicts for neophyte nurses since the subcultural values still are at opposite extremes of the continuum. Because they want to belong and reduce the conflict, they elect to abdicate the professional work system values. This choice may be functional and effective personally but, as with individuals in cultural shock, if they really "go native" they find their effectiveness is blunted. After all, they have been sent not to embrace the whole of the local culture but to effect fundamental changes in it. In a way, so also have the nurse graduates. There are many who believe that the impetus for improvement in the quality of health care lies with these new nurses (Kramer, 1974, p. 161).

Other nurses resolve the conflict between school and work values either by rejecting both sets of values and leaving the occupation completely or by becoming extremely complacent and verbalizing their anger at both since the profession placed them in situations in which they are experiencing pain, anxiety, and tension. In this case, the nurses actually may work as isolates and deal with the conflict by avoiding the pressures and conflicts of both stressors. Behavior in this realm is basically protective isolationism and usually is practiced by people experiencing this cultural shock. Biculturalism is a name given to this method of conflict resolution that neophytes use to resolve the value discrepancy that produced their moral outrage and rejection. In this case, individuals have not fused their values with those of the organization and permitted those values to be absorbed by the system, nor have they abdicated their professional values or behaviors. The net effect of this course of action can be examined by the level of patient care.

A question may be asked at this point: Is the care given by nurses in the throes of moral outrage, rejection, disillusionment, hostility, and despair less effective than that given by bicultural nurses—those who have managed the school-work conflict in a growth-producing way? Most assuredly, the care will be different and also less effective if it is agreed that the climate and milieu that surrounds the patients is instrumental in their health maintenance and recovery process. Nurses' impact is easily perceived by patients. Nurses who are severely in conflict and dissatisfied will experience difficulty in affecting the climate and relationship with their clients that is most conducive to the patients' well-being.

On a unit or health care system level, nurses who are unable to come to grips with the conflict experienced between their own value system and the predominant value system in the work world will be gravely handicapped in creating lasting and meaningful changes in the work situation (Kramer, 1974, p. 219). Ineffective methods of dealing with this conflict may be depicted by the nurses' refusal to assume any of the work values; rather, they hold a firm allegiance to the school values. These individuals usually maintain the conflict situation because of the demands put on them. The tension and conflict may be so painful that they feel they must leave the work scene either completely or by giving up their nursing practice for teaching or other occupations. They actually feel so powerless and frustrated that they have to leave a situation where the conflict is great since they are not helping to improve patient care or helping themselves.

Other nurses try to resolve the conflict and frustration by changing employers, fantasizing that other hospitals have different types of climates. These nurses hope that the investment they made in the tensions in one organization will be minimized and rewarded in others. This is not a viable or realistic option. The proverbial grass is not any greener in the new environment. As a result, frequent job changes because of dissatisfaction often become patterned methods to resolve conflict and have negative consequences on patient care.

At this point, nurses do experience burnout since they have a difficult time dealing with school-work value conflicts. They feel powerless to create changes and in essence give up and become apathetic or burned out. Nurses do want to improve the care for patients, but they feel so powerless and ineffective that they regard their ideas as being rejected completely. They now internalize their feelings and ideas, which makes it impossible for them to become advocates for the patients or even to interpret the clients' needs effectively.

Another major problem is that most of the nurses who are teaching are doing so because they dislike nursing practice or find it impossible to practice the way they believe it should be done. They do, of course, transmit these values to their students, who now arrive in the work environment with presocialized conflict regarding biculturalism. One of the more effective methods for nurses to resolve conflict is to be socialized and experience this conflict as employees in an interpersonal situation in which they can practice their skills at overcoming some of the conflicting barriers that come between the values experienced in school and those in the workplace. The process of developing biculturalism is similar for the socialization agent and the new graduate, but it probably will be more difficult. The faculty member already has experienced some degree of tension reduction through the previous flight behavior, and the tendency to resort to that solution once again probably will be very strong (Kramer, 1974, p. 224).

DOCTOR, HEAL THYSELF

Physicians, as well, become vulnerable to the same stresses as patients who may still be critically ill but may not be aware of this factor. Stress that physicians experience also depends upon their early psychological development. They bring with them to the complex health care environment their own conflicts and problems that may not have been resolved and, interestingly, may well be quite similar to those of the patients. Dying patients bring out these feelings of guilt and shame in nurses and physicians, who experience increased stress.

Specialists in critical care have several responsibilities. If they are to provide adequate psychological and medical care for the patient, they must understand the scope of psychological stress that both are experiencing. If they do this well, they will help the patient adapt to the situation, but they also must be aware that they, too, are experiencing this stress during such situations. If they do not cope with this stress, their relationship with a patient may be so affected that they become either overly involved or are forced to disengage so that they will be able to leave their patient when they are needed most. When health professionals become overly stressed, there may be a "conspiracy of silence" among colleagues and family members to protect them since social consequences can lead to license revocation in extreme cases.

Some of the problems of becoming ill, receiving treatment, and recovering bring about changing relationships between patients and health care professionals. At different stages in illness there are different relationships, depending on the phase of the illness, the patient's reaction to both the illness and to the physician and the doctor's style, and finally the physician's reaction to the illness. Five prerequisites for successful adaptation to a critical illness are:

1. the patient's ability to regress in the process of recovery
2. the patient's ability to maintain defenses against stresses brought out by the critical illness
3. the professionals' dealing with the patient's feelings and ability to communicate the client's needs to the health care staff

4.   the patient's trust in the physician and nursing staff
5.   the health care staff's demonstrating an empathetic and flexible climate for the patient

Physicians feel a need to cure all illnesses immediately and often view themselves most unrealistically. Some envision themselves as powerful healers where they have an intense need to save individuals in critical condition. When they do not succeed, some tend to wish the patient would die quickly. Other physicians feel they are indestructible and when they are caring for patients this evokes some anxiety in them regarding their own death, which they may not have dealt with at all. This identification brings about extremely stressful feelings and can result in regressive behavior. This anxiety often is rooted in physicians' anxiety that, in fact, they are not indestructible and cannot save every patient's life, just as their own lives may not be saved. Still other physicians assume they are extremely powerful and can cure any patient. At the same time, they also have the power to destroy patients who unconsciously refuse to get better even with all the advanced technology and expertise on the part of the physicians.

Specialists involved in critical care have a difficult time dealing with their unresolved feelings of being omnipotent and at the same time that they have problems adapting to situations that evoke feelings of guilt, shame, and inadequacy. One problem is how close they should get to the patient because this may stimulate feelings of failure and damage the relationship. These stressors affect everyone—patient, nursing staff, and administrators—and have a traumatic emotional effect on everyone involved. Methods for developing a psychological perspective in dealing with this critical care include the following (Strain, 1978, p. 44):

1.   The use of the team approach is particularly important, for if several persons are working with a dying patient, this decreases the possibility that one staff member would become overly burdened. However, the patient ultimately must view one staff member—ideally the critical care specialist—as the primary psychological caretaker.
2.   Typically, and understandably, the patient and/or family will feel hostile and angry at the critical care specialist for failing to save the individual. The patient and/or family should be encouraged to express these feelings.
3.   Anticipatory grief should be encouraged in the family when the fatal outcome of the patient's illness becomes evident.

4. The fantasies, myths, and misconceptions held by the patient and/or family relating to the disease or imminent death should be explored. For example, members of the family may torture themselves with the thought that death might have been avoided if the patient had been brought in earlier. A parent may assume blame for a child's death if there is a thought that the disease was genetic. A husband may feel secretly that the argument he had with his wife caused her myocardial infarction, or vice versa.

5. Members of the dying patient's family who are at a psychological risk should be identified. Preventive psychiatric treatment should be recommended for children under 2 who have not yet sufficiently separated psychologically from the object (parent). The aged person who will be alone when the spouse dies is a physical as well as a psychological risk; research studies have shown that the death rate among surviving spouses is seven times higher than the rate for the nonbereaved population (Parkes, Benjamin, & Fitzgerald, 1969, p. 740). Furthermore, the suicide rate of surviving spouses who live alone is three times that of persons in the same elderly age group who are not bereaved.

6. The patient's primary care physician (if one exists) should be contacted and details of the medical course shared so the doctor can work with the family during the process of bereavement.

7. If it is at all possible, arrangements should be made for patient and family to say goodbye so that feelings of abandonment, guilt, or regret, can be kept to a minimum.

8. Once the patient has died, the bereavement process should be initiated in the family. A request for an autopsy can even facilitate this process which illuminates the reality of the tragedy that is quite often repressed, leading to other problems.

9. The specialists must find their own level of tolerance for dealing with the dying and the feelings they evoke and must be able to accept their own limitations—to view them as human limits to their capacities rather than as personal inadequacies. If they are unable to do this—that is, if for whatever reason they feel unequal to the psychological tasks elucidated above—they should allow someone else to take on this responsibility and support these efforts.

While the physician is perceived as an omnipotent health care savior, little attention has been directed toward this individual who experiences personal stress and fallibility. The issue of personal illness for physicians is little discussed and needs to be opened up for personal insights and resolution.

Physicians are trained to treat individuals experiencing stress. But how do physicians who are affected adversely by stress deal with their own resolution and treatment? They have a difficult time treating other physicians who have been affected by stress and who may have additional psychiatric problems. They often will not accept the need for treatment and drop out of a therapeutic program prematurely intended to assist them in coping. They are interested in managing their own cases and feel they know more about their illness than other physicians to whom they have been referred. Physicians' orientation is social, psychological, and technical. When physicians encounter patients who are under stress and who experience problems associated with stress, they refer those persons to a colleague for psychiatric treatment. These patients are encouraged to be responsible for their own behavior and, or course, are encouraged to deal with feedback mechanisms concerning their problems so that interaction will enhance treatment.

When the situation is personal, the majority of physicians who need professional help do not accept the patient role with ease. In today's culture, the assumption of the sick role has five basic aspects:

1. People are not ill through any fault of their own.
2. They are viewed as having the right to care.
3. Their incapacity exempts them from usual social obligations.
4. They must realize they are ill and want to improve and return to functioning within the limits of their capacity.
5. They are expected to cooperate with their physicians and to adhere to the treatment regimen.

When some physicians acknowledge they are ill, they tend to blame themselves and to regard their ailments as entirely their own fault.

Characteristically, physicians are reluctant to give up their "usual social obligation" (namely, work) which serves as a vital psychological outlet for those who are psychologically vulnerable. Denial of illness is common, as shown by a reluctance to accept treatment. Cooperating with their own physicians and the loss of control that this implies also are threatening to physician-patients.

Physicians are reluctant to admit their problems and concerns. Perhaps one reason for this is that in "patient" roles, they must reveal themselves to colleagues and paramedical staff. At times, physician-patients may try to control the treatment, perhaps stating expectations for treatment in ultimatum form at the time of initial assessment. By outlining these expectations, they attempt to limit the influence other professionals have over them. Many physician-patients experience a lifelong pattern of isolating themselves. At times they rationalize this as a self-discipline necessary to carry the burden of a heavy practice. Neither colleagues nor family allow physicians to regress under stress nor do they tolerate regressive behavior. They act as social control mechanisms that make it possible to gain relief for role demands by playing the sick part. Physicians commonly avoid the sick role by maintaining their doctor role intact while hospitalized (Jones & Miles, 1976, p. 1315).

The dependency needs that arise from unfulfilled earlier childhood and adolescent desires are in conflict with the independent adult role physicians have been playing for a long time. This creates stress for nurses attending the physicians. The nurses are concerned that if they make certain recommendations, the physician-patients will deal with this in a negative way; and as a result, the nurses will pay for their intervention. If their recommendations are significant, then the physician-patients will not deal with them well, so nurses must learn to be very subtle.

It is not uncommon for nurses to identify with physician-patients and their problems. When they so identify through common experiences, this gives rise to nurses' doubts and fears. As nurses identify closely, they must wonder whether or not they are mentally ill or under stress as well. This identification often can cause nurses to deny the patients' problems. The dual role of the physician-patients may cause the nurses to treat them as professionals but not as private patients. This is very costly and actually tends to dilute the treatment.

The most effective management approach for dealing with physician-patients is by emphasizing and dealing with their feelings of vulnerability and helplessness. This is an important experience for health care workers who are treating physicians. Many such patients are reluctant to be treated, and nurses' demonstration of empathy for their situation becomes an important component in the care. However, it also may be important to confront physician-patients directly with certain abnormal patterns they are demonstrating that may be retarding their progress. It is not important for nurses to become involved with direct confrontations with these patients. They could be encouraged to deal only with current concerns.

If nurses actively attempt to prohibit physician-patients from maintaining their doctor role, they may be undermining a necessary defense mechanism. The doctors' life, education, training, and daily existence have meaningful values for development of personality assets. Such areas of maturity can be explored and exploited in psychotherapy. The physician-patients' dependence-independence struggle is the root of the behavior they use to avoid the patient role. A nursing approach that combines individual and group treatment fosters the development of dependence-interdependence and, finally, independence (Jones & Miles, p. 1317).

MANAGING TENSIONS: SOLUTIONS

Repugnant emotional states have an impact on the behavior of health care professionals. Those who feel anxious about dealing with individuals who have life-threatening illnesses may turn these patients off verbally and purposely develop a style that becomes repugnant, forcing the individual patient to feel uncomfortable in the relationship with such health care workers. These emotional states have an effect upon perception that affects behavioral patterns.

Cognition and perception are important factors in understanding the impact and behavior of health care professionals. They must manage their own emotional responses to patients. Their two resources to accomplish this are internal and external. Internal resources are the attitudes, values, beliefs, and abilities that enable individuals to handle difficult tasks. These help them to develop methods for solving problems and initiating new strategies. External resources are any individuals, groups, or agencies in the environment that can help these professionals handle stressful situations.

There are methods that can be employed. For example, to manage emotional responses and use internal resources, it may be necessary for health care professionals to give up their unrealistic need to be perfect in dealing with terminally ill patients. These professionals can invest in the process of helping without expecting some positive outcome such as a complete turnaround or cure. Health care workers are not employed to save every life—and they cannot.

Another method of managing internal emotional tensions is for professionals to accept their own feelings and live with them as a necessary component of the job. Feelings of anger, frustration, and depression are normal and are byproducts of a healthy, caring individual. Still another method is to analyze the problem and determine possible solutions. Health care providers may be reluctant to face their emotions and feel that some of these deep-seated feelings are taboo and unacceptable in their job. This creates tremendous stress and brings about unrealistic needs for perfection.

They must consider what alternatives are available and what is, in fact, the best course of action to be taken with the patient. They must maintain feelings of self-trust and understand that they are doing the best that they can under the circumstances. Health care workers cannot focus constantly on issues such as patient deaths because this consumes enormous amounts of energy, distorts perceptions, and affects them so negatively that their other patients are shortchanged and receive inferior care, which creates further guilt, anger, and stress. This is not to suggest that denial be used, but instead there can be selective focusing in which situations that actually have alternatives for resolution can be confronted and where the professional does not feel so helpless.

In addition to internal resources, health care professionals, as noted, have at their disposal external resources to help them manage and deal with emotional stressors. They may consider rescheduling time commitments. They face the common problem of burnout, which occurs when demands and emotional pressures of work cause them to become so calloused, frustrated, or anguished that they are forced to change jobs. One way to prevent burnout while maintaining vitality in a work setting is to schedule shorter rotations for shifts on which intense and emotionally draining interaction is the rule rather than the exception. It is essential to maintain inservice training. The need for staff members to assimilate new information and upgrade their skills is constant in organizations that are vital and changing.

Caregivers working with the terminally ill may have special needs in understanding loss and grief, learning techniques of coping with bereavement, and exploring their own emotional responses. Internal consultants from the institution itself or external consultants from other facilities should be components of any health care delivery service. Examination of the emotional needs of staff members who interact with persons facing life-threatening illness may require an experiential workshop format. The appropriateness of such methods will become clearer once the goals for inservice training have been elaborated.

It seems best to conclude by distinguishing between the role of saving and the role of helping. Helpers who take on the role of saving have an emotional investment in the patients with whom they interact. These helpers believe that their efforts determine the consequences for the patient (Bugen, 1979, p. 144). Health care workers who take on the role of helpers are less likely to avoid patients' emotional needs, are less likely to misperceive those needs, are more likely to be cognizant of their own emotional vulnerabilities, and are more likely to use both internal and external resources in managing their roles and stress.

THE FLEXNERIAN PROCESS: APPLICABILITY?

Health care professionals who focus completely upon patients use medical diagnosis and terminology to the exclusion of the social factors of disease, sickness, and death. This contributes to problems involving the professionals' adjustment to the social and psychological factors of their lives and creates a bias that not only affects the patient but also becomes more manifested in the health care system itself. Shifts in medical conception have made it difficult for modern research to emphasize the social problems that vexed the physicians of the social medicine movement.

Current medical theory and practice are based mainly on mechanistic and reductionist principles and do not accommodate social and psychological factors in etiology. Pivotal in the development of modern medical belief were two concepts: the doctrine of specific etiology, introduced in the late 1800s with the germ theory of disease, and the Flexner Report of 1910 (cited in Garfield, 1979, p. 34), in which the human body was viewed as a "machine" and in which a stringently reductionist, single-causal notion of pathogenesis was promoted. With its emphasis on specificity theory and biologic reductionism, the Flexner Report legitimized a paradigm that coincided with the interest of its corporate sponsors (Rockefeller and Carnegie) in minimizing the significance of social and industrial determinants of disease (Berliner, 1975, pp. 573-592).

Flexnerian medicine was compatible with the needs of the industrial sector of the economy to neutralize the political structure of the medical hierarchy. Until recently, medical processes in North America were based on the Flexnerian model, which attempts to neutralize and often not consider the social causes of disease by dealing with the biologic mechanism of disease and the individual. There was little emphasis on the etiological factors that affect the individual such as hazardous work conditions, psychological and physiological stress, and environmental carcinogens. This has been documented in several studies focusing on the indifference of physicians and health care institutions in particular to the psychological and sociological aspects of health care. Although these factors were neglected, they are major, significant etiological concerns. While social and behavioral sciences were emphasized in enriching the education of medical students, medical schools taught the biological and quantitative sciences that do not deal with necessary social-psychological factors. Flexner's model looks at illness as a separate function and not a system in which changes in one aspect of the human system affect other parts of the body. This is evidenced by the medical student who refers to a patient as "the coronary in Room 340."

In recognizing the connection between stress and pathology, self-care strategies delegate to the individual the responsibility for coping with stressful jobs and social conditions. Relaxation techniques, meditation, and biofeedback are offered to help people relax in and adjust to stressful environments that are accepted as givens. Most people who try these techniques discontinue them, however, largely because of the contradiction in trying to maintain a relaxed state in a high-pressure world. Strategies for changing the working and living conditions that demonstrably contribute to stress pathology rarely are proposed (Garfield, p. 36). This process and philosophy appears to have limited credibility in contemporary medical education and socialization. The emphasis placed upon Flexnerian medicine created a double bind and role conflict for the naive students who were shocked by the realities of health care when they entered their newly selected profession. Kramer (1974, pp. 67-102) has suggested an interesting approach for the socialization of nursing professionals that can be considered as a model to help resolve the stressful events and dysfunctional results that have occurred.

In recent years the emphasis has changed to exploration of the social causes of disease, as evidenced by the establishment of the National Institute on Mental Health, the Occupational Safety and Health Administration, and the National Institute for Occupational Safety and Health. Hopefully this will lead to more balanced health care, as well as better handling of the mind-body connection by health care professionals.

SOCIALIZATION MODEL (INSERVICE)

Kramer's (1974, p. 228) method considered effective in helping new graduates anticipate job conflicts and stress through socialization and all its related constraints involves six elements. The health care institution should:

1.   Acquaint all new graduate nurses with the socialization cycle and the underlying theoretical perspectives.

2. Help them establish clear-cut socialization goals for themselves.

3. Use socialization methods appropriate to achieving socialization goals.

4. Develop an awareness and sensitivity to the blind spots and distorted perceptions likely to occur during the moral outrage phase. Present ways of helping neophytes deal with their feelings of victimization so they can move from this closed, threatened position into an open, growing posture.

5. Upgrade the quality of role performance of the socialization agent. Develop role models who portray growth-producing conflict resolution behavior. (The kind needed by new graduates must be able to model effective influence postures and techniques from a relatively low status position, since that is the position of the neophyte nurse.

6. Develop skills of reactive compromise and the attitudinal perspective that adjustment does not mean enforced abdication of prior values.

This program may be accomplished by an inservice education department in the health care institution. This actually is a postsocialization process to be experienced by individuals who are attracted to an organization by the institution's own values that may be divergent from those experienced during presocialization orientation in nursing school. One of the important areas where inservice training may be helpful is in the management of conflict for neophyte nurses in a most constructive and growth-producing manner so that they are not traumatized by reality shock and then opt to become job-hoppers or subjects of burnout, which is dysfunctional to the health care system, the organization, nurses, and patients.

Inservice education can go a long way in fostering this postsocialization process since many neophytes find not only that their rational ideals are upset but also that they are becoming emotionally involved in ways they did not anticipate. New nurses soon learn that arriving at a rational, technical solution to a problem is not enough. One of the primary requisites for making the relatively small transition from school to work is the neophytes' self-confidence in their ability to learn and use their resources. This becomes a problem for the nurses caught between the values of professional schooling and of the workplace. Someone must be there to neutralize this transition somehow.

One of the best suggestions for resolving this conflict is by having the new nurses experience the present shock and anticipated cultural traumas through inservice training sessions that they will need to adapt more smoothly to the new constraints of the job. This may be antithetical to what is occurring in the professional schools, but it could be simulated by the inservice department in order to have individuals experience some of the dynamic factors that create conflict and stress in the turbulent climate.

Typically, work socialization agents such as head nurses and inservice educators do not get feedback from young graduates on the success of their socializing efforts. As a result, the socializing agents lack criteria upon which to judge the effectiveness of their programs and do not really know what they can do to help further the neophytes' socialization. This certainly contributes to the problem since the feedback loop is broken and the efforts intended to smooth out the conflict are not dealt with in a positive way.

It is important to note that if conflict is welcomed as a vehicle to encourage growth in health care organizations, then improvement in patient care and in staff morale and competence will result in a positive manner. This may be accomplished by working with the graduates involved in the socialization program and involving them initially in confronting their perceptions concerning the variance between the values transmitted from professional school training to the work situation and how the gap affects them. A participative management view such as this not only will help to involve the new nurses, but also will reduce job dissatisfaction and tensions, resulting in their much greater involvement in the work environment. Reality shock is real and it will not leave by ignoring it. It will take its toll in terms of those leaving the profession and those who decide to retire on the job—and patient care will be affected.

Dealing with this reality shock is crucial for personnel effectiveness and satisfaction. It must be dealt with through the role transformation of individuals coming from sterile learning environments into turbulent health care organizations. The two cultures have been antithetical and must be melded in a much more symbiotic manner. Unless valid, visible efforts are translated into actuality and are made operational, the affected personnel will not accept the value systems of their new organization and in all probability will reject the values of the professional environment from which they came, realizing that the conflicts inherent in both are too great a cost to pay. As a result of this stress, they will leave the profession and move into other areas, leaving health care to suffer additional human resource losses.

BIBLIOGRAPHY

Adams, M., Hanson, R., Norkool, D., Beaulieu, A., Bellville, E., & Morss, K. Psychological responses in the confused patient. *American Journal of Nursing*, September 1978, *78*(9), 1504-1511.

Benne, K., & Bennis, W. Role confusion and conflict within nursing. *American Journal of Nursing*, 1959, *59*(2), 196-198.

Berliner, H.S. A larger perspective on the Flexner report. *International Journal of Health Services*, 1975, *5*(4), 573-592.

Bugen, L.A. Emotions: Their presence and impact upon the helping role. In *Stress and survival: The emotional realities of life-threatening illness*. St. Louis: The C.V. Mosby Co., 1979, 138-148.

Cartwright, L.K. Sources and effects of stress in health careers. In *Health Psychology*. San Francisco: Jossey-Bass Publishers, 1979.

Crawford, R.L., & McCormack, R.C. Reasons physicians leave primary practice. *Journal of Medical Education*, April 1971, *46*, 263-268.

Dittrich, J.E., Lang, J.R., & White, S.E. Nurses' management problems and their training implications. *Personnel Journal*, May 1979, *58*(5), 314.

Duff, R., & Hollingshead, A.B. *Sickness and society*. New York: Harper & Row Publishers, 1968.

Garfield, J. Social stress and medical ideology. In *Stress and survival: The emotional realities of life-threatening illness*. St. Louis: The C.V. Mosby Co., 1979, 33-40.

Graves, H.H. Can nursing shed bureaucracy. *American Journal of Nursing*, March 1971, *71*, 491-494.

Jones, B.E., & Miles, J.E. The nurse and the hospitalized mentally ill physician. *American Journal of Nursing*, August 1976, *76*(8), 1313-1317.

Kramer, M. *Reality shock: Why nurses leave nursing*. St. Louis: The C.V. Mosby Co., 1974, 23, 95-96, 157, 161, 219, 224, 228.

Parkes, C.M., Benjamin, B., & Fitzgerald, R.G. Broken hearts: A statistical study of increased mortality among widowers. *British Medical Journal*, 1969, *1*, 740.

Patrick, P.K.S. Burnout: Job hazard for health workers. *Hospitals, JAMA*, November 1979, 87-90.

Pearlman, J., Stotsky, B., & Dominick, J. Attitudes toward death among nursing home personnel. *Journal of Genetic Psychology*, 1969, *114*(1), 63-75.

Seybolt, J.W., & Ross, S.C. Nursing staff expectations, commitment and turnover. *Proceedings of the Academy of Management*, Atlanta, 1979, 6, 10. (Paper)

Strain, J.J. Psychological reactions to acute medical illness and critical care. *Critical Care Medicine*, January-February 1978, *6*(1), 39-44.

Wolman, B.B. (Ed.) *Dictionary of behavioral science*. New York: Van Nostrand Reinhold Co., 1973, 350.

Chapter 6

Effects of Stress on the Family

CONSIDERATIONS FOR THE HEALTH CARE MANAGER

1. Health care personnel do not necessarily have to be involved directly with a patient to be affected emotionally because the hospital environment can create feelings of alienation that predispose the individuals and increase their vulnerability to stressful situations. Being placed in a compromising position with regard to values can contribute to alienation for the manager.

2. Hostility is the result of frustrated or unfulfilled needs. Repressed hostility is a major source of anxiety that is a major underpinning to stress. Repressed hostility becomes even more dysfunctional.

3. There are four types of marital relationships that have an effect upon stress for the individual who occupies multiple roles of spouse, parent, and health care manager:
    - a thrusting executive married to a caring spouse
    - a thrusting executive married to a thrusting spouse
    - a caring manager married to a caring spouse

- an involved manager married to a caring spouse

4. There is an implied marital agreement between professional manager and spouse as to what role each is to play in the quest to keep the marriage afloat and provide some support (even silent) for the professional's position.

5. An added stressor for the professional manager is the formula needed to balance private life and organizational commitment. There are combinations and permutations to consider.

6. The incidence of child abuse and delinquency problems is increased in families where anxieties and stress are not resolved by the professional manager and spouse and the residue is dumped on the offspring.

7. Where the family structure is disintegrating, the incidence of child suicide increases. Suicide is hostility turned against the individual who is crying out for help. Unfortunately, health care professionals under stress are unable to perceive the message.

8. Parents of children under stress have several options available: psychiatric intervention, family therapy, advocacy services, etc.

Managers of dynamic health care departments or organizations, experience complex emotional feelings that are connected indirectly to the health care environment and related directly to their own personality dynamics that may also have been a primary stimulus in the decision to enter this occupation and field initially. Health care personnel do not necessarily have to be involved directly with a patient to be affected emotionally because the environment in the hospital for any administrator can create feelings of alienation.

ALIENATION

Alienation can be described as the feelings individuals experience when they become disassociated from themselves or the groups in which they may be working. They feel powerless since the results of their behavior are not determined by them but by outside forces such as chance or happenstance. Individuals with external orientation often feel powerless to determine the consequences of their behavior. This feeling has a direct link to increasing their vulnerability to stress and its ensuing problems. There also are feelings of meaninglessness, and when individuals experience these, it becomes difficult for them to choose with any confidence an alternative course of behavior that may be available to neutralize these feelings. They also are unable to predict any outcomes when they do select a course of action.

There is also a sense of normlessness that can be compared to Emile Durkheim's concept of anomie (cited in Benoit-Smullyan, 1967, pp. 215-216). This is a situation in which the social norms have broken down or no longer are effective and individual values are in conflict or not available. This state of normlessness is what is considered to be anomie and can be experienced by individuals who feel alienated (Durkheim, 1951). Another characteristic of this alienation is the feeling of isolation, in which individuals do not expect to be accepted or included by the group with which they work and may experience feelings of self-estrangement, which is another form of alienation. Individuals are unable to find any activities rewarding in this instance.

Alienation actually is a problem for administrators to be aware of, and does occur when there is lack of congruence between individuals' perceptions of the real and ideal, or between aspirations and achievements. Alienation may come as the result of individuals' value systems. Health care administrators who are put into positions where they must compromise their values often feel alienated. It is important to determine the factors contributing to alienation for managers in health care institutions. Alienation results from a lack of ego identity and may even be induced organizationally.

Individuals with fewer resources and options may tend to experience more alienation, which in itself indicates to health care workers that isolated positions can be problems. As an example, when patients are hospitalized they go through feelings of alienation; they lack knowledge about their condition, their medication, and the expected course of treatment. This may lead to increased feelings of powerlessness and social isolation. Health care workers experience similar attitudes, generating a future collision course when they interact with patients in feeling similar ways, thus creating stress. Individuals who are deprived economically, socially, and educationally are more likely to feel that they lack the power to control and feel quite separate from other persons.

There appears to be a correlation between anomie or normlessness and inflexibility, anxiety, low ego strength, and generalized aggression. Based upon the rationale that unchecked feelings of alienation can lead ultimately to paranoid behavior (Bloch, 1978, p. 121), the need for social supports becomes even more significant. In studies of alcoholics in organizations, alienation and social isolation were considered to be integral parts of their feelings. Among alcoholics who participated in rehabilitation programs, the most alienated were those who were not successful in being rehabilitated. Powerlessness was a common form of alienation they experienced.

A study in Sweden, France, and the United States (Seeman, 1971, pp. 135-143) focused on four types of alienation: self-estrangement, feelings of powerlessness, social isolation, and cultural estrangement. A major conclusion was that the personal and social consequences of modern alienated personnel were important for organizations to consider; however, work alienation did not correspond with a general feeling of hostility. There was a definite correlation between powerlessness and hostility and apathy. Another conclusion was that people learn to live with "eight hours" of unrewarding activity.

Another study by Constas sought ways to reduce employee alienation. The key factors of alienation were defined as the individuals' sense of personal identity and the nature and quality of the interaction between management and support personnel. Following is a list of sources of alienation and recommendations for alleviating the situation (Constas, 1973, pp. 349-356).

Alienation was thought to manifest itself as:

1. absence of goals
2. lack of communication
3. poorly defined self-concept
4. apathy and boredom
5. resistance to change
6. limited exercise of alternatives, choices, and decisions

The management therapies suggested to counteract alienation included:

1. utilization of managers
2. mutual support systems
3. interaction and cooperation development
4. open information systems
5. an audit of objectives and goals on a continuing basis

Means of eliminating alienation included:

1. periodic identification and elimination of nonessential tasks
2. personnel auditing
3. manager responsibility for career planning and individual development
4. identification of personnel potential
5. implementation of a job enrichment program

Alienation is further illuminated in these health care organizations when the administrator's power and physicians' authority and power are brought to bear in direct conflict with nurses. The result may be alienation and the feeling that individuals cannot control their own destiny.

HOSTILITY

Hostility is an emotion and interpersonal-organizational problem that appears to be receiving a great deal of attention in health care literature and practice. It is an emotion experienced not only within individuals themselves but also between nurse and patient, between nurse and members of the patient's family, between nurse and physician, and between physician and the administrative staff of the institution. Hostility may be viewed as being on a continuum of manifestations ranging from being overly polite (passive) to extreme forms of hostility such as rage, aggression, homicide, depression, or even suicide as a final method of internalizing the feeling.

In health care institutions, the degree to which nurses are aware of their own hostile impulses and wishes, and of the behavior patterns they have adopted to cope with them, are crucial factors in determining how effective nursing intervention will be in dealing with patients' hostile behavior (Kiening, 1978, p. 129). Hostility has a destructive component that is quite different from anger, which does not have such a component. Being hostile involves some wish to inflict pain, harm, or destruction upon another individual. This could be a problem for health care professionals who are experiencing conflict and hostility in their private lives. Problems with marriage have been documented by several medical education researchers. In one study, 47 of the doctors responding reported poor marriages or divorce, compared to 32 percent of the control group (Vaillant, Sobowale, & McArthur, 1972). This factor certainly spills over onto the clients and peers of the health care system, creating stress.

Hostility also involves inflicting or trying to inflict either physical or psychological destruction upon another individual who is the target of the hostile act. When individuals are hostile, they have feelings of antagonism, accompanied by the desire to humiliate and hurt others while attempting to degrade them. This, however, may produce feelings of inadequacy and a loss of self-esteem. Hostility is the result of frustrated or unfulfilled needs, and repressed hostility is a major source of anxiety, which is one of the component underpinnings of stress.

Individuals who become patients in a medical system usually are under stress because of the uncertainty of their illness. They attempt to alleviate this anxiety or deal with these frightening feelings in ways that previously have proved only moderately effective. This may take the form of regression, in which the individual reverts to childhood patterns. When individuals are put in positions where they feel helpless, it is not uncommon to find that they select patterns of hostility in dealing with their interpersonal relationships.

Hostility that becomes repressed originates from two basic sources:

1. Individuals are fearful of jeopardizing authoritative relationships that are very similar to parental relationships because they must depend on these powerful adults in their organization as they did upon their parents for their very existence.

2. Individuals also have a fear of these authoritarian symbols in light of their own weaknesses and inadequacies and they desperately need the approval of these authoritarian individuals (usually managerial personnel) who psychologically assume the role of parent.

Therefore, based upon these two traumatizing events, these individuals develop a need to repress this hostility, which also comes from reflected self-appraisal. Individuals attempt to reject the negative imagery they have of their own behavior and the elements of their personality that previously brought them disapproval from adults in authoritative and/or parental positions. This rejection leads to further anxiety and they defend against these emotions by attempting to disown or disassociate the hostile feelings by projecting them onto others or pushing them out of their own stream of consciousness. The development of hostility may be initiated by individuals who have experienced frustration, loss of self-esteem, or unfulfilled needs for status, affection, and prestige. Hostility occurs in situations in which individuals hold certain expectations of self or others and the expectations are not met. Unfilled expectations are the focus of conflict and stress resolution.

EXPECTANCY BEHAVIOR

Complex situations can be described organizationally in terms of the expectancy theory introduced originally by Victor Vroom with regard to individuals in a job performance situation (Vroom & Yetton, 1973). The motivation to produce is presumed to be related positively to performance, and the perception linking these two together is described as expectancy or effort-performance probability. These extrinsic outcomes basically are determined organizationally and beyond individuals' power to control directly. Individuals are presumed to have a sense of goal accomplishment or attainment if the outcomes received have a personal, positive valence.

Expectancy theory predicts that individuals generally will be high performers when they see a high probability that their efforts will lead to high performance, and when they view these outcomes to be attractive to themselves. If any one or more of these conditions does not hold, the theory predicts that the individuals would not be high performers. When expectations are not met, frustration usually is one of the outcomes, with the individuals feeling inadequate and humiliated and experiencing stress. They then may experience anxiety in the form of hostility and can make decisions to behave in one of three ways:

1. They may repress the hostility and withdraw.
2. They may disown the feelings and overreact by being extremely polite and compliant.
3. They may engage in some type of overtly hostile behavior, either verbal or nonverbal (Kiening, 1978, p. 131).

Nurses and physicians often face patients with certain types of illnesses or physical disabilities who do not know how to deal with these problems and exhibit more hostility than others. Patients may be silent because they are resentful, withdrawing from a perceived threat or seething with anger to such a degree that they are fearful of speaking because of the rage they feel internally. They may be depressed, which is a sign of hostility turned inwardly upon the individuals themselves.

A perceptive health worker often picks up many nonverbal cues indicating that the patient may feel hostile. This can be determined, for example, through body language, facial expression, or posture that often describes internal turmoil and stress. Resentful silence or deliberate avoidance should be dealt with gently but directly before any positive or meaningful communication can occur between worker and patient. Accepting the patient does not in any way imply that the nurse should abdicate responsibility to set reasonable limits or controls should this become necessary. This lesson also manifests itself in the relationship between an administrator and subordinates. Most patients find it difficult to express anger or hostility toward authority figures, particularly if they themselves are authoritarian personalities. If the patients have invested the nurses with an authority role, these nurses may need to be even more perceptive in recognizing distress signals that appear in the guise of hostility (Kiening, p. 136).

This phenomenon is symbolic of the complex relationships between the institution's administrators and staff and its structure. People who exhibit hostile behavior have a unique background and reasons for behaving in that manner. It is not simplistic enough to distinguish between persons with hostility that may be motivated by the need to hurt or humiliate individuals, and persons who are self-assertive, which is a component of the human process of growth development and a demonstration of individual rights.

One of the indicators of emotional maturity is individuals' need to self-actualize (Maslow, 1954). This implies the ability to perceive what is occurring correctly in their world in relation to their own life situation and to assume some personal responsibility for their actions. While individuals' objectives are to self-actualize or become everything they are capable of being, this optimum element in the hierarchy of needs is not to be achieved at the cost of others' being annihilated along the way. This self-assertion, which is a part of the growth process, may be difficult to exercise in the structure of automated health care networks, which are mechanistic and often not engineered to consider the components of alienation and hostility. Unfortunately, unfulfilled expectations, hostility, alienation, and stress are not the exclusive domain of the health care environment. Too often, they spill over onto the family and other personal domains of the professional, who is affected.

THE FAMILY

Health care managers who experience stress often ponder the question: Can a family be a source of stress or is it a support system? This question usually is difficult to answer directly because of several factors that will be explored. Research findings may help to shed some light on this area.

Managers who were satisfied with their jobs had wives who were involved with their husband's work, who had a positive attitude toward their husband's working overtime, who let their husbands put their work first, and who thought their husband's salary was unimportant.

Executives with a frequency of stress symptoms had wives who were not involved with their jobs, particularly the content or the social side. Executives reporting physical symptoms of stress had wives who thought their husband's salary to be important and disliked their working overtime (Handy, 1978, p. 108).

Other research studies focused on the marriage relationship, level of satisfaction, and stress. In one study conducted by Burke and Weir, 189 husband-wife pairs responded to questionnaires concerning their marital relationships as moderators between stress and well-being. The data showed a positive correlation between satisfaction with the spouse's informal help and support and satisfaction with job, life, and marriage. Fewer psychosomatic complaints were related to satisfaction with the spouse's support. Stress was inversely related to measures of well-being and individuals who reported greater satisfaction with their spouse's help also reported less stress. The research suggested that a good marital relationship could help both to prevent and to reduce stress (Burke & Weir, 1977).

An interesting study by Handyside and Speak questioned whether general life satisfaction was the cause of job satisfaction or whether job satisfaction was related specifically to work and not to a general adjustment to life. The results indicated that these were separate, independent phenomena. In another study, Handyside found further support for the conclusion that a measure of job satisfaction was not merely a measure of overall satisfaction with life (Handyside & Speak, 1964, pp. 57-65).

One study concluded there was a close relation between job satisfaction and satisfaction with life in general: a person unhappy with life could generalize this to include dissatisfaction with job (Graham, 1966, pp. 544-547). There appears to be a "six-of-one, half-dozen of the other" situation with some research.

MARRIAGE MIXES

The need to examine satisfaction and a satisfying family and marital structure has broad ramifications as described in this study: Life style and habit patterns of men aged 40 to 60 who had suffered myocardial infarctions were compared with those of healthy control subjects. The subjects were matched by age. Interview data and clinical and laboratory tests indicated that subjects who had suffered myocardial infarctions reported higher incidences of divorce, loneliness, excessive working hours, fluid consumption, night eating, sleep disturbances, nervousness, anxiety, and depression. Glucose metabolism disorders, cigarette smoking, and lack of exercise also characterized the myocardial infarction group (Thiel, Parker, & Bruce, 1973).

There appear to be four types of marital relationships that have an effect upon stress. The first relationship is where individuals have high needs to achieve, dominate, and socialize. They want to belong to and be part of a group and maintain strong relationships. These managers often fill the role of staff or are in government. The next category is that of thrusting individuals, who appear to be the most successful in their areas of endeavor. These individuals are high achievers with a need for dominance and do not have great needs for affiliation or nurturing. They are not sensitive to the needs of their group and appear to be interested mainly in high achievement. The third group involves existentialists who do not have a great desire to control individuals or to be concerned with subordinates and other individuals in positions. They are inner-directed, not very ambitious, and set their own standards for their lives while being isolated. The fourth group is composed of caring and supportive individuals who are satisfied to look after other individuals on the job and are interested in being members of groups. The patterns and pairings are as follows.

Marriage Mix A: Thrusting and Caring Types

The most common combination of these four was a thrusting executive who was married to a caring wife. In this case, the husband works and the wife manages the home. She wants him and the children to be happy, although achievement and success above a certain point are costly to her. She is concerned with the activity arenas of the husband/wife relationship, the family, and their social network. Roles are clearly defined. The husband may help in the house and must make major policy decisions concerning it, but she is operationally in charge, just as he is in charge in the work arena.

Their common problems are in the family arena and may concern money, children, or mobility. She is unlikely to want to venture into a job herself unless there is a great need for money. The wife will be very supportive of her husband in his work although she may not in fact be very interested or involved in its details since his is not a shared domain. The husband's need to dominate and achieve is no problem to the caring wife, particularly if he satisfies these needs at work. The wife's task, as she sees it, is to absorb her own problems and not burden her husband. In the family arena, his activity will be channeled into his agreed roles, and in the husband/wife relationship, she expects him to dominate (Handy, 1978, p. 111).

These couples often have multiple social networks that may fall within his or her arena or even a joint arena. His network may have as its focal point a location outside the home but these couples overtly manage a regulated environment within the home. Their communications often are ritualistic in which they talk about the events of the day at work and at home, but do not get involved in deep discussions since they are fearful that these will create problems and, as a result, both consciously and unconsciously, they attempt to avoid tension. The wife does not want to impose her tensions on her husband or family, becomes extremely masochistic, and learns to suffer quietly. Tension is often felt but not discussed by the parties. The stress may be repressed temporarily since discussing it is not part of the relationship and this seems to be an effective formula for a traditional relationship that can be defined as successful.

Marriage Mix B: Thrusting and Thrusting Types

The next pattern involves a thrusting husband married to a thrusting wife. In this case both partners are interested in dominance and achievement. Both want an arena where they can hold onto responsibility and can demonstrate, at least to themselves, that they have achieved something. For the husband, the arena most obviously and frequently is his work. However, if he fails to find full satisfaction for those needs in that arena, he may turn to another—his family, a hobby, or the community.

The wife has equal needs, which may be met most appropriately by a work arena. This marriage may have seeds of considerable discontent. The wife, if children have arrived, finds inadequate outlets for her achievement and dominance needs, which she may transfer to the arena of the family and the marriage relationship. She may put perhaps unwanted pressure on both and create competition rather than support in the home (Handy, p. 112). The stress of this situation appears to be heightened if both wife and husband are involved in their own professional work arenas and the domestic foundation may tend to be shakier, more disorganized, and eventually shattered. Both of these types of people generally are aggressive, under pressure and, when they feel this stress, rather than supporting each other they usually move against each other and have many conflicts. These relationships often are turbulent. The chance for survival is greater if the competition between husband and wife is of equal proportions. This will occur only when there are no children and minimal support requirements. This enables both husband and wife to be thrusting in their own lives, and then get together after work for companionship, mutual support, and stimulation.

Marriage Mix C: Two Involved Types

The third type is the marriage of two people who are involved. Involved individuals usually are high achievers and very dominant but their personality styles usually are controlled or are confused by the significance they place upon caring and belonging. They have high social needs and want to belong to and be a part of a group. They often opt to share rather than separate their worlds. There are few clear duties. Whoever is available or has an interest may cook the meal, clean the house, or put the children to bed. Children tend to be full members of the family and can appear precocious or undisciplined. Tension is high in these marriages, perhaps because both partners are sensitive. Under tension, both partners first withdraw, then move toward each other, often talking things out for hours. These are very intense relationships with the potential for much mutual support. The high value these persons place on caring and belonging increases their tolerance for a situation that a purely thrusting wife would have resented more (Handy, 1978, p. 113).

Marriage Mix D: Involved and Caring Types

The last relationship is that of an involved husband and a caring wife in which he usually is involved with his work and in many cases under a great deal of stress. In this case his wife usually will support and protect him and be much more comforting. These relationships are more intense and emotional, more questioning and flexible, than the traditional marriage, but less competitive and striving than those with two involved persons. The husbands in these patterns usually work far more intensely and for far longer hours. As a result, the home for a caring wife can be a lonely place (Handy, 1978, p. 113).

It is interesting to note here that the factors that may produce stress in some situations generally are not noticed in others. What is essential is that the roles, the activities, and the perceptions of the partners must shift and change with the situations or stress will be prevalent at many points in their relationship. In many conventional marriages that appear on the surface to be satisfactory, and where one of the partners clearly is career oriented and the other clearly family oriented, not a great deal of satisfaction is experienced. Happiness in these relationships appears to decline as the number of children increases and the husband becomes more involved in his career.

The wives' caring component in these relationships does not appear to be enough to handle the amount of role separation brought about by a husband involved in his job and children who are demanding in their own right. If one of the partners becomes quite successful in work, greater pressure is exerted on the other partner to take on more of a domestic role, forcing the individual into a caring role that may not be a first priority. This incongruency may cause friction and stress in the relationship. The involved male is more likely to tolerate some failure or a levelling off in his career, since he now will be able to devote more attention to his family and its needs.

An added complication is that individuals in midlife career have placed their family above the fantasy of their jobs and gained greater satisfaction with this. When thrusting individuals are frustrated at work, they often find it difficult to develop other outlets for their needs to achieve and dominate. This situation results in stress in the domicile. Stress can be minimized and satisfaction increased if the activities, responsibilities, and roles of the two partners correspond to their personal dispositions. If their activities fit their natural marriage patterns, life will be easier than if they are forced by circumstances or convention to play the part of one marriage pattern while truly belonging to another (Handy, 1978, p. 116).

After the Children Leave

Stress also is felt by the wife who occupies a caring role when the children leave home. She no longer is needed for her managerial and supportive role at home and while the husband still is involved in his own commitment to his job, she now must seek out a new role for herself. This incongruency again may cause a great deal of stress because she must look at another career that may be similar to his and be forced to occupy the role of an achievement-oriented individual. Her basic instincts to achieve reach the surface and move her from a supportive relationship into the direction of a thrusting individual who may be quite threatening to her husband, who has not become conditioned to this and is comfortable with her in her normative role. If he is not sympathetic to her priorities and neglects her, then stress is felt and more conflict is experienced.

Partners must adapt to their changed roles and their priorities so that stress can be minimized. If tension is experienced in the family situation, it will affect the work environment as well. One of the key ele ments here is that work does occupy a significant role for both partners. When the occupational role is highly individualized, notably among the professions (physicians and nurses, for example), other high status occupations such as executives in large organizations demand a similar primacy of commitment, with perhaps somewhat less scope for individualized participation than the free professions, but with other incentives for a high degree of involvement. Where especially gratifying incentives do not exist, as in the lower status occupations, work has less salience or it may take on negative significance, with different kinds of repercussions on family life (Handy, 1978, p. 119).

It may be concluded that the shape of the marriage pattern will be determined for a long time for most individuals by the type of work they do and by its relative importance in their lives. This will be balanced out by looking at the significance of family and marriage as the underpinnings for a general feeling of satisfaction and congruency in their lives.

THE IMPLIED MARITAL AGREEMENT

In preindustrial and early industrial society, the family had been the unit of both production and consumption (as in farming or cottage industry communities), whereas in modern society, with large-scale enterprises and complex division of labor, not only have the units of production and consumption become differentiated, but more recently the locations of production and consumption widely separated. Thus, where once the husband worked at home with his wife (admittedly on different tasks, but with a high degree of mutual interdependence) now typically he not only works in a separate place (and at activities whose real nature his wife often can only guess) but one that may be miles from home and may exercise little direct influence on the community in which he and his family live and consume (Gowler & Legge, 1975, p. 71).

The relationship between the male who occupies the role of a manager and his wife is a most important one that borders both on differentiation and integration. Sometimes there exists explicitly stated between managers and their wives what can be referred to as a hidden contract, upon which many organizations depend when purchasing the services of managers. This contract is necessary for efficient and effective managerial performance. The contract also focuses upon the managerial career for the individual male. The occupational roles that are held require a high degree of commitment on the part of the individual and the organization. These individuals enhance their careers by moving from one job and organization to another, continuously collecting experiences that improve their performance for their next position.

If managers support this notion of career upward mobility, then a decision must be arrived at regarding their domestic life, for the energy and time invested in a career must be a decision that affects the emotional and intellectual resources that normally are used in a domestic environment but now must be directed completely to their occupations. For the wife, the admission of the demands of her husband's career and her providing a well-serviced and supportive domestic environment is in return for the development of a joint conjugal role relationship in other areas. Thus for example, support for the husband's career aspirations can be on the understanding that there will be joint decision making on the allocation of the material rewards that result from his advancement (Gowler & Legge, p. 74).

These situations become stressful when individuals feel unable to deal with the demands that these roles place on them, but the rewards and punishments of the demands are enticing. As an example, a laboratory director may consider that bringing work home from the hospital, working on weekends, or being willing to be geographically mobile upon request is very desirable for career advancement and will be its own reward. The director may rationalize that this heavy commitment to the job is possible because the person thus can support the family materially. But the cost is that there is no time or interest to be with that family to enjoy these rewards. The spouse may not accept the weight and priorities the director places upon the occupation, or the rationalization for this allocation of resources.

Latent stresses over the balancing of priorities and resources in the hidden contract emerge frequently and take on collision ramifications when they reach a crisis that may affect both the individual in the career and the spouse. A geographic move not only may place stress upon both partners in their own independent roles, but on the agreement itself within the marriage. The manager may feel in need of a supportive domestic environment, while the spouse who is coping with problems of self and of the children may not be interested or have the personal time to provide this nourishment and support. This, in effect, may be one of the first cracks in the agreement and relationship since the spouse may be seeking self-support that may not be an integral part of the initial relationship agreed upon between them. The spouse may feel forced and pushed into a role that is incongruous with a preferred level of equilibrium.

Many individuals try to cope with the problem of their own identity through their positions in organizations. This usually is the case for the manager but does not hold much credence for the spouse who does not view housework as an occupational role. The spouse has a difficult time developing and maintaining an identity since supporting the manager and raising children often are accomplished at the expense of the person's individuality, which also may stifle creativity.

Women have gotten married and have raised children at younger ages. In addition, actuarial data project an increased life expectancy for females. These factors not only give women the opportunity to be trained and actively employed after their children are well on their own way, but can give them career aspirations. This may produce a conflict for both partners since it brings a new dimension to their implied agreement. Although both husband and wife may be working at totally different jobs, many decisions affecting one partner's career (such as a promotion that involves geographic mobility, or a heavier commitment in time and other resources) are likely to have repercussions on that of the other. In this sense, their occupational roles tend to be more competitive and less complementary than those of couples where the wife's occupational role is that of a housewife and where the hidden contract still operates effectively.

A major advantage of the implied agreement is that the manager pursuing a career is provided automatically with a comfortable supportive domestic environment. It is the spouse's "full-time job" to do so and to mold this environment largely around the demands of the manager's occupational role. If both partners have careers, who is to provide the domestic supports that will encourage them and leave them free to realize their full career potential? (Gowler & Legge, 1975, p. 81). This is a question in need of an answer since these collision courses create stress for both partners, their children, and the organization employing the manager.

These complex situations not only are emotional but also are stress producing. Some families cope with the overload of stress by generating further stress. When husband and wife both are under stress, the domestic responsibilities generally will be reassigned in the direction of the more available partner. This may indicate that a husband may now find himself regularly handling traditionally female tasks such as cooking, cleaning, and raising the children. This, in itself, may be stressful to him since it creates role conflict and ambiguity. In these cases, either the husband or the wife can have a personal identity crisis that may be reinforced by environmental sanctions such as disapproval of their pattern of life by families oriented toward implied marital agreements. These situations appear to be ambiguous and these relationships generally are structured around the blueprint agreed upon by both members earlier in their personal and professional lives when needs, values, and anxieties were quite different and unanticipated.

BALANCING PROFESSIONAL AND PRIVATE LIFE

A major concern in the management of stress is the balancing of individuals' private and professional lives. It is important to determine whether there is a pattern in the method by which a manager copes with these dual commitments since the time demanded in a career-oriented and family-oriented milieu may be equal. A study by Bartolomé and Evans (1979, p. 5) found that 80 percent of managers surveyed attached a high value to both career and family and 50 percent of these found some aspect of their professional lives to be their major source of satisfaction. The other half said their major gratification originated from their private lives. The managers estimated that they spent an average of 62 percent of their time and 71 percent of their energy on their professional lives. Nearly twice as much time and three times as much energy was directed to work as compared to family.

When the spouses were interviewed, the primary complaint about the managers' life style was not the great amount of time spent travelling, working in the office, or working at home on the weekends. Rather, the major frustration was the invasion of the spouses' private lives. The frequent unhappiness or concern that the managers brought home from the office was a major element in their dissatisfaction. Asked about the conflicts involving their life styles, 44 percent of the managers appeared satisfied and 42 percent dissatisfied with lives in which they had difficulties in balancing family relationships and career aspirations.

The key issue is that most managers, who also serve the dual role of spouse and parent, do not want to make these choices. They would love to have the best of both worlds; they want their professional life and they also want their private life. At a rational level they realize that they cannot have their cake and eat it too, but at a fantasy level anything may be possible. Most of these individuals felt they were far from the ideal. This created ambivalance, dissatisfaction, and increased stress. Managers who usually are impulsive and are perfectionists are drawn to competitive situations and challenges that result in job overload and conflict. This is a problem because the managers drain a great deal of energy from the job and its requirements, leaving very little for the family and other personal problems that are in need of resolution.

The launching of a career for an individual in an organization is a beginning to a hierarchy of steps similar in nature to Maslow's hierarchy of needs. It appears that success experienced early in individuals' careers motivates them to seek more successful experiences and develop further opportunities in the form of more complex assignments and promotions. This in turn leads to a hierarchical need to be more successful. The net effect of all this is that the managers become more heavily involved in their careers in the early phases of their lives and marriages.

The spouses of these successful young managers often become dissatisfied and the whole institution of their marriage comes under scrutiny. This becomes further exacerbated when the managers are very sensitive to their careers and the associated tensions. They also experience greater tension from the demands made by their children. They seem to deal with this stress but need to reduce the tension by working longer and harder at their "craft." These individuals are preoccupied with developing their professional careers and view their family life as a support system that is there to give them the foundation necessary for their own advancements. When faced with tension in their personal lives, they believe the solution lies in working harder.

Younger managers are troubled by the job problems they encounter that seem to be without resolution, and they cannot diagnose what steps and directions they should be taking in solving them. They are psychologically committed to and involved with their careers. However, they are not getting a great deal of satisfaction and their basic investment is not coming to fruition. As a result, they experience considerable stress and anxiety and do not have any positive channels for coping. One step they consider as a solution is to withdraw from the family and the marriage psychologically, being there only physically.

The managers who adjust better to this dilemma of balancing career and personal life do so because of the priority they attach to the needs of their children, more than they do to the needs of their spouses. They seem to be content with maintaining a positive relationship with their children. While this is going on, the spouse has been playing a secondary role in the manager's life. The spouse's expectations of the marriage have been frustrated and have been heightened by the tension the manager is experiencing in the career that is spilling over to the marriage. When this is communicated to the manager, the dilemma becomes more intense and enigmatic. Not only must the managers balance their personal lives with career but they now experience new ambivalences that indicate quite clearly that the effect of the position and career are affecting the quality of the marriage. Their preoccupation with a supportive, gratifying relationship becomes an objective to achieve in addition to the other multifaceted organization goals the managers are carrying around as added baggage.

As they become more ingrained in their careers, the managers should become more adept at juggling both missions—professional and private—and should have more positive feelings concerning their marriages as supportive systems for their own lives. In the study being discussed, it was the career misfits among the midlife managers who were most likely to experience emotional strain. On the other hand, the managers who felt unhappy with their marriages were most likely to feel that strain, thereby experiencing a need to be left alone, feeling irritable, restless, and depressed (Bartolomé & Evans, 1979, p. 18).

The net effect of the managers' ambivalence and their need to juggle their professional and private lives can be reflected in the behavior of the spouse. When the spouses reach the mid-thirties, they may be on the verge of giving up in frustration. Resigned, they are ready to adapt themselves to this status quo. This adaptation may take several forms. Some reconcile themselves to finding gratification in supporting the managers and their careers. Others try to establish their own separate and independent lives by going back to work. For a few, this adaptation may take the form of separation and divorce. But the paradox is that many spouses are ready to give up their efforts to renovate their marriages and family lives precisely at the same time the managers become more concerned with the quality of their private lives and especially of their marriages. The managers' focus is shifting toward family and marriage. They are more willing to respond actively to the challenge of developing the marriage. It is ironic that one gives up when the other one is ready to give in (Bartolomé & Evans, p. 20).

At the same time, managers who are more heavily involved in their parental roles begin to realize the failures of their careers and find their personal gratifications missing. They also realize they are not going to conquer this organization and look for other supportive devices and other objectives. Some of these objectives may involve looking again at their families, what has happened to their children, and the quality of their relationships with the family and other individuals. When they realize that they have achieved their original objective, they then are ready to look at new roles in life that occur only around midcareer. It is at this point that they exhibit some interest in supporting younger managers and serving as organizational models for them.

It is interesting to note that most successful directors and chief executive officers of organizations do have stable marriages and fulfilling relationships involving family and a wide array of friends. This happens only when they have integrated their need both to achieve and to balance their own personal lives outside of work. It is unfortunate that this occurs only when the managers already have passed the "anxiety arising phase" of their lives and now are capable of handling both elements that are necessary for achieving their own personal objectives and reducing stress at the same time.

Various studies (Rapoport, 1977; Pahl, 1971; Levinson, 1978) have indicated that statistically, marital happiness is at its lowest in the late thirties of a manager's life. The results are reported as if real marital happiness were at an all-time low. This may be a result of the managers' being most sensitive to their marriage problems at that age. What is being evaluated at that time is a purely subjective perception of the marriage. An analysis would suggest that this perception in part reflects the managers' sensitivity to their marriage, a perception that changes throughout the career and life cycle. At a later stage in life, they may perceive their marriage to be very satisfying, not because of their behavior or that of their spouses has changed, but because they have learned to accept marriage for what it is (Bartolomé & Evans, 1979, p. 26).

Organizations must view managers as significant resources who must be looked at as being in a complex bind while juggling personal and professional lives. This creates as much anxiety and stress as the institution experiences when it attempts to juggle effectiveness and efficiency. The nomothetic (norm setting) and idiographic (behavioral-personal) dimensions of an institution are considered essential in evaluating organizational effectiveness. These measures are no more important than the need to help managers balance their professional and private lives without experiencing great conflict and counterproductive, dysfunctional behavior that can harm the organization and individual as well.

MANAGERS UNDER STRESS: WHAT ABOUT THE CHILDREN?

Abused Children

Child abuse is a family crisis or a symptom of a family that is experiencing severe stress in its inability to cope with life. What provokes and motivates adults to batter children and what are their personality dynamics that create this dilemma? Individuals under stress in their personal lives and/or their occupations may opt to "dump" their anxieties on socially safe targets such as children who cannot affect their security. There seem to be occasions on the surface, in the relationship between child and parent, when the desire to strike the child who may be acting up or being provocative appears to be valid. However, this is a way for adults to discharge some of their aggression and anger. Usually this potential act of violence is controlled by the individuals' ego defense mechanisms and concern with ramifications of the act.

Individuals who are affected by anxieties and stresses can become sociopathic. They bring into play the ego defense mechanisms of repression, denial, and projection that prevent the realization of the consequences of the violence about to be committed. Thus, abusing parents project their anger over other matters often related to frustrations on the job onto the child while denying it in themselves. In psychoanalytic terms, the proper development of the ego and subsequently the superego depends upon a satisfactory early parent/child relationship.

The majority of abusing parents were themselves abused or neglected as children. They may have been beaten physically, harassed emotionally, neglected in their nutritional or social needs, or even pampered materialistically while being deprived of attention by busy, selfish parents. Having never been adequately nurtured or parented, the children never learned how to love or to nurture others and grew up with this deficit. In the absence of proper gratification for the frustrations of infancy and childhood, the individuals lack ego strength and have a poor self-image. As they grow into adolescence and adulthood they develop subconscious, self-defeating mechanisms as support for their weak egos in the form of repression, denial, and projection. Their poor self-image and mistrust of others, usually identified as parent figures, afford them low frustration tolerance.

The yearning to be loved renders them vulnerable, especially the young women, for a poor sexual (not always a marital) union with weak characters like themselves or with domineering psychopaths (Blumberg, 1977, p. 208). As a result it is the child who appears to be the victim of the parents' maladjustment and frustrations because they are thwarted in their own drives.

This usually occurs when the male figure in the family is dominant and the wife is quite submissive. The relationship in the marriage therefore is unsatisfying and often turbulent, with both partners seeking out relationships with members of the opposite sex, which creates more anger and frustration. The woman who is passive and submissive often is dependent and ineffective as both wife and mother. The child therefore becomes entangled in a situation that is very frustrating and where he/she may become a victim. The probability that this will occur is quite high since the mother does not know how to do her job properly, is isolated and lonely, and has a low frustration tolerance. There is no support from the father and, as a result, she is not being given emotional support. She actually becomes psychologically abused by her husband and searches excessively for more love and support from the child, who is incapable of giving any due to its own immature development. She identifies herself with the child and, in failing to receive affection there, may project the anger she held toward her own unfeeling-ungiving parents onto the child and consequently inflict punishment upon it. If she feels helpless, she may project her anger toward her spouse onto their child when her frustration tolerance is at its low ebb, so the child becomes abused in this circumstance as well.

The busy father who is under a great deal of his own stress and anxiety may develop intense jealousy because his wife's attention is focused now upon the child. He may not be able to deal with his feelings of inadequacy and as a result may decide to abuse the child psychologically and/or physically. This decision often is arrived at an unconscious level. When an individual is under great stress and most vulnerable, the person resorts to abuse. Parents can beat their children thoroughly emotionally without doing so physically, which may have longlasting effects while being difficult to treat.

One way of handling this problem is to get both parents into a psychotherapeutic relationship so they may be able to understand and be aware of the impact their lives have upon each other and on the milieu of the family. The parents' intrapsychic conflicts, and not just the parent/child relationships, must be dealt with initially. If the parent/child relationships are stressed too greatly, the parents will feel threatened by the competition that they feel toward the child, who may be getting too much attention from the psychiatrist. This may lead to a role reversal on the parent-patient's part, and increased hostility toward the psychiatrist. The parent-patient usually has a poor self-image, lacks ego strength, and therefore is immune and a loner. Adversity and criticism are unacceptable and usually provoke impulse violence. Individuals live with fantasies relevant to themselves and their child. In the role-reversal episodes, they fantasize a change in position with the child (Blumberg, p. 211). Health care organizations should be encouraged to offer help to staff members who may be under stress and in need of it.

As important as therapy and catharsis are for the abusing parent, so, too, is the therapeutic involvement of the nonabusing parent if this happens to be the case. If it happens to be the father, he may be a dominant, aggressive husband who has been driving his wife to frustration and seeking a scapegoat for both of their inadequacies—and the victim may be their child. Or he may be extremely weak, lacking ego strength, and not giving his wife the moral or emotional support for which she is longing. His employment patterns or alcoholic/drug habits may keep him away from home for long periods. The intrafamily relationship in this arena of conflict must be understood by each member so that their problems and treatment can be congruent. If this can be achieved and if the parents can understand the proper combination of child-rearing practices, the family may very well be out of crisis in time and the child will not be subjected to abuse.

A great deal of stress is placed upon parents in this position and they do need help. These parents usually are immature, lonely people who have low self-esteem and lack great ego strength as a result of neglected or cruel parenting during their own childhood. Lacking normal ego mechanisms of reality testing and memory, the potential abuser resorts to self-defeating mechanisms of repression, denial, and projection as a defense mechanism. These prevent parents from realizing the consequences of their violence and permit them to vent their anger on an inappropriate object—the child. Fantasies and the mechanism of role reversal make the ego deficient parent more vulnerable to inimical environmental factors. Again the child may be the scapegoat (Blumberg, 1977, p. 214).

Child Delinquency

Family members experience stress in many ways. While child abuse is an extreme form of how parents deal with anxiety, there is another major problem: the delinquency rate affecting children of families where one or both members are under stress. A broken home or one where parents experience emotional problems has a direct effect upon all members of the family unit and may be one of the major factors that account for child delinquency. If a home has been fractured by divorce or separation, the case studies suggest that it is not the breakup of the home that promotes delinquency but the discord and problems in the family that are the foundations for the delinquency itself. This type of situation is characteristic of managers caught between the stresses of the institution, marriage, and intrapsychic conflicts.

Research studies by Offord, Allen, and Abrams indicated that alcoholism in particular was significantly more common in families involved in conflict where child delinquency was prevalent. Delinquents from families with parental disability appeared in juvenile court at a younger age and had more antisocial symptoms overall than those from healthy families. Leading the symptoms were both the severe (such as stealing and breaking and entering) and the nonsevere (bad associates and smoking). Children with delinquent patterns from nonintact homes had more antisocial symptoms, particularly severe ones, than those from intact homes. Prospective delinquents with mentally ill parents had their first court appearances at a younger age and had more severe antisocial symptoms than those whose parents had no mental illness (Offord, Allen, & Abrams, 1978, p. 233). Parental mental illness was significantly more common in families of delinquents.

As noted earlier, individuals involved in anxiety arising and stressful situations have a greater propensity for their own anxiety and psychosomatic disorders as well. It appears that a stage in the development of children's delinquent behavior involves insufficient parenting. This can occur when both parents are outward bound, or one parent is a thruster and the other is concerned with maintaining the social supports that seem to be absent. Insufficient parenting can take the form of one parent in the home and one outward bound, or parents who have psychological disorders, or parents who have many children to look after and fail to mobilize proper priorities and timing for them. Anything that reduces parents' resources to care for their children increases the risk of antisocial behavior and delinquency. The role of insufficient parenting in the development of delinquency should be understood against the background of the widespread occurrence of antisocial behavior in children and adolescents.

The major role of parents in dealing with the antisocial actions of their children is to provide controls and limits necessary to keep this behavior in check. This can occur only when parents are interested primarily in this role and when they are working together as an intact unit. Parents who are concerned with their own organizational lives and upward mobility pursuits and who claim they are concerned with maintaining the structure of the family run the risk of being overwhelmed with additional pressures and stress that ultimately are dumped upon the family unit and children who may not possess the emotional strength to deal with that pressure. This appears to be a cyclical pattern that has a most negative effect upon children.

Child Suicide

Another problem area for a family in crisis is the suicide rate of children of individuals who are under stress and where the family structure is disintegrating. Suicide is the second or third leading cause of death of young adults in almost every industrialized country. It is increasing in the United States, particularly among adolescents. The suicide rates for 15- to 24-year-olds rose 77 percent for men and 43 percent for women in the 1970s. In 1975, as an example, official figures show 27,000 Americans committed suicide, an estimated 250,000 others tried to do so, and many self-inflicted deaths were reported as accidents. Although far more women than men attempt suicide, more than twice as many men succeed, apparently because they usually select immediate irreversible methods of self-destruction while women generally choose slow-acting poisons or barbiturates. Statistical studies report that about 10 percent of all individuals who commit or attempt suicide are psychotic but more than 50 percent are intelligent, hardworking, ambitious people as reported by Dr. Ari Kiev of Cornell at the 1977 International Congress on Suicide Prevention and Crisis Intervention in Helsinki (Medical Newsmagazine, 1977, p. 55). They may be depressed, anxious, or agitated.

The concern here, of course, is the total milieu of the family and its connection with the husband who is also serving a dual role as a manager. It is essential to study these units to determine what happens to the children of marriages in conflict in which career and family life are in turbulence and on a collision course. The prevalence of depression and suicidal behavior in young people has been attributed to social turmoil, changing values, family disruption, use of drugs and alcohol, and the lack of trust in adults and in institutions. Most adolescents who committed suicide had frequent, unexpected separations from their parents in early childhood. This is not an uncommon pattern for children living in a family structure previously described (Medical Newsmagazine, 1977, p. 55).

An interesting yet disturbing situation occurs when physicians treating these turbulent families and their children are themselves in psychological pain. Physicians commit suicide at a rate equivalent to one graduating medical school class a year, according to a study conducted by Dr. Douglas Sargent at Wayne State University. Psychiatrists who have studied this factor feel presuicidal physicians usually come from disturbed families, had barren childhoods, were good students, are depressed, single or unhappily married, and abuse alcohol (Medical Newsmagazine, 1977, p. 56).

The overwhelming majority of both male and female doctors are satisfied or very satisfied with their careers (Cartwright, 1978, p. 419). At the same time so many of the ingredients of a meaningful life are present, there also is evidence that emotional distress is an occupational hazard for some health professionals. The pressures of training and practice, the number of patients seen, the psychological drain associated with assuming responsibility for others' lives, the affective climate surrounding disease, and contradictory and unrealizable aspects of current roles as healers are among the more obvious factors implicated in the search for sources of distress (Cartwright, p. 419).

Increasing stress on physicians and health care professionals in general is manifested in other ways. Drug abuse is a frequently noted problem. The incidence of drug abuse in physicians varies from 30 to 100 times that found in the general population. These findings from the United States are confirmed in England, Germany, Holland, and France, where 30 percent of the known drug addicts are physicians, nurses, or pharmacists. This percentage far exceeds the proportion of health professionals in the general population of those countries (Modlin & Montes, 1964, pp. 358-369).

Suicide is escalating not only for children but also for professionals in the helping professions. The rate of suicide is high in psychiatrists, anesthesiologists, and otolaryngologists, and low in pediatricians and pathologists. It was 1.15 times that of the general population in male physicians and 3.0 times the expected rate in women physicans during a five-and-half-year period surveyed by several physicians of The Medical College of Pennsylvania. The high rate of suicide in women physicians has been attributed to a sense of isolation and helplessness that some professional women feel in competitive nonsupportive roles. Ironically, suicide occurs more often among curable than incurable diseases and is uncommon with patients with cancer even when it is in advanced stage (Medical Newsmagazine, 1977, p. 56).

Suicide actually is a hostile pattern turned against the individual that psychiatrists view as a cry for help. It may be determined by the interaction of different motives in which depression may be a foundation for a feeling of hopelessness leading to suicidal behavior. It may be necessary to explore these feelings of hopelessness with the children of executives who are experiencing anxiety and stress. These children for the most part are modelling their lifestyles after individuals who cannot cope or set limits for their progenies' behavior. The children see their parents abusing themselves with conflict, anger, hostility, aggression, drugs, alcohol, self-destructive behavior, and any other methods that are comfortable and convenient for individuals actively practicing self-destruction.

Feelings of hopelessness exist where individuals feel trapped, not by forces that can be dealt with in an aggressive manner but by their own insecurities and their own turmoil. This occurs because they continue to look·to their own parents for support, nourishment, and guidance. It is very difficult for children to emulate models who are having a more difficult time coping with their own lives in an organization during the day and who return to the family structure, depositing their own frustrations and feelings of hopelessness on all members of the family as escape valves.

Potential suicides frequently become withdrawn, lose a great deal of sleep, become disinterested in sex and food, do not want to converse, are preoccupied with their own deaths, and the legalities of their wills, and begin to give away all the possessions that were important to them at one time. These individuals are feeling hopeless and helpless. Their behavior sets a unique pattern for children to emulate, which may contribute to many of the suicides. This also occurs for adults who use their supervisors as adult-parental paradigms and then experience failure.

Parents make a great mistake when they attempt to control the feelings and emotions their children experience as they are growing up. It is not uncommon to hear parents state that they will give their children all the material things in life that they themselves never had and will attempt to protect and save them from the frustrations, anxiety, and empty feelings they experienced. This is not the optimum way for children to experience the real world and its frustrations. Such protective decisions give the children great difficulty in coping with their own lives. They then look to their parents for guidance and modelling and become more frustrated when they see similar patterns. This becomes clearest when they see their parents groping in their attempt to deal with anxiety. Anxiety is normal in childhood. It is not the purpose of parents to try to remove every hurdle from the path of children as they grow up. Indeed, it would be unkind to do so, for the children must learn to cope with the frustrations and hurdles appropriate to their age. Parents must be sensitive to children's needs and should make certain that the hurdles they confront are not inappropriately high. Managers make this same mistake when they personally assume responsibility for their subordinates' welfare and try to clear the path to all goals, thereby increasing anxiety and reducing frustration tolerance.

Many children experience a relationship with their parents in which a parent is totally committed to and involved with the job. The parent often is overwhelmed by helpless feelings of inadequacy that are heightened by the manager's role in the organization and by a withdrawn and helpless spouse and partner who will not assume responsibility for their children, whose behavior then often turns to delinquency. Delinquents resemble children with diagnosed psychiatric disorders. Children in juvenile court clinics demonstrate psychotic and/or organic symptoms similar in nature to the symptoms of those from broken families who wind up at child guidance clinics. Social class and family size are two factors that can help to explain the difference in referrals. Court children tend to come from lower social classes and larger families.

Deprivation is not just an economic phenomenon but may be social and psychological. When a natural parent is not present, there may be no one to protect the best interests of the psychiatrically disturbed children and direct them to a therapeutic rather than a correctional facility (Shanok & Lewis, 1977, p. 1133). It may be easier in the end if the children act up and are brought early before a court for referral for treatment or even disciplinary intervention. Unfortunately, this does not occur often to middle class and upper class children or families going through their own conflicts. These children act up and are protected by their parents and the community even as the parents' behavior continues to stimulate children who really are attempting only to gain affection and nourishment. Parents also are not reluctant to demonstrate negative behavior that may be terribly self-destructive for the children in the long run. The parents are unable to recognize these symptoms and, as a result, attempt to hide their problems by allowing their children to act up more. The children may be screaming out at their parents to stop them. Too often, the parents cannot hear the message and the signal for help.

Parents who are heavily involved with their careers are willing to initiate an agreement with their children at an unconscious level similar to those both parents developed with each other via implied marital agreements. They will allow the children to continue deviating so long as they do not get into any "serious trouble." These parents feel that the delinquent behavior is normal for growing children and assume that the youngsters will magically become normal again when the parents' own anxieties are quieted and resolved within a reasonable time.

The parents do not understand that developmentally the children already have switched from one course of behavior to another and, as a result of this deviation, have opted voluntarily to try to cope with problems affecting the family and themselves in their own unique way, no matter how destructive this may be. The children are only emulating the behavior of their parents, who attempt to resolve their own conflicts by trade-offs, inequitable agreements, and self-defeating mechanical behavior intended to avoid feelings while arriving automatically at any solutions they feel will work in the short run just to reduce the stress. This is a pattern similar to the manner in which the manager-parents attempt to resolve their own conflicts on the job. Both efforts become unsuccessful.

Children who see the manager-parents arrive from a tough day in the organizational arena and tranquilize themselves with three martinis realize that they too can go out and achieve and also deviate in their own way to reduce their tensions. What's good for the parent certainly is good for the offspring. The children of these anxiety-ridden families are taught early in life that their parents can "cure tumors by applying a Band-Aid" and fantasize that the problem is resolved without any internal, emotional investment. This creates additional dependency needs for these children, who already feel helpless and have few supports to begin with.

ADVOCACY FOR THE CHILD

Child abuse and neglect, delinquency, and failure to thrive are known to have family, child developmental, and environmental antecedents. Social illnesses have a direct link and a common etiological foundation that may indicate significant elements of stress in the family before, during, and after the birth of the child. Of particular interest is the impact of stress on a family's protective capacity in the child's present life functioning. Different levels of stress in the child's environment definitely contribute to pediatric social illness.

It would appear that the child who is involved in conflict needs an intermediary or an advocate. Advocacy is an intervention concept that addresses family life functioning and related problems. By working to assure access to essential services (housing, health, child care, education, welfare, and legal, for example) family advocacy endeavors aggressively to change or to better the ecological setting for child rearing and to foster the development and functioning of adults and children. Advocacy services developed by governmental and social service agencies do not seek to replace other, more traditional forms of social intervention (Morse, Hyde, Newberger, & Reed, 1971, p. 613).

The advocate's role is to stimulate a much more appropriate response to the family's needs and to force more productivity from the system for the family and children involved in these conflict situations. By working with parents around specific personal and social issues, advocates often help these parents develop a renewed sense of personal effectiveness and control. It is at that point that parents begin to see themselves not as passive victims but as active individuals who now are capable of controlling the psychological and physical environment for their children. Advocates use several approaches to do this:

1. They make direct and intensive contact with the family at the time of referral through home visits, telephone calls, and office

accessibility. The goals are: (a) to develop an open and trusting relationship with the family, (b) to define in conjunction with the family the goals and scope of the advocate's involvement, and (c) to establish a division of tasks so that the achievement of goals will represent a joint effort between family and advocate.

2. They provide knowledge of the people, policies, and systems that are available to assist both the family and the advocate in resolving the problems that affect families.

3. They provide data and information in the course of helping families that can be pooled and generalized to support broadly focused efforts for institutional and social change (Morse, et al., p. 613).

When families do run into problems and psychiatric consultation is not desired nor available, the advocate's role may be a secondary support system or even an initial salvation for the family and child, who feel they are beginning to lose control and become more helpless. The users of advocacy as a group usually do experience social and family stresses similar to those involved in the etiology of pediatric social illness. This may be associated with the risk of child abuse in certain cases.

The ramifications of stress in child abuse cases is important to understand because it is essential to diagnose the cause and effect elements of this in order to avoid it in the long run. As the family is experiencing stress, child abuse becomes more probable, whether it be physical abuse or the even more devastating emotional abuse that leaves scars for life. The reduction of stress in the family and its members has a positive spillover for parental figures who are attempting to cope on the job and need more consonance in their personal domain and institutional arena as well.

BIBLIOGRAPHY

Bartolomé , F., & Evans, P.A.L. Professional lives versus private lives—Shifting patterns of managerial commitment. *Organizational Dynamics,* Spring 1979, 7(4), 3-29.

Benoit-Smullyan, E. The sociologism of Emile Durkheim and his school. In H.E. Barnes (Ed.), *An introduction to the history of sociology.* Chicago: University of Chicago Press, 1967.

Bloch, D.W. Alienation. In C.E. Carlson & B. Blackwell (Eds.), *Behavioral concepts and nursing intervention* (2nd ed.). Philadelphia: J.B. Lippincott Co., 1978, 116-127.

Blumberg, M. Treatment of the abused child and child abuser. *American Journal of Psychotherapy,* April 1977, *31*(2), 204-214.

Burke, R.J., & Weir, T. Marital helping relationships: The moderators between stress and well-being. *The Journal of Psychology,* 1977, *95,* 121-130.

Cartwright, L. Sources and effects of stress in health careers. In *Health Psychology.* San Francisco: Jossey-Bass Publishers, 1979, 419.

Constas, P.A. Alienation—Counselling implications and management therapy. *Personnel Journal,* May 1973, *52*(5), 349-356.

Disease of despair. *Medical Newsmagazine,* September 1977, *21*(9), 55-57.

Durkheim, E. *Suicide.* (Translated by G. Simpson.) New York: Free Press, 1951. First published in French as *Le Suicide.* Paris: Alcan, 1897.

Gowler, D., & Legge, K. Stress and external relationships: The hidden contract. In D. Gowler & K. Legge (Eds.), *Managerial stress.* New York: John Wiley & Sons, 1975, 70-85.

Graham, G.H. Job satisfaction. *Personnel Journal,* October 1966, *45*(10), 544-547.

Handy, C. The family: Help or hindrance. In C.L. Cooper & R. Payne (Eds.), *Stress at work.* Chichester, England: John Wiley & Sons, 1978, 107-123.

Handyside, J.D., & Speak, M. Job satisfaction: Myths and realities. *British Journal of Industrial Relations,* March 1964, *2,* 57-65.

Kiening, M.M. Hostility. In C.E. Carlson & B. Blackwell (Eds.), *Behavioral concepts and nursing intervention* (2nd ed.). Philadelphia: J.B. Lippincott Co., 1978, 128-139.

Levinson, D. *Seasons of a man's life.* New York: Knopf Publishing, 1978.

Maslow, A.H. *Motivation and personality.* New York: Harper & Row, 1954.

Modlin, H.C., & Montes, A. Narcotics addiction in physicians. *American Journal of Psychiatry,* 1964, *121,* 358-369.

Morse, A.E., Hyde, J.N., Newberger, E.H., & Reed, R.B. Environmental correlates of paediatric social illness: Preventative implications of an advocacy approach. *American Journal of Public Health,* July 1977, *67*(7), 612-615.

Offord, D.R., Allen, N., & Abrams, N. Parental psychiatric illness, broken homes and delinquency. *Journal of Child Psychiatry,* Spring 1978, *17*(2), 224-238.

Pahl, J.M., & Pahl, R.E. *Managers and their wives.* London, England: Penguin Books, 1971.

Rapoport, R., & Rapoport, R. *Career families re-examined.* New York: Harper and Row, 1977.

Seeman, M. The urban alienations: Some dubious theses from Marx to Marcuse. *Journal of Personality and Social Psychology,* August 1971, *19,* 135-143.

Shanok, S.S., & Lewis, D.O. Juvenile court versus child guidance referral: Psychosocial and parental factors. *American Journal of Psychiatry,* October 1977, *134*(10), 1130-1133.

Thiel, H.G., Parker, D., & Bruce, T.A. Stress factors and the risk of myocardial infarction. *Journal of Psychomatic Research,* January 1973, *77,* 43-57.

Vaillant, G.E., Sobowale, N.C., & McArthur, C. Some psychologic vulnerabilities of physicians. *New England Journal of Medicine,* 1972, *287,* 372-375.

Vroom, V.H., & Yetton, P.W. *Leadership and decision.* Pittsburgh: University of Pittsburgh Press, 1973.

Part II

The Management of Stress

Chapter 7

Coping with Stress

CONSIDERATIONS FOR
THE HEALTH CARE MANAGER

1. Coping with recent life changes involving such factors as health, work, finances, home and family, and personal and social activities can have an impact on individuals' tolerance for stress.
2. There are many styles for coping with stress, ranging from passivity to direct confrontation. The most important element is the ability to recognize when individuals are experiencing stress and its causes.
3. Coping consists of efforts to manage demands and conflicts that put pressure on or exceed individuals' internal resources.
4. One method of coping with stress is to change the environment/person relationship. Other methods include coping via information search, direct action, the inhibition of action, and intrapsychic modes.
5. Defense mechanisms often are used to avoid stressful events; these include rationalization, projection, reaction formation, repression, and sublimation.
6. Stress also can be coped with by cognitive processes and fantasy, by feeling, by con-

trolling, by assertive communication training, and by adapting.

7. When coping fails, individuals no longer are
able to deal with stress-producing agents
and may seek out drugs, alcohol, and
suicide as methods to deal with uncontrolled stress.

8. Failure to cope may indicate both denial
mechanisms and action-oriented approaches are not working.

9. Behavioral modification and behavioral
therapy are specific intervention strategies
whose purpose is to deal with the psychosomatic disorder resulting from stress.

10. Biological scientists and social-
psychological scientists should integrate
their expertise and efforts through a multidisciplinary approach to deal with stress
and coping that would benefit health care
managers in need of direction and
understanding.

Coping is taking charge of one's circumstances—so necessary in the
management of stress. Psychological stress on the job involves the destruction of a balance that produces certain types of reactions. The disruptions may come from guilt, fear, and anxiety. A condition of dysfunction occurs when individuals' drives are frustrated and are not
allowed to be discharged in a positive manner. Selye's (1978)
distinction between harmful and constructive stress-distress and
"eustress" highlights the positive factors that accompany coping with
problems. He notes that self-actualization and the spice of variety, as
well as simple enjoyment, follow the mastery of difficult situations. At
the same time, it must be borne in mind that the meanings attached to
potentially stressful events rely on the persons participating in them.
To a large measure, individuals interpret the meaning of their own
stress. Individual differences in capacity to cope with difficulty exist
and can make the difference between those who suffer deeply and are
immobilized and those who are challenged and grow (Pearlin &
Schooler, 1978).

Stress has an effect upon the ego. A crumbling superego is found in the face of stress, producing difficult situations with which individuals must cope. Many occupational stressors result in lowered self-esteem and often loss of support, for the ego and superego can manifest themselves in poor adaptation, with stress levels increasing. Superego conflict may occur when individuals are asked to behave in ways that violate their own internal standards and when they feel they are being compromised. The guilt that results from this is apparent and increases the stress level as well. Threats to adaptation are constantly stressful. When the unconscious psychological contract between individuals and their work organizations is threatened, a stress reaction is the common result.

At this point it is essential to distinguish among the stages of the organism's reaction to stress, such as acute discomfort, heightened defensiveness, and chronic residual pathology. The adaptive strengths with which people enter stressful situations greatly influence how they will react. For persons unprepared for stressful events, the vigor and appropriateness of the defenses may influence whether they or the stressor emerges as victor. Individuals need to incorporate actively into their work the awareness that the interaction between stress and the organism takes place at many conceptual levels that can be stated broadly to include (among others) the biological, the psychological, the interpersonal, and the sociocultural (Jenkins, 1979, p. 14).

People who have worked hard, who have done what is expected of them for their organization, and who suddenly find themselves out of a job, feel they personally have been dealt with unjustly regardless of the economic reason for this action. The adaptive task for people in management ranks involves increasing intensity of demand on their employees for performance, particularly in organizations whose heads are preoccupied with running them with the focus on quarterly reports to security analysts. Such a focus inevitably means that people are moved up and down an organizational hierarchy like yo-yos, with increasing pressure to make the results look good. Organizations, like competitive children, must look good to those whose approval they require (Levinson, 1974, p. 29).

Adaptation to these turbulent events basically involves managers' coping with their defense mechanisms and maintaining equilibrium efforts. Adaptation also involves managing personal tensions and drives and closing the distance between individuals' ego ideal and their self-image. This avoids producing a great deal of incongruency, creating more stressors and issues that cannot be resolved, and thereby creating a secondary level of stress. A manager's job carries with it the assignment of maintaining effectiveness in turbulent environments. Contemporary health care organizations encounter daily issues of change and adaptation. In recent years, managers have been required to respond to changing environments by adjusting and adapting to new structures, new politics, and new personality styles. All adaptation leads to increasing stress.

Managerial positions are so complex and turbulent that individuals holding these jobs have not been able to cope with foundation issues, let alone intricate problems in need of rapid, yet accurate, decisions. In health care organizations, the technological and behavioral demands are unique and without precedent and therefore administrators who are held accountable for the management of technology, structure, and behavior often have a difficult time in determining what the priorities should be. When this burden becomes overwhelming, the result is stress and emotional discomfort, accompanied by feelings of not being able to cope. These managers begin to feel that things are falling apart and that one is not in control, or have a general uneasiness that all is not well, without any particular apparent cause.

At the physical level, this feeling brings about such symptoms as loss of appetite, sleeplessness, sweating, ulcers, and a general susceptibility to a variety of other illnesses. In general, stress is a result of the body's mobilizing itself for activity or defense without the occurrence of the particular stimulus. The consequence is that the physiological system is thrown out of balance, with excess acids secreted in the stomach, adrenalin in the blood, heart rates higher, and other inappropriate reactions. All of these events have been covered previously. Chronic physiological preparation for action, without the action, leads to disease and disorder. Stress is fundamentally a psychophysiological phenomenon. It has to do with feelings and emotions and how the body reacts to these (Howard, 1978, p. 61).

Some studies (Howard, 1978, p. 62) were undertaken regarding tensions on the job. Respondents indicated that they used various methods in coping with potential stress-inducing situations:

1. building resistance by regular sleep, exercise, and good health habits
2. compartmentalizing work and nonwork life
3. engaging in physical exercises
4. talking through problems with peers on the job
5. withdrawing physically from the situation
6. changing to a different work activity
7. changing strategy of attack on work

8. working harder
9. talking problems through with spouse
10. changing to a nonwork activity

The value of good health habits was demonstrated by Lester Breslow (cited in Howard, 1978, p. 62) in a six-year study with 7,000 persons. The positive habits under study included: eight hours of sleep a night, breakfast every morning, no snacks, maintaining weight within limits, no smoking, moderate alcohol consumption, and moderate exercise. It was found that at age 45, those following six or seven of these habits had an additional life expectancy of 33 years, while those at the same age following three or fewer of the habits had an additional life expectancy of only 21 years. Breslow also found the effect to be cumulative—the more of these habits the individuals followed, the better their health. This approach to coping appears to be a reasonable buffer for stress and its results.

COPING WITH LIFE CHANGE EVENTS

The recent life change events of individuals appear to be an important element in explaining the onset of physical and emotional illness. Coping with these events impacts upon individuals' stress tolerance characteristics such as social support systems, psychological defenses, coping capabilities, and illness behavior tendencies. The following life change list covers 102 items but there is no unanimity of opinion among researchers as to which ones are most representative and/or meaningful in a person's life. It is known that they do create stress and must be dealt with via coping mechanisms (Dohrenwend, Krasnoff, Askenasy, 1978, pp. 205-229).

Dohrenwend List of Life Change Events

Health

1. Physical illness?
2. Injury?
3. Started menopause?
4. Physical health improved?
5. Unable to get treatment for an illness or injury?

Work

1. Changed jobs for a better one?
2. Changed jobs for a worse one?
3. Changed jobs for one that was no better and no worse than the last one?
4. Conditions at work got worse, other than demotion or trouble with the boss?
5. Conditions at work improved, not counting promotion or other personal successes?
6. Took on a greatly increased workload?
7. Sharply reduced workload?
8. Promoted?
9. Found out that was not going to be promoted at work?
10. Demoted at work?
11. Had trouble with a boss?
12. Started a business or profession?
13. Expanded business or professional practice?
14. Suffered a business loss or failure?
15. Retired?
16. Fired?
17. Laid off?
18. Started work for the first time?
19. Returned to work after not working for a long time?
20. Had significant success at work?
21. Stopped working, not retirement, for an extended period?

Financial

1. Started buying a car, furniture, or other large purchase on the installment plan?
2. Took out a mortgage?
3. Foreclosure of a mortgage or loan?
4. Repossession of a car, furniture, or other items bought on the installment plan?
5. Took a cut in wage or salary without a demotion?
6. Suffered a financial loss or loss of property not related to work?

7. Went on welfare?
8. Went off welfare?
9. Got a substantial increase in wage or salary without a promotion?
10. Did not get an expected wage or salary increase?
11. Had financial improvement not related to work?

Home and Family

1. Moved to a better residence or neighborhood?
2. Moved to a worse residence or neighborhood?
3. Moved to a residence or neighborhood no better or no worse than the last one?
4. Unable to move after expecting to be able to move?
5. Changed frequency of family get-togethers?
6. Remodeled a home?
7. Spouse died?
8. Child died?
9. Family member other than spouse or child died?
10. Close friend died?
11. Married?
12. Trouble with in-laws?
13. Married couple separated?
14. Married couple got together again after separation?
15. Divorced?
16. Birth of a first child?
17. Birth of a second or later child?
18. Adopted a child?
19. New person moved into the household?
20. Someone stayed on in the household after he was expected to leave?
21. Became pregnant?
22. Abortion?
23. Miscarriage or stillbirth?
24. Found out that cannot have children?
25. Relations with spouse changed for the worse, without separation or divorce?

26. Relations with spouse changed for the better?
27. Marital infidelity?
28. Person moved out of the household?
29. Serious family argument other than with spouse?
30. Lost a home through fire, flood, or other disaster?
31. Built a home or had one built?

Personal and Social

1. Started school or a training program after not going to school for a long time?
2. Changed schools or training programs?
3. Graduated from school or training program?
4. Had problems in school or in training program?
5. Failed school, training program?
6. Did not graduate from school or training program?
7. Took a vacation?
8. Was not able to take a planned vacation?
9. Increased church or synagogue, club, neighborhood, or other organizational activities?
10. Went to jail?
11. Started a love affair?
12. Became engaged?
13. Engagement was broken?
14. Broke up with a friend?
15. Assaulted?
16. Robbed?
17. Accident in which there were no injuries?
18. Involved in a lawsuit?
19. Accused of something for which a person could be sent to jail?
20. Lost drivers license?
21. Arrested?
22. Got involved in a court case?
23. Convicted of a crime?
24. Acquitted of a crime?
25. Released from jail?

26. Didn't get out of jail when expected?
27. Took up a new hobby, sport, craft, or recreational activity?
28. Dropped a hobby, sport, craft, or recreational activity?
29. Acquired a pet?
30. Pet died?
31. Made new friends?
32. Entered the Armed Services?
33. Left the Armed Services?
34. Took a trip other than a vacation?

An important question for health care administrators is how the majority of individuals in that environment tolerate their recent life change experiences and remain healthy. Usable results are needed from current research in the areas of stress, social supports, life satisfactions, and psychological defense-coping structures. Attempts have been made to add such stress tolerance variables to life stress and illness studies. One such study, in Sydney, Australia, incorporated measures of persons' social support and of their psychological defense "maturity" into life change and psychological disturbance measures (Andrews, Tennant, Hewson, & Vaillant, 1978, pp. 307-316). The investigators found that when all three variables were considered, the discriminative power between sick and healthy persons was increased greatly. Persons with low stress, high social supports, and mature psychological defenses had only a 12 percent psychiatric impairment rate versus a 42 percent rate for those with high stress, low social supports, and immature defenses (Rahe, 1979, pp. 2-10). Health care administrators have in their sphere of influence the power to neutralize the stress level and social supports extended to those individuals with less than optimum psychological perspectives. This is a beginning in coping processes.

Passive Coping Styles

There are various styles of coping. The following coping styles are used by passive individuals who are not totally in control of change and of the stressors that will affect them. These styles are considered to be least effective in dealing with stressful events. These individuals:

1. react passively to life's events
2. leave their lives to fate, tend to cram rather than plan activities

3. have little foresight or anticipation of events
4. allow events to accumulate until they are unable to cope when the unexpected arises
5. perceive the environment, and most change events, as generally threatening
6. tend to react compulsively, most often in a stereotyped manner, when faced with potential stressful change
7. may unconsciously choose coping mechanisms that actually increase stress reaction through adverse consequences
8. continue to tax their psychophysiological capacity to the limits as stress symptoms accumulate (Rahe, 1979, pp. 2-10).

Active Coping Styles

There are effective styles of coping with change that, if followed actively, can be stress reducers and can be used to avoid some of the anxieties that become very counterproductive and dysfunctional. Individuals with these styles:

1. participate actively in life
2. maintain life change events within tolerable limits by making a conscious selection of controllable activities
3. anticipate and prepare for likely events in the foreseeable future; have good foresight
4. build and maintain reservoirs of untapped time and energy to deal with unexpected events
5. use the environment objectively; sort events into categories of importance, urgency, and degree of actual threat
6. take time out when faced with potentially stressful changes to evaluate alternative strategies, perhaps even adopting a novel solution to a novel problem
7. try, after careful evaluation, to adopt the mechanism of coping most apt to reduce potential stress and aid in successful adaptation
8. effectively eliminate or reduce stress, continue to operate well within their adaptive range, and avoid overtaxing their psychophysiological capacity

Other indicators to determine whether or not stress is creating additional emotion disruptions are significant in attempting to determine methods of coping. The most important factor for managers in coping with stress is the ability to recognize when they are experiencing stress and what some of the acute causes may be. When the methods they use are not working, the chances are that the individuals already are experiencing serious stress and are not capable of identifying the factors and their severity. Signs to look for immediately include: high blood pressure, headaches, fatigue, muscular tension, upset digestive tract, lack of sleep, etc. When individuals recognize that these coping mechanisms are not working, then they actually are operating at a more serious and advanced level in trying to deal with the stress. There are methods to help individuals identify stress factors. This self-inventory includes these questions:

1. Are minor problems and small disappointments throwing me into a dither?
2. Am I finding it difficult to get along with people, or are people having trouble getting along with me?
3. Do I fear people or situations that never used to bother me?
4. Am I suspicious of people or mistrustful of friends?
5. Do I suffer from self-doubt?
6. Do I constantly worry about the future?
7. Do I accomplish more, but seem less satisfied?
8. Am I physically exhausted when I haven't done any physical activity? (Rummel & Rader, 1978, p. 307).

A positive response to these questions may be an indication that positive action is needed immediately to deal with the stress and its usual heightened, dysfunctional level. Adapting to stress is one method of coping in order to reduce accompanying tensions that may not be resolvable immediately.

Adaptation

The central theme and problem of adaptation is not focusing purely on stress but the critical problem of how people cope with stress. There are variations in individuals as to how much stress they can face. But by and large, stress is an inevitable part of an individual's life and the difference lies in how people manage it. One of the most important elements is not just how and what individuals do, but what they tell themselves and believe about their ability or vulnerability regarding coping.

Coping consists of efforts to manage demands and conflicts that put pressure on or exceed the individuals' internal resources. This stress is reflected in a relationship between individuals and their environment. This relationship may be one in which the individuals' resources are taxed. In psychological stress, the difference is the cognitive mediator that makes individuals recognize that their resources are indeed limited. This includes both intrapsychic and action-centered methods. Coping is not just what individuals do; it includes a variety of interesting and important intrapsychic devices.

There are many situations that cannot be controlled and that become stressful. These situations and stressful events require coping, and coping management is a way of attempting to be able to control a dynamic turbulent person/environment relationship in which individuals are involved. Humans strive to remain adapted to their environment, but adaptation can hardly be described using only positive terms because they cannot anticipate what change in the environment may disrupt that adaptation. Primitive people tend to be healthy and vigorous as long as they are isolated and retain their ancestral way of life. But when they make contact with new societies, catastrophic disadaptation often results. In today's ever-changing society, people do not have time to reach a state of adaptation.

"The nearest approach to health is a physical and mental state fairly free of discomfort and pain which permits the person concerned to function as effectively and as long as possible in the environment where chance or choice has placed him" (Dubos, 1965, p. 351). This may include tolerating a bad situation that cannot be changed or controlled or accepting the situation the way it is and attempting to neutralize it. This whole concept of how coping affects adaptation can be expanded since adaptation is concerned with social functioning, morale, and health.

Coping in its generic form is an effort to manage and is not a totally positive function. Some efforts to manage are successful, others are not, and there are costs involved. The cost of coping in which a decision must be reached as to whether a situation should be changed should be evaluated with regard to personal costs involved. Changing a situation or relating it in certain ways to the environment may make it worse. Individuals adopt many bad habits that damage their health and also are part of the coping process. Examples are smoking, drinking, overeating, or (the opposite extreme) refusing to eat.

Individuals who are cognizant of and practice coping mechanisms have a greater probability of living a longer life than those who do not. But coping with stress does not mean adapting to the situation causing the pain and accepting it as a chronic future life style. This can be managed.

SOME STUDIES OF COPING

Some forms of coping involve mobilization of the body and of the individual. To deal with crisis that may be in the form of the fight-or-flight reaction (see Chapter 4), prolonged and excessive mobilization can produce tissue changes developing from hormonal secretions associated with stress or with mobilization and can be quite destructive. This may produce ulcers or psychosomatic diseases and colitis, migraine headaches, and disabling psychosomatic disorders. All diseases are multidetermined. Stress and the mobilization of stress create bodily changes that could be contributing factors.

The Type A behavior studies of Friedman and Rosenman (1973) examine the connections between cardiovascular diseases and the physiological mechanisms that may be involved in coping. It is important to distinguish between mobilization to deal with everyday problems and the demands that are placed upon individuals and their own commitments for dealing with stress. Most individuals do not easily give up, pull back, or disengage from a crisis—which is a method of coping. They cope in a way that impairs their health and interferes with adaptive behavior, that is, behavior that is necessary to maintain life and function properly. Avoidance and denial are intrapsychic methods of coping and are worthy of analysis.

There have been large numbers of women who have had breast tumors and whose biopsies indicated the tumors were malignant. It was found that one of the most common methods of coping with the discovery of the breast lump was avoidance—that is, avoidance of dealing with the physician, contacting the hospital, and denying there was anything of concern. These patients arrived late for diagnosis, by which time the disease had progressed quite rapidly from the first localized stages of cancer. When it reached the second stage, this meant considerable spreading outside of the local area and a movement to the third stage, where the prognosis was quite poor. This is a case of using denial in coping and for a time actually was quite successful in having the individuals feel less threatened and less distressed and enabling them to go about their normal everyday tasks. However, this is an extremely dangerous method of adaptive behavior. Some denial may be helpful, but in the long run it becomes damaging because it interferes with positive adaptive behavior requiring direct action and intervention.

There are other experiences focused on adaptive behaviors. One examined individuals suffering from coronary heart disease. Men who had suffered heart attacks waited up to 36 hours to get medical attention for their symptoms. Some of these individuals experienced some temporary relief and temporary remissions. But in other cases, those with a history of indigestion felt the attacks were just more severe cases of it. These people were insensitive to the nature of their symptoms and felt that by using denial, there actually was no problem. This was another method of coping that produced maladaptive outcomes because it interfered with adaptive behavior.

Men have suffered coronaries and during the heart attack utilized the defense mechanism of denial by doing vigorous pushups and running up and down many flights of stairs to prove to their physicians that they could not possibly be experiencing an attack since they were not dying at that moment. They did in fact experience heart attacks and some fortunately did survive. A good example of the maladaptive behavior was how they coped with the situation. This type of coping, however, has serious health consequences.

SOME VALUES OF COPING BEHAVIOR

Coping actually can facilitate health if it is used effectively and not maladaptively by the individual under stress and into denial. Coping can help by initiating effective action that improves the stressful situation or the troubled confrontation the individuals are encountering in the organization and with other people. When action is taken, it can change the managers so they begin dealing with the stressful relationship they are experiencing. In such instances, they attempt to prevent future problems and further confrontation.

People often do this when they are expecting a forthcoming appraisal interview, evaluation interview, or an interview for a new position. They prepare and simulate the situation. This preparatory activity reduces a great deal of the threat of the confrontation that may be festering. Planning, role playing, and experiential learning are significant in helping anxiety-ridden and problem-laden individuals who are experiencing stress and need buffers.

Many acute stresses arise because of individuals' vulnerabilities and ineptness in dealing with common, chronically repetitive situations. These chronic conflicts have been cycling unresolved throughout the individuals' lives and reflect agendas that they bring with them from earlier stages of their development. The conflicts illuminate their vulnerabilities, difficulties with authority figures, problems in dealing with people who confront them, and their general ineptness in handling interpersonal situations in the health care environment. Individuals who have a difficult time in dealing with these confrontational issues at work may have an equally difficult time in dealing with relationships with their spouses and children and therefore increase the stressors geometrically.

Another method of coping has facilitative value to lower stress or mobilization level. Many forms of coping have the intrapsychic capacity of lowering stress levels. What they do is reduce the turmoil individuals experience physiologically and deal with the diseases of adaptation at a less acute level. As people attempt to cope with these stressful situations, they resort to various decision-making apparatuses to deal with their dilemmas. They may use denial (as previously discussed) or misperceptions, or they may intellectualize or become extremely detached, viewing the situation that created the stress in a manner similar to a scientist performing a laboratory study at a distance. Denial, intellectualization, and other methods can reduce the initial level of stress and may even, in the short run, be an elixir. This method has ramifications for the health care manager who is a decision maker and counsellor simultaneously.

Individuals' personalities determine how well their decision-making models work and how well they cope with them. But what works well for one individual does not necessarily work as well for another. The nature of the personality, the situation, and the fit between the environment and the individuals all affect how capable these persons are at reducing the stress level.

Managers attempt to use an interesting device that is antithetical to mobilization. It is referred to as insulation. Research conducted with individuals suffering from hypertension found that those who could detach themselves and maintain insulation from external stimuli could in fact affect and reduce their level of hypertension. Insulation is a way of disengaging from an environment that may be turbulent and is an effective coping strategy that can reduce the level of disturbance. The only problem with insulation is that while it reduces stress in the short run, it does not cope effectively with basic problems in need of resolution; it does not facilitate health, which is one of the basic objectives in the coping mechanism; and it does not reduce the vulnerability or risk of illness; rather, it actually serves as a temporary tranquilizer.

There are interesting ways of coping that do not connote insulation. One notable example was a personal account by Norman Cousins, editor of the *Saturday Review* (Cousins, 1976, pp. 1458–1463), who reported his unusual experience involving a connective tissue disease from which he was suffering. There was general consensus that this disease was a serious collagen illness entitled ankylosing spondylitis. The chances for recovery were one in five hundred. He later published this account in the *New England Journal of Medicine.* He decided to reverse the pessimistic psychological disposition he experienced when he learned he had the usually fatal disease. At that time his outlook was quite grim. Cousins decided to turn to humorous audiotapes and videotapes that would make him laugh. He systematically stimulated and developed a positive environment and found he was spending much time experiencing positive emotions and laughing rather than dwelling upon the negative, threatening, depressive aspects of his disease. He was, in effect, practicing holistic medicine. Cousins felt that if negative emotions produced negative chemical changes in the body, then the transference to positive emotions had optimistic potentialities and in fact might produce positive chemical changes. His results were encouraging.

This concept is most interesting for those in helping professions such as nursing and medicine as a preventive device. It would be interesting in terms of potential intervention if this positive method of coping could be studied systematically and used as an alternative consideration.

Along this same line, studies of coping mechanisms for cancer patients sought indicators by exploring the connections between the disease, modes of coping, biological outcomes, and health-related results (Lazarus, 1979). Several researchers looked beyond the classic validity methodology of looking at coping with regard to outcomes. They found that patients who in general became depressed through the onset of the disease felt isolated and could not ask for help nor relate well to others. They showed negative outcomes and their prognosis was not positive. On the other hand, patients who maintained positive relationships with others while gaining their support and help were not alienating themselves by seeking out this assistance.

Another study, by Aldridge and Menkoff (in Lazarus, 1979), examined the mobility and relocation of aged patients. It was considered important to study the increase in mortality rates of older patients who were moved from one institution for the aged to another. It was found that during the relocation and in the first six months afterward, there was an increase in mortality. The group that had the most difficulty in coping encompassed the most poorly adjusted, psychotic, and depressed. These persons were disoriented and least able to cope, and their outcomes were terminal. Patients who adjusted more easily were those who reacted in a positive manner and took the total move in a most philosophical way by stating "this is the way it is."

A further study of coping (Lazarus, 1979) was conducted by Frances Cohen on patients the night before they were scheduled for surgery in a hospital. The patients who initially appeared to have a difficult time coping were those who were not interested in discussing their case and were considered avoiders and deniers. Patients interested in knowing all the details about their surgery and outcomes were most positive only on the surface and, interestingly, recovered at a much slower rate and with more complications than did the deniers. Popular opinion would speculate that the positive individuals should have had more healthful outcomes. This point is in need of explanation. The individuals interested in being very active and getting all the answers also were in need of controlling their environment. In the hospital, however, there was little they could do about that and they were unable to sit back passively and allow the medical experts to perform their magic (art and/or science). The deniers and avoiders were able to mobilize themselves at a much lower level and were not interested in controlling their environment nor in changing their relationship with the hospital and the physician.

Coping does not necessitate being in total control of a situation that an individual in fact cannot control. It may mean that a person has to maintain a low profile and at the same time have certain confidence in the authority figures in control of this situation. This has far-reaching managerial ramifications. In some situations in need of immediate coping, denial is not pathological and self-deceptive. There are times when denial as an intrapsychic device is useful and can reduce stress to a manageable level. The hospital patients who were using denial maintained a lower stress level in the short run that was essential for that particular event and stressor.

There are certain types of stresses that do not react positively to inputs or interventions. While individuals under stress may attempt to be positive and control situations that may appear to be out of hand, their attempts only create more frustration that they ultimately repress and therefore it may become more damaging. The data from all of these studies indicate there is no clear-cut mechanism for immediate mechanistic stress reduction and that different forms of coping have different potential effectiveness. It is extremely difficult to generalize, and the issues of coping and adapting may have broad-ranging ramifications for organizations in need of alternative strategies for managing operations and personnel.

AREAS OF COPING WITH STRESS

One way of coping with stress is to change the environment/person relationship that may be damaging and stressful. A second way is to lower the level of stress and the response to stimuli on which people habitually have patterned their behavior. Humans generally do pattern their behavior on direct action as a coping device or on some form of denial. Those intrapsychic factors, intellectualizations, or other alternatives seem to fall into both broad categories. The avoidance of issues and denial as coping mechanisms are two different processes that are constantly confused. Denial means that the person is saying "I am not sick or I am not dying, and I am denying these feelings." Not many professionals can assess denial simply because the individuals are not providing any information. The surface assumption is that they are denying when in reality they actually may be avoiding.

People actually operate a highly intricate defense mechanism by not wanting to think about nor talk about an object that is oppressive to them. Some stressful events necessitate denial while others lead to avoidance. However, avoidance may be dealt with ultimately by denial by individuals who are faced with a stressful confrontation and do not want to use direct conflict as an alternative response.

There are several other classes of coping that could be considered:

1. *Coping via information search*—in which individuals under stress seek information as to the nature of the situation and what could be done to alleviate the pressure.

2. *Coping via direct action*—in which individuals under stress attempt to change the situation by altering the fit between themselves and the environment.

3. *Coping via the inhibition of action*—in which individuals under stress do not attempt any direct action as just proposed, but maintain a psychological distance from a situation by waiting until the initial tension and ensuing reactions are at a lower level.

4. *Coping via intrapsychic modes*—in which individuals under stress use defense mechanisms (discussed in the next paragraphs) as attention deployment alternatives.

There seems to be no one best way of dealing and coping with stress. It may be easier to describe the nature of stress than to tell individuals what to do about it. Some of the many ways of dealing with stress (some discussed previously in describing defense mechanisms) include:

1. *Rationalization*—in which individuals seek relief by blaming other individuals or circumstances for the problem.
2. *Reaction Formation*—in which people seek relief by concealing undesirable motives through opposite behavior.
3. *Projection*—in which persons seek relief by attributing undesirable characteristics to others.
4. *Repression*—in which people seek relief by denying the predicament.
5. *Sublimination*—in which people seek relief from social condemnation by engaging in socially acceptable behavior.

These mechanisms usually are handled unconsciously in attempts to cope at this level. The coping process will not be successful if it is dealt with at an unconscious level and must be brought to the conscious level in order to attempt to control stress. Additional methods of coping with stress are as follows.

Coping by Cognitive Processes and Fantasy

In this case individuals project a "guesstimate" that they are under stress because of recent symptoms and behavior, then attempt not to think about the situation. They use avoidance thinking in which they escape stress by turning their attention away from the stress-creating situation and by fantasizing about other positive events. Since it is quite difficult to forget problems and since additional data about potentially stressful situations are not always available, the concept of fantasy is a good alternative for a coping mechanism.

Some of these fantasies may be daydreams of flight or may deal with unpleasant psychological states of anxiety in which failure and guilt emerge. The other type of fantasy may be positive daydreaming as a way of dealing consciously with the stressors. Some studies have indicated that individuals who do a great deal of daydreaming have fewer nervous breakdowns than those who do not. Daydreamers can use fantasy to escape boredom, conflict, pressure, and frustrations that are foundation blocks for stress. Certain behavior modification methods such as systematic desensitization do require individuals to create some imagery while they are being deconditioned, and therefore this can be an effective method for coping and reducing stress.

Since fantasy is considered a good coping device, it is essential to consider this as a developmental task. Fantasy and daydreaming can be simulated for health care managers who are experiencing stress throughout the day so that they can decompartmentalize their thinking patterns, avoid some of the debilitating factors creating additional stress, and attempt to regroup their thinking through a positive vehicle.

Coping by Feeling

Humanists and psychologists contend that individuals do not cope well with stress because they are "not in touch" with their inner feelings. Stress is accepted as a fact of life in health care environments and it is a continually growing and changing dynamic force. It can be a detriment to managers' growth if it becomes distress because it affects their potential and basic coping skills. Successful coping is the result of releasing individuals to actualize their potential, which in effect actually helps to reduce stress. Maslow was one of the pioneers who felt that individuals moved from physiological to self-actualization needs in their quest for development. It certainly can be hypothesized that the need for the reduction of stress increases as individuals move up the hierarchy of needs (Maslow, 1954). This has not been tested empirically but can be viewed in an organizational reality in which managers constantly struggle with the need to reduce stress during their upward mobility drive. The juggling act results in equilibrium, which is the favorable state these individuals were seeking initially. Stress builds to the point where individuals cannot deal with their potentialities since they are preoccupied with their priority for stress reduction. To cope with the stress, these individuals must get in touch with their own feelings of vulnerability to somehow develop the mechanisms needed to reduce the anxieties that can be so dysfunctional.

Coping by Controlling (Biofeedback)

Coping by controlling is a method used to reduce stress. Individuals can achieve this objective by manipulating their environment and modifying behavior that has proved to be a problem. Biofeedback is one of the suggested methods for this process. Biofeedback is being used with increasing regularity to help business people cope more effectively with stress. Various biofeedback devices and techniques, such as the electromyograph (EMG), electroencephalograph (EEG), thermal indicators, and the galvanic skin response (GSR), allow the subject to see or hear symbols that reflect internal states.

Through this direct feedback of internal events, individuals can learn to attain some level of control over their own visceral body reactions. By first attempting to alter an external signal (such as a click or flash of light), subjects eventually can learn to direct control of the internal body process that the external signal reflects. In this manner, hypertension and other symptoms of stress can be controlled (L. Smith, 1977, pp. 59-61). When an alpha state is achieved, the machine converts the brain waves into a tone that individuals can hear through earphones. An alpha state is one that occurs as the result of sensitization. At this point, the individual discovers certain subjective feelings or sensations in the body that are associated with the feedback. Thus, the individuals maintain continuous feedback about the electrical activity in their brain during different phases of mental activity since the brain sends out different waves.

With biofeedback, subjects learn to produce a rhythm that comes close to their alpha wave by controlling their physiological and mental processes. This procedure has been shown to be useful in treating tension headaches and certain cardiac conditions and may be effective in treating certain chronic stress-induced conditions such as high blood pressure. This method of using individual mental powers to control stress has been making quiet but impressive advances in the medical community in the last few years. After biofeedback training, diabetics claim to have reduced their dependence on insulin. Epileptics have avoided seizures and victims of hypertension have been able to keep their blood pressure at the low end of their usual range. Sufferers from debilitating migraine headaches report they definitely have been able to ward off attacks with the help of the technique.

Biofeedback, or visceral training as it is also known, generally is lumped together with Zen, Transcendental Meditation, and other disciplines in the human potential and mind control movements, but it differs from them in important ways. Its primary objective is to improve physical health and not to produce mind-expanding, other-world experiences. It got its impetus from Western science, not from Oriental mysticism (L. Smith, p. 60). In biofeedback training, as already described, the subjects are connected to one or more of the half-dozen biofeedback devices and the electromyograph (EMG) records muscle tension. The subjects actually watch dials and listen to these clicks and can tune in on what the body is doing. By using their thought processes, they are able to regulate their systems. The feedback from the instruments tells them whether their mental strategies are working and whether they are in control of them.

One of the fastest growing applications of feedback is on the part of executives who are in need of improving both their personal lives and their managerial and organizational performance. The focus is on particular recurring events that they find stressful. Once they have learned to control their anxiety under one set of circumstances, they have the confidence to control them under other scenarios as well. In some cases, gaining control over anxieties may give managers a positive, competitive advantage that they never experienced before. Stress basically forces managers to focus their attention on a single concern that may be mobilized into multiple patterns while becoming more dysfunctional in the long run. Managers are so intent upon solving this one problem that they become completely preoccupied by it and, as a result, become quite dysfunctional by not dealing with other issues and tensions in need of resolution.

Individuals who have learned to relax in stressful situations have testified that their perception of events slows down, becomes clearer, and moves at a more orderly, predictable, and controllable pace. Relaxation is a method of coping being used in the management of stress. Environmental stress produces a host of physiological changes that collectively are known as the fight-or-flight response. Specifically, there is an increase in metabolism, blood pressure, heart rate, breathing rate, amount of blood pumped by the heart, and amount of blood pumped to the skeletal muscles. Chronic elicitation of the fight-or-flight response leads to hypertension, which is associated with heart attack and stroke. Hypertension is found in 15 to 33 percent of the adult population in the United States, and heart attacks and strokes account for more than 50 percent of deaths in the nation each year.

To reduce these dangers, it is recommended that business people learn how to elicit the "relaxation response, an innate, integrated set of physiological changes opposite to those of the fight-or-flight response." Four conditions are required for this response: a quiet environment, a mental device, a passive attitude, and a comfortable position (Benson, 1974, pp. 49-60).

A study was conducted to demonstrate the relaxation response in dealing with tension and stress. Two hundred subjects were divided randomly into three groups, A, B, and C. A fourth group, D, consisted of subjects who did not volunteer initially to participate in the experiment. Four weeks of baseline measurements, including blood pressure, were obtained from each subject. Group A was taught a special relaxation response, group B simply sat quietly during breaks, while groups C and D received no special instructions. The treatment groups (A and B) took two relaxation breaks of 15 minutes each day. Only group A demonstrated a significant decrease in blood pressure. Questionnaire data concerning general health, performance, and sense of well-being replicated the blood pressure results. It was concluded that relaxation breaks are feasible in the world of work, and can be associated with improved general health, performance, and well-being, and with lowered blood pressure (Peters & Benson, 1978, pp. 120-124).

Coping by Assertive Communication Training

This process and technique is one by which anxiety habits of response to interpersonal communicative situations are overcome by encouraging the individual to openly express other spontaneously felt emotions in the actual situation. Assertive communication training enables staff and managers to deal with one another, and with patients and clients when necessary, in straightforward ways that recognize the rights and needs of all the individuals involved. Assertive communication training provides certain specific verbal skills employees can use to avoid being intimidated or manipulated by others, thereby reducing anxiety.

This concept arose from the recognition that virtually everybody has defensive feelings, learned early in life, that sometimes can come into play at inappropriate times. These defensive feelings often lead persons to yield to the intimidating behavior of others, to accept situations or make agreements that they know are detrimental to their own interests, and to negotiate ineffectively.

Assertive communication techniques essentially are verbal strategies, coupled with revised attitudes about self and self-esteem. They help in coping with stressful situations. Assertive training differentiates very carefully between assertive behavior, which is seen as constructive, and aggressive behavior, which is seen as antisocial and detrimental to people's own interests in the long run. Whereas an aggressive approach to dealing with another person—an irate patient, for example—involves a win-lose mentality, an assertive approach involves finding a balance of the two transacting personalities, with respect for the interests of each and with a workable compromise as the espoused goal of the transaction.

Two individuals can communicate and solve problems together much more effectively if both understand and can use assertive techniques. However, even if only one of them understands the concept, that person still can do a great deal to steer the transaction along a constructive course, even if the second person is upset, angry, or aggressive.

The basic assumption behind assertive communication is that individuals' self-esteem does not need to come into jeopardy in dealing with others, even if they lack the skill or consideration to approach the transaction constructively. People can only be manipulated by others, for example, if they let ancient guilt feelings come into play when the other persons make statements intended to "hook" into such feelings. Other forms of manipulation involve the use of accusations, leading or loaded questions, sidetracking the conversation with irrelevant diversions, and questioning people's honesty or integrity. The directness of this method is one way to overtly control feelings of helplessness that lead to anxiety and eventually a stressful situation.

Advantages accrued from this experience include the following:

1. Patient-contact health care employees function more effectively, alienating fewer patients-peers and maintaining a positive institutional image.
2. Assertive professionals experience much lower levels of job-related stress because they feel a greater sense of potency and experience fewer strong emotions in their job situations.
3. Health care managers learn to deal with staff in more open, straightforward ways, deploying their formal authority gracefully and sparingly.
4. Formerly inhibited employees who often have good ideas develop greater confidence in themselves and express their ideas more forcefully.
5. Morale and social climate generally improve in a work unit after its members have been trained collectively in assertive communication techniques.
6. Employees may take greater initiative and innovate more as a result of increased confidence in their ability to promote and defend their ideas (M. J. Smith, 1975).
7. Adaptation to conflicting situations becomes easier when staff members use assertive communications. All are made aware of needs and directions.

Coping by Adapting

The basic nature of coping by adapting has been described in Selye's General Adaptation Syndrome (Selye, 1978, p. 79). The G.A.S. is a manifestation of stress in the whole body as it develops in time. It evolves in three strategies already described in Chapter 3 on Occupational Stress and Coronary Disease: alarm reaction, stage of resistance, and the stage of exhaustion. The sources of stress may be great and may be varied, and individuals cope with stress by adapting to it. At that same time, they adapt by coping at a new level that becomes physiologically harmful to them. As a result chemicals are released that affect hormonal production and attack organs and tissues in the body through three stages:

1. the alarm phase
2. the resistance phase
3. the exhaustion phase, in which the total organism breaks down, with death as a possible outcome

Stress produces the same reaction within individuals, who as a result suffer dysfunctional emotional and physical problems unless stress-producing situations are identified early.

When coping fails and individuals no longer can deal with stress-producing agents, they may look to alcohol, drugs, or suicide as methods of dealing with stress that apparently is now out of control. Everyday factors responsible for stress include frustration, conflict, and anxiety. Causes of other stresses may be psychological or emotional or may be organizational. Whatever the cause, stress produces problems of personal and social adjustment and, in certain cases, can kill the individual.

In coping with stress it is essential to be able to identify the stressors, enlist other people to help, or at certain appropriate times to sit back and do nothing. Coping with stress means basically that managers are either initiating an action-oriented approach or are dealing with denial. When they fail to cope, the denial mechanism or the action-oriented approaches may not be working either. At this point it may appear to be a logical but irrational act to consider drugs, alcohol, and/or suicide. These alternatives become a final decision when individuals no longer can cope or reduce the stress creating the acute pain. Adaptation is accomplished through preinductive, anticipatory socialization in which individuals who are to experience stressful situations are exposed initially to at least a part of the conflict so that a resolution can be developed in the quest to adapt.

BEHAVIORAL MEDICINE

Psychosomatic medicine is concerned with disease and the interaction between both physiological and psychosocial variables. It is associated with a broad range of interests and rationales concerning health, coping, and diseases.

Behavior modification and behavior therapy are more specific terms in the field of behavioral medicine, conveying a particular type of intervention as well as a strategy for assessment and methodology for research:

- Behavior modification uses principles derived from the experimental analysis of behavior and social learning theory to modify maladapted behaviors. Although procedures for intervention are delineated clearly, application is not limited to any particular area, although in practice it has been associated with behavioral intervention in educational and rehabilitative settings.
- Behavior therapy on the other hand consists of activities that seem closer to the idea of behavior role medicine, implying a contractual agreement between therapist and patient or client to modify a designated problem behavior. Behavior therapy, however, has been concerned historically more with the problem of neurosis and effective disorders and less with physical disease (Pomerleau, 1979, p. 655).

At this point it is important to explore what behavioral medicine is and how it may be used to deal with psychosomatic disorders through behavioral modification therapy. Behavioral medicine can be defined as the clinical use of techniques derived from the experimental analysis of behavior—behavior therapy and behavior modification—for the evaluation, prevention, management, or treatment of physical disease or physiological dysfunction; and the conduct of research contributing to the functional analysis and understanding of behavior associated with medical disorders and problems in health care (Pomerleau, p. 656).

Biofeedback is one of the processes of behavioral medicine, has special application for operant conditioning, and has limited application in dealing with hypertension, tension headaches, asthma, functional diarrhea, and other psychosomatic disorders. Biofeedback, however, may not be capable of solving these problems. In dealing with self-management attempts must be made to change certain aspects of the environment. This is an important point in considering the health care environment. These changes then modify the problem behavior, and the behavior change techniques, in turn, modify the problem behavior. The behavior change techniques and ultimate altered behavior are essential in adapting to stressful situations. At present there are four methods of development associated with clinical behavioral medicine:

1. an intervention intended to modify overt behavior that is a problem

2. an intervention intended to modify behavior of health care personnel to improve their service, which ultimately will benefit the patient.

3. an intervention intended to modify adherence to prescribed treatments

4. an intervention that attempts to modify behaviors that constitute risk factors in disease

An interesting area of development has been modification of the behavior of medical personnel to provide more cost-effective care to patients or clients. In a study by Pomerleau, the behavior of health care aides was considered a limiting factor in the rehabilitation of highly disruptive psychotics in a state hospital, in that baseline observations concluded that the aides typically ignored patients unless they were causing trouble. Special contingencies of reinforcement were introduced to increase the number and quality of therapeutic interactions between aides and patients. The amount of disruptive or inappropriate behavior by patients on the ward as a whole was found to decrease in direct proportion to the amount of monetary incentive given to the aides for attending to the behavior of those patients (Pomerleau, p. 658).

Another application of this theory and practice is worth exploring. It is a fact that major causes of death for adults are coronary disease, cerebrovascular diseases, and malignant tumors resulting in death. It appears that specific aspects of individuals' life styles such as their activity, diet, and consumption of alcohol and drugs have an effect on this mortality rate. Health practices, as well as individuals' personal practices, can be modified through behavioral medicine to help retard these diseases. Research on the prevention of coronary heart disease provides a model demonstrating that certain activities are connected to behavioral medicine. Many risk factors and behaviors do occur in clusters and their effects combine multiplicatively.

In applied research, clinical trials have been attempted to determine whether behavioral risk factor modification will lead to corresponding improvements in the physiological indicators of risk and ultimately to decrease the morbidity and mortality from heart disease. Modification of individual risk factors has been attempted in numerous instances, particularly for obesity, smoking, and hypertension. There is even evidence that the highly resistant Type A behavior pattern defined as aggressiveness, ambition, competitiveness, and a sense of time urgency can be modified with some degree of success (Pomerleau, 1979, p. 660). This approach reduced the stress and increased the individual's chances of coping and, ultimately, surviving.

A MODEST SOLUTION

In a paper presented at a conference, in Boston, Mass. on the Role of Stress in Hypertension, the theme for the entire conference was The Crisis in Stress Research. Richard Lazarus critiqued the limitations of contemporary epidemiological research on adaption, coping, and stress. His major contribution from the conference report was:

> I plan to argue that an important reason for our ignorance is methodological, that we need to focus in our research far more on process and less on structure, and to adopt intraindividual or normative strategies in which the same persons are studied repeatedly and in depth, rather than following interindividual or normative strategies....

There are two main reasons why previous psychosomatic research has not led to understanding: First, there has been a failure to understand the concept of stress itself at each of three levels of analysis—social, psychological, and physiological. The key defect is the continuing tendency to separate artificially the two major classes of interacting causal antecedents of the stress response, namely, the external environment and the characteristics of the person. Again and again, writers seem to be saying that stress is either out there in the social or physical environment, or within the person as an intrapsychic defect. However, stress is a special kind of transaction or relationship between a particular kind of system (a person, social unit, or tissue structure) and a particular kind of environment. Although all levels of analysis are equally important, stress has quite different meanings at each.

Second, at the psychological level, stress depends on the ways individuals cognitively appraise a transaction and cope with it. They may view it as threatening, challenging, or benign. They may cope by direct action to change things or by intrapsychic processes such as denial, detachment, or trying to avoid thinking about the negative aspects. These mediational processes profoundly alter the persons' tissue state and hence their prospects of developing a psychosomatic disorder such as hypertension. Until individual differences in the processes of appraisal and coping are understood and brought into the equation, the role of psychological stress in hypertension and other somatic disturbances cannot possibly be understood, and research will continue to fail to specify adequately the crucial personality and situational variables that are causal because they affect the way individuals appraise their relationships and how they cope (Conference Report, 1979, p. 11).

A general message synthesized from the conference suggested a shift in the basic conceptualizations and future research of behavioral scientists working in the areas of stress and coping:

- The social and psychological scientists learned that they could not work on psychosocial parameters alone, isolating themselves from the biological scientists and the issues they investigated. They also learned that identification of variables and measurement capabilities in their fields needed refinement, if not overhaul, in order to win acceptance by those in the biological sciences who would work with them.

- The biological scientists learned that research in the future, by virtue of funding as well as analytic requirements, would take on a greater multidisciplinary context, and that it therefore would be beneficial for them to become acquainted with, and knowledgeable about, the psychological and social methodology and terminology of their colleagues.

- Both groups of scientists discerned clearly that the crisis in stress research on hypertension had come about in large part as a result of lack of communication and interaction among disciplines, and that they all were necessarily involved in formulating appropriate questions and seeking the same ultimate understanding of the puzzles that surrounded hypertension (Conference Report, p. 22).

This summary of the conference has broad-ranging ramifications for health care managers dealing with their own and others' life change events, adaptation, and stress. Coping with stress is not adapting to a complex, difficult situation that often becomes escalated, organizationally dysfunctional, and personally painful. Personal coping is analogous to the purpose of any health care organization: perpetuation and survival.

BIBLIOGRAPHY

Andrews, G., Tennant, C., Hewson, D.M., & Vaillant, G.E. Life stress events, social support, coping style and risk of psychological impairment. *Journal of Nervous and Mental Disorders,* May 1978, *166*(5), 307-316.

Benson, H. Your innate asset for combating stress. *Harvard Business Review,* July 1974, *52*(4), 49-60.

Conference Report. The role of stress in hypertension. *Journal of Human Stress,* June 1979, *5*(2), 7-27.

Cousins, N. Anatomy of an illness (as perceived by the patient). *New England Journal of Medicine,* December 1976, *295*, 1458-1463.

Dohrenwend, B.S., Krasnoff, L., Askenasy, A.R., Exemplification of a method for scaling life events: The PERI life events scale. *Journal of Health and Social Behavior,* February 1978, *19*(2), 205-229.

Dubos, R.J. *Man adapting.* New Haven, Conn.: Yale University Press, 1965.

Friedman, M., & Rosenman, R.H. *Type A behavior and your heart.* New York: Fawcett Cress Publishing, 1973.

Howard, J.H. Managing stress and job tension. *The Labour Gazette,* February-March 1978, pp. 61-64.

Jenkins, C.D. Psychosocial modifiers of response to stress. *Journal of Human Stress,* December 1979, *5*(4), 3-15.

Lazarus, R. The crisis in stress research: A critical appraisal of the role of stress in hypertension, gastrointestinal illness, and female reproductive dysfunction. Conference Report. The role of stress in hypertension. *Journal of Human Stress,* June 1979, *5*(2), 7-27.

Lazarus, R. Coping with stress: Effects on somatic illness, morale and social functioning. *Stress and Behavioral Medicine,* Gary Schwartz, Ed. Bureau of National Affairs, Inc. New York, tape presentation, 1979.

Levinson, H. A psychoanalytic framework. In A. McLean (Ed.), *Occupational stress.* Springfield, Ill.: Charles C. Thomas Publisher, 1974, 27-30.

Maslow, A.H. *Motivation and personality.* New York: Harper & Row, 1954.

Pearlin, L.I., & Schooler, C. The structure of coping. *Journal of Health and Social Behavior,* 1978, *19*, 2-21.

Peters, R.K., & Benson, H. Time out from tension. *Harvard Business Review,* January 1978, *56*(1), 120-124.

Pomerleau, O. F. Behavioral medicine: The contribution of the experimental analysis of behavior to medical care. *American Psychologist,* August 1979, *34*(8), 654-663.

Rahe, R.H. Life change events and mental illness: An overview. *Journal of Human Stress,* September 1979, *5*(3), 2-10.

Rummel, R.M., & Rader, J.W. Coping with executive stress. *Personnel Journal,* June 1978, *57*(6), 305-307.

Selye, H. The stress of life. (Rev. Ed.) New York: McGraw Hill Book Co., 1978.

Smith, L. Fighting stress. *Dun's Review,* January 1977, *109*(1), 59-61.

Smith, M.J. *When I say no, I feel guilty.* New York: Bantam Books, 1975.

Chapter 8

The Troubled Employee

CONSIDERATIONS FOR THE HEALTH CARE MANAGER

1. A personal crisis situation involving marital, family, financial, or legal troubles is considered the most prevalent problem among all employee groups. Alcoholism is ranked next.

2. With increasing costs to organizations experiencing these problems, it becomes evident that a movement toward prevention and alleviation of these stress-related disorders by providing employee counseling services is gaining momentum.

3. Alcoholic employees have twice the incidence of longer lasting disabilities than other employees, deteriorated work performances resulting in undue turnover, and cases of early retirement.

4. Early identification and referral of the alcoholic by the supervisor is important since the prognosis for successful treatment becomes less favorable toward the latter stages of the disease.

5. But early identification may be delayed because the employee is able to conceal the problem and the supervisor does not want to become involved. The symptoms

are not difficult to diagnose since decrease in job performance is the focal point.

6. It is recommended that formal policy statements be presented within the organization to ensure the commitment of top management and provide a procedural blueprint for the supervisor and affected employee. This actually legitimizes the treatment approach.

7. Failure comes not only because alcoholism is not recognized as an illness but also because there are serious obstacles to treatment, thereby intensifying the problem and creating greater stress.

8. The responsibility for change always rests with the individual affected by alcohol and/or drugs, and performance is the only objective method of evaluating the employee's effectiveness.

9. Managers also come into contact with drug-related problems. An effective way to approach this dilemma is to understand what drugs are and what they do. This reduces anxiety and stress when problems with opiates, amphetamines, barbiturates, hallucinogens, and marijuana occur. Drugs are used as coping mechanisms by those experiencing stress in the organization. Diagnosis and treatment are quite similar to alcohol problems. It is management's responsibility to reduce stresses and provide needed support.

10. Occupational physicians can help a tense organization going through traumatic changes by working both with managers and with employees experiencing stress in dealing with anxieties and alternatives.

11. Occupational physicians can help management identify the conflicts creating stress in individuals seeking help and relief. Health care managers affected by this tur-

bulence also can employ these physicians as internal consultants to mediate the conflicts in need of resolution.

12. Conflicts between occupational physicians and managers of anxiety-ridden departments must be resolved initially with each individual assuming roles of consultant and decisionmaker prior to any help's being offered or accepted.

13. Problems requiring intervention by an occupational psychiatrist include intrapyschic, interpersonal, work group, family, corporation, and community.

14. Occupational nurses can intervene in systems experiencing conflict and stress by assessing individuals with problems and planning therapeutic treatments. They also are involved in the prevention and control of the destructive effects of occupational stressors.

15. Occupational nurses experience problems and stress while attempting to help clients under stress:
    - They may be poorly trained.
    - They have little freedom to exercise professional judgment.
    - They are poorly compensated.
    - They have limited organizational status.
    - Those who are women experience the conflicts of being female in male-dominated organizations, and male nurses face the same problems in female-dominated areas.

16. Organizations may be reluctant to employ occupational therapists since problems then are transferred to the system from individuals under stress. The occupational medical department is viewed as a physical-oriented, not merely emotional-oriented, function.

17. Health care organizations have a difficult
time dealing with individual's weaknesses
that stigmatize emotional health and actually create additional stress in the system.

Alcoholism, drug abuse, emotional illness, and family crisis are employees' personal problems that spill over into the environment of the health care organization and ultimately affect the individuals' job performance while becoming a complex issue for the administration. A personal crisis situation involving marital, family, financial, or legal troubles is considered the most prevalent problem among all employee groups, affecting an estimated average of 10.9 percent of production workers, 7.2 percent of office clerical employees, 6.1 percent of technical and professional staff, and 5.8 percent of managerial personnel according to a 1978 survey (ASPA-BNA, p. 1).

The study found that alcoholism was ranked second to personal crises, affecting 4.6 percent of both professional and managerial employees compared to 3.8 percent of office-clerical workers and 7.7 percent of the production service group. The incidence of emotional illness requiring psychiatric treatment was higher in 1978 than in 1973, according to 26 percent of the respondents, and 25 percent reported an increase in marijuana abuse over the preceding five years.

While there are many types of troubled employees, the immediate focus here is on alcoholic and drug-addicted workers, as both groups affect organizations and their cost structures. Mental disorders can be classified according to retardation, psychosis associated with organic brain syndromes, nonpsychotic organic brain syndromes, schizophrenia, neurosis, paranoia, obsessive/compulsive personalities, passive-aggressive personalities, and psychophysiological disorders. It is not essential to perform a taxonomy of these to determine the net effect of stress experienced by health care administrators attempting to achieve the goals of their organization and meet the needs of employees who also are undergoing stress.

THE COST OF ALCOHOLISM

In 1974, the National Institute of Mental Health reported that the annual cost of disabilities resulting from mental disorders alone exceeded $10 billion. Subsequently, The Cornell University-New York State School of Industrial and Labor Relations estimated that absenteeism, personnel turnover, industrial accidents, and alcoholism related to mental disorders exceeded $12 billion a year. No matter how they are measured, the inescapable conclusion is that mental, emotional, and personality disorders are costly to employers and can have a substantial effect upon the national economy. The yearly wage loss alone has been placed at $432 million. The loss of goods and services, poor productivity, faulty decisions, and personnel turnover resulting from alcoholism have been estimated to cost $1 billion to $2 billion annually (Follmann, 1978, p. 73).

Scientists at Harvard University's School of Public Health in 1974 determined the cost to business and industry of alcohol-related problems to be about $5 billion annually, with the problem drinker missing an average of 22 work days a year and a probability of incurring an accident at a rate two to four times greater than that of the nondrinker. This report also said three times as many medical benefits were being paid to alcoholics as to other workers. Another estimate put the average loss to a company at 25 percent of the drinker's salary (Filipowicz, 1979, p. 18).

The National Institute on Drug Abuse and Alcoholism estimated 25 percent of employed alcoholics were white-collar employees, 30 percent were manual workers and 45 percent were professionals and managers (Goldberg, 1978, pp. 78-79). The National Association for Mental Health said a total $17 billion annual productivity loss to business in the United States was due to emotional problems of employees, with individual workers costing their organizations an average of $1,622 per year. Some estimates regard these figures as most conservative (Filipowicz, 1979, p. 18). While some of the data are at variance from others, the studies do indicate that the costs can be crippling.

When the impact of inflation is added to these data, the need for preventing and alleviating these stress-related disorders through employee counselling services is very evident.

In a 1973 Special Task Force on Work, United States Department of Health, Education, and Welfare researchers reported that nonsupportive jobs in which workers received little feedback on their performance appeared to cause the kind of anxiety that could lead to alcoholism. Work conditions, occupational obsolescence, role stress, and unstructured environments (for certain personality types) appear to be other important risk factors for both alcoholism and drug addiction (Filipowicz, 1979, p. 18).

Phillip Goldberg in a study (1978, pp. 78-79) indicated:

- Premature employee deaths cost American industry $19.4 billion a year, more than the combined 1976 profits of *Fortune*'s top five corporations.
- An estimated $10 billion to $20 billion is lost through executives' absence, hospitalization, and early death.
- About 32 million workdays and $8.6 billion in wages are lost annually to heart-related diseases.
- The American Heart Association reported the cost of recruiting replacements for executives felled by heart disease was about $700 million a year.

The American Medical Association recognized alcoholism as an illness in 1956. The American Hospital Association in 1957 and the American Federation of Labor-Congress of Industrial Organizations in 1959 followed suit. Alcoholism is considered by many to be a manifestation of a psychiatric illness, although this concept lacks unanimity. Its cause is not known, but unquestionably individuals' stress factors such as mental, emotional, and personality disorders can be attributed to alcoholism. The toll of alcoholism is serious. The alcoholic person has a 12-year shorter life span and is more illness prone than the nonalcoholic. Half of all motor vehicle fatalities, half of suicides, a third of homicides, and the vast majority of drownings are said to be involved in one way or another with drinking problems. Of all admissions to hospitals, 13 percent are reported to result from alcoholism, and 10 percent of the resident population of public mental hospitals are alcoholic.

The abuse of alcohol is the major cause of cirrhosis of the liver. The cost of alcoholism in the United States has been estimated by the Department of Health and Human Services (formerly HEW) to exceed $25 billion a year. This is the highest estimate yet with regard to all the varied data. Of this amount, more than $9 billion is reported to result from lost production, more than $8 billion from the cost of medical care, and more than $6 billion from motor vehicle accidents (Follmann, 1978, p. 222).

Alcoholics at the workplace have two and a half times as much absenteeism as other employees, three and a half times as many absences due to off-the-job accidents, twice the incidence of respiratory and cardiovascular diseases, and three times the incidence of digestive and musculoskeletal disorders. Alcoholic employees have twice the incidence of disabilities lasting 30 or more days than do other employees and six times the incidence of disabilities lasting 90 or more days. Other effects include lateness, deteriorated work performance, faulty decision making, employee friction, impaired customer relations, reduced efficiency, material wastage, and on-the-job accidents. These factors may entail undue labor turnover and cases of early retirement.

Some case studies in 1976 by the National Institute on Drug Abuse and Alcoholism of employers' estimates of annual costs of alcoholism may be of interest:

- North American Rockwell Corporation , with 100,000 employees, $250 million a year, or $50,220 per alcoholic employee.
- Gulf Oil Canada, Ltd., with 11,000 employees, $400,000.
- The United California Bank of Los Angeles, with 10,000 employees, $1 million a year.
- The Illinois Bell Telephone Company, employees, wage replacements alone, $418,500 a year.
- The United States Postal Service, with employees, $168 million.
- The United States General Accounting Office reporting on the 2.9 million federal civilian employees, $550 million a year.

Despite such findings, many employees are unaware of the problem of alcoholism in their work force, others are concerned about the effect upon their public image should they admit the presence of alcoholics, while still others simply discharge the detected cases.

On the positive side, an increasing number of employers are establishing alcoholism control programs to help employees with drinking problems. The National Institute on Drug Abuse and Alcoholism estimated that 12,000 such occupational programs were operative by the end of 1976, double the number a few years earlier. Certain of these programs that are considered significant have been established by Anaconda, American Brass Company, the Canadian National Railways, Canadian Pacific, Western Electric Company, Lockheed-California Company, and the Dow Chemical Company (Follmann, 1978, p. 224).

Symptoms of Alcoholism

In 1968, an article in *Business Week* titled "Business Copes with Alcoholics" was one of the initial attempts to look openly at some of the strategy, methodology, and treatment programs that organizations used in dealing with alcoholics. An executive of a large corporation in Texas stated, "We don't have a problem, we fire our drunks."

Six months later, this same executive died of acute alcoholism. This problem certainly is not limited to the rank and file.

Identification of alcoholics is extremely difficult, particularly at middle and upper management levels where adequate work records seldom exist and where a sense of loyalty impels executives to cover up for fellow managers. There appears to be a Machiavellian factor at work: A manager may not blow the whistle on a colleague, consciously or unconsciously, because both may be competing for a top management spot. The theory: It's better to let him stub his toe than see him receive treatment.

Alcoholism, however, is not always accompanied by deteriorating performance. Dr. Thomas Wickes, Medical Director of T.R.W., Inc. in Cleveland, Ohio, comments, "Surprisingly, the quality of an alcoholic's work usually goes up, not down. The quantity suffers, but not the quality." He describes typical alcoholics as charming, open, sensitive, slightly dependent, and quick to form warm relationships. Consequently, supervisors may try to cover up for them. More alcoholics are to be found in middle management and the technically skilled levels from ages 35 to 50 than in top ranks. Alcoholism is only one facet of a broad spectrum of personal problems that impinge upon performance and productivity at the workplace.

There are certain factors to look for in attempting to diagnose who the alcoholic individuals facing this problem may be. One set of criteria:

- excessive absenteeism patterns: Monday, Friday, and days before and after holidays
- unexcused and frequent absences
- tardiness and early departures
- altercations with fellow employees
- causing other employee injuries through negligence
- poor judgment and bad decisions
- unusual on-the-job accidents
- increased spoilage and breaking equipment through negligence
- involvement with the law, such as wage attachments
- deteriorating personal appearance (Filipowicz, 1979, p. 20)

Since the care of alcoholics and problem drinkers traditionally has been the responsibility of clinicians, it is perhaps understandable that there has been a widespread use of clinical perspectives in trying to understand how and why people drink. This has resulted in a distinct tendency even among nonclinicians to adopt as their own the concepts of clinical theorists such as the existence of the alcoholic personality. It is useful to think of drinking as involving several distinct patterns of behavior. One pattern is represented in the efforts of people to deal with emotional distress arising out of the circumstances of their lives (Pearlin & Radabaugh, 1978, p. 992). Individuals' levels of anxiety appear to be related to the intensity of the economic stress experienced. This anxiety may be associated closely with the use of alcohol as an attempt to control emotional distress. Alcohol is not an equally attractive coping mechanism for everyone. When individuals seem to be able to control their environment and have a healthy concept of self-esteem, they are likely to deal with their anxieties in more effective and productive ways.

The use of alcohol apparently does control and reduce the pain and discomfort of stress for some, but it is a coping mechanism that becomes so serious a problem and so uncontrolled that the costs exceed the benefits in nearly all cases. Alcohol is an instrument of social control and appears to provide short-term relief from the unpleasant effects of conflict and strain; at the same time, it may help to maintain the very circumstances that contribute to such symptoms (Pearlin & Radabaugh, 1978, p. 994).

Early identifcation and referral of alcoholics is important because the prognosis for successful treatment becomes less favorable toward the latter stages of the disease. However, early identification often is delayed because employees are able to conceal the problem or perhaps supervisors do not want to become involved. In other cases, the supervisors may be drinking with the individuals and do not wish to expose their own personal problems. Rather than looking for a drug or alcohol problem, it is suggested that managers be concerned with identifying employees who are not performing.

Some of the symptoms of alcoholism are absenteeism, tardiness, increase in physical symptoms, irritability, changes in motor activity, smell of alcohol on breath, repeated arrests for drunk driving, excuses for absence, and a decrease in job performance. Managers must know their employees quite well, along with their normal patterns of behavior. If these patterns are not known, then managers may not be able to identify the changes. If the employees demonstrate some of the symptoms previously described, there is a good chance that the identified problems may be connected with alcoholism.

Once the problem begins to manifest itself on the job, managers should be held responsible for dealing with it directly. They should talk to the employee, indicate their awareness and concern, and specify the degree to which the worker's job is being affected. The supervisors should not try to do rehabilitative counselling but should focus upon a change in behavior. Many managers do attempt this and find that it not only interferes with the managerial-subordinate relationship but also prolongs the problem and makes it more difficult to handle when a referral finally is made.

HOW TO APPROACH EMPLOYEES

There is a way of approaching troubled employees who may be in need of help through early diagnosis and intervention. Under this procedure, managers should:

1. Establish levels of work performances they expect.
2. Be specific about supportive behavioral criteria for problems such as absenteeism, poor job performance, and others.
3. Be consistent.
4. Try not to diagnose the problem.
5. Restrict criticism to job performance.
6. Be firm.
7. Be prepared to cope with employees' resistance, defensiveness, or hostility.
8. Try to get the employees to acknowledge the problem.
9. Show them they cannot play against higher management.
10. Point out the availability of counselling services.
11. Discuss drinking only if it occurs on the job or the employees obviously are intoxicated.
12. Get a commitment from the employees to meet specific work criteria and monitor this with a plan for improvement based on work performance.
13. Explain that the employees must decide for themselves whether or not to seek assistance.
14. Emphasize confidentiality of the program (Filipowicz, 1979, p. 22).

What may be most important is that the managers are aware of available resources and can encourage the employees to make an appointment. It is advisable for managers to follow up with the identified employees to ensure that they are obtaining the help needed. Organizations should make available for their managers lists of referrals and alternatives needed in dealing with problem employees.

If employees do not want this help, it should be made clear that their continued employment will depend on effective performance and the elimination of the problem, which is affecting the workers, the managers and the organization milieu. In some cases, alcoholics will not want to change and eventually will be discharged. However, the majority can be helped. It is important to diagnose the incidence and intensity of the problem.

Alcoholism: Stage 1

When individuals move into the first stage of alcoholism, they usually are recognized as being different from other drinkers. The first symptom of this stage is the blackout that results in temporary amnesia. After several drinks, early stage alcoholics may carry on fully rational conversations or go through a series of complex activities but will be unable to recall these events the next day. The blackout is not connected with actually passing out or becoming unconscious. The increased frequency of this symptom indicates the individuals' increased susceptibility to alcohol.

In the early stage, alcoholics begin to undergo personality changes. These result from their increasing dependence upon alcohol and their need to hide this dependence from other people. The personality changes are demonstrated in many ways such as avid drinking, guilt feelings about drinking, and avoiding any reference to alcohol. The prognosis of cure is most favorable if alcoholics can be started in treatment programs at this early stage.

Alcoholism: Stage 2

After several months or perhaps years, the individuals enter the second stage of alcoholism. The primary symptom here is loss of control. This may appear when one drink begins a chain reaction that lasts until the individuals actually are drunk. For this reason, alcoholics must avoid even that first drink if they are to be rehabilitated. When tensions arise and stresses are great, a drink is a natural remedy for these persons; each time, they are convinced they will have only one or two.

Throughout the second stage, untreated alcoholics develop other symptoms that reflect their change in personality. They begin to rationalize their drinking by making up excuses to explain their behavior to themselves and to persuade themselves that they have not lost control because of their habit. At this point, they will develop persistent remorse and periods of total abstinence as changes in their drinking patterns. They may even attempt to switch the kind of beverage they drink. All symptoms are attempts to deal with the problem without admitting dependence. When they find these attempts are not working, their drinking increases again. They will have a loss of outside interests, marked self-pity, geographic escape, changes in family habits, and unreasonable resentments. All such behavior is a sign of continued withdrawal from other activities and other people, and increasing dependency.

In the latter phases of the second stage, the individuals begin to undergo organic changes. At this time, many alcoholics who have not been under treatment will receive their first hospitalization for physical complications.

Alcoholism: Stage 3

With early morning drinking, alcoholics pass into the third and chronic stage. Prolonged intoxication is the first symptom of this stage. Chronic alcoholics may leave their jobs early or fail to go to work at all. The prolonged intoxication results in marked ethical deterioration and impairment of thinking. The alcoholics' general behavior no longer has the appearance of responsibility, and their judgment in most types of situations rarely is reliable. In about 10 percent of the cases, alcoholic psychoses may develop. Observable patterns include drinking with persons far below one's social level, and drinking technical and household products containing alcohol. If old friends disapprove, chronic alcoholics will change friends. In the chronic stage, there is a decrease in alcohol tolerance, indefinable fears, tremors, and psychomotor inhibitions. This stage is most serious. Once the supervisor diagnoses alcoholism as an organizational-individual problem, a formal program should be at their disposal to which to refer afflicted individuals for treatment.

ORGANIZATIONAL PROGRAMS: SOME ROADBLOCKS

There is a basic problem in studying management systems that are programmed and intended to deal with stress because of the communication gap between the organization's managers and occupational health practitioners. This dilemma affects the pool of expertise needed to deal with these problems. Unfortunately, there are many managers who will have no difficulty arriving at unfounded conclusions regarding how to improve communications and how to remove problem areas. They accomplish this via impeccably structured and stated standard operating procedures that ultimately result in low productivity and poor financial results. They claim they understand problems involving human resources but they rarely will consult the health staff to deal with these dysfunctions. One explanation may be that many health specialists now operating organizations do not generally feel comfortable dealing with management problems. Moreover, they don't think managers are eager to have them do so.

Physicians, psychiatrists, counsellors, and personnel experts dealing with stress in organizations currently see their principal role as performing therapeutic services for individual employees. Supervisors in general do not look at the incidence of unfavorable stress reactions in relation to their effectiveness as managers, nor do they see stress as an impediment to achieving organizational goals. On the contrary, some observers suggest that the ability to overcome (not reduce) stress is considered a "badge of honor" among managers (Schwarz, 1974, p. 81).

The systems in many organizations do not accept any intervention by occupational therapists since the problem is transferred from individual distress to a total systematic dysfunction. When chief executive officers are questioned as to what they perceive the medical department to be doing, they generally will respond that they are there for the treatment of sick individuals. Their concept of "sick" is physical, not emotional, distress. The effect of those executives' perception tends to establish an insulated zone in the organization that does not deal with emotional problems leading to stress reduction. Physical well-being and mental health are viewed separately and the health care staff is excluded in participating in many management decisions that affect the organization as a totality.

Managers generally seek power, which is the ability to influence decisions, and possessing it and/or losing it can be a major factor in producing stress. This is an important consideration because outside of their own department, medical directors do not have the hierarchical power that is derived from an established structure; they do not have coercive power or reward power (to "hire and fire"). They do possess expert power that is based upon their special technical competence that is not necessarily shared by anyone else in the organization. One of the problems with this is that these medical directors' inputs are viewed only as staff offerings and administrators tend not to accept them with a great deal of credibility.

In a large health care complex, hierarchical power defines the structure in a triangular manner, with functions being separated up and down the chain of command. This system creates limitations and problems, with the functions being separated along the chain of command. For example, messages traveling from the top down can become diffused. Response messages can get choked as they travel toward the top. Many managers do not deal well with human resource problems and their concept of feedback about people in their organization usually is in the form of statistics regarding the number employed, wages and salaries, absentee rates, turnover, and other data that can be measured.

The concept that psychological stress will be manifested in part by a significant change in some physical parameter provides the basis for developing useful early warning signals of incipient problems. Collecting and interpreting these data should be an appropriate function of the medical department. Many such departments, often in conjunction with the internal counselling service, already have data of this type available, but the channels for using them effectively are inadequate for organizational improvement (Schwarz, 1974, p. 87).

Since work is so inextricably tied in to the individuals' own concepts of self-esteem and of identity, normal patterns become unpredictable when, as an example, they are faced with a stressor such as unemployment. This phenomenon was identified clearly in a 1975 article in *The New York Times* describing the reaction of a recently fired 52-year-old executive:

> As an infantry veteran of World War II in the South Pacific, I have had some experience with fear, and how men deal with it. I like to feel that I don't scare any easier than the next guy, but to be 52 years old and jobless is to be frightened—frightened to the marrow of your bones. Your day starts with it, and ends with it. It is all-pervasive. It is numbing. It is mind-boggling (Furey, 1975).

Even when work is not ideal, it still is important for individuals' basic existence. Freud felt that two of the most important elements of adult development were the ability to love and the ability to work. In the classic book *Work in America* (1972), the function of work is described as a process offering economic self-sufficiency, status, family stability, and an opportunity to interact with others in one of the most basic activities in society.

More than 90 million persons occupy jobs in the work environment in the United States and many experience job performance difficulties because of emotional problems. Their ability to carry out the components of their tasks, to respond to routinized work demands, and to maintain their interpersonal skills and relationships all may be affected by stress factors. The nature of the workplace, however, does not encourage individuals to seek out help when they are having a difficult time functioning.

In making health care organizations receptive to differences, and at the same time dealing with individual weaknesses in which compassion and support are component parts of functioning, a different type of climate must be created. This climate must be one that can reduce the stigma of individuals' not being totally in control of their emotional health and at the same time accepting them with their emotional problems by an organizational commitment flatly stating that "it's OK to not be perfect." This is an affirmative method of reducing occupational stress by accepting individuals as they are without applying extra pressure for perfection.

MODEL ORGANIZATIONAL PROGRAMS

Approximately 300 out of hundreds of thousands of organizations are beginning to offer special programs to enhance their employees' physical and emotional health. Kimberly Clark Corp. has instituted a comprehensive exercise and diet training system along with elaborate exercise facilities for its workers. More than 120 companies provide their employees opportunities to learn Transcendental Meditation and some provide special rooms for meditation. The Equitable Life Assurance Company has implemented a biofeedback program with training for its employees to use this form of tension reduction in company-owned and -operated laboratories.

The purpose of these efforts is to provide workers with better psychological and physical resilience to stress. The programs are designed as preventive measures, to reduce the physical and emotional disease consequences of chronic stress such as high blood pressure, heart disease, stomach ulcers, emotional disorders, and alcoholism. This makes good sense since stress disorders cost organizations an estimated $17 to $25 billion each year in lost performance, absenteeism, and health benefit payments (McGaffey, 1978, p. 26). It is important that stress prevention programs rely on the voluntary use of these exercise and biofeedback programs. However, the voluntary programs do miss a large segment of the employee population. It is unlikely that Type A highly driven middle managers who are interested in upward mobility and promotion will leave their desks to get involved in programs intended for their own health and welfare.

The model endorsed by such organizations as the Kaiser Permanente Medical Center in San Francisco is called the Comprehensive Health Model and underscores the need for multifaceted and integrated treatment programs for stress-induced diseases. For example, in the case of a patient with high blood pressure or alcoholism, not only is medical treatment provided but also there may be psychotherapy, vocational counselling, family counselling, and other forms of treatment and adjustment skill training. This necessitates the expensive services of physicians, psychologists, social workers, family therapists, and vocational counsellors. In spite of the expense, these types of professionals are invaluable to the development of stress prevention programs for organizations (McGaffey, 1978, p. 27).

These components must have as an objective early intervention in the stress disorder since correction measures at the initial stage are important in stemming declining performance. Unless this occurs early, employees will deteriorate even more due to stress-related factors. Early intervention also addresses the complexity of various needs and treatments in order to deal with stress and its inherent problems. Management control systems for dealing with employee stress are essential because they have viability and credibility when workers are aware that top administrators are endorsing the programs. These programs, when combined with other stress prevention methods (nursing, social work, etc.), serve as foundation blocks for creating managerial systems to combat organizational stress.

Model programs for employee assistance efforts based on a contract between the workers and the organization entail the following:

1. The contract spells out what is involved with regard to the rights of both parties, costs, and opportunities for the reduction of stress.
2. The role of the supervisor in the employee assistance program is essential.
3. Training in performance assessment and dealing with confrontation of employees who are experiencing poor performance should be a prerequisite for managers.
4. Supervisors will become the key links in the program as long as the employees are not performing and the managers have the option of referring the workers to an in-house coordinator for help.
5. The latter could be an occupational physician, nurse, or psychiatrist. It then is determined whether a corrective component is needed for any diagnosed performance deficiencies.
6. Training may sensitize supervisors to stress disorder signals but they certainly are not responsible for diagnosing alcoholism or drug abuse problems or any deep-seated emotional disorders. The supervisors actually are the initial links in determining

whether the individuals are performing at optimum levels and what barriers are preventing them from performing effectively.
7. The contract should make clear that the supervisors' job is not to "psychologize."

With this contract between individual and organization, the elements of an employee assistance program are spelled out as follows:

1. A policy statement should outline the elements of the performance contract, specifically identifying the view that many performance problems are due to factors out of the individuals' control, that the organization will not accept continued poor work and absenteeism, but that it will help employees obtain assistance with the causal problems.
2. In institutions with labor organizations, union representatives should be integrated into the philosophy of assistance to troubled employees and should endorse the program and its benefits to workers.
3. Definite work performance standards should be defined and assessed clearly by supervisors and managers; there also should be adequate training performance assessment. Managers must be willing to record unsatisfactory performances and bring them to employees' attention.
4. Supervisors and employees should recognize that performance problems will have a range of causes that may include alcoholism, emotional and physical disorders, family conflicts, marital and/or vocational problems, financial difficulties, etc. Performance may be affected by any one of these factors or combinations of them.
5. A diagnostic, referral, and intake resource should be established. It should be professionally competent to sort the primary and secondary problem mix and to make a definitive and accurate referral to the appropriate help-providing agency.
6. A Comprehensive Health Model treatment system that can respond to the diagnosed problem should be available. This system may be a single agency or a combination of community treatment resources.
7. Assurance benefits available to workers should be aligned so that treatment may be covered for all the disorders included in the employee assistance program system. Alcoholism, emotional disorders, and the treatment to be provided for these must be covered specifically.

8. A system of evaluation to gauge the impact of an employee assistance program and its effectiveness should be set up. Included in a minimum assessment profile would be absenteeism, performance change data, and benefits usage data for referred employees. Information on treatment outcomes also should be obtained. This allows the organization to monitor the employee assistance program for its contribution to the goals of improving performance and reducing absenteeism and to assess the degree of effectiveness of the treatment system (McGaffey, 1978, p. 28).

These programs have provided much data on individuals referred into the program. The employees averaged about one year of treatment for conditions including alcoholism and emotional disorders. The results led to associated changes of a positive nature in work performance as measured by supervisors' ratings and other assessment means. The alcoholics who received treatment through these types of programs were considered to be satisfactory or improved in their work performance measures for 85 percent of the treated cases. Understanding the nature of employee alcoholism programs is essential for both the health care organization and affected employee. Therefore, these efforts need to be formalized and legitimized.

EMPLOYEE ALCOHOLISM PROGRAMS

The BNA study previously referred to suggested several important approaches that organizations should use in developing counselling policies and programs for employees with problems. These include:

- Policy statements or written suggestions and lists of outside referral sources are the most common techniques for helping supervisors deal with troubled employees. Training sessions to assist supervisors are conducted in approximately one-fourth of the organizations responding, somewhat more frequently for alcoholism than for drug abuse, emotional illness, or personal problems.
- Supervisory consultation and referral to an outside agency is the most common approach and nearly half of the organizations noted that this action was recorded on the employees' personnel records.
- Some type of in-house counselling, usually informal, is provided by nearly half of the organizations that respond to employees'

problems involving alcoholism, emotional illness, or personal crisis.

- Less than half of the respondents developed any type of organizational program to alert employees to problems associated with alcohol. Educational programs focusing on drug abuse and emotional or family problems were even more uncommon.
- The overwhelming majority of companies rated the effectiveness of their current programs or methods for dealing with troubled employees as only fair or poor (BNA, 1978, p. 1).

This last point should not be considered global evidence of failure. Interestingly, organizations with the greatest success in identifying alcoholics early and motivating them to accept treatment often have these processes and procedures in common:

- These organizations consistently applied disciplinary procedures for declining work performance.
- Line management held supervisors responsible for observing employees' work behavior patterns and for taking consistent steps to correct deteriorating performance.
- Supervisors avoided discussion of drinking problems and focused on work performance unless intoxication was observed on the job.
- A management-union alliance was considered unusually good in dealing with the behavioral-medical problems.
- Personnel and work record systems were designed to be used as early warning systems.
- Employees who had recovered from alcoholism played a significant role in small informal employee groups.
- One or more staff or line managers had definite responsibility for observing personnel practices and reporting to top management when any supervisor neglected to follow approved·personnel procedures (*Business Week,* 1968).

There are several key elements in an employee alcoholism program that must be considered in the quest to assist the individuals experiencing difficulties and, at the same time, to attempt to make the health care institution less stressful and more effective. The organization should:

- provide for a third party payment for the treatment of alcoholic employees in the group health insurance policies

- have a policy for dealing specifically with alcoholism alone, a policy that should be known to all employees and should delineate clearly a positive procedure aimed at helping alcoholics recover
- develop specific procedures for handling and referring employees experiencing performance problems
- establish a definite referral system and procedures with alcoholism diagnostic facilities and identify personnel who possess qualifications needed to assure that alcoholics will be referred to the proper rehabilitative agency
- train managers at all levels so they will be able to understand the process of identifying alcoholic employees and what the alcoholism policy and procedures are
- create an educational component designed to inform employees about contemporary approaches to alcoholism that includes a full description of the institution's policy
- provide an effective medical recordkeeping system that assures confidentiality to the individual employee while furnishing evidence of the operation's effectiveness through statistics and reports necessary to identify what has occurred developmentally with regard to the effectiveness of this program
- compare data in these reports with results of other operating programs so that meaningful measures of their relative worth can be completed and their cost effectiveness evaluated

All of this detail is essential because in most organizations, alcoholic employees are handled in a similar way to the family that keeps the relative with a mental disorder safely locked in the attic.

Alcoholism occurs at different socioeconomic levels in society and in organizations. Executives and nonexecutives often are treated in the same way. It is not considered efficient to have two separate programs with two standards since the disease manifests itself in a similar fashion in all individuals. The individual's spouse may be an alcoholic, too. Rehabilitation must be redirected within the family unit, or the managers suffering from this problem as a result of other stressors will not be supported adequately and the therapy and rehabilitation will be ineffective.

It is not uncommon to discover some behavioral regressions, but this does not indicate that the individuals' rehabilitation is unsuccessful. It is only after the individuals admit that alcoholism is the major cause of performance and personal problems that any success can be achieved through rehabilitation. The institution must be involved personally, as previously described; this can be demonstrated by an employee alcoholism program's being legitimized by a formal policy statement.

In actual practice, these programs usually work when the designated personal assistance office is contacted by the affected employee's manager. This occurs when the employee is beginning to demonstrate poor performance under normal management systems. After the manager has discussed the worker and apparent performance problems with a counsellor from the employee alcoholism program, a performance evaluation is completed along with any other documentation necessary to support the manager's initial diagnosis.

At this point, a staff member of the employee alcoholism program and the manager discuss the strategy of just how to deal with the employee. An interview is recommended for the employee with a program staff member who outlines its operation. This primary process is handled confidentially. The employee also is informed that if the individual does not keep the interview date and at the same time the job performance does not improve, disciplinary action will follow. This direct confrontative act seems to be a motivator to direct the employee into this crucial, initial phase. The manager then is informed that the employee actually is attending the program. This usually makes it much easier for the manager to attempt to diagram the worker's progress with the focus always upon performance to determine whether or not any remissions have occurred.

The responsibility for change always rests with the individual, and performance is the only objective method of evaluating the worker's effectiveness. Throughout the program, the individual is considered to be deviating from the norms of performance, and not of behavior. If the employee aborts the program at any advanced stage and performance problems persist, the individual is warned that dismissal may be the next step. Similarly, if the worker blatantly refuses to cooperate with the manager and the personal assistance program, dismissal must ensue. This also happens to be a therapeutically sound procedure for both the employee and the manager.

Once the individual who was performing poorly and diagnosed is encouraged to participate in a psychotherapeutic program, the person usually responds well since the psychotherapy reduces the incidence of greater emotional and physiological disorders. These programs are effective as stress control mechanisms because intervention is based on work performance and not on changes in personal habits. In these programs, individuals are confronted regarding their performance problems before they lose their jobs. This gives them the option of deciding unilaterally whether they want to be fired or turn themselves around. Most of them are not interested in being unemployed since, as stated previously, Freud found that individuals were connected to their jobs as a direct link to reality. Losing a job is a tremendously stressful event and increases the problem.

These programs must include considerations of multiple factors that produce stress. Treatment usually is focused on dealing with family conflicts, financial problems, emotional problems, and psychological disorder. This milieu and network of stimuli and services can be directed to dealing with a multiple number of stressors, with their identification and treatment being important in the initial stages. There are needs for multiple stress prevention programs designed for organizations that should include workshops not only for dealing with effective functioning on the job, but also relating to the family, marriage dynamics, and other significant factors that are stress producing.

The biggest and most difficult problem to overcome is the feeling on the part of managers who refer workers to employee alcoholism programs that these actually are a punishment and not a benefit. When management can deal with this factor, an important issue in coping with stress from a managerial perspective will be resolved. Of course, these efforts are not successful in enough of the cases; in many, the individual does not want to be helped. This is a serious problem since the organization must make a decision as to what it must do now with the nonresponding employee.

The basic question usually asked about discipline and even separation is: "What action would be consistent with the way the company would handle the situation if there were some other chronic illness affecting performance to a similar degree?" (Lavino, 1978, p. 42). If alcoholism is to be treated as a disease, then this is an important position and should be handled in an extremely neutral fashion, as with any other psychophysiological problem affecting an employee.

The national experience indicates that 5 percent of any employed population will present problems of alcohol abuse. If it can be assumed, as an example, that an organization employs 250 individuals at an average annual salary of $10,000, the alcoholic expectancy rate of 5 percent at minimum indicates that 13 individuals will present alcohol abuse problems. These persons will cost the organization $130,000 as a base payroll cost for the "troubled employee" population.

Definable and nondefinable costs to an employer will total 25 percent of the average annual wage of employees not experiencing the alcohol abuse problems. This 25 percent of the $130,000 annual wage being paid to the 13 individuals in the sample organization yields a $33,000 definable and nondefinable cost of alcohol abuse. This cost and problem should lead a health care institution to seek out a program intended to help the employees in treatment for alcohol addiction, since addictive illnesses are part of a large family of related disorders that have a number of characteristics in common.

Failure comes not only from not recognizing alcoholism as an illness but also because there are serious obstacles to the treatment, such as:

- Most alcoholic employees are hidden and protected. The family or the immediate manager usually will try to deal with the problem in their own ineffective way.
- The alcoholic employee denies drinking heavily and has little motivation to seek help.
- The alcoholic employee cannot be forced to seek help.
- There has been a lack of consensus about the cause of this disease so, although the medical profession recognizes there are different types of alcoholism, treatment has developed in a haphazard, empirical fashion.
- There has been professional apathy toward treating alcoholics. This starts at the medical and nursing school level where, even now, courses in this illness are grossly inadequate.
- Alcoholism has been recognized as a disease only recently.
- Hospital facilities have been inadequate to care for and rehabilitate alcoholics.
- Law enforcement agencies and businesses alike generally have taken a punitive attitude toward alcoholics (Hilker, 1977, p. 204).

The city of New York, an employer of more than 300,000 persons, was forced to initiate an Employee Counseling Service (ECS) when it was estimated it had approximately 30,000 workers with alcohol problems, 12,000 with drug-related issues, and 3,000 others in need of mental health services. When the city decided to attack the issue, it already had escalated greatly. The ECS focused on all behavioral-medical problems of troubled employees. Supervisors made referrals—solely on the basis of changed or declining employee job performance—to the therapeutic department empowered to handle that issue.

In 1978, ECS held 4,125 interviews, an average of 16 per day. Of this total, 529 represented new referrals, while the rest were accounted for by follow-ups and by individual and group therapy sessions. Although the program originally was established to help alcoholic employees, by 1978 they accounted for only 17 percent of new referrals. The majority of new referrals (55 percent) were those with other psychiatric or emotional problems. This seems to bear out the view that alcoholism is only a part of a wider spectrum of employee behavioral medical problems and justifies the decision to expand the scope of the service's activities (Rostain, Allan, & Rosenberg, 1980, p. 307). Health care organizations also must deal with employees' drug addiction as well as alcoholism since this is another issue involving the troubled worker. A model human resources counselling program is proposed for this issue.

THE MODEL: HUMAN RESOURCE COUNSELLING

One of the most effective methods for working with employees experiencing difficulty on the job is to develop a human resource counselling program which focuses upon the development of individuals' career paths. If an organization employs a specialist in personnel and/or psychology to deal strictly with the troubled employee—the alcoholic or drug abused employee—then the impact and effectiveness of this objective will not be actualized. This type of pathological effort is quite similar to a "witch hunt." If performance is the focal point of career development then any problem or regression serves as the focal point for serious analysis as to why the individual is fixated in his/her career and not progressing.

The goal of this program is to aid managers in maximizing their career potential through fully exploiting their assets and covering deficits. The philosophy of the Human Resource Counselling Program is a positive one wherein past and present performance and achievements play a dominant role. The program assumes that the managers' self-interest, incorporated with the third party objectivity of their own supervisors and the human resource counsellor, will result in a maximum contribution for the organization and the individual. The ten steps of the program are as follows.

1. The professional (counsellor) completes a history and profile on the troubled employee (counsellee) during the initial interview.

2. Counsellor scans individuals who work with counsellee and also personally observes counsellee's performance on the job.

3. The managerial profile is developed and actually becomes a negotiated document. All differences of opinion between both parties must be discussed and resolved.

4. A formal meeting is arranged to discuss the career assessment and planning program, exploring strengths and weaknesses and making plans for change.

5. Counsellee must make a decision to pursue certain options and directions while counsellor advises the counsellee.

6. Counsellee is required to summarize the attached report. This feedback session is intended to clarify the counsellee's strengths and weaknesses and also affords the opportunity for the counsellee to clarify the report, which separates high potential candidates from those with problems.

7. Further sessions are arranged between both parties and plans are developed to correct any problems highlighted in the report (e.g. declining performance, behavior change, etc.).

8. A confrontation counselling session is arranged to deal with serious personal problems, such as alcoholism and drug abuse, which may or may not have been illuminated in the report.

9. Open discussion session is held with counsellor, counsellee, and supervisor, and an action plan is developed to correct problems and support career assessment and planning program.

10. The following evaluations are completed.
    • Management Diagnoses Profile (See Exhibit 8-1)
    • Managerial Insight Analysis (See Exhibit 8-2)
    • Performance-Behavioral Profile (See Exhibit 8-3)
    • Supervisory Appraisal (See Exhibit 8-4)

The human resource counsellor requests the counsellee, and often troubled employee, to complete the Management Diagnoses Profile (Exhibit 8-1) to ascertain how the individual perceives his/her interests, activities, and goals. This is usually completed prior to the session between the two parties. In addition, the counsellee is also asked to complete the Managerial Insight Analysis Exhibit 8-2) which is a human resource accounting of both psychological and social factors important to the counsellee within the work environment. Both evaluations serve as the individual's own blueprint which will be altered somewhat after the supervisor of the counsellee submits his/her own personal insights about the individual, his performance, and any problems.

Exhibit 8-1 Management Diagnosis Profile:
Human Resource Program

Directions: The purpose of this exercise is to get you to do more in-depth
thinking about your own abilities, interests and aspirations in
preparation for meetings that you will be having with the Human
Resource (Personnel) Department.

1. Describe the 3 or 4 critical "make or break" elements in your present
job (i), and how you are doing (ii).

(i) a) _____   (ii) a) _____

    b) _____   b) _____

    c) _____   c) _____

    d) _____   d) _____

2. Within the next 2 years, what do you see yourself promotable to do?

   _____

   What do you see as your long range career potential?

   _____

3. a) What is your major strength in relationship to those you supervise?

   _____

      Major weakness? _____

   _____

   b) What is your major strength in relationship to your peers?

   _____

      Major weakness? _____

   _____

4. What is your major strength in relationship to your immediate
   supervisor? _____

   _____

   Major weakness? _____

Exhibit 8-2 Managerial Insight Analysis

What do you feel will be your major contribution in the position you currently
occupy?

What do you feel you could contribute most in the position you aspire to?

What do you regard as your most important assets?

What do you regard as your limitations?

What three things in your life provide you the greatest personal satisfaction?

What qualities do you admire most in subordinates?

What qualities do you admire most in associates?

What adjectives do your friends use to describe you?

For what are you most often complimented?

For what are you most often criticized?

Please briefly state:
  Three things you want most in life:

  Three things you want most in your job:

DATE_____ NAME_____

The supervisor of the troubled employee completes the Performance-Behavior Profile (Exhibit 8-3) and describes the counsellee's personal characteristics, problem solving ability, work capacity, attitudes, and personal relationships. At this juncture both strengths and weaknesses are highlighted and can be contrasted with the Management Diagnoses Profile and the Managerial Insight Analysis, previously completed by the counsellee. In addition, a Supervisory Appraisal (Exhibit 8-4) is also completed to yield a complete picture of the individual as seen by the supervisor.

Now that both sides of the situation are on record, an open discussion and confrontation can take place between the human resource counsellor, the supervisor of the counsellee, and the troubled employee (counsellee) to develop an action plan intended to support his career development and correct any problems which may be thwarting that plan. *At no time is the accusation of alcohol or drug abuse brought up. Only the performance criteria and progress are discussed.* Quite often the counsellee openly discusses his alcohol or drug problem as being the roadblock to a more effective performance. Since declining performance cannot be rationalized by the counsellee as fantasy, a reasonable reason must be given to explain problems and career arrest. This reason will eventually emerge in this supportive, yet objectively-structured climate. Troubled individuals react more favorably to structure than to insincere repressed support on the part of an unenlightened management.

If the employee aborts the program at any advanced stage and performance problems continue to surface, then the employee is usually informed that dismissal is the next step. If the individual blatantly refuses to accept this interview, then dismissal procedures are initiated. The responsibility for change always rests with the individual, and performance is the only objective method of evaluating the individual's effectiveness.

Exhibit 8-3 Performance Behavior Profile

Manager's name _____ Date_____ Evaluator_____

Position_____ Company_____

Personal Characteristics & Disposition

Put "M" by Five Most Accurate.
Put "L" by Five Least Accurate.

Reasons:

1. Self-confidence _____ _____
2. Self-reliance _____ _____
3. Persistence _____ _____
4. Forcefulness _____ _____
5. Enthusiasm _____ _____
6. Optimism _____ _____
7. Adaptability _____ _____
8. Calm _____ _____
9. Cautious _____ _____
10. Cheerful _____ _____
11. Conforming _____ _____
12. Dependable _____ _____
13. Energetic _____ _____
14. Easily aroused emotionally _____ _____
15. Feels emotions without showing them _____ _____
16. Hard Boiled _____ _____
17. Impatient _____ _____
18. Impulsive _____ _____
19. Individualistic _____ _____
20. Inhibited _____ _____
21. Inclined to be cynical _____ _____
22. Imaginative _____ _____
23. Limited Interests _____ _____
24. Mature _____ _____
25. Often feels lonely _____ _____
26. Over-sensitive _____ _____
27. Quick-tempered _____ _____

Exhibit 8-3 continued

Problem Solving Ability

Put "M" by Three Most Accurate.
Put "L" by Three Least Accurate.
Reasons:

1. Exceptional high level of intelligence _____ _____
2. States ideas clearly _____ _____
3. Ability to solve problems quickly _____ _____
4. Ability to develop solutions showing good judgment _____ _____
5. Persuasive ability _____ _____
6. Creativeness _____ _____
7. Analytical ability _____ _____
8. Decisive _____ _____
9. Quick _____ _____
10. Resourceful _____ _____

Work Capacities & Attitudes

Put "M" by Four Most Accurate.
Put "L" by Four Least Accurate.

1. Amount of time he/she is willing to spend on the job _____ _____
2. Amount of money he/she wants _____ _____
3. Ability to organize his/her work _____ _____
4. Self-starter _____ _____
5. Avoids responsibility _____ _____
6. Ambitious _____ _____
7. Conscientious _____ _____
8. Competitive Spirit _____ _____
9. Diplomatic _____ _____
10. Enjoys hard work _____ _____
11. Finds it difficult to concentrate _____ _____
12. Feels criticism too much _____ _____
13. Good self-expression _____ _____

14. Has initiative _____ _____
15. Indecisive _____ _____
16. Likes responsibility _____ _____
17. Lacks initiative _____ _____
18. Methodical _____ _____
19. Original _____ _____
20. Often Procrastinates _____ _____
21. Poor in leadership _____ _____
22. Pre-occupied _____ _____
23. Reliable _____ _____
24. Resistant _____ _____

Relations with People

Put "M" by Three Most Accurate.
Put "L" by Three Least Accurate.
Reasons:

1. Ease in establishing contact _____ _____
2. Pleasant _____ _____
3. Takes the lead in conversation _____ _____
4. Service-minded _____ _____
5. Cooperative _____ _____
6. Easily annoyed _____ _____
7. Excitable _____ _____
8. Easy going _____ _____
9. Good listener _____ _____
10. Good sense of humor _____ _____
11. Good natured _____ _____
12. Generally liked by others _____ _____
13. Good team worker _____ _____
14. Loyal _____ _____
15. Likes to lead and supervise others _____ _____
16. Reserved _____ _____
17. Retiring _____ _____
18. Socially skilled _____ _____

Throughout the program, the individual is considered to be deviating from the norms of performance and not behavior. If the individual will not cooperate with the manager and the human resource counsellor, then disciplinary action is the next logical step. This happens to be a therapeutically sound procedure for both the affected employee and the manager.

It is not uncommon to discover some behavioral regressions occurring but this does not indicate that the individual's rehabilitation is unsuccessful. It is only after the individual admits that alcoholism and/or drugs is the major cause of performance and personal problems that any success can be achieved via rehabilitation. The organization must be personally involved, and this can be demonstrated by a human resource counselling program legitimized by a formal policy statement and a concerned management

DRUGS AND DRUG-RELATED PROBLEMS

Drug abuse and addiction are considered to be manifestations of psychiatric illness since they indicate disordered mental functioning. They may take any one of essentially three forms:

1. the abuse of drugs and medications commonly purchased, such as barbiturates and antihistamines
2. the misuse of prescribed drugs by overuse
3. the illegal use of mind-altering drugs such as heroin and marijuana

Most of the drugs considered in this part of the chapter have legitimate uses in coping with many physical and mental disorders so long as there is a strict adherence to the regimen prescribed by the physician. However, some physicians' prescribing habits for these drugs are under legal and ethical criticism. Most of these drugs can be habit forming and dangerous. Dependency can result, the functioning of the mind can be affected, and mental disorders may ensue. Physiological consequences including hepatitis, bacterial infections, and skin diseases, may develop. Death can result from drug abuse.

While alcohol is the most abused drug, managers will come into contact with other problems, and the most effective way to approach them is with the knowledge and understanding of what drugs are and what they do. In this way there will be less panic, fear, and hostility when a drug situation arises. Individuals in a health care institution who are involved with drugs should be looked upon in the same way as are

Exhibit 8-4 Supervisor's Appraisal

	I am his/her	self___, sup.___, sub.___, peer___, functional___
Manager's name		

a) Technical Skills	Strength	Weakness	CA*	N/A	Comment
Technical knowledge					
Ability to apply technical information					
b) Decision Making Skills					
Problem solving					
Creativity					
Understanding complex technical problems					
c) Receiving Information Skills					
Interpersonal sensitivity					
Company environment sensitivity					
Listening					
Reading					
d) Expressive Skills					
General:					
Writing					
Formal speaking					
Persuading others					
Group:					
Leading meetings					
Participation in meetings					
Individual:					
Order giving					
Handling disciplinary problems					
e) Process of Management Skills					
Planning					
Control					
Delegating					
Budgeting					
f) Management Development Skills					
Counselling					
Coaching					
Appraisal					

CA*: cannot answer

Exhibit 8-4 continued

g) Select five skills from the preceding profile in which you consider
him/her outstanding.

1) _____

2) _____

3) _____

4) _____

5) _____

h) Next, select the five which he/she needs to improve most greatly
upon.

1) _____

2) _____

3) _____

4) _____

5) _____

those involved with alcohol or other diseases. There are those who use
them and those who abuse them, and this distinction is important for a
rationalistic approach to the problem.

Managers should understand a drug problem will affect more than
merely those involved with illegal drugs since many drugs are legal
and easily obtained by prescription and across the counter. The reactions of many individuals toward drugs and drug users are based not
on facts but on emotions. Many employees can rationalize their personal use of alcohol, sedatives, or even aspirin and yet have a closed
point of view about drugs they do not use.

The drugs with which managers most frequently have to deal fall into six families: opiates, amphetamines, barbiturates, alcohol,
hallucinogens, and marijuana. Employees who abuse drugs have been
found to be those with personal adjustment problems, who are aimless,
lack clear goal direction, or are suffering from alienation and
loneliness. Other characteristics include a mistrust of others, a tendency not to respect authority, or propensities toward self-destruction.
Peer group pressures can affect individuals in need of support. Other
persons who have a high degree of self-esteem and a concept of self-
worth usually are not vulnerable to drug abuse.

Drugs are an important issue in studying organizational stress since many individuals in the institution who are subject to stress use drugs as a coping mechanism, which leads to further problems in a family hierarchy of habit stressors. One reason why drugs have not approached the scope of alcoholism as a problem is that only about a third of drug abusers are employed. Because the problem is a relatively recent one, there is not a great wealth of data on the net effect of drugs in the employment climate. It is evident that drug abuse increases the incidence of absenteeism and accidents, and reduces job performance. Premature death may be the result.

One study (Rush, 1971) found that 44 percent of the drug abusers were factory workers, 35 percent clerical workers, about 10 percent professionals, 5 percent in supervisory positions, and 3 percent occupied managerial and executive level positions. One point that stands out clearly is that drug abuse occurs in professional ranks as well as with managers, executives, and unskilled individuals. A study by the National Industrial Conference Board (Rush, 1971) indicated that 67 percent of organizations responding found drug abuse to be a major problem. However, they did not identify this problem as being one of their own.

Where employers have attempted to take a constructive approach to the problem of drug abuse, they have followed a route similar to that taken in coping with alcoholism, and it need not be repeated here. Once top management has established policy and delegated responsibility, managers are trained to observe unsatisfactory job performance and they then make referrals to the medical department or consultant or wherever appropriate treatment is recommended. Refusal of treatment calls for disciplinary action. Health education on the subject is provided. Furthermore, many employers today will employ addicts if they have undergone treatment and rehabilitation and if they are recommended for employment by a responsible treatment agency (Follmann, 1978, p. 230).

An interesting addition to this procedure can be found in the experience of the Weyerhaeuser Company as an organization with a management policy dealing specifically with drug abuse. Weyerhaeuser identifies addicts on the basis of deteriorated job performance and it educates managers to detect such situations. Treatment then is recommended and there is follow-up on the rehabilitative process. The buying and selling of illicit drugs on company premises is not condoned. It is interesting that known addicts are not denied employment. In 1972, Weyerhaeuser found that 59 percent of its employees used marijuana to some extent, 29 percent used psychedelics, 15 percent took sedatives, and 28 percent used speed.

The extent to which such usage constituted abuse was not known (Follmann, 1978, p. 230).

Drug abuse is only a small aspect of a "chemical age" and involves only the relatively few drugs just mentioned that have become popular as "psychological toys" but that frequently evolve into emotional catastrophes.

Drug abuse is not a problem that can be traced to one chemical agent, one set of social conditions, or one particular psychological type. It is unbounded by time and circumstance and only slightly affected by knowledge. In fact, if there is a common thread woven throughout the entire history of drug abuse, it is ignorance. The one thing that distinguishes alcohol from most other dangerous drugs is the fact that its moderate use is socially acceptable and disguised. That makes it neither less nor more dangerous, but it adds a broader scope to the problem of its abuse. The same problems do not exist with other drugs that are abused and that need explanation. Brief descriptions of these drugs, reactions to them, and symptoms to help managers' understanding of them follow.

Psychoactive Chemicals

Psychoactive drugs are intended to alter individuals' moods and perceptions of reality and appear now to be a permanent part of society. The majority of these drugs are useful, indeed often indispensable, in alleviating physical and mental disease and were developed for those positive purposes. Some drugs, such as alcohol, are accepted and institutionalized by society as pleasure-giving mild sedatives. A few, such as heroin and LSD, are aberrations that appear to represent nothing but problems for users and organizations that employ such individuals. It appears that the psychoactive drugs are permanent fixtures because some are necessary, and they are extremely difficult to eliminate socially, economically, and legally.

Narcotics

Narcotics technically are opiates that depress the central nervous system, causing stupor and insensibility. Opium in its natural form has been used for thousands of years. In addition, synthetic opiates, such as methadone, have been formulated for use in drug abuse therapy. Narcotics have wide though not casual use in medicine. Medical use of morphine and other opiates is controlled tightly and the likelihood that an individual will become dependent upon these accidentally is extremely small. Some narcotics manufactured for medical purposes do find their way into the illegal drug market, but this is a minor source for abusers. Narcotics abuse primarily involves heroin, a substance that more than any other has come to symbolize the drug problem in North America.

Heroin is not used now in medicine in the United States. It is particularly dangerous because it quickly can create a physical and psychological dependence. Although some people use heroin periodically without getting "hooked," experimenting with the drug is extremely risky and the chance of addiction is high. Withdrawal from heroin can be an agonizing experience, but it rarely is life threatening. Actually, in some cases, the physical dependence can be overcome more quickly and with less risk and pain than withdrawal from heavy use of alcohol and some other drugs. The physiological dependence remains, however, and the psychological dependence on heroin seems to be deeper than that associated with the abuse of any other drug.

Heroin may enslave users so thoroughly that they become totally occupied with obtaining their next dosage. Few legitimate occupations produce enough income to support the habit; therefore, many heroin addicts are forced to turn to antisocial methods of getting money to make their buys. This has a major effect on an organization that employs these individuals because it actually may become a source for this subversive, additional funding. The drug is available only from illegal sources and control over quality and potency is lacking. By the time it reaches the street, the drug usually is diluted to less than 10 percent of its pure strength. Heroin usually is taken intravenously and the users run a high risk of hepatitis from infected needles. Other drugs in this area of concern are Demerol, morphine, and cocaine. The user can inhale, inject, or take these drugs by pill.

While opiates are physically addicting, this does not mean that everyone who takes them will become addicted immediately. Some who experiment with them escape addiction. However, the extreme potential of addiction makes such experimentation very risky. Death occurs through overdoses and dirty needles. Although there will be some heroin addicts in organizations, these will be fewer than users of other drugs because of the increased expense. Opiates give temporary escape to those who feel insecure and frightened and who believe they lack any opportunity to change their environment. These drugs give users a very warm, comfortable feeling so that their problems seem to vanish. Narcotics are known to relieve physical pain but users also find they have the potential to relieve mental pain only initially before the secondary problems begin.

Barbiturates

Barbiturates are depressants with wide medical use that, when abused, are even more dangerous than heroin. Used under strict medical supervision, barbiturates are safe and effective in sedating patients, relieving anxiety, and controlling high blood pressure, epilepsy, and chemically induced convulsions. The physical effect of the drugs is to depress the central nervous system and the psychological effect is similar to that of alcohol. When abused, they are potentially lethal, and death can result either from overdoses or unsupervised withdrawal.

Barbiturates are the drugs most often associated with accidental poisoning and suicide. What makes them so dangerous is that they can distort judgment, which can lead to an overdose because individuals may not remember how many pills they have taken. When used in combination with alcohol, the danger is compounded. Once a pattern of abuse develops, a physical and psychological dependence occurs, just as with heroin. As more of the drug is used, a tolerance develops, requiring greater amounts to produce the desired effect but further increasing the danger of an overdose.

Barbiturate abusers resemble persons intoxicated from alcohol. Their speech is slurred, they lose physical coordination, they frequently injure themselves, and they are emotionally erratic. Unlike opiate ad dicts, barbiturate users do not want to escape their world—they just want to make it more tolerable. Many users indicate that they take barbiturates only to calm their nerves. However, once they stop, their nervousness increases, creating a need to take more in order to relax but without their realizing that the nervousness is their bodies' reaction to the absence of the drug. Addiction to barbiturates often is easy to camouflage because of their accessibility and general acceptance by society.

Tranquilizers are in the same category as barbiturates. They are depressants possessing a number of legitimate medical uses. They are used to counter psychotic conditions, to treat mild or emotional upsets, as muscle relaxants, and as sedative-hypnotics, of which methaqualone is the most prevalent among younger adults. High chronic use can create a barbiturate-like dependence with similar dangers and deaths resulting from methaqualone abuse.

Amphetamines

Amphetamines often are referred to as "uppers" because they stimulate the central nervous system and are used medically for fatigue, certain types of mental depression, and sometimes obesity. Outside of medicine, they frequently are used by long-distance truck drivers attempting to stay awake, by students cramming for exams, by athletes trying to get "up" for a big game, or by housewives who need a little more "pep." Some, but not all, of the unprescribed uses of amphetamines lead to abuse, and there always is a danger that dependency can develop. One of the more common stimulants abused is methamphetamine, which is called "speed." This drug is injected into a vein, but death rarely results from abuse. However, acute psychotic episodes involving hyperactivity, paranoia, and hallucinations can result.

The use of amphetamines increases individuals' ability to work and makes them feel stronger and more powerful. They do reduce individuals' need for sleep and speed up all bodily functions. The drug has been used by individuals to avoid depression. With an increased new energy level, they frequently organize projects and make plans they probably never will execute. When the effects of the drug wear off, users are fatigued and usually feel "down." The extent of this "letdown" creates a greater depression and a need for other methods of coping that may come in the form of other drug dependencies.

Hallucinogens

LSD (full name lysergic acid diethylamide), commonly referred to as acid, became a serious drug abuse problem in the middle 1960s, attracting much public attention. Individuals involved with this drug are said to be taking a "trip" in which they leave a reality situation and move on to a psychedelic fantasy.

LSD is the best known of hallucinogenic drugs that include mescaline and "angel dust." These drugs severely distort reality and induce a mystical state, frequently with visual hallucinations in the form of changing colors in geometric patterns.

Although hallucinogenic drugs do not create physical dependency in the user, there is some dispute about psychological dependence, which may be quite dangerous. The bizarre mental effects of LSD have resulted in a number of deaths when users have taken falls from heights or have died in other accidents. Suicide is another danger, with individuals experiencing severe psychotic flashbacks and turning their anger on the object they like least—themselves. These drugs often are used in combination with others for more bizarre effects.

The increased sensory perception the drug produces is stimulating. The drug breaks down users' defenses and normal roles while permitting them to see the unconscious. Danger arises, of course, when this occurs so rapidly, particularly with those having strong defenses and playing many roles.

Marijuana

Marijuana is the most widely used and possibly the most controversial drug under discussion. It has been roughly estimated that approximately 20 percent of the population of North America has used this drug at some time. The current thinking is that not enough is known about the long-term effects of this drug and therefore it is difficult to decide whether to accept or reject it.

Marijuana comes from the cannabis plant, which grows wild in many parts of the world, and is known also as pot or grass or dope. Once the specialty of artistically inclined professionals, this drug is now widely used. It sometimes is classified as a hallucinogen. It is an intoxicant, and its effect on the user is similar to that of alcohol or other hallucinogens. It creates euphoria and a dreamlike sense of well-being. Perception may be distorted and accidents may result. Research is being conducted on the long-term use of this drug and its effect upon humans' genetic chemistry.

The facts presented here are only a few of the major points regarding marijuana and other drugs. It is hoped that they can serve as an introduction to these drugs as potential and even real problems in the health care organization. Managers who suspect employees of using drugs should not approach the problem with fear or with immediate condemnation of the user. It is helpful to determine whether the employees are experimenting with or using or abusing the drug. The managers should approach the workers with a desire to be understanding and helpful and should make referrals to help them change their drug behavior if this is the route the organization wants to follow.

The programs for rehabilitation are the same as for alcohol. It is extremely difficult to determine the degree of success in dealing with drug abuse cases. The drug programs are new and are succeeding in only varying degrees. Administrators must assume a portion of the responsibility for dealing effectively with this problem, which may be related directly to the management of stress. For organizations to deal effectively with the stress-induced problems of drugs, alcohol, and emotional disorders, formal programs need to be established in a manner similar to the previously described employee alcoholism programs. The use of the organizational physician and nurse as a support system is a solid beginning.

HELP! IS THERE A DOCTOR IN THE HOUSE?

These alcoholic, drug, and emotional problems may bring about the need for an organizational physician who can deal with those affected by the stress of change and help individuals cope in a more positive manner. A gradually developing role for the physician is that of consultant to the organization. The aim is to help identify organizational conflicts, the resolution of which can improve the well-being of employees, reduce the level of stress, and prevent casualties. By acting as a consultant, the physician can help, albeit indirectly, many more individuals than by remaining a specialist who deals only with the victims of change.

Managers, believing their difficulties as due to subordinates who are suffering from symptoms of stress and who therefore are a medical problem, may only want advice from the doctor on how to cope with these employees or seek relief by transferring responsibility directly to the physician. However, the physician, on the basis of knowledge of the organization, its structure, and its administration may feel duty-bound to call attention to difficulties in areas that might be contributing to the symptoms of stress. Thus, without realizing it, manager and physicians have conflicting basic aims and so can quickly lose patience with one another (Brook, 1977, p. 98).

Managers may be concerned with overcoming the anxieties of the individuals they are supervising and the frustrations, uncertainties, and feelings of helplessness that they personally experience that may be the result of the change effort. The difficulty for the physician is how to cope with both the distress of the supervisor and the uncertainties and anxieties that the supervisor may illuminate in the physician. The relationship between the physicians and the managers is intensified by the anxieties of the workplace. As a result, their mutual concerns and their own inadequacies may become entangled and create a breakdown in a potentially valuable working relationship. While responsibility for decision making involving change is the managers', it is only when conflict in the physician/supervisor relationship is resolved that the doctor's assistance can be sought out and be valuable to the managers, who need all the help they can get. Personal incompatibility between the physician and the managers may be a problem but it usually can be worked out since both parties are interested in establishing a positive relationship pattern and successful performance.

A collaborative system must be developed between the physician, the psychiatrist in an organization, the manager, and the individual client. There are many systems of collaboration. Some involve the psychiatrist as a true member of the occupational health team even if on a limited consultative arrangement. In addition, a number of industrial physicians and psychiatrists can get together in small groups to study problems creating stress that may be multidisciplinary and affecting the organization's management, personnel, and mission— paramount factors in health care organizations experiencing change, conflicts, and stress.

Only recently have psychiatrists and organizations agreed to work with each other. Before the enlightened 70s there were few connectors, but now all-encompassing emotional problems serve as necessary links. Psychiatric clinicians are hired in industry on a part-time basis as consultants to high-level executives experiencing depression, alcohol dependency, deterioration of job performance, and other problems significant to the effectiveness of the organization. Several interrelated problems that occur in organizations affect the individual in need of psychiatric consultation:

- Intrapsychic: loss of self-esteem, hunger, and need for sedation.
- Interpersonal: regressive demands for emotional supplies.
- Work group: role expectation, attitudes toward failure to perform, morale, and esprit.
- Family: the role as spouse, parent, the family's response to withdrawal, and alcohol-related problems.
- Corporation: policy and unofficial approaches to poor work performance, and intervention by management, personnel, and medical department.
- Community: resources for treatment, including Alcoholics Anonymous, outpatient and inpatient psychiatric services, and attitudes toward drug abuse (Robbins, 1977, p. 109).

It appears that an effective method of reducing the prevalence and incidence of these health problems is to alter the environment in the institution and remove conditions that create stress. Initial prevention of psychiatric illness requires the involvement of management, the community, and the psychiatrist.

OCCUPATIONAL NURSING AND SUPPORT SYSTEMS

Nursing is a profession, process, and organic system whose objective is to give direct service to persons under stress relative to their basic human needs and provides emotional and physical support for these individuals and their well-being. In this case, needs are defined as the requirements of individuals who become patients of a nurse that, when supplied, will reduce immediate attention and relieve distress or improve their basic sense of adequacy and well-being. The services are provided by many health care organizations seeking some relief from these distressing problems.

A nurse is aware of the destructive nature of stress, which is not always recognized and identified by the patient. This comes about from the patient's persistent anger, fear, and frustration or free-floating anxiety. These stresses threaten the health and well-being of the patient and the nurse, who usually is attempting to identify the symptomatology and to deal with some of the stress reduction and coping mechanisms. Each crisis an individual encounters is precipitated by a hazardous event, is followed by a period of acute psychological upset, and ends in resolution. The period of upset is characterized by feelings of anxiety, fear, guilt, or shame along with some disorganization of function. A crisis is resolved when the individual establishes a new pattern of coping with the situation. The new pattern would be at the same level of functioning as the individual's precrisis state, but may be at a lower level.

The organizational nurse has many opportunities to work with numerous patients who are experiencing stress. The industrial-organizational environment lends itself to various conditions that constantly cause anxiety and frustration. There is constant work stress where employees not only deal with supervisor and peer friction but also face a number of critical possibilities: losing a job and financial security, losing a coveted position and prestige, being forced to accept a job that is less demanding but more demeaning, and undergoing the uncertainty of fulfillment of short-term and long-term goals. Concurrently, they also are coping with such factors as illness or death in the family, marital problems, personal illness, destruction or loss of home, reversal of an expected gain, or some other life stress. To add even more frustration, there is the possibility of traumatic injuries' occurring on the job that may lead to permanent impairment or short-term or long-term disability (Baughn, 1976, p. 16).

The organizational nurse has the rare opportunity of being influential in assisting individuals during times of stress. Successful intervention may help the individuals reestablish their prior level of functioning and reduce their increased levels of tension and anxiety that, if unchecked, lead to a state of crisis and stress. The process of intervention as initiated by the occupational nurse includes assessment of the individuals and their unique problems and planning a therapeutic program. Crisis resolution and crisis preplanning may be prescribed as well. This usually occurs when a nurse suspects that a patient is either approaching a crisis or is being deeply involved in stress and overwhelmed by it.

When nurses assess the situation using their observational and interviewing skills, they usually look for physical signs of increased anxiety and tension or of indications the individual is experiencing psychosomatic disorders that are creating counterproductive behavior and organizational inefficiency. After observing or identifying those factors through information collection, the nurses can assess the situation further and then develop a strategy for intervention.

The reduction of tension and the development of a reality focus is very significant in this intervention process. One of the component parts of any successful intervention is the privacy afforded the patient and the opportunity for emotional ventilation. Intervention methods the nurse can use include the encouragement of adaptive behavior, a support system, manipulating the environment for much more positive results, and the exploration of previous and present mechanisms for coping. In addition, referral may be appropriate. Managers and nurses must be aware of the fact that these patients seek help because of multiple problems that become compounded, brought about by the effects of stress when they are unable to cope any longer with this mechanism. They seek help because they are in pain and in need of some supportive device to reduce the crisis and its ensuing stress. Occupational nurses do attempt to develop support systems for their clients seeking relief from problems and stress.

Nursing is a caring process, and occupational health nursing deals with the net effects of all occupational stressors upon individuals. One of the problems in occupational nursing is the potential of nurses' overinvolvement in developing emotional support systems. This interferes with the individuals' basic development of their own support systems by giving too much nourishment, direction, and support to those in need of coping at their own comfort level.

Occupational health nurses are involved in prevention and control of the destructive effects of work stresses. They assume independent roles in programs and implementation and are involved in actually working with individuals in the organization to deal with problems that affect their emotional—physiological health and productivity. More of these nurses also are involved in studying the work environment since its health hazards are key factors in certain problems. These nurses coordinate their activities with those of the physician and psychiatrist by collecting data about the demands of the job and stressors and by providing follow-up care. Some industrial organizations committed to this approach even go so far as to provide home nursing visits for individuals who have been severely affected.

In areas of mental health, occupational nurses are trained more heavily than ever before in identifying and counselling alcohol and drug abuse cases and in developing referral networks for these individuals. Occupational nurses are extremely visible in the organization and generally are thought of as the health care contact for employees under stress. Frequently, they will initiate activity through the personnel function when they perceive that their clients are in trouble. Nurses also have firsthand knowledge of individuals and their cases because of other health problems that may have arisen. Nurses can coordinate programs for employees who are in treatment for related emotional disorders, working in conjunction with the psychiatrist and occupational health physicians because of common interests and orientation.

Nurses can provide support for the patient, the supervisor, and the occupational physician without becoming caught in the middle. They may become aware of potential employee relations problems because of the dynamics experienced in dealing with managers and personnel who may be under stress and who at the same time ventilate their frustrations to the nurse. This provides a diagnostic intervention that will benefit the troubled employee, the manager, and the organization. Nursing success will depend upon organizational policy and relationships with supervision.

Nursing actually is a process in which substantial specialized knowledge derived from the biological, physical, and behavioral sciences is applied to the care, treatment, counsel, and health teaching of persons who are experiencing changes in the normal health processes. It is applied also to those who require assistance in the maintenance of health or in the management of illness, injury, or infirmity, or in the achievement of a dignified death; and such additional acts as are recognized by the nursing profession as proper to be performed by a registered nurse. This role definition was developed by the American Nurses' Association and Model Nurse Practice Act and was published in the *American Journal of Nursing* in January of 1977 (Klutas, p. 104).

The report of a Department of Health, Education, and Welfare committee (1972) on extending the scope of practice further defined the broader functions of the profession to state that the qualified nurse will:

1.   Obtain and record a health and development history and make a critical evaluation of such records.

2.   Perform basic physical and psychological examinations and interpret the data into required nursing action.

3.   Discriminate between what is normal and abnormal with regard to physical and psychological examinations.

4.   Make decisions about treatment in collaboration with physicians.

5.   Initiate actions and treatment within the range of acceptable collaboration by medical and nursing personnel—such as adjusting medication, ordering and interpreting laboratory tests.

What does the occupational health nurse need to meet the demands for quality and health care of workers, so as to be ready to help them cope with the myriad of job stresses they face? It appears that the acquisition of "substantial specialized knowledge" in the following critical areas enhances the occupational nurse in dealing with organizational-individual problems:

- toxicology
- industrial hygiene
- occupational diseases
- epidemiology
- health evaluation and assessment
- emergency care
- health teaching
- safety
- business and personnel management
- interpersonal relations
- communication skills
- labor principles and practices
- legal and regulatory aspects of occupational health
- program planning, evaluation, and reporting
- nursing administration

Nurses need knowledge and competency in these and other areas whether they work in a large or small industry, and whether in an office or chemical industry (Klutas, 1977, p. 105).

SOME PROBLEMS OF HELPING

Occupational nurses are affected by certain stressors in their own occupation, such as being isolated, being separated from peers, and feeling abandoned and ignored. They also suffer the anonymity of being on a large staff while being a small piece of the total pattern. They do not have a great deal of opportunity to develop special skills and they still are serving as the extensions of the physician without having the freedom to exercise professional judgment. The frustration of not being trained adequately for their job creates another difficulty and generates in them certain conflicts that they pass on to their clients (the employees), further increasing personal and professional problems of stress for both parties. They are not adequately compensated and their status in the organization is limited. This is fully discussed in Chapter 5, which deals with nurses and their problems.

Nurses have restricted career patterns because they have selected an occupation that seems to have a very low ceiling. They must be attuned to dealing with many complex personal value systems while attempting to appear to be neutral and not exercising judgments regarding the personal life styles of the patients who come to them for assistance. They must control their helping instincts so they do not completely overcontrol the patients when it is the latter who must create some of the changes needed to reduce their stress. Nurses face certain stress in dealing with administrative nonnursing duties. They may experience the conflict of being female in a generally male-dominated organization (or male in a female-dominated career) and suffer conflicts of personal vs. professional time and professionalism.

A question occurs as to how these professional nurses balance and juggle their own lives as individuals who may be spouse to a busy manager and parent to children who are making demands. The helping professions experience this stress as well as their clients but are expected to resolve the conflicts easily and without loss of effectiveness. This unrealistic demand is stressful in itself. Who will nurse and support the occupational nurse?

BIBLIOGRAPHY

Akabas, S.H. Mental health program models: Their role in reducing occupational stress. In *Reducing occupational stress: Proceedings of the National Institute for Occupational Safety and Health,* White Plains, N.Y.: U.S. Department of Health, Education, and Welfare, 1977, 186–195.

American Society of Personnel Administrators–Bureau of National Affairs. *Counseling policies and programs for employees with problems.* Washington, D.C.: Bureau of National Affairs, March 1978, Survey *34,* 1–10.

Baughn, S.L. The role of the nurse in dealing with stress in the industrial setting. *Occupational Health Nurse,* April 1976, *24*(4), 15–16.

Brook, A. The role of the occupational physician: Coping with the stress of change. In *Reducing occupational stress: Proceedings of the National Institute for Occupational Safety and Health,* White Plains, N.Y., May 1977, 93–100.

Business copes with alcoholics. *Business Week,* October 26, 1968.

Department of Health, Education, and Welfare. Extending the Scope of Nursing Practice. A Report of the Secretary's Committee to Study Extended Roles of Nurses. Washington, D.C., 1972.

Filipowicz, C.A. The troubled employee: Whose responsibility? *The Personnel Administrator,* June 1979, *24*(6), 17–22.

Follman, J.F., Jr. *Helping the troubled employee.* New York: AMACOM, American Management Association, 1978, 222, 224, 230.

Furey, E.P. *New York Times.* April 1, 1975.

Goldberg, P. *Executive health.* New York: McGraw Hill Book Co., 1978, 78–79.

Hilker, R.F.J. Alcohol abuse: A model program of prevention. In *Reducing occupational stress: Proceedings of the National Institute for Occupational Safety and Health,* White Plains, N.Y., May 1977, 202–215.

Klutas, E.M. Occupational health nursing and occupational stress. In *Reducing occupational stress: Proceedings of the National Institute for Occupational Safety and Health,* White Plains, N.Y., May 1977, 101–107.

Lavino, J.J., Jr. Personal assistance program. *The Personnel Administrator,* November 1978, *23*(11), 35–43.

McGaffey, T.N. New horizons in organizational stress prevention approaches. *The Personnel Administrator,* November 1978, *23*(11), 26–32.

Pearlin, L.I., & Radabaugh, C.W. The sociological study of a social problem: A reply to Ronan. *American Journal of Sociology,* January 1978, *83*(4), 991–994.

Robbins, D.B. Psychiatric consultation in the world of work. In *Reducing occupational stress: Proceedings of the National Institute for Occupational Safety and Health,* White Plains, N.Y., May 1977, 108–110.

Rostain, H., Allan, P., & Rosenberg, S. New York City's approach to problem-employee counseling. *Personnel Journal,* April 1980, *59*(4), 296–307.

Rush, H. The drug problem in business. *The Conference Board Record,* March 1971.

Schwarz, D.T. Health status assessment: An untapped source of management information. In A. McLean (Ed.), *Occupational stress.* Springfield, Ill.: Charles C. Thomas Publisher, 1974, 80–89.

Work in America, Report of a special task force to the Secretary of Health, Education, and Welfare. Massachusetts Institute of Technology Press, 1972.

Chapter 9

Participation and Enrichment: Quality of Work Life

CONSIDERATIONS FOR THE HEALTH CARE MANAGER

1. A possible solution to alienation involves the use of leaderless work teams. Alienation occurs because of conflicts in values concerning the use and misuse of power. These contradictions create anxiety and stress for managers.
2. Participation seeks to achieve high productivity and a satisfied work force through the involvement of subordinates in the decision-making process.
3. Job enrichment is the redesign of a position to include tasks and activities that promote the psychological involvement of the employee in the work itself. In this process, individuals often can work at their own pace, which can reduce a number of physical and emotional problems.
4. The most effective leadership style is where managers perceive themselves as sharing problems with subordinates as a group and do not try to influence the group to adopt their solutions. They are willing to accept and implement any solution that has the support of the entire group. This style leads to low conflict, low stress, and high goal congruence.

5. Middle level managers lack organizational authority and power, both of which are withheld from them, thus creating uncertainties. Survival becomes contingent upon vague events that cannot be measured, which creates anxiety.

6. Managers experience stress because of a lack of information to carry out a job, conflicting demands made by others, being forced to do things against their better judgment, and because the scope and responsibility of the work are vague.

7. In Scandinavian countries, legislation has been drafted to include physical, psychological, and social factors in its definition of the working environment. As a measure to combat distress, compensation is payable for psychological and/or psychosomatic injuries found in the job environment.

This chapter explores organizational behavior theories and practices used in attempts to manage stress in the health care environment. When examining the managerial stressors, it is common practice to refer to the popular theory of participative management, which has made significant contributions to the administrative process and its effectiveness. The absence of a participative climate can create stressful problems that need managers' solutions. In looking at participative management as a component to managing stress, it is necessary to examine the underpinnings of the participative management process, which actually is *delegation*.

Delegation is not always a completely voluntary act on the managers' part. Managers may feel forced to delegate to subordinates when they are under certain organizational pressures and cannot perform the functions that they are competent to do under normal circumstances. At the same time, the subordinates may have little or no input concerning the acceptability of those new delegated responsibilities that are being dumped into their domain. These individuals may find that they do not have the capability, experience, or authority to achieve these newly delegated objectives. For delegation to be participative, at least in the sense that it stimulates commitment, involvement, and job satisfaction, a particular combination of factors has to exist (Donaldson &

Gowler, 1975, p. 104). Delegation is explored fully in Chapter 12, focusing on the management of time.

PARTICIPATIVE SYSTEMS

A pure participative climate is ideational, thus creating frustration. There are certain incongruencies between the actual organizational powers and the formal powers that become sources of managerial anxiety and stress. This stress usually is experienced in situations where managers believe they cannot carry out their formal duties and obligations, with ambiguity and alienation occurring as a result of these conflicts in delegation. Alienation is an important concern for health care managers. A 1972 study by Richard Walton focused on solutions to worker alienation in a plant that are transferrable to the health care system. One solution suggested using work teams performing without supervisors, with decisions to be based upon employee consensus and with most staff functions assigned to live operators. A total systematic restructuring of the way work was done was needed.

Employee dissatisfaction can be reduced by actions such as the following:

- change in authority and status structures
- redesign of the division of labor
- change in control procedures
- emphasis on career paths
- allocation of economic benefits
- change in the nature of social contacts among workers (Walton, 1972, pp. 70-81).

Managers often find themselves confused, alienated, anxious, and angry. These anxieties stem from the erosion of their powers just described. Managers often find themselves in ambiguous situations where they expect their authority to be supported by the organization and its vast powers. Unfortunately, this does not always happen and the managers begin to experience more anxiety while questioning the need to delegate at all. This can create a climate of alienation that may stem from changes in values concerning the use and misuse of power and of authority. Managers become alienated when they begin to use illegitimate means and an overbearing authoritarian style to implement legitimate organizational objectives.

These contradictions in value systems and organizational commitments create feelings of alienation and anxiety for the managers, who generate greater stress by passing these on to subordinates. The subordinates simply may not want to participate in activities—a decision that may make the managers feel angry, inadequate, guilty, and anxiety ridden when their attempts at encouraging a participative system are not viewed with great enthusiasm by their subordinates.

The traditional pyramidal structure and managerial controls tend to place individuals and departments in constant interdepartmental warfare, where win-lose competition creates polarized stances that tend to get resolved by the superiors' making the decisions, thereby creating dependence on them. This situation has been described in the writings of Chris Argyris (1967, p. 32), who indicates that this conflict is a major element of stress.

If managers actually do believe participation to involve the delegation and/or sharing of their powers, in all likelihood they will believe that it also involves the delegation and/or sharing of their earned rewards as well. These circumstances are likely to arouse in them a sense of loss and deprivation. Consequently, any managers who feel this way are likely to view the prospect of increased participation by others in decision making with resentment or anxiety about the possible loss of status and/or rewards. Moreover, given these reactions, those involved resist the introduction of participative activities or indeed any form of innovation (Donaldson & Gowler, 1975, p. 111).

Executive stress may occur as a result of this implementation of managerial systems such as a participative process. Stress is created by the perceived mismatch between the organization's actual powers and formal powers. This problem becomes accelerated when managers envision participation to be a form of delegation when actually their subordinates realize that the executives' powers are quite limited in the organizational milieu; the false sense of participation management thus projects a source of conflict and stress.

JOB ENRICHMENT

In addition to participative management, health care administrators have another option to use in conjunction with a participative approach that seeks to achieve high productivity and maintain a satisfied work force. Participation seeks to achieve these goals, as noted, through the involvement of subordinates in the decision-making process, presuming that participation will increase satisfaction, stimulate interest, and thus induce high productivity (Lundgren, 1974, p. 337).

Job enrichment is an approach and philosophy intended to increase satisfaction and achieve objectives. Job enrichment is the redesign of work to include tasks and activities that promote the psychological involvement of the employee in the function itself. It includes rearranging tasks and processes, adding new ones, increasing feedback on results and performance, increasing work variety, and increasing the level of contact with other employees.

The need for job enrichment was recognized when such behavioral scientists as Douglas McGregor (1960) and Frederick Herzberg (1966) pointed out that most individuals were more motivated when they were given opportunities to exercise discretion and given more responsibility. McGregor's Theory Y sees humankind as essentially creative beings who will seek responsibility, exercise discretion and self-control, and see achievement as its own reward. According to Herzberg's motivation/hygiene theory, individuals are motivated when they are given opportunities for self-advancement, self-development, achievement, recognition, and promotion arising from an interesting and demanding job.

Although American writers have had more to say about job enrichment than European experts, companies in the latter area probably have experimented more with it (Butteriss & Albrecht, 1979, p. 12). The essential ingredients of job enrichment are:

Methods of Job Enrichment

1. Giving a worker a whole job with an identifiable end product and allowing the individual more freedom to set targets.
2. Redesigning work so that a whole job or an identifiable unit of work is carried out, and so that a person or team is given authority and discretion for that unit of work.
3. Reducing or changing the level of supervision. Supervision becomes supportive, concentrating on advising work groups on how to achieve their targets, rather than on exercising close control. Controls therefore are removed, but the individuals still are accountable for their tasks.
4. Offering discretion over work pace. For instance, in the Saab car assembly plant in Sweden, one assembler can complete one car engine alone in 30 minutes or three can work together and complete the job in 10 minutes, thus allowing choice over work method and pace.
5. Introducing more difficult and exacting jobs and giving more immediate feedback of results. This has a direct application to the health care system., which has used the industrial sector as a model for management.

Rationale for Job Enrichment

1. High wages have led to the need for better use of people; some form of job restructuring can achieve this result.

2. Today's workers often are better educated than their older counterparts, and consequently expect more from the job. If dissatisfied at work, individuals can express this attitude by poor workmanship, absenteeism, and high labor turnover. For these reasons Saab and Volvo in Sweden redesigned their assembly lines, in an attempt to prevent high absenteeism and labor turnover. It is felt, although not yet proved, that better motivated people may result from such operations.

3. Changes in the production line systems of the British car industry, where labor turnover is low, have been undertaken largely for technical reasons such as cutting costs, improving production, increasing flexibility, and enhancing the quality of the product. Job enrichment in this case has been concentrated largely on the individual rather than on the work team.

4. Job enrichment in health care systems has been considered from an economic and control perspective, since cost containment and productivity do link with satisfaction and efficient work design.

Some Benefits

A study of the case histories of organizations that have introduced this system indicates that several advantages accrue:

1. It leads to a multiskilled work force that can do a number of jobs, so there is no real problem if key people are absent.

2. Individuals can work at their own pace; this self-pacing can reduce a number of physical and emotional problems.

3. Because individuals and work teams are semiautonomous and do their own checking and inspection, fewer supervisors are required.

4. This technique leads to a reduction in absenteeism and turnover, although further research is required to see how much job enrichment really is responsible for these changes. Further, an increase in productivity and an improvement in the quality of work usually occur.

Although there are advantages to job enrichment, this technique does engender a number of problems that must be considered before implementing of any such plans.

Some Problems

1. This system highlights the need for good selection and training so that suitable people, who like increased responsibility, are hired and then trained thoroughly.
2. The climate and culture must be right. All levels of management, not merely lower-level workers, must be committed to change or the system will not work. An effective system of communication is essential.
3. Job enrichment is not easy to introduce or execute in operations such as research that usually do not result in a tangible end product in such case, who contributed most to the scheme is difficult to say.
4. Job enrichment may take a while to introduce as people take time to adjust to changes and to function under a new method requiring cohesive work teams (Butteriss & Albrecht, 1979, p. 18).

Job design and structure are essential elements in enrichment efforts and proposed work satisfaction remedies.

One study investigated the effects of reorganization of the management structure of a chemical manufacturing unit of a large British enterprise. The unit had a mechanistic, hierarchical structure. Its reorganization involved:

1. simplification and clarification of authority lines
2. increased communication channels
3. shortened chains of command
4. fewer managers responsible to more than one supervisor
5. additional personnel at lower echelons
6. median income raise of 33 percent
7. encouragement and availability of formal management training (Blain & Keohane, 1969, pp. 23–28).

The reorganization resulted in improved communication and knowledge and a 5 percent or greater increase in favorable attitudes toward work challenge and variety. Managers felt that work was worthwhile and meaningful and that their standard of living had improved. An increase in meaningful work may signify some decrease in the perceived alienation of personnel, which is so necessary to improving satisfaction and congruence.

Another study, by Hackman and Lawler (1971, pp. 259-286), also focused on design and satisfaction. Data were collected from 208 employees and 62 supervisors in 13 different jobs in the plant and traffic departments in an eastern telephone company. The researchers reached these conclusions:

1. The motivational potential of jobs can be realized only when psychological demands and job opportunities fit well with the personal needs and goals of workers employed in them. There is no single best way to design a job.
2. Many employees want to obtain higher need satisfactions from their work; few are overwhelmed by the psychological demands of their jobs.
3. Both vertical and horizontal job redesign allow employees to feel responsible for the outcome and thus work becomes more meaningful (Hackman & Lawler, 1971).

Enrichment is an option for managers considering the most effective mix of resources at their disposal.

LEADERSHIP AND STRESS

Contemporary theory has focused on the significance of contingency models of leadership behavior that is determined by the traits of the individual, the nature of the situation, or a combination of both. Leadership and its determinants often create stressful situations in which there is high conflict between managers and subordinates and among subordinates in the organization. In such occurrences, stress is felt at its peak and produces a dysfunctional organizational system that is one of the byproducts of negative leadership. There are a number of leadership styles to be considered, with several focusing on the decision-making process:

Style No. 1:   Manager or leaders perceive themselves as solving the problem or making the decisions alone, using information available to them at the time.

Style No. 2:   Managers or leaders perceive themselves as obtaining the necessary information from their subordinates, then deciding upon the solution alone. They may or may not tell their subordinates what the problem is as they collect this information, but they perceive their subordinates' roles in the decision-making process as those of providing necessary information rather than of generating or evaluating alternative solutions.

Style No. 3: Managers or leaders perceive themselves as sharing the problem with the relevant subordinates individually and getting their ideas and suggestions without bringing them together as a group. The managers then make the decision, which may or may not reflect the subordinates' influence.

Style No. 4: Managers or leaders perceive themselves as sharing the problem with their subordinates as a group while collectively obtaining their ideas and suggestions. The managers then make the decisions alone, which may or may not reflect the subordinates' influence.

Style No. 5: Managers or leaders perceive themselves as sharing the problem with subordinates as a group. This group then generates and evaluates alternatives and attempts to reach agreement on a solution. The managers perceive their role as somewhat like that of a chairperson. They do not try to influence the group to adopt the managers' solution, and are willing to accept and implement any solution that has the support of the entire group (Yetton, 1975, p. 93).

With Style 1 and Style 2, the subordinates' level of participation is quite low; this can lead to feelings of anger and stress in the future. With high levels of stress, individuals experience high levels of conflict and low congruence for achieving goals; with low stress, conflict is low and goal congruence is high. In medium levels of stress, conflict is low or high, with the corresponding goal congruence being either low or high as well. When managers are more participative, they realize that their subordinates' acceptance of a solution is important to these employees personally and, as a result, stress is low. This leads to the fact that the congruence of goals between managers and subordinates is high and conflict among the subordinates is low. This situation appears to be optimal and could be a model for managers to follow.

When managers need to develop subordinates' acceptance of decisions, they usually will be much more participative when the workers' acceptance is not very critical. This participative mode is not utilized readily in high stress and medium stress situations because managers will feel uncomfortable and unable to cope with group decisions that they normally would be looking for in other types of situations. In high and medium stress situations, goal congruence between managers and subordinates usually is incompatible, which may indicate that the managers are functioning in an autocratic manner. When managers are faced with problems that are likely to be resolved despite disagreement with their own subordinates, they may be unwilling to share the issues with these employees as a group. Their style may be characterized now by a low level of participation and by high conflict. Stress therefore is related to the situation and is experienced by both subordinates and supervisors as psychological disequilibrium.

Goal congruence between managers and subordinates and the level of conflict among the latter are important issues in determining whether the stress is at low, medium, or high levels. Managers appear to be more participative in low stress situations but less participative in high stress ones, which may create additional conflict.

Several studies focused on the impact of leadership upon satisfaction, stress, etc. One of these explores relationships between the subordinates' perceptions of their immediate supervisor's behavior and the level of satisfaction experienced with their job and the organizational environment. This was reflected in the satisfaction of subordinate role expectations. The data indicated that when leaders demonstrated consideration for their subordinates, this was related strongly to satisfaction. The degree to which these leaders initiated structure by setting clear objectives and procedures on the job with their subordinates also was positively related to satisfaction. The decisiveness of leaders had a direct linkage to subordinate satisfaction (House, Filley, & Gujarati, 1971, pp. 422-432).

Measures of job satisfaction have proved to be fairly good predictors of absenteeism and turnover. The study of their relationship to performance, however, has yielded discrepant results. Porter and Lawler (1968) suggest that satisfaction or dissatisfaction with a job may not affect the workers' performance directly; rather, it reflects the degree to which the organization is rewarding them properly for what they are doing. These researchers feel that if an organization actively and visibly rewards its workers in proportion to their quality of performance, higher satisfaction should be more closely related to higher performance. In reference to the models proposed earlier, Porter and Lawler note that previous assumptions about the effects of high levels of job satisfaction were greatly oversimplified, if not clearly incorrect. Any view that because workers are satisfied, they must be highly productive performers obviously is naive. The first lesson to be learned is not that job satisfaction is an inconsequential variable, but rather that its relationship to performance is more complex than previously recognized (Porter & Lawler, 1968, p. 120). Enrichment, participation, and leadership are internal processes that have been explored. It now is necessary to examine the other environmental factors affecting organizational functioning and dysfunctioning.

ENVIRONMENTAL STRESS

The amount of stress felt by individuals in an organization is a function of their own personality, resources needed to deal with the source of stress, previous experiences dealing with stressors and with nonstressors. There appears to be a relationship between the situation and the individuals' mechanisms to use internal controls. This relationship affects individuals' ability to make decisions in stressful situations.

Managers who are externally oriented feel they gain their rewards from forces outside themselves and that these forces happen to be connected to chance. Those who are internally oriented believe they have the personal controls to influence decisions; when confronted with situations dealing with stress, they explore alternative models for coping. Individuals who are externally oriented do not do this but try to adopt a coping approach more congruent with their own personal styles.

Another important aspect in trying to understand individuals' reactions to a radically altered task environment is the resource fund available for these persons, who are trying to cope with the stressful situation. These resources (monetary, physical, plant), have been considered important intervening variables between the source of stress and individuals' reaction to it. In addition to monetary and physical resources, past personal experiences with similar stressors may assist individuals in deciding which types of resources and strategies may be most helpful in reducing the stressfulness of the situation (Anderson, Hellriegel, & Slocum, 1977, p. 261).

There appear to be three coping mechanisms used by managers who have undergone changes in their own task environment. This has resulted in several alternatives they can decide upon that are significant in pooling their own personal resources, their personality styles, and their managerial styles. The synthesis of these styles will determine the individuals' perceived level of stress and directly affect the type of coping mechanism they use. These styles of behavior can be classified as follows:

Class 1:   Behaviors aimed at resolving the problem, i.e., dealing with the objective situation. These mechanisms may involve reduction of stress-related problems by obtaining resources to counter the initial loss.

Class 2: Behaviors that deal with tensions, threat, and other emotions. These mechanisms are reactions to emotional consequences rather than objective characteristics. These include withdrawal, affiliation with the immediate work group or with external task forces, and hostility and aggression.

Class 3: Behaviors that deal with secondary or derivative problems resulting from coping attempts, primarily failure during initial coping attempts (Anderson, Hellriegel, & Slocum, p. 265).

These studies indicate that individual managers who were internally oriented were much more likely to use Class 1 mechanisms and the externally oriented were more likely to resort to Class 2 mechanisms. Organizational effectiveness was related directly to the relative use of Class 1 alternatives and inversely related to the use of Class 3 mechanisms. Managers' use of Class 1 coping behaviors was related to organizational effectiveness while their use of Class 2 behaviors was inversely related to the effectiveness of the organizations. The internally oriented managers were better able to adapt to rapid environmental changes than were externally oriented ones, and there was evidence to suggest that at least one personality factor (externality) was common to both high stress and defensive coping behavior.

It is possible that defensive coping is a necessary first step for some managers before problem solving can begin and that performance style may be satisfactory in the long run for these organizations. On the other hand, defensive coping may be an early indicator of ultimate failure. The effectiveness of an organization's response to its environment appears to depend, to a large extent, upon the coping behaviors of its managers. These coping behaviors result more from the personal characteristics of the decision maker than from the work objectives, environmental demands, or organization resources available under those conditions of stress. This suggests that increasing the decision-making effectiveness of managers under conditions of stress should take the direction of altering their coping orientation, rather than simply providing other types of resources to aid recovery (Anderson, Hellriegel, & Slocum, 1977, p. 271). Managers are mediators of both internal and external factors in their quest to achieve the goals of the health care organization and to fulfill the needs of their human resources. A brief examination of their conflicts is in order.

FOCUS: THE MANAGER

In looking at organizational stressors, it becomes necessary to examine the managers' role in the health care institution and some of the conflicts they experience. The position of middle managers who do not possess power often is perilous, with very little intrinsic security. If things go well, their tenure is guaranteed, but if they go badly these individuals may become the scapegoats. Since many of the factors that affect their performance are out of their control, they constantly are subject to the threat of an uncertain collision course and its associated anxiety and stress. Their only hope for surviving under these conditions is to gain power and to be able to hold onto it. Unfortunately, at middle levels this is not a very realistic alternative. One of the problems is the status of middle managers. This usually is held and controlled in limbo. These managers lack organizational authority because it too is withheld from them, which creates basic uncertainties. Survival becomes contingent upon vague events that cannot be measured.

Health care administrators usually are middle managers who can become obsolete as a result of technological change, poor interpersonal skills, changing cultural values, internal politics, and economics. This also occurs when their aspiration levels are incongruous with the reward networks of the organization. When middle managers become obsolete, the indications that this is happening are apparent. Their decisions are not made at the right time, their decisions are not accurate and effective, their innovation and creativity decline severely, and they exert little if any motivation upon their subordinates. Other events occur:

1. Middle managers are unrealistic concerning their environment, facilities, and programs. They are not cognizant of the factors against which their programs are evaluated.
2. Middle managers are unrealistic concerning their role in the organization. Top management sees them as interfering in the administrators' roles as decision makers and wants them to carry out the other activities they feel middle managers should be doing, whatever they are.
3. Middle managers are not really in a position to alleviate pressures exerted upon top management. Some are told they will not be involved in the decision-making process. The decision then is up to them: they can leave the job, leave their organization, or withdraw from the work environment psychologically and assume only a few risks, which is safer.
4. Middle managers have no influence with key leadership in the organization, which dilutes their effectiveness and impact. Even when the middle managers cannot exert change at the top, they are equally vulnerable by not being able to provide a rationale why their requests are rejected.

5. Middle managers are indecisive because they usually must "plead their case" before top leadership, which serves as another hierarchical stifling block.
6. Middle managers are considered as having undesirable jobs to which subordinates do not aspire. It is a negativistic motive for a junior manager to seek a middle management job when one of the best things that can be said about it is that it serves as a buffer for the rest of the organization (Appelbaum, 1977, p. 41).

Some of the conflicts these middle managers experience are brought about by these constraints and demotivators:

1. Middle managers are expected to function in a manner that will not provoke any negative reactions from their supervisors. They exhibit a favorable attitude toward authority.
2. Middle managers must demonstrate a strong competitive trait and desire to compete for the available rewards.
3. Middle managers must play a role in which they are assertive and driving as required by society.
4. Middle managers must exercise power over subordinates and direct all efforts toward achievement of the institution's mission and goal.
5. Middle managers must behave differently from the manner in which subordinates function. They must be willing to want the spotlight and be distinctive.
6. Middle managers must be able to handle responsibility and routine daily, and at the same time gain satisfaction from it while being productive (Appelbaum, 1977, p. 42).

The result of all this is that extraordinary and unrealistic stress is put upon these managers to perform in an environment that is programmed for failure. They also are under the pressure of dealing in an uncertain work environment and at the same time coping with their own midcareer life crises. Changing social norms and individuals' inability to deal with conflicts and changing family relationships, personal roles, and dissatisfaction with traditional behavioral guides can result in stress for many of these middle managers in this pressure cooker. Changes in the workplace in the form of task overload, job ambiguity, and conflict with an organizational culture are equally stress producing.

The human resource also has undergone considerable change in value systems and self-image. On the average, people are living longer; are healthier for longer periods of time; are better educated; and have much changed perspectives of social and moral issues, of the role they see themselves playing, and of their role in the working environment (Blau, 1977, p. 130). These managers are caught in a bind in which they are attempting not only to maintain their financial security, but at the same time to seek out certain job satisfactions and contribute to their own growth emotionally. The quality of working life is significant in these managers' day-to-day environment, and this bind has a negative effect upon them since they are pressured to perform at unrealistically high levels. Many midcareer managers experience the conflict and crisis between the ages of 35 and 55. They are under a dual set of pressures in the work environment and familial structure since diverse pressures are exerted by their institution, family, and society. These stressors usually are accompanied by free-floating anxieties. The middle managers attempt to direct the anxieties in the direction of the unfulfilled promises and performances, as they now have reached the midpoint of their careers and have not moved along any further than they were as junior managers.

All of these factors exert pressure and can produce stress in the organizational environment, particularly at the midcareer point where individuals often reevaluate their lives to try to see where they have been, where they are now, and where they may perceive they are being forced to go. These variables, in addition to others, bear very strongly on the behaviors of people—particularly middle managers—at work (Blau, p. 132).

Managers can be trained to recognize significant changes in their subordinates' behavior as these actions affect job effectiveness and stress levels. Initially, midcareer crises are dealt with in relationship to observed changes in the quality and quantity of individuals' performance and effectiveness. Managers can be trained and sensitized to seek out these symptoms in their employees. They may be able to correct them in part since they want the individuals to function effectively and efficiently and not be thwarted by stressful and emotional problems.

While they may be trained to do this externally, managers may not perceive their own inadequacies and their own vulnerability to these same stressors. It is interesting that as managers are observing their subordinates being affected by stress, they themselves are coping with this dilemma impersonally as evidenced by the external perspective and position they assume. Midcareer crises and stress cannot be prevented by optimizing workplace perceptions and relationships since the severity of these stressors can be reduced somewhat by minimizing contributing factors that have been identified as those that overload the managers in their own environment.

A study was conducted (Rogers, 1979) in which perceptions of stress among managers in Canada and the United States were measured. The stressors that were felt most heavily by managers in both countries were as follows:

1. lack of information to carry out a job
2. conflicting demands made by other people
3. quality/quantity conflict in work
4. being forced to do things against their better judgment
5. scope and responsibility of the job were unclear
6. inability to influence superior's decisions
7. too little authority to carry out responsibility
8. superior's evaluation of their performance is unknown

For many of the managers in the United States, organization structure appeared to be a less frequent precipitator of stress than workload or decision making. For many of the Canadian managers, the workload was perceived as a more frequent precipitator of stress than were organizational structure, decision making, and performance. For Canadians, all of the eight stressors were considered to be precipitators of stress. The most important difference between managers in Canada and the United States seemed to be the relative frequency with which the latter perceived decision-making responsibilities as stress precipitator relative to organization structure and workload. For the average Canadian manager there was little difference in the frequency of stress precipitated by organization structure or decision making. Finally, the data indicated that 30 percent of the managers in the United States experienced a very low frequency of stress due to all the stress items while only 4 percent of the Canadian sample fell into this category.

In Canadian organizations, high stress more often than not is precipitated by inadequate or inappropriate institutional design resulting in heavy achievement-centered behavior and denial of self-actualization needs. In the organizations in the United States, high stress is precipitated more often by the anxiety related to decision making, resulting in ambiguous behavior and a high survival orientation. This is marked in the one case by an overemphasis on risk avoidance or in the other case in a high emphasis on self-actualization that could be interpreted as a withdrawal from traditional organizational values and imperatives (Rogers, 1979, p. 12).

The study indicated that organizations in the United States appear to have a higher degree of bureaucratization and a higher emphasis on managerial accountability. They seem to perceive communications as inadequate and there was a lack of trust between supervisors and subordinates. The result is a high degree of insecurity manifested in a fear of making suboptimum decisions. This is expressed in suppression of achievement-centered behavior, which carries a higher risk factor than ambiguity-based behavior. Organizationally this can result in an increasing emphasis on bureaucratic imperatives—that is, structural emphasis, vertical integration, increased rigidity and inflexibility, more demands for complete information, and more criteria for the decision-making process. Canadian organizations, in contrast, are marked by inadequate or ambiguous definitions of scope, authority, and responsibility; in short, poor organization design.

A byproduct of this phenomenon is the whole issue of performance evaluation, Without precise and measurable objectives—emphasizing authority, responsibility, and related definitions—realistic performance appraisal is difficult. The results are frustrated attempts at self-actualization because the individuals do not know whether they have achieved their objective because they have only limited feedback and high degrees of role conflict and role ambiguity. It is interesting again to note that in this cross-cultural study and analysis, both groups of managers experienced different stressors and different degrees of stress, but the unique factor was that all eight of the stressors cited were counterproductive and at the same time very dysfunctional to organizational effectiveness. These stress items also diluted the quality of work life experienced by the managers in their organizations.

QUALITY OF WORK LIFE

Participative management, job enrichment, environmental factors, and satisfaction all are components of the general rubric of the quality of work life.

Recent research has produced insights into the importance of stress factors that are prevalent in the working climate and their impact on the emotional and physical well-being of employees. It appears difficult to legislate against hazards that affect individuals in the workplace. This has been tried, and while some experiences with certain aspects of the Occupational Safety and Health Administration

(OSHA) have been encouraging, changes in the social fabric of organizations seem to occur mainly as a result of threats and legal entanglements. However, this has indicated that institutions appear unwilling to voluntarily change hazardous environmental factors affecting the quality of work life. The United States is not a leader in this domain and must look elsewhere for models and effective efforts.

THE SWEDISH CONNECTION

In the Scandinavian countries, as an example, job legislation passed in 1976 included physical, psychological, and social factors in its definition of the working environment (Wahlund & Nerell, 1977, p. 63). In addition, Sweden in 1979 adopted an Industrial Injuries Insurance Act that opened possibilities for compensation for completely new and different types of injuries not found previously in the catch-all of broad-based industrial injuries. Compensation now is payable for psychological and/or psychosomatic injuries in the working environment.

In a related research study, an analysis of the responses of 133 first-line supervisors surveyed by questionnaire supported the hypothesis that managers' environmental control orientation was related to work strain, job satisfaction, and positional mobility. Findings indicated that, although the exact nature of these relations was not understood, the greater the belief in the ability to influence the environment, the lower the reported job strain and the higher the reported work satisfaction and positional mobility (Gemmill & Heisler, 1972, p. 241-250). This type of control factor is essential in the management of stress since the legal environment is necessary for some controls and inhibitors needed in the organizational culture.

Studies of the Swedish work environment found that career systems could lead to social isolation, since individuals did not readily discuss personal problems with competitors their own age, with their managers who were to evaluate their performance, or even with subordinates and peers. This underlines the fact that relationships at a workplace for the most part reflect the scheme of organization existing there.

A psychosocial environment can cause problems in human relations (Wahlund & Nerell, 1977, p. 65). This situation can be transferred to health care institutions since in the medical sector, the work environment of health care professionals (as supervisors or managers) often suggests intense competition between conflicting interests. The employer organizes the wards, work schedules, and personnel pool; the patient expects continuity of care and human contact. The actual business of medical work is fragmented by a host of paperwork routines, as a result of which the nurses barely recognize the profession for which they trained. At the same time, their situation as supervisors involves problems because they are forced to delegate responsibilities to personnel who are untrained for the tasks (Wahlund & Norell, p. 65). This situation, which is quite prevalent in North American health care institutions, creates certain stresses for nurses caught in this bind. The problems of being involved in situations such as this are significant since they create stressful situations that can be difficult to resolve.

Confinement to work, i.e., difficulties in getting away from the job for a short while or in taking a half a day or a whole day off at short notice, proved to be connected with mental strain experienced by personnel in Swedish health care organizations. Almost three times as many persons who were "experiencing frequent stress" felt they were unable to leave their duties for even five or ten minutes, while twice as many of those who said their work was mentally strenuous felt they were unable to leave for half an hour, an hour, or a day at short notice. This situation is particularly crippling for individuals involved with a hectic pace and under constant pressure to achieve high productivity, who at the same time are responsible for the maintenance of patient care. Wahlund and Nerell (1977) also found psychological reactions clearly were connected to perceived mental strain: 12 percent of respondents in the high strain groups reported that they often felt uneasy or reluctant about going to work, as against 1 percent in the low strain group. And 48 percent of respondents in the high strain group said they were too tired after work to engage in anything active, such as hobbies or meeting friends and acquaintances, as against 11 percent in the low strain group. At the same time, 46 percent of respondents in the high strain group found it hard to get their minds off their work during leisure hours, as against 8 percent in the low strain group.

Behavioral reaction patterns also were found to be connected with mental strain. Of persons who often experienced mental strain, 43 percent had seriously considered changing jobs as against 24 percent in a group that seldom or never experienced mental strain at work. The group often experiencing mental strain at work, moreover, took more drugs—above all, more sedatives and tranquilizers—and smoked more than the group experiencing little mental strain.

There was no great difference between the two groups where sickness and absence were concerned. The main difference concerned absenteeism and was ascribed to weariness or fatigue in connection with the work; the high strain group reported three times as much absenteeism on this score as the low strain group (Wahlund & Nerell, p. 70). These issues are addressed in Chapter 5 (Impact of Stress on Nursing) and Chapter 6 (Occupational Stress).

This research suggests strongly that many factors casually considered previously are now to be classified as stressors. It also suggests that monotonous and rigidly controlled jobs and those involving uncertainty and conflict lead to nervous complaints. The frequency of nervous complaints among groups with these stress factors was greater than among those experiencing mild, generalized strain. The notion of a legal remedy for managing stress has as its basis the concept of a democratic organizational structure since institutions do not voluntarily alter the technical-managerial-behavioral process in the quest to fulfill the needs of their personnel while actualizing health care goals.

DEMOCRACY AND PARTICIPATION

Organizational democracy is an objective that could emerge in actual management practice as a result of a policy under which all members of the institution have an opportunity to participate in the decisions that affect the quality and quantity of work and its components.

Participation in organizational and personnel decisions is essential for individuals who feel they are part of the system employing them. Some personnel policies contribute to alienation among employees and directly affect all individuals. These areas are problems since the policies needed to manage these components effectively often are vague and lead to conflict and ambiguity. They include:

- promotion policies
- inflexible requirements
- outside hiring
- wage and salary policies
- incentive plans
- employee counseling
- work rules
- employee services
- educational aid
- insurance plans
- compulsory retirement age (Brown, 1970)

Among the basic prerequisites of the classical theory of democracy are two that are important:

1. **A minimum of freedom:** If individual members are to exert any influence, they must be able to relate to the issues, to establish

contact with other people, to exchange views, and to form social links. Those who do not have a certain freedom of movement—not only physically but also psychologically and socially—cannot take part in a democratic process.

2. **Skills and competence:** Any organization confronts a number of issues that must be discussed and settled. Since much of the structure is dependent upon how issues are settled, it follows that those who are to take part in generating structure must have a reasonable level of competence and insight in relation to such issues (Gustavsen, 1977, p. 161).

The focus of this democratic movement is to bring into cognition the need to legislate job reform since organizations do not opt voluntarily to improve the climate and quality of work life.

LEGISLATIVE ISSUES: NORWAY

In 1976, the Norwegian Work Environment Act shed light on the issue of job reform. Elements of that act's Section 12, concerning the design of jobs and work, follow:

1. **General Requirements:** Technology, job organization, work time (e.g. shift plans), and payment systems are to be designed so that negative physiological or psychological effects for employees are avoided as well as any negative influence on the alertness necessary to the observance of safety considerations. Employees are to be given possibilities for personal development and for the maintenance and development of skills.

2. **Design of Jobs:** In the planning of work and design of jobs, possibilities for employee self-determination and maintenance of skills are to be considered. Monotonous, repetitive work and jobs that are bound by machine or assembly line in such a way that no room is left for variations in work rhythm should be avoided. Jobs should be designed to provide possibilities for variation, for contact with others, for interdependence between elements that constitute the work, and for information and feedback to employees concerning production requirements and results.

3. **Systems for Planning and Control:** Employees or their elected representatives are to be kept informed about systems used for planning and control, including changes in such systems. They are to be given the training necessary to understand the system and the right to influence their job design.

As far as is known, this is the first example of job design/work organization issues' being treated legally in terms of specific requirements. These legislative considerations were deemed to be significant because they addressed physical health, mental health, psychosocial life qualities, accident prevention, and employee activity. It is interesting to note that job dissatisfaction, for example, has been found to correlate with psychosomatic illness symptoms, work-related fatigue, injury and illness rates, heart disease risk factors, nervous diseases, depression and problems with sleep, and pains in the back, shoulder, and stomach.

The increasing amount of research on the term stress shows links between job experiences and physiological as well as psychological stress (Gustavsen, 1977, p. 165). It is intriguing that something can be done about psychosocial issues, an approach that is a prime step in the change. This is indicated by the scope of Section 12, which focuses on technology and work organization. It also is necessary to look at all of these areas in the aggregate and not as isolated systems. When the legal ramifications are treated as a total unit, it is much more cogent to look at methods of job reform in the context of the organization as a system.

A further point of importance is the use of legislation in itself. This is not primarily because legislation introduces a set of binding rules and regulations. Of greater importance might be the point that an act of Parliament (or Congress) in itself is a valued declaration since it gives sanction to certain points of view and makes others less legitimate. Law generates the possibilities for raising new questions and putting forth new arguments. This is significant for employees and health care institutions attempting to wrestle with the dilemma of managing stress, maintaining productivity and worker satisfaction, and achieving ultimate organizational perpetuation.

To further support this line of analysis, the Swedish National Association of Salaried Employees in 1974 reported that 33 percent of employees in a research project experienced stress at work quite often. An additional study, for the Swedish Confederation of Professional Associations, demonstrated conclusively that 42 percent of all academically trained professionals reported such phenomena (Levi, 1977, p. 218). Briefly then, 42 percent, or almost one out of every two professional individuals studied, said they experienced this stress; for other professions such as teachers and social workers, such reports came from two out of every three. This is an essential statistic to consider since these individuals in an academic and health care environment are counted upon heavily for their reliability, stability, and capacity to serve as a ventilation outlet for individuals experiencing stress themselves.

There appear to be fewer outlets for professionals than for clients of a system. There are other indicators of a poor person-environment fit such as alcoholism, suicide, and mental and psychosomatic disorders. These are very common phenomena in all types of society throughout the world, although the close connection between them and occupational stress has not always been proved in the literature, but it is suspected in many cases. Some 25 to 30 percent of all public mental service involves diseases that are mainly psychosocially induced and those that focus heavily upon the stress component.

What must be considered is how organizations can begin and continue to protect individuals—and managers in particular—against these stressful and counterproductive situations. A good formulation is given in a 1963 resolution from the Parliament of the International Labour Conference that concluded:

> Work should respect the worker's life and health; this is the problem of safety and healthiness in the work place. Work should leave the worker free time for rest and leisure. This is the question of hours of work and their adaptation to an approved pattern for life outside work. Work should enable the worker to serve society and achieve self-fulfillment by developing his personal capabilities; this is the problem of the content and organization of work.

It appears that these three aspects are essential, and if they could be legislated they would legitimize some remedies that would be nonnegotiable.

Individuals' requirements at work need to be spelled out since it is essential to determine the arrangement between the institution and its employees with regard to safety, health, wages, hours, and security. Workers have the following requirements:

1. the need for a job to be reasonably demanding in terms other than sheer endurance, and to provide at least a minimum of variety
2. the need to be able to learn on the job and to continue learning
3. the need for some area of decision making that individuals can call their own
4. the need for some degree of social support and recognition in the workplace
5. the need to be able to relate what they do and what they produce to their social life
6. the need to feel that the job leads to some sort of desirable future (Levi, 1977, p. 219).

PARTICIPATION: QUEBEC

While these suggestions border on the human resource-legislative boundary, a synthesis is needed between what can be enacted legislatively and what can be instituted by organizations in order to handle the welfare, well-being, counterproductiveness, and stress reduction of individuals involved in turbulent employment climates. One of the popular managerial systems introduced by Douglas McGregor (1960), Rensis Likert (1967), Chris Argyris (1967), and other management theorists was that of participative management. This was a managerial process used in the 1960s by many behavioral scientists who were attempting to democratize the organizational climate. As an example, if participative management is significant as a management technique, is it not advisable to employ this behavioral process in health care organizations through legislative reform and structure?

This issue was examined in 1967, when the Quebec Ministry of Health formed a commission to study the possibilities of reorganizing the health service system. The commission's report led to 1971 legislation calling for a major reorganization of the province's health and social care system so it could adapt to and improve the health of the population. The principles of participation were recognized by the reform. Since then, unfortunately, the development of the participative structure has been somewhat thwarted by wide public debate, which is characteristic of this society.

The health care system was built originally upon the medical model and its expansion was limited to that model. The commission concluded that if the population's health was to be improved, the definition of health services had to be expanded outside the medical model. It was recognized that working environment, eating habits, hygiene, epidemics, social diseases, living habits, and many other factors affected individuals' health (Bégin, Bherer, & Hobbs, 1979, p. 3). It also was realized that hospitals and physicians, particularly specialists, appeared unable to give adequate consideration to social and environmental aspects. It is not difficult to see why legal intervention is necessary when social movements erode. The basic argument was that if the professional personnel and clientele could participate in the management of the health care system, it would be possible to bring about a more congruent demand for services.

The reform proposed that hospital boards of directors be composed of administrators, personnel, patients, representatives of community organizations, and representatives of affiliated institutions in the province. This was truly a participative approach. The legislation also proposed changing the administrative process in the hospitals. It attempted to integrate medical and administrative interests at all decision levels. Prior to the reform, medical and administrative personnel belonged to different worlds, with sparse communication between them. The reform also proposed the creation of multidisciplinary teams composed of community health and social service personnel. This can be viewed as another form of participation growing out of legislative enactment. The reform recommended that a group of professionals composed of doctors, psychologists, social workers, and community organizers could better judge patient and community needs than a physician alone (Bégin, Bherer, & Hobbs, 1979, p. 4).

However, at the hospital board level, there was little participation. The problems at the board level are clear because in hospitals today there are two diverse groups—the administrators who know very little about medicine and the physicians who ignore the basic elements of administration. It is difficult to meld both views into an effective and efficient organization. Forced participation is an alternative.

Participation, therefore, seems to be an essential need in which a legislative stimulus is an equally vital ingredient for perpetuation. The problem of connecting both disciplines (administration and medicine) has been one with which hospitals and other health care organizations have been wrestling historically. Multidisciplinary teams may be a way to correct this situation since both functions—management and medicine—appear to be in conflict otherwise. Under the label of multidisciplinary teams is a profoundly divided group of professionals, each trying to acquire or conserve for themselves or their professional core the maximum of autonomy, well-defined fields of action, and the power to control certain activities and their own clientele. If "team" means pooling individual contributions toward a common goal, then there has been little experience with teams operating in this type of environment. Teams seem to connote the concept of participation in health care organizations. Even though this participation appears to be forced by structure and/or legislation, it is a significant foundation for creating a much more positive climate.

However, one of the problems in dealing with the Quebec situation is the social-political heritage. This problem continues to exist in the politically changing province. Quebec society often has been open to values of mutual aid and cooperation. But the political structures at all levels have never been able to tolerate the ambiguity and uncertainty that, at least in the beginning, accompany all true decentralization of decision making (Bégin, Bherer, & Hobbs, 1979, p. 10). While this model is not perfectly operative, it is a beginning and conceptual blueprint which is being emulated in varied forms in other provinces.

Participation means dealing with an integrative procedure. Integrating people from the liberal professional domain into participative management presents special problems. The reform assumed that the professionals would be able to deal efficiently with administrative matters, both on an operational and a strategic level. Whether it be a question of personality or training, professionals seem to have difficulty grasping administrative problems. Furthermore, professionals show more allegiance to their colleagues and their professional core than to the organizations that employ them.

To operate this participative system with professionals, educational technology and processes should be planned and used. In the case of Quebec's health care system, it appeared that no preparation was provided. The structures were developed as quickly as nominations could be made. The medical profession generally reacted negatively to social and preventive medicine, to the multidisciplinary teams, and to community health and social service centers that were developed based upon the participative model created by legislative edict.

Some conclusions can be drawn from this experience in legislated participation:

1. If participation is to have a chance of succeeding, some way must be found for ensuring more tolerance for ambiguity in the political structure.
2. The choice of the participative models should be made explicit.
3. It should be decided first to what extent participation is a terminal or an instrumental value.
4. Room should be left for experimentation and diversity.
5. Careful consideration should be given to the fundamental opposition to this procedure.
6. If the use of organization development techniques is necessary in making small changes in existing institutions, these certainly should be considered when dramatically changing a whole sector of activity in creating a new organization.
7. The participative model appears to be a viable remedy, and the use of legislation to initiate this procedure should be one of the stimulating options available when the program is brought to a halt by conflicting values of medical, administrative, and/or board memberships.

While this chapter has dealt with the management of stress via participative management, job enrichment, quality of work life, and international experiences, the following chapter focuses upon the predecessor of stress—conflict—and ways to attempt to manage its dysfunctional aspects.

BIBLIOGRAPHY

Anderson, C.R., Hellriegel, D., & Slocum, J.W., Jr. Managerial response to environmentally induced stress. *Academy of Management Journal,* June 1977, *20*(2), 260-272.

Appelbaum, S.H. The middle-manager: An examination of aspirations and pessimism. *The Personnel Administrator,* January 1977, *22*(1), 39-44.

Argyris, C. *Integrating the individual and the organization.* New York: John Wiley and Sons, 1966.

Argyris, C. Today's problems with tomorrow's organizations. *The Journal of Management Studies,* February, 1967, *4*(1), 32.

Bégin, C., Bherer, H., & Hobbs, B. Experiments in participative management in Quebec's health care system: An appraisal. *Academy of Management* meeting, Atlanta, August 1979, pp. 3-10. (Paper)

Blau, B.A. Organizational structure and mid-career stress. In *Reducing occupational stress: Proceedings of the National Institute for Occupational Safety and Health,* White Plains, N.Y., May 1977, 130-134.

Blain, I., & Keohane, J. One company's management structure before and after a change. *Occupational Psychology,* 1969, *43,* 23-38.

Brown, D.R. Do personnel policies alienate employees? *Personnel Administration,* January/February 1970, *33*(1), 29-36.

Butteriss, M., & Albrecht, K. *New management tools.* Englewood Cliffs, N.J.: Prentice-Hall Inc., 1979, 12.

Donaldson, J., & Gowler, D. Prerogatives, participation and managerial stress. In D. Gowler & K. Legge (Eds.), *Managerial stress.* New York: John Wiley & Sons, 1975, 102-114.

Gemmill, G.R., & Heisler, W.J. Fatalism as a factor in managerial job satisfaction, job strain and mobility. *Personnel Psychology,* Summer 1972, *25,* 241-250.

Gustavsen, B. A legislative approach to job reform. In *Reducing occupational stress: Proceedings of the National Institute for Occupational Safety and Health,* White Plains, N.Y., May 1977, 160-174.

Hackman, J.R., & Lawler, E.E., III. Employee reactions to job characteristics. *Journal of Applied Psychology,* June 1971, *55,* 259-286.

Herzberg, F., Mausner, B., and Snyderman, B. *The motivation to work* (2nd ed.). New York: John Wiley and Sons, 1966.

House, R.J., Filley, A.C., & Gujarati, D.N. Leadership style, hierarchical influence and the satisfaction of subordinate role expectations: A test of Likert's influence proposition. *Journal of Applied Psychology,* October 1971, *55,* 422-432.

Levi, L. Psychosocial stress at work: Problems and prevention. In *Reducing occupational stress: Proceedings of the National Institute for Occupational Safety and Health,* White Plains, N.Y., May 1977, 216-222.

Likert, R. *The human organization: Its management and value.* New York: McGraw-Hill Book Co., 1967.

Lundgren, E.F. *Organizational management: Systems and process.* San Francisco: Canfield Press, 1974, 337.

McGregor, D. *The human side of enterprise.* New York: McGraw-Hill Book Co., 1960.

Porter, L.W., & Lawler, E.E., III. What job attitudes tell about motivation. *Harvard Business Review,* January 1968, *46*(1), 118–126.

Rogers, R.E. Perceptions of stress among Canadians and American managers: A cross-cultural analysis. *Academy of Management* meeting, Atlanta, August 1979, pp. 12, 14. (Paper)

Wahlund, I., & Nerell, G. Stress factors in the working environments of white-collar workers. In *Reducing occupational stress: Proceedings of the National Institute for Occupational Safety and Health,* White Plains, N.Y., May 1977, 62–72.

Walton, R.E. How to counter alienation in the plant. *Harvard Business Review,* November–December 1972, *50*(6), 70–81.

Yetton, P.W. Leadership style in stressful and non-stressful situations. In D. Gowler & K. Legge (Eds.), *Managerial stress.* New York: John Wiley & Sons, 1975, 89–101.

Chapter 10

Management of Conflict

CONSIDERATIONS FOR THE HEALTH CARE MANAGER

1. Conflict is both natural and to be expected in interdependent relationships.
2. Conflict requires a state of interdependency if it is to occur at all.
3. Conflicts often are seen as collision courses of personal goals of one or more of the individuals involved in the relationship. Goal collisions can be mutually exclusive, distributive, or pathway.
4. Conflicts are resolved by dissolving incompatibilities or removing preconditions and by exerting controls over factors that appear to be contingencies.
5. When boundaries are clear, all individuals know what is expected of them. As a result, the more basic conflicts are resolved.
6. Conflicts increase when individuals are dependent upon each other for the performance of tasks.
7. Some types of conflicts are perceived, felt, or manifested.
8. Methods of conflict resolving include:
    - win-lose
    - yield-lose
    - synergistic
    - lose-leave
    - compromise

9. Effective managers resolve their conflicts in this order:
   - confrontation
   - smoothing
   - compromise
   - forcing
   - withdrawal
10. Shared data between departments promotes trust and reduces differences while lowering potentials for conflict.
11. Health tension can stimulate learning, increase critical self-appraisal, and induce decision makers to examine conflicting values more discerningly when taking actions.
12. Organizations bring about change through a process of unfreezing—education—refreezing.
13. Changes instigated entirely in the interests of the organization without consideration of effects upon personnel are potent factors in causing stress.
14. Occupational health physicians can be involved as consultants to management by identifying internal conflicts that increase stress on the part of individuals caught in the middle of dynamic change.
15. Interdependence, specialization, and heterogeneity of personnel in levels of authority all appear to be related positively to conflict.
16. Health care administrators and physicians both are trying to increase their power base, professionalism, and status in their institutions, which becomes a collision course.
17. A valid change effort in an institution can avoid dysfunctional conflict by encouraging self-governance, individual responsibility, mature interdependence, and mutual organizational goal setting.

Contrary to conventional wisdom, the single most important thing about conflict is that it *is* good for you. While this is not a scientific statement of fact, it reflects a basic and unprecedented shift of emphasis—a move away from the old human relations point of view where all conflict was seen as basically bad (Kelly, 1970, p. 103). Conflict per se is a neutral concept and is not good nor bad, right nor wrong, nor imbued with any of the meanings that people attach to it. Conflict-dynamics are approached as simply a very natural facet of human interaction. The particular meanings are defined and imposed by those who are parties to the conflict.

CONFLICT: SOME CAUSES

The basic theory is that people dictate what conflict situations mean and what their consequences will be. The fact that conflict too often is conceived of and treated as if it possessed some inherent qualities all its own serves to obscure the critical role that individuals play in conflict resolution. Individuals' view of conflict and their predisposition to handling it in certain ways are more important determinants of the outcome than the nature of the controversy. It is this very conflict that is part and parcel of the health care environment. Therefore, an understanding of the problems involved with conflict and some remedies are essential for administrators attempting to resolve and manage this reality of health care organizations' life.

Conflict is both natural and to be expected in interpersonal relationships. Individuals are preoccupied with conflict, promote certain rules of thumb for resolution, and attempt to teach subordinates and others acceptable and effective ways of conducting themselves in such situations. This is another way of saying that most people learn about conflict and its implications for them from the behaviors of others.

Assuming there are wide ranges of learning opportunities among people, many different approaches to the management of conflict are encountered among as many individuals. So it is that one individual may come to believe that winning is the most important objective in conflict, while another may believe that turning the other cheek and displaying charity are the most appropriate behaviors. Others may have learned that winning is not nearly as important as how they play the game, and when these *acquired values* are magnified by the importance of the issues, they emerge readily to shape and guide individuals' behavior in conflict situations.

One important consideration is the context in which conflict occurs and the personal significance of the issues involved. There are two primary areas of concern to individuals in conflict—context and personal relevance—that are taken as the two basic dimensions of conflict management. The degree of concern individuals express about one or the other, or both, serves as an indicator of the kinds of action alternatives or styles they will perceive as appropriate for dealing with the situation. It is important to note that they learn to attach importance to both considerations and how much importance to assign to each. These learnings are significant in individuals' conflict management style.

The interpersonal context in which conflict occurs, whether it is a two-person encounter, small group situation, or confrontation between groups or cultures, represents a relationship in a very real sense. Concern for the relationship is interpreted as one of the motivational factors operating to encourage the use of particular behaviors during conflicting situations. As an example, if individuals attach great importance to the well-being and durability of the relationship, they are quite likely to view conflict and react to it differently from persons who attach relatively little importance to it.

The importance of the relationship dimension and the reasons for concern about it may be traced to the nature of conflict dynamics: Conflict requires a state of interdependency if it is to occur at all. The state of interdependency when the actions and values of one individual have direct implications for the well-being of others is the foundation of relationships, but also the spawning ground for conflicts. The relationship per se becomes the ostensible focus of much that occurs in conflict situations, and individuals reveal many of their feelings about their relationships through their behaviors in managing conflicts.

The concern for relationships is only one dimension of individuals' approach to managing conflict. The personal relevance in terms of their own goals is important as a motivational force. Conflict may be interpreted further as a collision course of the personal goals of one or more of the individuals involved in an interdependent relationship. Personal goals may collide in several ways and, depending upon the nature of the collision, may be valued in differing degrees. The more common instances of goal collision are:

1. mutually exclusive collisions, in which, if one goal is entertained or achieved, it is at the cost of and to the exclusion of another
2. distributive collisions in which similar goals are desired by parties but involve commodities that are in short supply and therefore not available to all
3. pathway collisions, in which the same end objectives appear to be desired but the means for their attainment are perceived quite differently

4. value collisions, in which individuals' subjective evaluations of right and wrong are involved and many have elements of other forms of collision imbedded in them

An example of this occurs when administrators of a health care institution may be in agreement on the desirability of achieving a bottom line figure but differ on how to attain it. Another example may be when health care administrators agree upon an objective of maintaining a satisfied work force but differ on the managerial practices needed to achieve this mission.

While there may be many types of goal collisions, the importance individuals place on attaining their personal goals becomes an important determinant as to how they will behave in conflict situations. The individuals' ultimate style of conflict management is the essential factor in determining how the relationship will be maintained. There is a problem in understanding conflict because there is no universal concept concerning the terminology. Conflict carries many different connotations, ranging from behavior that is unacceptable to a very positive method of functioning in an organization. The way individuals value conflict is based on their own perceptions and prior experience.

MANAGING CONFLICT OR HANGING ON?

There is a difference, however, between managing and resolving conflict. For conflict to develop there must be two parties or analytically distinct units and a situation either of position scarcity or of resource scarcity. Position scarcity is a condition in which an object cannot serve two different functions simultaneously, a role cannot be occupied simultaneously or performed by two or more actors, and different prescribed behaviors cannot be carried out simultaneously. Resource scarcity is a condition in which the supply of desired objects or states of affairs is limited, so parties cannot have all they want of anything (Pood & Glenn, 1979, p. 3).

Conflict occurs when some level of mutual incompatibility occurs between two or more parties based on goals or methods that are evaluated in terms of outcomes. A goal that is incompatible with another goal or method actually interferes with the achievement of the latter and makes it less effective than another objective. This often is confused with verbal disagreements in which individuals are thwarted in their quest to achieve an objective.

Disagreements and arguments may be viewed at best not as conflict but as a response to a conflict. This is essential to understand, since the conflict is a mutual incompatibility based on the communication regarding the conflict. The individuals dealing with this issue have a difficult time determining whether to resolve the conflict or to manage it. Conflicts are resolved by dissolving the incompatibilities or removing preconditions; conflicts are managed by exerting controls over factors that appear to be contingencies. This is the basic difference between these two processes.

The management of conflict involves the control and direction of the total situation, which may include the communications and responses of the individuals involved. The resolving of a conflict may even ignore the individuals' communication behaviors entirely. In this way, people do not get a really clear view of how the basic issues of scarcity of inter-personal conflict were brought about. The characteristics of these conflict situations can be described as follows:

1. At least two parties, individuals, or groups are involved in some kind of interaction.
2. Mutually exclusive goals and/or mutually exclusive values exist, in fact or as perceived by the parties.
3. Interaction is characterized by behavior designed to defeat, reduce, or suppress the opponent or to gain a mutually designated victory.
4. The parties face each other with mutually opposing actions and counteractions.
5. Each of the parties attempts to create an imbalance or relatively favorite position of power vis-a-vis the other (Filley, 1975, p. 4).

Another issue in the management of conflict is that the internal psychological reactions of individuals may or may not be consistent with external communications. Therefore, the management of conflict necessitates that some attention be given to the reactions of the parties as well as to their communication behaviors. While conflict apparently is being managed effectively, the failure on the part of managers to recognize the possible inconsistency between the reactions and the responses of the parties may lead to negative results. Over time, the intensity of the relationship between these two managers or groups may increase and lead to unregulated confrontation, which is extremely destructive. Conflict management involves attempts to control or direct the internal feelings as well as the communication behaviors of the parties. Attempts to regulate the communication responses may not produce desirable outcomes if they are inconsistent with the reactions of the participants (Pood & Glenn, p. 10). Conflict has positive values, and some conflicts that are deeply ingrained in an institution are important as preventive measures against more destructive types of behaviors.

However, conflict can create tensions in an organization that can be resolved only through joint problem solving, which is one way of ultimately coming up with a solution. Conflict may increase the cohesion of the group experiencing it and of the performances of some of the members involved who must now cooperate with each other to avoid further competition. Conflict usually is intense when the boundaries for departments and individuals in the organization are ambiguous. When boundaries are clear, each individual knows what is expected of each member with regard to roles, so some of the more basic conflicts become reduced. If the parties are separated physically in the organization, the opportunity for a conflicting situation becomes greater because of the escalation of intrapsychic tension, and no apparent resolution is made.

Conflict results when individuals are dependent upon each other for the performance of tasks. This also occurs when task-oriented groups find their levels in the organization are raised and their specialization is increased as well, further intensifying a conflict-laden situation. Joint decision making appears to be a positive suggestion that many organizations use as a device to propose solutions, but conflict actually has been found to increase when decisions are made in a group manner. This occurs when individuals forced to become involved in group decision also are forced to reach a consensus; this usually heightens the intensity of the situation.

SOME TYPES OF CONFLICT

Perceived Conflict

It is likely that individuals attend more readily to conflictive conditions that they perceive to have easily accessible processes for resolution or for which accessible outcomes are available. There seems to be a preference for attending to conflictive situations involving relatively fewer negative attitudes (Filley, 1975, p. 13). Individuals' lucid perception of events and conditions regarding the conflict may even help reduce it since clarity is involved.

Felt Conflict

The most important consideration in determining the outcome of the conflict is whether the situation is personalized or depersonalized. Personalized situations are those in which the whole being of the other party is threatened or judged negatively (Filley, 1975, p. 14). When trust exists between the parties, it certainly can affect the outcome of a potentially negative conflicting situation. This may be an important consideration for institutions attempting to develop methods of resolution.

Manifest Conflict

Competition, dominance, aggression, and defense are part of an established process learned unconsciously in the family, in the school, and in the other social institutions. Problem solving, on the other hand, appears to be learned less frequently through developmental experiences. Conscious effort is required to develop and practice problem-solving skills. The appearance of anger, aggression, apathy, or rigidity in conflictive situations reduces each party's effectiveness in gaining a relative advantage and makes it difficult for both to terminate the interaction (Filley, 1975, p. 16). This manifest behavior may be identified as being that of an individual, group, or organization. Manifest conflict resolving or problem solving can be programmed in the organization as a method of dealing with this situation. This leads the managers to the position of deciding whether or not conflict should be resolved or suppressed.

RESPONSES TO CONFLICT

One way of dealing with conflict is by *avoidance*. This is the 'nonresponse" reaction that is quite similar to managers' deciding "not to decide." Avoidance behaviors are oblique in that they do not respond directly to a conflict. The respondent may try to ignore the incompatibility, hoping it will disappear, or may feign ignorance to prevent possible unpleasantness. Clamming up and refusing to talk or totally withdrawing indicates that the respondent for some reason does not believe that meeting the issue directly would be productive.

A second method of responding to conflict is via *confrontation*, which is the set of all behaviors that respond directly to the conflict. Confrontational responses range from mediational moves on the one hand to anything from simple disagreement to violent warfare on the other. All responses that are not avoidance responses are confrontational. The word confrontation, much like the word conflict, provokes a negative response. Although confront can mean oppose, less limiting and more accurate synonyms are to face up to, encounter, or meet directly (Pood & Glenn, 1979, p. 11).

Confrontation, however, is not a system that, once employed, need become uncontrollable. It actually is a resolution process that can be either regulated or unregulated. A regulated confrontation is one in which responses that neither avoid the conflict nor attempt to injure or eliminate another party are controlled. Boundaries are used to control explosions. The lower boundary of regulation begins just above avoidance, while the upper boundary ends just below injury or elimination of the other party. These are controlled responses that make the use of conflict an equitable solution. An unregulated confrontation method is a response aimed at eliminating or injuring the other party. This can be done through violence, destruction, hostile behavior, or verbal abuse. When these are used, the situation usually gets out of hand.

Management in many cases cannot prevent a conflict situation from occurring. However, a competitive climate can manifest itself and all efforts to reduce its intensity should be mobilized. A competitive organizational climate fosters the increase of hostility, with corresponding decreases in communications and interaction, further reinforcing negative, stereotyped images and associated distorted perceptions. Results usually include a breakdown in communication networks and fractured interpersonal relationships. When competition is perceived and practiced extraneously, a limited reward program manifests apparent and hidden systems of intergroup conflict.

One element of confusion that intensifies intergroup conflict is the method used in evaluating and rewarding competing groups by placing them in a goal-role ambiguity situation. Confrontation is diagnosed by the groups involved as a system superior to others that were examined and tried for conflict resolution, since opposing groups are made aware of the problems and encouraged to discuss openly their views, feelings, and expectations concerning the functions of competition.

Confrontation requires a sophisticated and skilled level of interpersonal peacemaking and conflict resolution that can be painful for the problem-solving participants or unavailable in departments and organizations (Appelbaum, 1975, p. 15). Conflict can occur because objectives are nebulous, groups are oriented to different organizational goals, and only one reward is in evidence. All win-lose situations should be avoided by not placing groups into competitive positions with limited organizational rewards/resources as stimuli. Differences of philosophy are essential to progress since an open, dynamic climate where conflict is accepted and where conformity is not rewarded can motivate any organization to actualize its mission, which is basically the perpetuation of itself (Appelbaum, 1975, p. 16).

RESOLUTION OF CONFLICT

Some of the methods of conflict resolution are manifested in the styles employed by managers in the institution:

The Win-Lose Style

Those who prefer the win-lose strategy as a dominant style typically view conflict situations as having but one of two possible outcomes—winning or losing. More often than not, winning somehow is associated with managers' status and competence, either in demonstrating these or simply maintaining them. The threat of losing is seen as tantamount to a loss of status and a display of incompetence and weakness.

Such ego-arousing values result in an approach to conflict that places prime importance on personal goals to the virtual exclusion of any concern for the relationship. Indeed, social survival is at stake and individuals who favor this approach typically seek to win at any cost. The outcome is an aggressive, dogmatic, inflexible, and unreasonable approach to conflict management in which the goal is to overcome the adversary. The effect of such tactics on the relationship usually is not even considered until after the conflict has been resolved. Suppression and coercion are the central mechanisms used, and the protection of personal goals is taken as an index of a successful encounter.

The Yield-Lose Style

As a dominant conflict management style, the yield-lose strategy reflects individuals' concern for the effect of conflict on the well-being and durability of their relationships. At the same time, it reflects an implicit assumption that human relationships are so fragile that they cannot endure the trauma of working through genuine differences. Often revealing more about people's need for affiliation and acceptance than it does about the true nature of relationships, this style seeks to appease others by ignoring, denying, or avoiding conflict. Should differences still persist, giving in and submitting to the goals of another are seen as effective ways of protecting the relationship at the cost of personal objectives.

The result is a hesitant approach to handling differences that more often than not is revealed in false cooperativeness and agreement, if not commitment. A forced, happy climate of compliance may characterize the strategy but the cost to the user is cumulative. As such, the burden of the relationship may become enormous to maintain. Personal objectives are set aside and the relationship lends itself to one-sided domination.

The Lose-Leave Style

Hopelessness is the basic feature of this strategy, which is designed to protect individuals from the useless and punishing experience of being caught up in endless struggles that they feel they cannot win. An expectation of losing characterizes the style. Rather than undergo such a frustration, persons using this style simply leave the conflict, psychologically and physically. A withdrawn and detached observer quality characterizes the style, and its users are willing to give up personal achievements as well as any positive contribution to the relationship in return for noninvolvement.

Depersonalization and careful avoidance characterize the style further. It is a way out for individuals who previously have placed unsuccessful confidence in other styles and then have decided that they cannot win. It results in compliance without commitment and more often than not leaves the users with feelings of frustration and hostility.

The Compromise Style

A little bit of winning coupled with a certain amount of losing is characteristic of this style. Reflecting essentially a variant of the win-lose philosophy, the strategy attempts to soften the effects of losing by limiting the rewards. This is seen as a means for making the situation more tolerable to individuals while somehow implying that everyone's time for winning will come along shortly. It is a persuasive and manipulative conflict management style in which both ends frequently are played against the middle in an attempt to "come out clean" while ensuring a moderate amount of success in maintaining a position.

It results in a confusion of values and a climate of paranoia among the parties. It is opportunistic and often its ends justify the means. For many people who try this style, the notion of compromise is so ingrained in their personality and their own method of operation that they lose sight of the duplicity of its strategy. They may even support their negotiations and bargaining with a great deal of verbal merchandising for their style in which they "sell" this approach as being the ultimate of the democratic method. Relationships, as well as goal achievements, usually are modest in this style.

The Synergistic Style

As a dominant style for managing conflict, the synergistic approach attaches major importance to the goals of the participants and to their relationship and its well-being at the same time. The two are not seen as mutually exclusive and therefore all goals must be served if the relationship is to endure. Differences are confronted in a problem-solving method and serve primarily as symptoms of incomplete understanding and less than acceptable levels of commitment on the part of the members of the relationship.

An implicit faith in the process of conflict resolution characterizes this approach. The faith rests on the assumption that a working through of differences may lead to a more creative solution of both personal and interpersonal problems than can be achieved by any individual. Tolerance for differences and recognizing the legitimacy of individuals' feelings are central to this strategy. In turn, this promotes a trusting climate among the individuals and develops the foundation for more objective and open appraisals of issues and their significance. Hidden agendas are brought into the open so that they may be dealt with, and relationships actually may be strengthened as a result of congruency between the goals of the individuals and the organization. This style is founded upon the concept that everyone wins and everyone also profits from resolving the conflict while maintaining the relationships.

It is important to understand that individuals use different styles based upon different situations. These styles are available to individuals involved in a conflict situation, but it often is found that once individuals have identified a dominant style, they merged it into their own network of responses. As a result, it is very difficult for them to explore other styles or to change some of them. It should be noted that a change of dominant style and other backup styles may occur in the individuals' relationship in the organization based upon similar changes in the power structure and the goals to be achieved. No one is locked into a given profile simply because it characterizes that person at a particular point.

Effective Styles

Current research on conflict resolution indicates that the most effective managers and organizations resolve their conflicts in the following order:

1. confrontation
2. smoothing
3. compromise
4. forcing
5. withdrawal (Filley, 1975, p. 31)

An added dimension and explanation of these five styles is essential in presenting their strengths and characteristics as resolution strategies. Confrontation involves an open exchange of information in which both parties in conflict work through the situation to achieve a result. This has proved to be the most effective in health care systems. Smoothing—the second most popular choice—involves playing down differences and appealing to common interests. This leads only to a worsening of problems since no action is taken. Compromise, the third method, is one in which no one wins or loses and essentially is a groping search for a halfway something. Forcing, the fourth method, produces a winner and a loser, is competitive, and polarizes the parties. Withdrawal, the last and least effective, is a strategy in which it is easier to refrain than retreat from an argument. Problems therefore never are confronted and remain unsolved (Appelbaum, 1974, pp. 24-25).

SOME REMEDIES FOR MANAGING CONFLICT

One of the initial ways of exploring remedies to resolving conflict is to consider the development of a joint agenda on the part of the groups involved. If there can be open disagreement, then a great deal of the uncertainty of a situation will be reduced. The organization can train individuals in the theory and techniques of resolving conflict and may even involve them in developing commitments for problem solving through a win-win solution, rather than a win-lose or an "all-out war." It may be important to initiate open conferences where individuals may explore their feelings and anger toward each other. This may be the appropriate place to resolve some of the conflicts, avoiding the complex organizational health care situation where it becomes very costly and counterproductive.

In some studies (Filley, 1975) examining the structure of individuals in groups it was found that conflict could be reduced when individuals worked in a close side-by-side arrangement leading to cooperation. When they were placed in a face-to-face structure, this led to competition and an ensuing no-holds-barred confrontation that was quite destructive. Management must resolve boundary decisions so that individual jurisdictions can be clarified, ambiguity reduced, and the conflict itself ultimately cooled. The following questions and suggestions could be explored with regard to boundary and personal space:

1. Do the spatial arrangements promote equality and avoid divisiveness? Problem solving should take place on neutral territory with

parties arranged in a nonconfrontational manner that directs attention and energy to the problem.

2. Are time constraints minimized? Problem solving occurs most readily where the parties are not pressured by a deadline.

3. Is group size controlled to facilitate interaction and avoid divisiveness? Groups of five to seven persons are most appropriate for interaction and member satisfaction. Larger groups may be used, but member interaction is reduced and restrictive.

4. Is the communication process arranged so that all members communicate with each other rather than having communication channeled through a single group representative? The former arrangement will promote problem solving and the latter conflictive relations.

5. Is the leader controlling the process rather than the content of group interaction? Process leaders make sure that the necessary steps in the problem-solving system take place, rather than promoting their own preferred solutions; content leaders do the same.

6. Is information shared by all parties rather than hoarded by some to be used for their own strategic advantage? Shared information promotes trust and reduces differences of power associated with information monopolies. Hoarded information reduces trust, creates power differences, and increases the potential for conflict.

7. Are opportunities provided to deal with problems as they occur rather than reserving them for discussion at a later date? Delays permit facts to be lost and positions distorted; problem solving is facilitated when parties can handle problems as they arise (Filley, 1975, p. 96).

Perceptions are important in exploring remedies since managers grapple with some type of reality testing to determine whether or not their views are correct in situations that appear to be negative conflicts. These perceptions should connect to individuals' evaluation of conditions surrounding these events. If individuals involved in a conflict situation see only limited solutions, then the problems will continue. One way of perceiving events in a limited manner is for managers to feel that conflict, by definition, is avoidable, when in fact it is inevitable. They may feel that conflict is caused by troublemakers and people who enjoy doing this when conflict actually may be determined by the physical structure of the organization—the shape of the room, the geographical disbursement of individuals involved, and the nature of the structure. Other factors that may pose problems involve individuals who perceive that going through channels creates conflict when conflict actually is an integral part of the nature of change.

These perceptions are problems that affect individuals in health care organizations through the attitudinal structure. In dealing with these perceptions, it is important to get a reading on the attitudes and feelings of the individuals involved in a problem-solving situation since some of these may be explicit enough to deal with behavioral manifestations and some may even lead to conflicting situations themselves.

Persons who are low in self-esteem are more vulnerable, feel threatened, have a great need for structure, exhibit aggression, and yield more to group pressure than those who possess higher self-esteem. To resolve this conflict it is important to weigh the individuals' perceptions and level of self-esteem, since added knowledge regarding the cause of conflict for these individuals is colored by their personal characteristics, previous training, motivation, and ability to learn and change. People will resist using new knowledge, attitudes, and skills until their organization supplies social supports to reward the new behavior. When problem solving rather than unresolvable conflict and competition is encouraged by top leadership, the process becomes institutionalized and more readily accepted by those involved.

There is a link between managing conflict and the anxiety that individuals experience. Anxiety creates feelings of uncertainty, and in managing conflict people usually are dealing with individuals who demonstrate aggression that often becomes a part of their managerial style. The manner in which conflict is managed and not repressed contributes heavily to the organization's effectiveness. Uncertainty is a major component of the managers' existence, creates anxiety, and must be dealt with throughout their problem-solving tenure with their organization.

In the turbulent environment of contemporary business suffused with ambiguity, the hard-headed executive with strong nerves and a feel for the moment of drama that a crisis affords has the chance to restructure the organizational scene in a way that may meet both the administrator's needs of self-fulfillment and the interests of the institution.

Closely involved with conflict is tension. Research evidence suggests that tension needs to be reappraised and that the exploitation of healthy tension can:

- stimulate learning
- serve to internalize the problems of other managers
- increase critical vigilance and self-appraisal
- induce decision makers to examine conflicting values (including their own) more discerningly when they are making decisions (Kelly, 1970, p. 106).

There appears to be an optimal level of anxiety and conflict that an individual can experience to function effectively. However, when the conflict and anxiety lead to severe stress and this threshold is exceeded, certain problems arise that become very counterproductive to both the organization and the individual. As noted particularly in Chapter 6, this vicious cycle affects the manager's family and other personal relationships. Managers must understand that the organization exists in a turbulent environment in which the rate of change is accelerating at a great pace. Normally the institution has difficulty adjusting to this, which makes it more difficult for individual managers to cope personally, since they themselves are having a difficult time adjusting to the demands of macrosystem and to change itself.

WHAT ABOUT CHANGE?

The management of change and the management of conflict do occur in health care institutions. Some of the resulting individual problems manifest themselves in organizational problems. Individuals experiencing change may feel apprehensive, anxiety ridden, or dissatisfied, or tend to lose interest in their work; others cope with their anxiety and stress by avoiding work or by retiring temporarily on the job. Some develop anxiety symptoms, become depressed, and fall victim to psychosomatic disorders. The effect of change on individuals accounts for some of the psychological and organizational problems experienced such as alcoholism, drug abuse, emotional illness, and family crisis as already discussed.

Change does have positive aspects. One of the most important factors to consider for a healthy outcome is that the organization is perceived as trustworthy. Changes generated by management must be seen by employees to be in their best interests for the future or problems will occur. However, anxieties concerning change do arise, some of them largely rational and concerned with such topics as job security, work satisfaction, uncertainties about the new situation, career prospects, status, pay, and differentials. In particular, individuals may be far from certain that they want to adapt to the change or have the ability to do so, and may have many doubts about the adequacy of their skills or personality resources to meet the challenge of a new situation (Brook, 1977, p. 94). Many change-oriented situations force individuals to reexperience earlier personal anxieties that may be deep seated, based upon episodes that affected their lives, family, and work situation. These traumas may reappear in the present existence of individuals who are unable to resolve these conflicts.

CLIENTS OF CHANGE

Change and anxieties bring out primitive infantile feelings experienced at earlier points in individuals' lives when they were more helpless. These feelings have been repressed and kept tightly under control. As adults develop their attitudes about change, these feelings may be negative. These individuals may be forced to become integrated with their own contemporary group with which they identify socially and intellectually. Even though they have intellectualized their anxieties over sudden changes in their environment, they have not actually internalized such personal events and continue to experience fears and uncertainties that lead to confusion and helplessness.

This is one of the areas in which an occupational psychologist or physician can be essential to the organization because individuals may wish to discuss their perceived anxieties about change. They may find this difficult to do in an objective, rational manner with their managers. As a result of this blocked ventilation valve they become invalids due to primitive irrational feelings. Individuals become anxiety ridden and vulnerable and are affected by changes and events over which they have no control. If a work situation is uncertain, then the individuals can take this unstable climate as an opportunity in which to project their internal conflicts in order to eliminate them. They then believe that all their problems are organizationally based and that their supervisors are the reason for their anxiety and stress. Irrational reactions to sudden change have a major effect on these persons. The outlet for this may be alcohol, drugs, or a turbulent family environment.

People are vulnerable to changes who have attained a certain goal in life that they feel has been connected to reaching the peak of their abilities. This also affects those who are in late middle age and not adapting well. These people react negatively to change, they resist it, or they may have physical or emotional problems and feel forced to leave the institution. Others affected are in jobs where the changes involved withdrawal of some of the satisfactions they had worked so hard to achieve.

Other individuals who are vulnerable have personality difficulties and compensate for their disappointment in other areas of their existence by taking the job and making it the major component of their way of life. This, of course, leads to extreme disappointment, disillusionment, and the need to be dysfunctional. Individuals with obsessional personality structures, who need a routinized way of life through their jobs as reinforcement against their anxieties, react poorly to changes.

The middle managers in health care institutions can be particularly vulnerable in a time of change. They often are expected to reconcile pressures from above for initiation of the change in the interests of the organization, they face the resultant resentment pressures from below. They may act indecisively, which subordinates may take as a justification for regarding the managers as inadequate and thus intensify their criticisms. How well managers cope depends on the understanding and support they receive from their superiors. Experience suggests that a change that is instigated entirely in the interests of the organization without proper consideration of its effects on the people concerned is a very potent factor in causing stress (Brook, 1977, p. 97). While change often is exciting, it creates stress both for those who are involved and those who are uninvolved directly. Change often is a prerequisite for conflict that must be managed before it becomes counterproductive and dysfunctional.

Some of the research (Brook, 1976, pp. 484-492) focusing on change has indicated the following concepts for consideration in the health care environment:

Positive Aspects of Change

This usually is characterized by an attitude on the part of those affected by change of a positive nature and who expect the change. It may even be a relief for them that an unsatisfactory condition now has been offset and that their satisfaction at work will increase as a result of a new system. One of the best things about this is that the outcome is considered to be positive for the organization and for the individual.

Anxieties About Change

Individuals experience rational anxieties about changes that affect their job security, work satisfaction, general uncertainties, career changes, salaries, and status. They may not know what will be happening to them and have certain questions about their adaptability and whether or not they still will be able to use skills that now may not be adequate. At the same time they may feel angry because they have been dependent upon management and now changes have occurred that create newer anxieties.

Early Personal Anxieties

Any change that managers go through in the organization helps reacquaint them with deep-seated fears that occurred at earlier stages of their lives when they were least prepared. Even though these individuals reach adulthood, an infantile component exists that brings out confusion and tremendous fears of the unknown. At this juncture, the anxiety can lead to stress that interferes with normative functioning if not managed.

Group Anxieties

The customary working methods of a group form a social structure that helps keep anxieties under control. Change is regarded as such a threat because it involves the removal of this special defense against anxieties. This is one aspect of group resistance to change. If the anxieties are unusually intense, certain forms of group behavior may predominate over individual reaction. Without realizing it, the individual may become trapped in certain forms of group behavior. One example is a fight-or-flight group that takes action as a means of coping with its conflicts. As a flight group it may retreat to known boundaries and be totally resistant to change. As a fight group, it may label management as the source of confusion and irrational behavior (Brook, 1978, p. 11), thus accelerating conflict and resulting stress.

People who experience severe anxiety have a difficult time readjusting and are vulnerable. For example, they may be caught in a double bind of having to adjust to internal conflicts of their own personality dynamics while at the same time experiencing a midcareer life crisis with an accompanying change in the organization. These persons may attempt to point their finger angrily at the organization, realizing that management was responsible for their conflict.

Individuals become vulnerable when they reach a certain goal in their life and then, for no apparent logical reason, must readjust again and move into a new situation that the organization brainstormed and implemented unilaterally. When they have reached personal goals and have experienced personal satisfaction in life, they feel a sense of deprivation when they are forced by their organization to learn new behaviors. This sudden change creates a disruption to their equilibrium that is referred to as cognitive dissonance (Festinger, 1957, pp. 1-31). This is an antecedent condition leading to activity oriented toward reducing the dissonance that may be a psychologically uncomfortable inconsistency and motivates individuals to attempt to reduce or avoid the associated stress.

These feelings of stress and tension bring about needs for change in individuals because they are forced to realize that their old methods and behaviors are creating serious problems since the organization now is "encouraging" them to adapt to a new system. They actually are helped to unfreeze old methods-techniques and repress feelings they experienced while in equilibrium, that are not now positive. This unfreezing also is associated with personal acceptance and responsibilities for old patterns of behavior that, in many individuals, are not one of their hallmarks of mental health.

In many cases, individuals are not aware of the alternatives available to them and unnecessarily feel trapped. When they do attempt to select an alternative and experience some success with the new behavior, this becomes a stimulus. As a result, they discover that the unfreezing process was essential and now they are not as reluctant to adapt new behaviors through a refreezing process since this is the path to the successful goal of changed behavior. They also are willing to assume personal ownership of their new behavior and may even experience higher levels of self-esteem with increasing positive new social relationships.

Ineffectiveness and counterproductivity occur when the institution socializes individuals who are in vulnerable roles and whose positions and interrelationships are redundant. When their objectives are obscure, the role requirements become confusing and the individuals experience anxiety and conflict. Middle managers are expected to reconcile all the anxieties and pressures experienced by the organizations' top level executives and act as buffers so the vibrations will not be felt by those at the bottom of the hierarchy. The objective is to avoid a reverse backlash where dissatisfactions and associated problems are not transmitted up the organizational structure. This is a difficult position to put someone in since it creates other turmoil and conflict. Individuals are vulnerable when put into positions that have structural difficulties associated with them.

An interesting study (Dornstein, 1977, pp. 253-263) focused on conflict and role stress experienced by top management in voluntary organizations. State-owned corporations in Israel are reported to be inherently ambiguous in structure in that they are expected to be economically rational and efficient at the same time as they achieve objectives in the public interest. It was assumed that chief executives, being directly responsible for organizational conduct, would be vulnerable to role conflict in regard to corporate objectives and modes for their attainment. A sample of 59 chief executives and board members from 17 corporations was interviewed. The data suggest that role stress among chief executives is related positively to role conflicts within the board regarding disagreements about organizational means and ends. Role conflicts within the board were related to feelings of isolation among chief executives. Isolation can lead to intrapsychic tension and ultimate stress that both executive and subordinates will experience.

Experience suggests that a change instigated entirely in the interests of the institution without proper consideration of its effect on the people concerned is a very potent factor in causing stress. It has been shown that the most effective way of arousing hostility to change is to exercise unyielding pressure and not to listen to what the work force has to say (Brook, 1978, p. 13).

MANAGING CONFLICT IN HEALTH CARE

Elizabeth Kubler-Ross in her book *Death: The Final Stage of Growth* (1975) collected impressive evidence to show that most people experienced five distinct stages after a significant change had affected the stability of their lives:

1. denial or shock
2. anger
3. bargaining
4. depression
5. acceptance

These states have applicability to organizational behaviors and problems associated with changes that, interpreted psychoanalytically, connote separation and death. Too often the trauma associated with even the slightest change is discounted. It is important to note that the magnitude of the change must be judged by the person experiencing it, not by the supervisor. In other words, managers must make themselves aware of how those affected receive the changes (Morano, 1977, p. 21). This is demonstrated by institutions employing change agents to help deal with the shocks of stress.

Occupational health physicians are involved increasingly in acting as consultants to organizations to help them identify internal conflicts, the resolution of which can improve the well-being of employees, reduce the level of stress, and prevent casualties. By assuming this role, the physicians can help, even indirectly, many more individuals than by remaining specialists who deal only with the victims of change. Managers, attributing their difficulties to subordinates suffering from symptoms of stress who are therefore medical problems, often only want advice from the physician on how to cope with them or seek relief by a straight transfer of responsibility to the doctor. The latter, however, on the basis of knowledge of the organization and its structure and administration may feel that it is a professional duty to call attention to intrinsic weaknesses that might be contributing to the symptoms of stress.

Thus, without realizing it, managers and physicians have conflicting basic aims and so can quickly lose patience with one another. For managers, this problem may be expressed as how to cope with both the anxieties of the people over whom they have responsibility and the frustrations, uncertainties, and at times sense of helplessness that may be aroused in themselves in the process. For physicians, the problem is how to cope with both the distress of the managers and the worries and uncertainties that the latter may cause (Brook, 1978, p. 14).

The problem of coping with change and resolving conflict is essential in the health care environment in which the perceptions of the individual diagnosticians as well as administrators is so critical for the effectiveness of delivering service. When individuals are under stress they experience a narrowing of perception and an increased rigidity. They may be unaware of what is occurring around them, they focus virtually all their thinking on the situation producing the stress, and they tend to become immobilized.

Some persons have a greater tolerance for some stress, probably because of their genetic predisposition or makeup. It is important, therefore, to distinguish among individuals in the institution and decide who is more vulnerable to pressure and stress. By gearing the amount of stress to individual tolerance, managers can obtain maximum performance and efficiency and prevent disruption. The concept or belief that stress is additive explains some seemingly irrational behaviors on the job. A manager may ask a clerical employee why a report wasn't in on time, only to have the worker explode over what normally would be a relatively innocuous question. The subordinate may have had trouble with the children, the spouse may have wrecked the car, or the person might not have been feeling well or might have had other problems. The employee just reached the threshold stress level, and irrational behavior resulted. The fact is, the worker simply had not had time to recover from all the accumulated woes.

Only rarely do individuals experience a single severe stress (Morano, p. 24). The importance of this is that the life style demands and individuals' ability to handle stress are not mutually exclusive. There is a direct link between excessive demands on the individual and unanticipated consequences of behavior. This indicates that an essential method for managing stress and attempting to resolve it is to reduce it before it blows out of proportion.

Managers in health care institutions do have a responsibility to develop these insights and gain expertise in the operation of their organizations so that the deleterious effect of stress can be minimized and both the individual and the organization can experience a certain degree of satisfaction. This situation can be exemplified by conflicts that break out into the open between administrators and the medical staff. These conflicts seem to be increasing as charges of inefficiency are directed at the administration. The administrator continually faces pressures from different directions and eruptions in the various departments. Certain solutions can be applied to resolving these unanticipated conflicts. Most of the major conflict resolution processes have been addressed, but there are several more that have been used in these environments. The resolution of conflict in the health care institution is important because there is a direct link between the intensity of a conflict being experienced by an individual working in the system and the quality of patient care.

This situation is quite serious since stress management by the health care provider and professional has a direct impact on the quality of care and, often, on terminal behavior. It is the health professional's behavior that is most sensitive and reactive to the stressors and problems encountered in practice. Anxiety and tension impede the natural flow of communication. Stressed providers cannot listen empathetically nor can they respond sensitively. Constructive involvement in the problems of others requires concentration, energy, and peace of mind.

Although research is sparse, there is mounting evidence that stressed providers suffer measurable impairment in cognitive and technical competencies and relationship skills (Maslach, 1979, p. 112). Rigidity in thought processes, inaccurate diagnoses, and attribution of triviality to patients' complaints leading to incomplete workups are among the deficits in the performance noted in a broad spectrum of stressed health care professionals, including nurses, physicians, and administrators. Major conflict is experienced by all caught in this bind, which unfortunately is often unresolvable.

When a synergistic relationship exists among physicians, nurses, and administrators, the quality of care in the institution is higher. Researchers (Thompson, 1961, p. 519) who study conflict suggest that conflict fosters institutional creativity and progress. While this may be a valid point, the welfare of the patient certainly is a major consideration and is affected directly by this situation. In addition, unresolved conflict can be debilitating for the participants if not managed, and the total system can experience disequilibrium and may become entropic.

Certain internal characteristics inherent in the hospital organization foster conflict. For example, interdependence, specialization, and heterogeneity of personnel in levels of authority all appear to be related positively to conflict. In fact, few institutions are composed of as many diverse skills as the hospital, which generally has nearly three employees for each patient and a heterogeneous health team influenced by more than 300 different professional societies and associations.

Individuals' roles in the hospital can have a major effect on the intensity of the conflict they experience and to which they are subjected. Their personal characteristics and previous experiences will determine the effect of their coping mechanism on role conflict. Physicians, for example, function as agents for individual patients, their own specialties, their profession, their staff, their institution, their community, and their own welfare as individual practitioners. The welfare of these individuals and groups, and obligations of the physicians to them and to themselves, are in conflict periodically.

Role ambiguity is related to role conflict. Role ambiguity can be defined as uncertainty about how superiors evaluate work, scope of responsibility, opportunities for advancement, and what others expect in the way of job performance. A variety of studies (Kahn, 1964) demonstrate that there frequently is a wide disparity between what a superior expects of subordinates and what the subordinates think the superior expects of them (Schultz & Johnson, 1976, p. 163). These professionals experience the ambiguity and conflict as they too often are components of the job description and organizational climate as well.

These conflicts must be dealt with by administrators who are caught in the middle of this bind. Retreating into their own area of expertise and not attempting to exert their influence in arenas in which they may feel their competence is not up to par will not resolve conflict nor reduce stress. The implication is that the administrators can minimize their tension, anxiety, and conflict by maintaining a reduced influence and lesser role. However, the nature of managerial work indicates clearly that these executives have interpersonal roles, informational roles, and decision-making roles that can influence seemingly uncontrollable conditions (Mintzberg, 1973). They often are figureheads, spokespersons, disturbance handlers, negotiators, leaders, entrepreneurs, and resource allocators. The multiplicity of these roles implies the need to influence decisions and behavior in the organization. These administrators work with influence, authority, and power that can be defined as the maximum ability of a person or group to influence other individuals or groups. Authority has been defined as legitimate power. Filley and House (1969, p. 60) have summarized the basis of power as being derived from:

1. legitimacy
2. control of rewards and sanctions, including money
3. expertise

4. personal liking
5. coercion

Hospital administrators usually have (1) legitimacy from delegated authority over hospital affairs from the governing board; (2) effective control of funds, beds, and other resources; (3) increasing expertise, particularly as management information systems improve; (4) personal liking, and (5) the ability to coerce through demand of such sources as the Joint Commission on the Accreditation of Hospitals. Studies by Perrow (1963, pp. 112-146) and Georgopoulos and Mann (1962, p. 567) confirm the increasing dominance of administrators. However, recent demands by the American Medical Association and medical staffs in many hospitals for medical staff representation on hospital boards tend to confirm the administrators' declining influence (Schultz & Johnson, 1976, p. 165). This trend can only increase the anxiety and stress experienced by administrators who are attempting to balance their domains.

Surveys in health care institutions indicated that the medical staffs and the trustees did not view the health care administrator as the leader but one who was extremely passive and a go-between or intermediary for the board and the medical staff (*Modern Hospital,* 1968, p. 29). In addition, the administrators' drive for professionalism tends to leave the idea that status seeking is essential in the quest to maintain a power base. Physicians also are attempting to increase their power base. This creates a conflict situation in the institution. Physicians and nurses do have an initial allegiance to professional status and not to the needs of the institution, which seems to be the primary focus for health care administrators.

Certain hospital inefficiencies are due to dual management responsibilities and the conflict between bureaucratic structure and individual patient care. This situation could be alleviated with a more flexible organizational structure focusing on the needs of both diverse groups. Chris Argyris (1965, p. 62) focused on this in some of his earlier research and indicated that the nursing staff believed administrators actually were second-class citizens while viewing their own occupation as a profession. This adds to conflict of status. The conflict in the hospital must be reduced to a functional level and at the same time, the effectiveness and satisfactions of the parties in the organization must be increased.

One way to do this would be to redesign the managerial systems as open, organic structures in the quest to resolve the initial conflict. The managerial styles, structures, technologies, and networks responsible for this initial problem could be used antithetically to reverse the direction of the problem so that equilibrium could be maintained and the system balanced. Some approaches to solving these problems are:

- comprehensive institutional goal setting
- organizational changes and public relations programs
- community goal setting
- management by objectives
- job descriptions and organizational structuring
- creative problem solving
- constructive confrontation
- participative management
- team training and building
- sensitivity training.

The conflict in the health care environment is complex, but it can be dealt with by diagnosing the issues that are relevant and looking at who the conflicting participants are. This is an essential mission in need of unravelling. The clients of the hospital are participants in the conflict, as are the administration, the medical staff, and the nursing administration. All parties should be involved in the resolution of the conflict.

These conflicts are individual, intraorganizational, and many times interpersonal. When these issues are diagnosed properly and separated into components, it is easier to discern some of the primary sources of the conflict. The following areas are related sources of conflict in the health care environment; a model for health care administrators can be used to serve as a corrective device. The sources are:

1. goal displacement
2. inadequate communication
3. role conflict
4. role ambiguity
5. disagreements
6. antagonism
7. balance of power
8. status
9. unfulfilled expectations
10. free-floating stress

In the quest to change certain systems that have proved counterproductive and dysfunctional, it is important to note that the change process in itself is an anxiety-rising experience for individuals. An ideal change process should give the individuals a sense of the operation itself and leave them with an understanding of the means through which they can continuously monitor and alter their behavior in situations in the organization and within their own personality structure and dynamics.

The goals, the philosophies, and the techniques of any change program in the health care system intended to strengthen a management program and reduce conflicts and anxieties should encourage or at least be consistent with the values of self-governance, individual responsibility, mature interdependence, organizational goals, and finally the individuals and their own unique nature.

When this system is congruent, then the milieu of behaviors and ultimately the responsibilities will be in equilibrium with the health care environment. An excellent method to clarify relationships and reduce conflict is the process of management by objectives, the focus of the next chapter.

BIBLIOGRAPHY

Appelbaum, S.H. Changing attitudes: A path to the management of conflict. *The Personnel Administrator,* June 1974, *19*(4), 23-25.

————. An experimental case study of organizational suboptimization and problem solving. *Akron Business and Economic Review,* Fall 1975, *6*(3), 13-16.

Argyris, C. *Diagnosing human relations in organizations: A case study of a hospital.* New Haven, Conn.: Labor and Management Center, Yale University, 1965, 62.

Brook, A. Psychiatric disorders in industry. *British Journal of Hospital Medicine,* 1976, *15*, 484--492.

Brook, A. The role of the occupational physician: Coping with the stress of change. In *Reducing occupational stress: Proceedings of the National Institute for Occupational Safety and Health,* White Plains, N.Y., May 1977, 93-100.

————. Coping with the stress of change. *Management International Review,* 1978, *18*(3), 9-15.

Dornstein, M. Organization conflict and role stress among chief executives in state business enterprises. *Journal of Occupational Psychology,* December 1977, *5*, 253-263.

Festinger, L. *A theory of cognitive dissonance.* Palo Alto, Calif.: Stanford University Press, 1957, 1-31.

Filley, A.C., *Interpersonal conflict resolution.* Glenview, Ill.: Scott Foresman and Co., 1975.

Filley, A.C., & House, R.J. *Managerial process and organizational behavior.* Glenview, Ill.: Scott Foresman and Co., 1969,

Georgopoulos, B., and Mann, F. *The community general hospital.* New York: The MacMillan Co., 1962, 567.

Kahn, R. *Organizational stress.* New York: John Wiley and Sons, 1964.

Kubler-Ross, E. *Death: The final stage of growth.* Englewood Cliffs, N.J.: Prentice-Hall, Inc., 1975.

Kelly, J. Make conflict work for you. *Harvard Business Review,* July-August 1970, *48*(4), 103-113.

Maslach, C. The burnout syndrome and patient care. In *Stress and survival: The emotional realities of life-threatening illnesses.* St. Louis: The C.V. Mosby Co., 1979, 112-128.

Mintzberg, H. *The nature of managerial work.* New York: Harper & Row, 1973,

Morano, R.A. How to manage change to reduce stress. *Management Review,* November 1977, *66*(11), 21-25.

Perrow, C. Goals and power structure. *The Hospitals and Modern Society,* E. Friedson, ed. New York: Free Press, 1963, 112-146.

Pood, E.A., & Glenn, E.C. Conflict management and communication: A conceptual model. *Academy of Management* meeting, Atlanta, August 1979,   (Paper)

Schultz, R., & Johnson, A. Conflict in hospitals. In J.L. Gibson, J.M. Ivancevich, & J.H. Donnelly (Eds.), *Readings in organizations: Behavior, structure and processes.* Dallas: Business Publications Inc., 1976, 161-173.

Thompson, V. Hierarchy, specialization and organizational conflict. *Administrative Science Quarterly,* March 1961, *5*, 485-521.

Trustee's view of administrators told. *Modern Hospital,* October 1968, 29.

Chapter 11

Management by Objectives

CONSIDERATIONS FOR THE HEALTH CARE MANAGER

1. Management by Objectives (MBO) is a process intended to bring about the formulation of clear goals, the development of realistic action plans to achieve goals, and the necessary steps to achieve results. It is closely linked to participative management and develops a commitment to the organization.

2. It is crucial to balance a variety of needs and goals in every area where performance and results directly and vitally affect the survival and prosperity of the organization. These objectives must be defined in terms of the manager's contributions to the overall unit of which they are a part.

3. Many managers do not plan for the setting of objectives because they may be extremely orthodox and rigid in their thinking, which makes it difficult for them to make organizational decisions. Managers who are not totally immersed in the traditional methods of managing appear to do much better in MBO programs.

4. MBO is a systems approach to operating an organization. It is not a technique and goes far beyond mere budgeting. The objectives

are states of individual motivation derived from the needs of particular individuals. The objectives are values to be achieved by both the individuals and the organization.

5. The output of an employee of a health care organization is difficult to determine, particularly when objectives are to be stated. Before pay can be related to production, a viable method of measuring individual performance must be developed.

6. Group goal setting is essential since the goals of a health care organization personify the image of a well-managed institution. Goals should be defined as to the amount and direction of change that is desired from the present in a given period of time. This is a needs analysis.

7. Goals and objectives must be specific, defined in terms of measurable results, linked to overall organization aims, given a specific time period for review and accomplishment, required to be flexible, established under a plan of action to accomplish results, and, finally, prioritized.

8. As long as managers appraise only the end result of an operation without giving adequate weight to the means result, there will be problems with this process.

9. A new appraisal system may be needed that is a behavioral job description and not the traditional substantive method that has created problems and dysfunction.

10. The MBO interview process is crucial for the success of this method where objectives can be negotiated in a reality-based manner, and even openly renegotiated. This commitment is essential also for the feedback element of this process. Without feedback, support and control are virtually diluted.

11. The guidelines for developing an MBO plan must include the quantitative statement of an attainable objective with an accompanying weight for priority. Standards of perfor-

mance and terminal dates should be suggested for solidifying the agreement between the parties.

One of the efficient and effective methods of increasing managerial
expertise and skill is by the use of a managerial and behavioral process
called management by objectives. This process, when executed in the
most efficient and effective manner by skilled managers, is an important component in developing a model intended to reduce ambiguity,
anxiety, and stress. While management by objectives (commonly
referred to as MBO) has its roots in the industrial domain, its application in government agencies and health care institutions is common
and studies have demonstrated substantial success in its use.
However, this book looks exclusively at MBO in the health care domain while drawing from the organizational model that has proved
valid and reliable.

Hospitals are different and deal with people, with lives, with patient
care. The goal is not increased production, increased sales, or increased
profits. But before it can be concluded that the methods of General
Motors or other business managers cannot be helpful, it first must be
demonstrated that industry also does not deal with people, with lives,
with the physical, emotional, ecological well-being of people (Deegan,
1977, p. 2). The environment of a hospital is quite complex, based on
the interrelated services and value systems of those working in such
an institution. The complexities and dynamics of this environment require a system of management that is intended to focus more on
results and less on activities. The essence of this is a management by
objectives process and program.

MBO is not a new concept. In fact, it really is just common sense,
and most competent managers apply its principle, even if they do not
call it "MBO." However, many managers work toward their own
departmental objectives rather than toward the overall company
goals, thus sometimes creating a disparity between the two. Many
managers never know what objectives they are trying to achieve,
which is a problem even today.

The term MBO was used first by Peter F. Drucker in *The Practice of
Management* (1954, pp. 128-129). He made three main points:

1. For a business to be successful, all managers' jobs must be
   directed toward the objectives of the business.
2. Managers should set their own objectives and be able to control
   their own future.

3. Management development is essentially self-development of the manager under the guidance of the boss.

Not until the mid-1960s did systems develop that could incorporate Drucker's ideas effectively.

The process is important in helping health care managers to differentiate between what should be and what is. This system of personal responsibility is essential since results are the barometer used in allocating the rewards and human resources of the hospital. These results often are used for approving new programs, modifying some programs, or eliminating others that have proved to be unfeasible or unworkable. Overall organizational objectives, once they are developed and applied, are significant targets in the success of a health care organization. They provide the basis for selecting and allocating resources and serve as foundations for long-range and short-range goals, policies, and procedures. The plans help the organization evaluate the performance and progress of its resources.

These activities assist the management of a health care institution to guide operations and plan for future contingencies. Therefore, it is important that precise objectives and subgoals are agreed upon by the parties involved or individual efforts may not contribute to the essential overall success of the organization. These broad-based goals must be translated into specific, pedestrian objectives that are meaningful and that can be achieved.

The MBO process appears on the surface to be simplistic, but the dynamic impact of the internal and external environment and other intraorganizational phenomena create certain problems that are discussed in this chapter. The very nature of management involves coordinating the activities of individuals toward the attainment of objectives and goals. Managers have as their major task the definition and interpretation of broad organizational goals and their translation into operational targets for subordinates. The integration of these objectives must be understood completely by everyone involved and must carry top management's commitment.

MBO—A PHILOSOPHY AND/OR A METHOD?

Management by objectives is a philosophy of management and not a reactive way of running an organization. The emphasis on MBO is the attempt to predict and influence the contingencies that affect the institution and not react to events that have occurred already. A major focus is on change and improving the organizational and individual contributions of this dualistic system. The MBO process is important for a participative management system since it is an interdependent and interrelated system based upon:

- the formulation of clear statements of objectives
- the development of realistic action plans needed to achieve these objectives
- the systematic management and measurement of achievement and performance
- the taking of necessary steps to actualize the results.

MBO is well connected to participative management as a philosophy and technique intended to give employees an adequate input into issues concerning their careers and welfare and to improve the organizational climate most effectively. Feelings of personal significance, involvement, and sense of efficacy gained from having a say in the overall operation can lead individuals to develop not only a sense of commitment to the health care institution but also a desire to see it succeed. Although feelings of pride in one's organization seem relatively rare in health care, participative management programs can help foster such feelings. These positive attitudes tend to prevent or reverse the frequently negative effects of unresolved conflict battles. Specific advantages include:

- improved morale
- more efficient communications up and down the organization
- earlier detection and action on operational problems
- simultaneous improvement in worker satisfaction and productivity
- increased trust between employees and managers
- reduced absenteeism and turnover
- greater willingness by management to institute changes beneficial to workers
- greater employee support of management plans and actions
- improvement in the competitive position of the institution through greater operating efficiency
- making the MBO program alive and legitimate through participation

The MBO process is a system of management intended to illuminate planning, control, organizing, problem solving, decision making, and motivation. It allows certain aspects of organizational processing to be handled in a logical, systematic, and human manner. It involves performance appraisal, organizational development, managerial development, compensation, and personnel planning as integral parts of the total system. Management by and with objectives is an extremely important aspect of controlling some organizational processes and costs.

While health care executives who are not medically trained often assume the role of administrator in a health care setting, it is the physicians who have managed the institution and have made key operating decisions, even though they often seem poorly prepared for this role. The following is an account of a consultant in a health care institution who worked with medical staff on managerial processes:

> In the past years we have taught accounting and finance to hundreds of doctors who have charge of large and powerful healthcare institutions. Although they are enormously talented and industrious individuals, very few could read or understand his or her own financial statements. The sums wasted because of lack of managerial skills must be substantial. Conversely, the acquisition of general management skills by doctors will enormously enhance the efficiency and effectiveness of the healthcare system. Training and organizational behavior, financial mechanisms, investment management, and techniques for capital and operating budgeting is easy to acquire (Herzlinger, 1978, p. 107).

At the same time, management by objectives should be considered as a foundation for a managerial appraisal system that has proved to be effective and significant for the comprehensive operation of a health care organization. This process links many aspects of management tasks and responsibilities that must be under the control of the health care administrator. Drucker feels that the solution to hospital problems, which is becoming increasingly clear, will lie in thinking through objectives and priorities (Drucker, 1977, p. 140). He appears to suggest that the job of management is to balance a variety of needs and goals in every area where performance and results directly and vitally affect the survival and prosperity of the organization.

The first requirement in managing is determining what the organization wants to accomplish through the various management units or, in other words, the actual objectives for the units. Drucker's contention was that these objectives should be defined in terms of the managers' contributions to the overall units of which they are a part. Therefore, to assure that unit goals are congruent with the total organization, each manager must develop objectives supporting the objectives of the next higher unit, or as Rensis Likert (1967) hypothesized, the development of a linking process. Drucker described the total process as follows:

> The goal of each manager's job must be defined by the contribution he has to make to the success of the larger unit of which he is a part. This requires each manager to develop and set the objectives of his unit himself. Higher management must of course reserve the power to approve or disapprove these objectives. But their development is part of a manager's responsibility; indeed, it is his first responsibility.

It means, too, that managers should participate responsibly in the development of the objectives of the higher unit of which they are a part. Precisely, because their aim should reflect the objective needs of the business, rather than merely what the individual managers want, they must commit themselves with a positive act of assent. They must know and understand the ultimate business goals, what is expected of them and why, and what they will be measured against and how. There must be a meeting of the minds in the entire management of each unit. This can be achieved only when each of the contributing managers is expected to think through what the unit objectives are and to participate actively and responsibly in the work of defining them.

Drucker emphasized that top management commitment to, and participation in, MBO is essential. Top management's overriding responsibility for overall organizational planning has long been recognized by management theorists and practitioners alike.

In an excellent and comprehensive treatment of MBO, George Steiner (1969, pp. 103, 104) made the following observations that support Drucker's view:

1. Corporate planning will fail in the absence of the chief executive's support, participation, and guidance.
2. Corporate planning is the responsibility of the chief executive and cannot be delegated to a planning staff.
3. The chief executive is responsible for assuring that a proper organization for planning is created, that the manner of its functioning is clear and understood, and that it operates efficiently and effectively.
4. The chief executive must see that all managers understand that planning is a continuous function and not one pursued on an ad hoc basis or only during a formal planning cycle.

5. The chief executive should see that all managers recognize that planning means change and that the interaction of plans with people and institutions must be understood and considered.
6. Once plans are prepared, top management must make decisions on the basis of those plans.

It is essential that the chief executive and the top administration in the health care organization provide the direction and thrust for the total MBO system. Steiner's message is clear and direct for the survival of the hospital's management system. Managers must become actively involved in formulating long-range goals and strategic plans and in developing the mechanism for their implementation. They also must be involved intimately in developing short-run objectives needed for the health care organization. This is essential to an MBO process that is based on an integrated system. As Drucker implied in the earlier quotation, (1954, pp. 128-129), these goals and ensuing action help communicate to all members of the organization the level and intensity of top management's philosophy and commitment to the process of managing by objectives.

One of the most significant methods for implementing MBO is to know the basic philosophy of management by objectives. Without the fundamental trust in employees that MBO engenders, attempts to implement the system will become exercises in frustration. Another important aspect is to understand the total process well. Implementation is based upon the simple notion that the manager and the subordinate can reach agreement as to what needs to be accomplished. The notion also assumes that most people like knowing what they are being held accountable for achieving and do not like expending effort on vague or inappropriate tasks. When top management defines and communicates the overall goals and objectives of the organization, the lower level managers should be able to develop appropriate objectives for coordinating their unit's activities with the institution's expectations (Ford & Bell, 1977, p. 16). However, not all objective-setting commitments are effective and even logical, as originally advertised.

THE IRRATIONALITY OF LOGICAL PLANNING

MBO creates a situation that ostensibly forces managers to communicate their needs and mission to their subordinates. The establishment of rigid objectives actually is not a very creative process. Managers are considered to be superior when they establish the goals that have to be reached and set the path for subordinates to attain those objectives. This results in a positive experience for both parties. The major concern of the theory proposed by Robert J. House and Terence R. Mitchell, *Path Goal Theory of Leadership* (House & Mitchell, 1974, pp. 81-97), is how the leader's behavior is motivating or satisfying because of its impact on subordinates' perceptions of their goals and the paths to those outcomes.

A leader, through the use of positive and negative task and interpersonal rewards, can have a major impact on these perceptions. The leader can specify goals that are more, or less, attractive to subordinates and can make it easy or difficult to attain these objectives. Thus, a leader can influence both the type of outcomes experienced by subordinates as well as clarify the behavior-outcome relationship (Mitchell, 1978, p. 318). This process helps the manager to actualize complex aspects of both the job and the planning cycle that are needed in MBO. People have a tendency to perform programmed work at the expense of spontaneous work; a good MBO system adds flexibility and necessitates a contingency approach to provide for handling unexpected events and problems.

One problem managers usually encounter is that they feel that once the planning has been achieved they can go back to their own work without any follow-up. This implies that planning is separate from doing and therefore is such a unique and separate process that it is not integrated into the general work flow, which allows this aspect of managing by objectives to be overlooked. When MBO is used successfully, the manager of a department is not needed on a daily basis to make things happen because the blueprint has been outlined. If a manager is needed for every major decision, then the organization is ineffective.

MBO is a unique process when used to reduce problems in a health care institution. The purpose of the manager is to achieve results in identifying those problems. The system does not work properly when the planning phase of MBO is not put into operation. Some managers do not plan for setting objectives because they state, incorrectly, that the process forces them to make decisions. This is problematic but not an unusual decision-making style. They claim they do not have a basic philosophy about management and have not developed an effective managerial system. Oftentimes their best decision is deciding not to decide. They are extremely orthodox and rigid in their thinking and it becomes difficult for them to make organizational decisions.

It is unfortunate, but those who make the most progress in an organization are managers who are not orthodox and often appear to be unreasonable. In an MBO program, managers must think in macrovision. This grand approach is essential since in MBO programs, security-oriented managers often block the achievement of the goals and of the organization. Again, it would appear that managers who are not socialized by the traditional, seemingly reasonable methods of managing appear to do much better in MBO programs.

This is important because the setting of objectives is determined by how the managers actually conceptualize. This process is based upon their needs, their value systems and how they perceive the institution's mission. Good objectives are measured by time, by innovation, by quantity, and by quality. All of these characteristics are highly valued characteristics of ambitious managers who are interested in succeeding and not reluctant to take chances. In many organizations, when managers attempt to try to understand why objectives cannot be achieved, this is considered to be a trip through the maze. They try hard to be extrinsically rational and logical, as suggested in contemporary managerial literature. However, their being unreasonable and demanding that objectives be accomplished by their subordinates in conjunction with themselves seems to be a key ingredient in reaching the targets.

Objectives are states of individual motivation derived from the needs of particular individuals. These objectives usually are personal and are attached to individuals and not to organizations. The objectives are values to be achieved but are sought by both the individuals and the organization. This often creates conflict for both parties. The values defined by a major department or an institution constitute organizational objectives. While MBO is not a measure of individual behavior patterns, it is an attempt to measure the individuals' job effectiveness in comparison to the institution's overall goals.

In his book, *How to Manage by Results,* Dale McConkey (1965) states: "M.B.O. is a systems approach to managing an organization—any organization." It is not a technique, or just another program, or a narrow area in the process of managing. It must be an integrated, well-designed program that will be accepted by the managers for that very fact. For this to occur successfully, the managers must be introduced personally to the MBO process. They must know what it is all about, what it is used for, and how it connects with other processes and functions such as performance evaluation, budgeting, salary, motivation, promotional review, and organizational effectiveness.

The goals envisioned by top management are not always viewed by subordinate managers with the same knowledge or value system, which can create problems. One reason is that most top managers are interested solely in problem solving because they feel this is what they are being paid for. Middle managers are more concerned with problem identification, which is actually the initial step in this process. This conflict is essential in the introduction and acceptance of MBO organizationally because it is a process of both managing and appraisal. Once managers understand these elements of the MBO process, they have taken the initial step in accepting and using it. This commitment leads to results anticipated through the mechanism of goal setting. With this as a direction, the emphasis now is future oriented, and changing the organization is a major concern. Since an objective is a state or condition to be attained at some time in the future, more emphasis is placed on where the health care organization is going and how it must reach this target through accomplishments.

Objectives can be thought of as statements of purpose and direction that are formalized into a system of management. The goals may be either long or short range. They may be general, to provide direction to an entire organization, or they may be highly specific, to provide detailed direction for given subordinates (Carroll & Tosi, 1973, p. 69). Managers generally set objectives for two reasons: (1) because the clearer the direction of where they are trying to go, the greater the chance that they will get there; and (2) because progress can be measured only in terms of what they are attempting to achieve.

The goals for the organization are the most difficult to establish. They must be based on projections and a clear understanding of the health care institution's strengths and weaknesses. To do this, the organization must consider its economic forecast and outlook, including an examination of the industry of which it is a member. Human resources and financial constraints should be considered as well, since opportunities and problems the organization may encounter will affect these elements. This leads managers to consider the development of programs that will take advantage of future opportunities and at the same time displace present problems through a contingency approach.

Before managers can begin stating measurable goals and objectives, they must be clear with regard to their ultimate purpose. In the health care setting, this means reviewing and restating the charter of the institution. It is the responsibility of the health care executive team to be certain that the statement of purpose is well understood by all managers and that all of these goals have been worked out in light of the purpose. The health care administration actually delegates the implementation of most responsibilities to various managers down the line. The managers look at the "menu" or charter of goals and use it as a point of reference in setting their own initial goals. Broad health care goals provide a stimulus to managers to attain the responses and results expected from them. This, of course, necessitates the setting of a priority listing so that everyone understands what is expected of them.

Health care administrators often are asked what they feel the institution's basic goals or objectives are. They must perceive that the quality of patient care and the efficient utilization of financial resources are primary objectives. For example, personnel turnover rates for hospitals ranged from 36 to 72 percent ten years ago—a serious problem resulting in spiralling costs. The need to reduce this variable is essential, so turnover reduction may be a precise objective today in light of the efficient utilization of financial resources as a broad-based goal. The output of employees of a health care organization is difficult to determine and becomes a problem when objectives are to be stated. Output often is confused through the use of macromeasures and is measured erroneously by the amount of cost reduction attained over a period of time per employee. However, before pay can be related to productivity, a viable method of measuring individual performance must be developed (Hand & Hollingsworth, 1978, p. 209).

There must be direct linkages between perceived pay and performance, and money must have some value to the individuals. There also must be very few negative consequences associated with high performance. Conditions should be developed so that employees could receive intrinsic as well as extrinsic rewards. These types of measures are essential and should be included in the health care administrators' goal setting operation.

SUPPORTIVE STUDIES

The MBO process ties together the functions of health care managers and the overall mission of the institution. The development of an effective managerial climate depends upon the clarification of objectives to be reached and the methodology of getting there. It seems reasonable to conclude that objective-oriented programs increase the clarity of job requirements, resulting in a more comfortable feeling on the part of subordinates regarding the type of criteria to be used in evaluation.

This position was supported by two research studies attempting to demonstrate linkages between the setting of objectives and resulting stress reduction in organizations. The first study, in human motivation and performance in industry, found that people responded better to specific goals than to abstract ones such as "do your best." Setting goals was found to be a possible antidote to boredom and a means of increasing motivation if manipulated properly. The best procedure suggested by the study was to use the workers' previous achievements as the base goal and then to encourage them to surpass that level of performance. This prevents the frustration of attempting an impossible goal that could be the result of random selection, yet it is high enough to stimulate interest and desire. In the end, such a procedure leads to higher output and higher satisfaction (Locke & Bryan, 1967, pp. 120-130).

The second study, an in-depth survey of 150 executives drawn from *Fortune*'s list of large corporations, explored a number of stress-related factors including psychological stress, self-defeating behavior, corporate limitations and objectives, the management of personnel, mechanisms for change, firing and retirement, and the corporation vs. the individual. The survey's author concluded that:

- Corporate and personal goals should not be confused.
- Self-actualization through worthwhile performance is the best motivational strategy.
- Rules and temperaments should blend (Kiev, 1974).

Studies in hospitals and industry have illustrated the importance of job satisfaction is curbing turnover. A project at the Mount Sinai Hospital in New York City found four major causes of employee separation: unsatisfactory interpersonal relationships, dissatisfaction with ratings, dissatisfaction with pay systems, and general disappointment related to expectations (Hand & Hollingsworth, 1978, p. 212). There appears to be a direct link between developing job performance measures and individual levels of satisfaction and/or dissatisfaction.

In another study focusing upon goals, performance, and stress, several common managerial concepts were examined in light of recent information concerning the effects of stress on performance. The survey reported that the perceived level of stress was subjective, depending on the individual appraisals of employees. Thus, simple statements regarding the impact of rewards on performance are not always true. Major attention should be given to evaluation methods. Managers should try to maintain low levels of stress for employees who have not had sufficient time to learn their jobs well, and for those with very difficult tasks. Higher stress levels should be maintained for workers who have learned their jobs well. When excessive stress is obvious, managers may take steps such as these to help to alleviate it:

- adjust standards for quantity or quality
- reduce job responsibility
- separate the review process from normal contact with the employee

- clarify performance standards as much as possible via objective setting

The author of the study also suggested that steps opposite to those listed can serve to increase performance in instances when job stress is low (Meglino, 1977, pp. 22-28). Individual goal setting in the MBO process is not an exclusive component of the activity. Health care institutions also are moving in the direction of group goal setting as an interdependent task to promote participative management. The reviews on this effort are somewhat mixed to date. An examination of both positions is a starting point.

PROS AND CONS OF GROUP GOAL SETTING

MBO is a vehicle that serves as a link between interdependent areas. Group goal setting is a foundation for employee involvement; most managers indicate that they feel goals can be accomplished because individuals decided voluntarily to make the commitment to achieve objectives with which they can identify. If opportunities for seeking goals were present in health care institutions and in the jobs themselves, the assumption was that people will participate.

In 1977, a study was conducted in Toledo, Ohio, in a 340-bed, 1,300-employee hospital (Sherwood & Varney, 1979, p. 125). (This case study is presented to yield an overview of what actually occurred.) The purpose of the study was to find methods to improve the institution's effectiveness in terms of operational measures as well as individual employee fulfillment and job satisfaction. The program began with an assessment of a number of variables relative to how people felt the organization was being managed and operated. Later in the study, management designed a set of statements that described how the organization should be managed and how employees should behave and work together in the organization.

It was decided that the task of the management group was to develop training programs, redesign policies and practices, and organize various team activities to move the hospital in the direction of its basic goals. It was assumed that if the organizational goals could be achieved, the end result would be improved performance for the entire hospital and satisfaction for the individuals.

As the program progressed, employees began to question what role they were to occupy in helping to achieve organizational goals, which led to an examination of the process of goal setting. The goal-setting process was based on a theory of social dynamics in which it was assumed that the level of commitment to a goal was related directly to the degree of ownership of the goal and the extent of peer awareness of individual commitment. Group goal setting was considered to be important in performance improvement. One of the conditions that prompted consideration of a team approach to goal setting was that the previous one-to-one relationship had not dealt effectively with the interdependency of management positions and the related activities associated with each position. The blueprint included these points:

- In the beginning of this process, an orientation session was held and group goal setting programs were presented through experimentation.
- The managers then met with their respective subordinate administrators to review the targets and resolve operational problems while making sure that all methods needed to accomplish the goals were made available to the departmental group.
- Activities were initiated with regard to the goal setting procedure including the types of targets, rules and regulations, principles and criteria for effective objectives, and training exercises in goal clarity.
- Once this was accomplished, departments in the hospital were able to link their own goals with those of the organization while establishing specific plans.
- All managers were asked to complete goal-setting worksheets with their groups and identify the major outcomes or results for which their departments were responsible while establishing the areas in which objectives would be developed. The groups then identified the result variables for each major outcome. It was emphasized that when a group based a goal on a specific end result, it must be able to transcribe that result into quantitative terms.
- Each department next shared its goals with other departments in an effort to include everyone in the quest for improved communication and to provide reinforcement and stimulation for all groups so that a commitment was well established and communicated throughout the organization.
- The department administrators and the health care manager then discussed and agreed upon all of the essential goals. The result was a high level of commitment by the executive staff of the hospital as well as a mechanism for review and adjustment. This program has been operating for several years and is considered by the consultants who initiated this effort to be a most positive one. This model can be adapted to health care systems with modest adjustments.

Problems

While group goal setting seems to be a unique procedure, it poses certain problems. Subordinates often feel pressured into agreeing to goals. When some individuals feel the objectives have been forced or imposed upon them, they become reluctant to inform their management that some of the goals are inappropriate. The primary objective of building a stronger, more effective organization often gets lost in the nerve-racking effort to keep fantasizing about true involvement in this process.

However, there is a way to compensate for some of the problems in goal setting. Managers must not focus on the routine, everyday chores that the subordinates have agreed upon and must allow them to take in the forest before notching the trees. Basic to the goal-setting concept is the idea that objectives must be concrete and well defined—for example, not "improve productivity" but "increase productivity by 10 percent." It is essential that managers and subordinates work together in determining what the goals should be and always keeping the basic problem up front during all their communication interactions.

Goal setting is an extremely important process in the total MBO experience. The goals of the health care organization personify the image of a well-managed institution. Managers must always question which of the institution's goals are their personal and principal responsibilities. To check the completeness of the setting of goals, department heads and middle managers may examine the issues through some provocative questions:

1. If I were the executive director of the hospital, which key result areas in my own department are under control?
2. As head of this department, have I given all of my key personnel a focus for accomplishing their goals?
3. Prior to meeting with the executive director of the hospital and committing my department to a goal-setting procedure, have I clearly examined all of my plans for my key personnel with regard to goals?
4. Do I have all of their ideas squared away?

These questions are important to ask because group goals should be defined as to the amount and direction of change that is desired from the present in a given period. This can begin with an analysis of just where the department and hospital are now. This type of auditing may be referred to as a needs analysis. The needs analysis examines four issues:

1. What is the basic purpose of the health care institution?
2. What are its strengths?
3. What are its weaknesses?
4. What trend should be envisioned in important key areas?

An examination of the differences and variances between the weaknesses and strengths will help the administrator to look at objectives that should be established immediately to compensate for these weaknesses. An audit of the strengths will give the administrator a standard method of evaluation so that the weaknesses can be dealt with through a strategy of establishing group objectives for departments. Goal setting clearly is a component and essential ingredient of this MBO process.

The Viewpoint of the Experts

Most experts agree that goals and objectives should be specific and that they should be defined in terms of measurable results. Individual, group, and organizational goals should be linked to ensure congruency and satisfaction. In a management survey, selected MBO experts were asked to look at goal setting as a component of the process and indicate what activities they felt were the most essential. Their answers are listed in their order of priority:

1. Goals and objectives should be specific,
2. Goals and objectives should be defined in terms of measurable results.
3. Individual goals should be linked to overall organizational goals.
4. Objectives should be reviewed periodically.
5. The time period for goal accomplishment should be specified.
6. The indicator of the results should be quantifiable wherever possible; otherwise, it should at least be verifiable.
7. Objectives should be flexible but should be changed as conditions warrant.
8. Objectives should include a plan of action for accomplishing the results.
9. Objectives should be assigned priorities of weight (McConkie, 1979, p. 32).

Major authorities whose theories agreed with this goal-setting process as reviewed in the literature were Peter Drucker, Douglas McGregor, Rensis Likert, George Odiorne, Bert Scanlan, Henry Tosi and Stephen Carroll, Harry Levinson, William Reddin, Harold Koontz, John Humble, Anthony Raia, and Glenn Varney. These experts also suggested that heavy subordinate involvement in goal setting was essential and they felt those employees should set goals and present them to top management to review, critique, and approve.

They also indicated that superiors and subordinates should set the goals jointly and that some combination of these previous two processes could be effective and efficient. The experts also agreed that objective criteria and performance standards must be clearly laid out in the MBO process or the ensuing appraisal process would be a problem. The consensus of MBO experts seemed to be that where performance was measured, performance improved (McConkie, 1979, p. 33).

THE MBO PROCESS AND RELATED PROBLEMS

Managers using MBO should always be prepared for problems. No system is foolproof. If new managers are in the position of coaching people they are unfamiliar with, or must work with objectives for jobs they know little about, the potential for problems will be great and the total project will be somewhat conflict laden.

Basic and Minor Problems

Eighteen of the more basic and minor problems associated with MBO are:

1. Some systems involve much paperwork. The major pitfall to be avoided is the natural tendency to concentrate at the outset on the system itself and the associated documentation rather than on the purpose and the concepts involved.

2. Through poor implementation, MBO might be seen as a gimmick; people may go through the motions and fill in the appropriate paperwork, but the spirit will be gone.

3. Achievable and meaningful goals are difficult to set, especially as they involve the future, with all its uncertainties. The major problem is to set goals that are reasonably but not easily obtainable. These must not be too difficult to achieve, nor too easy; employees who are not stretching their abilities become frustrated.

4. MBO could lead to so much attention being paid to setting and achieving a few major objectives that managers will overlook other aspects of their jobs, or they may push their own objectives at the expense of the organization's.

5. One of the great weaknesses of using performance against objectives as the standard of measuring managerial action is that managers can meet or miss goals through no fault of their own. The appraisal may be centered on personality rather than performance.

6. Although MBO is a simple system, it is not easy for people to learn and it is not self-teachable, because it is difficult to plan for clear end results.

7. Maintaining an environment that makes MBO work takes effort throughout the organization and it may take as long as three years to get full understanding and commitment.

8. One of the major reasons for ineffectual MBO is the failure to give the guidelines to the goal setters. They need to understand the end result for which they are responsible and how this result contributes to corporate objectives.

9. When goals are being set, one manager's objectives may be inconsistent with those of another, so goals must be interrelated and supportive.

10. Goals must not be forced onto an individual by the boss, or the system may not be truly participative.

11. Fuzzy objectives must be avoided and goals should be verifiable in a quantitative or qualitative way so that at some specific time in the future managers can know whether or not they have reached the targets.

12. Inflexibility is a latent danger. Events may require a change in goals that in fact may not take place.

13. Review and counselling of managers may not be adequate. A boss must have regular information on subordinates and not just forget about them.

14. If management development is carried out only on the basis of data from the performance appraisal, it may be unsatisfactory, as other factors should be considered.

15. The system must be appropriate to the organization; the support of everyone in a given sector is required or the system breaks down.

16. Training is required to carry out appraisals.

17. MBO may be seen by management as a means of controlling subordinates since these employees no longer can pass the buck. Some, too, may see it as a refined piecework system to keep increasing subordinates' output.

18. MBO may become too narrow and remove initiative; also, motivation may fall off after a while (Butteriss & Albrecht, 1979, pp. 129-130).

Value Dilemmas

One thing managers must do is develop solid operating plans. MBO success is a direct result of good planning. Without a thoughtful planning document, the system may be haphazard and incomplete. MBO should be based on managerial value systems that provide an overall frame of reference for the goal setting. These values are normative and are held by managers at both conscious and unconscious levels. These values are used to supply the standards by which subordinates respond in their quest to reach goals. Organizations also have values and define them precisely by trying to demonstrate just how they influence goal setting and decision making.

Some problems occur from potentially conflicting values in which organizations may be striving for cooperation, while individuals in certain units may be responding to a competitive type of environment. Every individual brings a certain set of values to the organization even as other value inputs from external sources affect the institution equally. The values come from individual, group, and organizational levels, from constituents of the task environment, and from cultural inputs. The value system provides a framework for setting objectives. It also provides a means for determining which goals are legitimate and helps evaluate the relative merit among several objectives, along with potential methods of achieving them.

Individual values are those held by persons that affect their actions, while group values are held by small informal and/or formal groups. They also may affect the behavior of individuals. Organizational values are held by the total institution, which is a composite of individual, group, and cultural inputs. The values of the constituents are held by those in direct contact with the organization such as customers, competitors, and governmental agencies. Cultural values are held by the entire society. The combination and milieu of all of these values have major impact upon the objectives an organization and its leadership are to achieve. In addition, these values create conflict and stress for health care managers attempting to juggle and balance these diverse and complex elements.

No system is foolproof, and no matter how complete the planning for an MBO system is, a number of unanticipated problems will arise. Many of them are overlooked, as are limitations associated with this procedure, since MBO is not a panacea even when it is used with maximum effectiveness. Levinson in his article on "Management by Whose Objectives?" comments on the MBO process since:

> it is based on a reward/punishment psychology, the process of management by objectives in combination with performance appraisal is self-defeating. Moreover, this technique is one of the greatest management illusions, serves simply to increase pressure on the individual. I do not reject the MBO process itself, but the technique can be improved by examining the underlying assumptions about the motivation, by taking group action, and by considering the individual's personal goals first (Levinson, 1970, pp. 125-134).

While MBO incorporates many assets, it does create hostility, resentment, and distrust between management and subordinates. It was designed to be a fair, impartial, and reasonable process to determine job performance and appraisal. It also was designed to allow individuals the opportunity to be self-motivated by setting their own objectives. Yet MBO often begins to do the opposite of what it sets out to do: to take the individual into consideration (Levinson, 1970, pp. 125-134).

Some organizations may have been attracted to the system initially by its claimed advantages and may even have begun installing it without being fully aware of the concomitant organizational and individual problems that can and will arise. When these subsequently occur, the organization may not have been prepared sufficiently to deal with the difficulties and the success of the scheme will be in jeopardy.

More Problems . . . Major Ones

1. *Centralized Decision Making:* If the MBO program in the health care organization is characterized as a highly centralized decision-making and authoritarian management process, the program is likely to fail. Individuals in the institution—managers and subordinates alike—must be permitted to participate fully in the program to the extent where their input is used and where this occupies a high positive valence. With preestablished goals, little weight can be given to individual creativity, so this often becomes stifling. In too many cases, top management establishes the goals and then makes a very quick exit, never to be seen again. At a later date, these executives cannot understand why the program has failed. The fact that MBO brings with it organizational change is probably one of the most important reasons for top management commitment and control.

2. *Guidance from the Top:* MBO is a good indicator of the effectiveness of top and middle management. Without guidelines and direction from the top, the organizational ship may be abandoned and begin to sink. This lack is one of the concerns cited most frequently in management literature. Failure to provide executive support can cause resentment on the part of the managers, who may feel the process is being forced upon them without a true top-level commitment. Top level direction for the program enables all managers to understand their role in the process. Their individual objectives thus must be set in conjunction with the next higher level in the institutional hierarchy.

3. *Lack of Teamwork:* If MBO objectives are set too quickly and the program becomes faddish, there is not enough interaction between the different levels of the institution. This demonstrates a lack of teamwork and control mechanisms and the program becomes another headache in need of a solution.

4. *Team-Building Techniques:* It can be unrealistic to require managers to achieve goals for which they must rely on others interdependently or to supply them with personnel over whom they have no control. To avoid this problem, the MBO program should focus upon team-building techniques that would help correct this. This suggestion would take into consideration group goal setting and group appraisals—all based upon group performance—that actually would protect an employee against being castigated for making an individual mistake in a group climate. This allows managers to control their goals more fully based upon group value systems.

5. *The One-to-One Split:* Conversely, MBO also tends to become a one-to-one process, causing a split in the unit's team approach that may lead to other problems. The one-to-one approach does not account for the interdependent nature of most jobs nor does it ensure the optimal consideration of objectives. One of the advantages of MBO is that the objectives for all managers in the work unit are integrated. The responsibility for such coordination rests entirely upon the managers, since they are the only persons in the process who have formal contact with the network of all subordinates. One-to-one interaction does not encourage maximum coordination of objectives, even though it has been extolled for improving superior-subordinate relationships. Research has found that after an intensive and carefully planned MBO program that stressed subordinate participation, most managers felt that relationships with their workers had improved. This is a major consideration in looking at MBO for flaws.

6. *Conflict in Objectives:* The conflict between organizational and personal objectives can be critical. Most MBO processes concentrate primarily on the institution's aims and tend to ignore personal goals. If

both objectives are in conflict, then the individuals may be forced to compromise their personal values in favor of organizational objectives or leave the institution and pursue their own objectives elsewhere. Therefore, an MBO system must consider personal objectives with the same importance as organizational ones.

7. *Danger of Overemphasis:* MBO should not be overemphasized at the expense of other tasks. There is a danger of putting so much emphasis on the system that individuals may overlook other aspects of their jobs or may pursue their own objectives at the expense of the total organization. This then becomes the problem of suboptimization, discussed later in this chapter. Managers may make decisions that in the short run appear to be beneficial but in the long run may create problems. It is important in this case for managers always to discuss both the subordinates' and the organization's goals to determine if there is some degree of congruence. The important point is that although both parties' needs should be compatible, personal goals never should be met at the expense of the institution.

8. *Counterproductive Cost Cutting:* The MBO commitment is overemphasized when health care managers state that under their own plan they expect to cut costs in their department 20 percent by the end of the year. To accomplish this, they may decide not to hire additional personnel, which would lower costs but at the same time reduce the quality of health care.

9. *Dictated Objectives:* The issue of deciding just who sets the objectives can produce conflict. Instead of trusting subordinates to develop meaningful objectives for themselves, managers often dictate the goals, so there is no opportunity for compromise or joint meetings. This autocratic objective-setting system is self-designed for failure.

10. *Identification of Objectives:* Managers must develop skills in identifying and establishing key performance objectives and must have the ability to express them in clear and precise terms. Expertise in coaching and counselling and in giving and receiving feedback is essential. These managers need a great deal of training on the job to understand the requirements of MBO and their personal involvement.

11. *Multifunctional Objectives:* Multifunctional objectives tend to be difficult to implement and measure. For example, the accounting department and the personnel department in the health care institution could have a joint MBO to develop a compensation and wage and salary program. It must be clearly defined which departments will perform what tasks and by which date. Problems arise when one department does perform as initially committed and the other department fails to do so. This prevents the total objective from being fully achieved. Managers who review such situations must consider the performance of

each individual in the MBO process since it is not equitable, for example, to hold the entire second department responsible for the failure even though the total MBO procedure was not completed. It is essential to be able to diagnose and to segment functions in a multidisciplinary approach in which team objectives are perceived by management as being significant. Currently, more and more objectives are being formulated as interfunctional objectives because institutions are beginning to use a total systems approach to management that encompasses multifunction planning.

12. *Goal Measurement Difficulties:* Managers find difficulties in measuring and quantifying MBO goals. Certain positions and their respective performance are difficult to evaluate. This may be due to the nature of the job, lack of data, or lack of experience with goal orientation. If this is the case, management should stress the MBO system and not the specific objective itself. As time goes by, the individuals involved will become more proficient in developing the MBO components around quantifiable information. This leads to feedback and performance criteria.

13. *Poor Performance Appraisal:* A crucial concern in the process is that of the poorly conducted performance appraisal review. The total MBO program will be undermined by poorly conducted reviews and evaluations. Most appraisal and review systems are based upon standards that merely make it simple for reviewers to fill out checklists of redundant criteria and recite the results to the employees while forcing them to conform to the unilateral rules of the game. If the evaluation system is poor and performance standards are vague, the procedure will suffer from either the "halo effect" or the "horns effect." The former consists of preconceived notions relating to rating an employee in a most favorable manner. This can be caused by managers' perceptions of past performance, compatibility with others, or a "no complaint" bias. In the "horns effect" which is the opposite of the "halo effect," individuals are rated extremely low. Some of the reasons for this may be that the supervisors are perfectionists, or the personality patterns of both are in conflict. Needless to say evaluations based on aspects that are not subjective are not recommended.

14. *Performance Rewards Issues:* A stumbling block for MBO is the failure to reward performance, since the linkage between rewards and performance in the system is not entirely clear. Many managers feel the process has nothing to do with the actual compensation of the employee. This seems to emphasize the need to link performance to rewards. The issue can be examined by looking at factors such as the quality of health care, the quantity of effort expended in a job, and the actual "pot" of monies available to departments that are considered

effective and efficient and to managers who implement their objectives successfully. This, of course, is dependent upon the organization's doing an analytical job of determining the nature of jobs and their value to the institution. It is to be hoped that this does not mean that a competitive system will develop as a solution to the historic problems outlined.

15. *Misuse as a Punitive Device:* MBO can be used as a punitive device. The system has been abused by managers attempting to control their subordinates and by their getting commitments from employees on goals that the workers must achieve alone. If they act without consulting the subordinates, the managers abuse the system. There always is the danger that goals will become obsolete through change or unforeseen circumstances, and the system must be flexible enough to allow individuals to adjust their objectives by working with their managers. When managers resist making changes in the MBO program and inform the subordinates that agreement already has been established, this generates resistance to the system and becomes an extremely negative control device. Subordinates usually try to sabotage the efforts of their managers when they are backed into a corner in this manner.

16. *Time and Deadlines:* MBO can produce an obsession with time and "deadlineitis." For some odd reason, management seems to tie MBO directly to a calendar or fiscal year, with little or no flexibility. This means that once a year an organization will decide its objectives for the forthcoming year. This is done even when institutions are cognizant of the contingencies and opportunities that can arise at any time. Therefore, the MBO system should be oriented toward performance and results and not related to a time element. It is natural to set goals for short periods of time—less than a year or even quarterly. Based on this rationale and the dynamic changes in organizations, there is no reason for goals to be set for the long run when short-run results are less difficult to establish and evaluate. However, organizations seem to need time periods for evaluation and appraisal that connect directly to the computer, compensation systems, fiscal periods, and top management's personal idiosyncrasies.

17. *Overemphasis on Numbers:* Managers often relate total outcomes to quantifiable MBO results. This overemphasis on numbers can force individuals to avoid objectives that cannot be quantified in the short run. A different type of verification is required so that qualitative aspects of the process are considered as well. It is essential to have a system in which complex objectives tend to be produced as hedges against unsatisfactory performance. It is the managers' responsibility to put a realistic approach into the objective setting of their subordinates.

18. *Paperwork Dilemmas:* Managers create dilemmas by becoming so involved with the paperwork generated by MBO that this maze actually becomes the end result and the system serves only as the means. A successful procedure should be simple and as relatively free of paperwork as possible. Paperwork should be involved only where it is essential.

19. *Managerial Obsolescence:* Managerial obsolescence is an important factor in the MBO process. Managers who are in the midcareer life stream may not have been exposed to MBO and its ramifications when they were junior executives or even as students 20 years or so ago in universities. By not being aware of the latest "state of the art" of management science, these managers often find MBO or any innovative system extremely difficult to comprehend. They view the system as threatening and as a fad, not as an integrative element to be incorporated into their system.

A SMALL SOLUTION

After examining the 19 major problems encountered with MBO, it should be clear that the system still has many merits. The process can work well in health care organizations and should be given a full chance, since most other processes are either fads or failures. By identifying the problems that can bury this process prematurely, the decay can be stopped and even turned completely around so that the commitment to and operation of MBO will be successful. While this very small solution is quite basic, it is the only one that will work. Reverse the problems stated so that a positive situation will be perceived. Then implement it as a tool to clarify objectives and ultimately resolve conflicts and stress caused by muddled goals.

APPRAISAL OR A MANAGEMENT SYSTEM?

MBO, while being a basic management system, also is a method of appraisal. For purposes of this chapter, performance appraisal has four essential functions:

1. Performance appraisal should provide feedback to all individuals regarding their performance.
2. Performance appraisal should serve as a basis for altering the behavior of individuals so they will use more effective work patterns.

3. Performance appraisal should provide data for managers who are evaluating individuals with regard to compensation and other job assignments.
4. Performance appraisal should focus on the outcomes of individuals' behavior and not on the behavior itself.

As long as managers appraise only the end result of an operation without giving adequate weight to the means of getting there, there will be problems with the total MBO process and any type of evaluation mechanism considered. Most appraisals that become problems when they are connected directly to an MBO system are very static and do not take into consideration any of the critical incidents that managers face on a day-to-day basis, nor any of the conflicting roles that individuals must play.

In many institutions using a very structured and static MBO process, the procedure is based on job descriptions. These static job descriptions often are at the root of the inadequacies of performance appraisal and should indicate that something is not congruent. Static job descriptions can be catastrophic for managers. Job proficiency and goal achievement usually are necessary but not sufficient conditions for advancement; the key elements in whether individuals make it in an organization tend to be political. The collective judgments made about people, which rarely find their way into performance appraisals, become the social web in which they must live (Levinson, 1976, p. 32).

The traditional methods of appraising performance in the MBO process deal only with information that is very substantive and does not clearly describe the factors for which the managers are being held accountable. What may be needed is conversion to a behavioral job description that is better able to deal with the pure dynamics of the job such as:

- How does the manager handle affection and a need to be liked?
- Does this job actually bring out feelings of dependency for the manager?
- What demands are placed on the manager's ego needs?

These questions must be considered in the evaluation procedure. While it might seem difficult to analyze performance in terms of aggression, affection, dependency, the ego ideal, or other psychological concepts, this is no different from the traditional uses of economic, financial, or accounting criteria. Many managers already discuss these types of issues by using other terms: "Taking Charge" vs. "Being a Nice Guy," "Needing to Be Stroked" vs. the "Self-Starter," "Fast

Track" vs. the "Shelf-Sitter." Some practice in using this concept together with support mechanisms can help make this method effective.

Performance appraisal cannot be limited to a yearly reward-punishment judgment usually handed from the top of the organization down to the lowest ranks. Appraisal should be a part of a continuing process that helps guide both managers and employees. In addition, it should enhance an effective, superior/subordinate relationship. To accomplish these aims, performance appraisal

- must be supported by mechanisms that enable managers to master their own inadequacies and to cope with their feelings of guilt (regarding the appraisal of subordinates)
- must have a record of the part of their work that occurs outside the purview of their own boss (such as task force assignment that requires someone to appraise a whole group)
- must modify aspects of the superior's behavior that hamper the manager's performance

All of this requires an upward appraisal process (Levinson, 1976, p. 40).

The whole concept of review of performance and appraisal is a key ingredient of MBO, which should include a method for handling this very delicate process. It is clear that many of the negative features of the traditional performance appraisal systems can be corrected by the subordinates and the managers jointly establishing objectives against which performance can be measured.

A classic article in the *Harvard Business Review* by Meyer, Kay, and French (1965, pp. 123-129) suggested that individuals who usually did not participate in work planning decisions should consider job goals set by their managers to be more important than goals they set for themselves. If this conclusion is correct, it affirms the belief that there are employees who would prefer being told what to do and could be expected to be happy with a one-to-one appraisal where the managers tell the subordinates what is expected (McConkie, 1979, p. 36).

Levinson (1972, pp. 3-8) indicated that the MBO process had a built in reward/punishment psychology that had grown out of the one-to-one relationship of goal setting and the ensuing appraisal method. While some of the criticisms of the MBO procedure are valid, the overwhelming evidence indicates that the goal-setting process in which participation is a major component still is a superior method for managing the health care institution's human resources and at the same time viewing satisfaction and performance as positive dimensions. Further MBO theories and practices have indicated that individuals who systematically are encouraged and assisted in setting their own levels of achievement do much better than those who are not. Groups and individuals appear to perform better and reach planned objectives more quickly when they are provided with reliable and objective information (appraisal) about their progress.

One of the important components of appraisal is goal setting in the initial development of common aims. The common goals of the health care institution or department must be the first area of discussion and of agreement between subordinates and managers prior to any appraisals. Before individuals can plan their own work there must be a clear understanding of, and commitment to, the common goals of the organization. Once that agreement is reached and there is commitment to the common goals, there is less likelihood that individuals will try to establish their own targets in a different direction. In organizational theory this event is referred to as suboptimization.

A study by Appelbaum (1975, p. 13) of middle managers in a multinational corporation found that organizational suboptimization occurred in situations in which group goals assumed priority over institutional goals. These group goals were created through a simulated intergroup competition situation so the participants could experience the negative effects of competition and could understand the need to develop alternative cooperative-collaborative relationships. The group goals discussed in the study were not collaborative but were those of departments in competition with other departments. A much more supportive base for problem solving and goal achievement is essential, and MBO appears to be the vehicle to accomplish this. The goals developed by and with subordinates should be appraised, should be short term, and should be most specific. These goals should be stated so clearly that when the individuals achieve their missions, they will know that they have in fact arrived. This must be demonstrated throughout the appraisal process. Statements of goals should be accepted only if they are extremely precise and measurable. A goal might be described by the direction and the degree of change desired for future readings based upon current events. Then it can be evaluated.

THE MBO INTERVIEW

An important component of the MBO appraisal process is the conference or interview between supervisor and subordinate to discuss setting objectives and accomplishing them at a later date. The process is necessary for clarifying all responsibilities, reducing conflict, and maintaining organizational effectiveness.

Before the Meeting

Prior to the interview, the supervisors should ask the subordinates to develop preliminary objectives that have clear performance standards and completion deadlines. These should be given to the supervisors within the week so they can evaluate them and be able to understand what to respond to during the interview.

Once the supervisors receive this set of objectives, they should look at each goal to see whether it represents a priority need. They should check to see that the goals are technically sound, that they have clear performance standards, that these standards are realistic, and that deadline dates are specified. The supervisors must be able to specify any special personnel coordination that may be needed to achieve an objective and to supply additional resources that may be necessary. The managers should examine all of the subordinates' responsibilities to see if any are being neglected and determine whether any additional objectives are appropriate.

The Interview Setting

The managers should take the lead by selecting convenient locations that stress the significance of the meeting. The managers should be prompt and allow sufficient time for uninterrupted discussion. It is important that they request from the subordinates an explanation of each objective, because the method by which people write goals in many instances is very different from the manner in which they verbalize them. The managers may ask the subordinates to explain each objective and should listen to these explanations with a great deal of interest.

The subordinates next should be asked how the managers can help the employees do a better job. The managers should not place the subordinates in a defensive position by evaluating these objectives critically and extremely pessimistically. It is essential that there be no clashes with regard to personality differences and past mistakes. It also is essential that the managers provide positive comments where appropriate and be quite open about exchanges of ideas.

One of the important goals in this session is to help the subordinates gain insight into their own behavior and concentrate on anticipated performance, with the future improvement of those goals and objectives as the basic focus. The managers should see that all final objectives meet technical requirements where performance standards exist and that there be a completion deadline. Managers always must remember that the setting of objectives is a joint process in which compromise is essential.

The Responsibility of the Subordinate

The subordinates should present their objectives vigorously, and be thorough and confident in discussing each one since they form the employees' own blueprint for a specific time period. The individuals should listen carefully to the managers' responses, which may be both positive and negative because these are indicators of priorities of the department, the organization, and the managers. The subordinate should insist on final agreement on the MBO and not leave the meeting with issues "put on the table" for a later settlement. It is important that agreement be reached during the session so that if any changes occur, they can be done on an amendment or addendum basis.

This session is extremely significant and sets the framework for the manager-subordinate relationship through communications and effectiveness. It probably is one of the most important aspects of appraisal, since the interview is the only point in which objectives are pinpointed as operational activities and form the main interest linking both parties, who often are competing and not collaborating. This interview is the basic capstone of the feedback element of MBO that is so valuable. A managerial intervention without feedback is of extremely restricted value.

MBO AND FEEDBACK

Once the MBO program is put into operation, the managers should be on the lookout for problems it may generate and should examine the goal-setting process with a view to possible changes. Dale McConkey in his work on *How to Manage by Results* (1965, pp. 115-120) comments that it is unfortunate and contradictory if a provision for change is not built into the system since MBO essentially is a major change technique. Failure to provide for change causes managers to feel they are locked into their goals and that nothing can help in solving new problems that arise. Since management is a dynamic process, events and circumstances will change during the MBO target period. Managers must be prepared to control the situation once they receive feedback and are ready to make corrections. The initial tailoring of feedback to each individual manager can be very time consuming and laborious the first time around. Nevertheless, it is a mandatory step that will be eminently worthwhile in future years.

While part of the total acceptance of MBO in practice has arisen from the manner in which the concept is applied, it now appears that simply adapting and readapting the various formal elements of a program will continue to miss the mark in the pursuit of greater results (Sokolik, 1978, p. 23). One of the basic needs today in MBO is awareness of the difficulties involved with the process and actions to achieve a continuous feedback and control mechanism on all of the major steps in the quest to achieve objectives and goals. MBO theorists and practitioners will not continue to make the necessary investment in researching the process, let alone realize its full promise, until they are fully cognizant of the strategic importance of the continuing feedback and control device.

Only through the feedback loop can the information and basic consensus so important to understanding problems that arise be managed. Feedback also is needed to gain support from top-level managers and others and in the building and maintaining of task-oriented relationships. Some of the greatest problems in the use of MBO, as discussed, come as a result of the failure to implement and carry out an effective feedback program during the entire managing process. To make MBO functional and operative, there must be a frequent and systematic method for maintaining the timely discovery of problems so that they can be resolved. This need is essential in communicating information between managers and subordinates so that changes can be corrected promptly.

Certain problems seem to be responsible for the lack of feedback. These problems are in the form of stereotyped, dimensionalized thinking, and misconceptions on the part of managers who participate in the following fallacious theorizing:

1. The focus should be on results and, if it is, managers don't need to be concerned with the actions taken to realize them.
2. Managers need to review activities as frequently as possible, but significant results take time and therefore they can't review their subordinates' performance more often than once a year.
3. Supervisors are involved in an MBO program for the very reason of not wanting to exert control over their subordinates; to engage in intermediate performance reviews would indicate that they would be working at odds with their intent.
4. Intermediate feedback and control in an MBO program invariably involves appraisal or evaluation of subordinates' performance and it is difficult enough when these appraisals are made every six or twelve months.

5. The supervisors' periodic efforts to obtain feedback on progress under the MBO can only create dependency for their subordinates and ultimately retard their accountability for results.

6. Supervisors face up to the fact that setting objectives and measuring results at year-end takes time and generates paperwork for them. If they also have to conduct monthly or semimonthly reviews they will not have time to do anything else (Sokolik, 1978, p. 25).

These reasons and questionable rationale are the commentary given by managers who do not use the feedback mechanism so essential in the MBO procedures. Most organizations unfortunately lack the managerial capacity to engage in such feedback on a continuing basis. They do not always integrate the MBO process into their own management systems and styles and therefore it actually becomes external to the operation of the organization. Managers also do not have the interpersonal skills to be involved in a continuing feedback process with their subordinates. This lack of human relations skills appears to be widespread in management and in the training of managers. The need to correct this flaw has been retarded because of economic pressures and other priorities. These managers do not have the proper tools to examine this process analytically and it is important that their training concentrate on feedback. When managers are incapable of executing effective feedback, it actually is their lack of the psychological insight and skills necessary to bring about, as Chris Argyris has put it, "double-loop learning." He goes so far as to state that only three forces have led to successful double-loop learning in the past, each entailing serious long-range problems (Argyris, 1977, pp. 115-125).

1. a crisis precipitated by some outside economic, competitive, or societal event
2. a change in top management
3. a crisis created by existing management to shape up the organization

Argyris's goal is for managers to realize that alternative learning methods do exist. The managers must take the risk as well as expend the energy and effort so important in engaging the double-loop learning process without the intervention of one of the forces just cited. This process yields another perspective on why the feedback and control mechanism has posed problems: The more an organization envisions itself as successfully operating the MBO process and the longer it continues to feel this way, the more likely it will find itself dealing with problems with the system that should have been resolved in an earlier phase. By this time, it may be too late to change a system that is operating ineffectively and inefficiently. It also may become more difficult to transmit the theories into actual MBO systems.

A HOW-TO GUIDELINE FOR MBO

Setting objectives, subobjectives, and goals for a future period is a critical step in the MBO process. As already noted, an objective is a desired state or accomplishment, a specified and desired result to be accomplished within a given period of time. It represents progress, a gain beyond past accomplishments, a tangible improvement over existing conditions. Objectives and goals must be set for each of the key areas identified. Managers should focus on the following questions in developing objectives with subordinates:

1. Which organizational goals and higher level management objectives require the managers' support?
2. What specific functions, tasks, and activities of the managers provide this support?
3. What is the managers' current level of performance in these areas?
4. What tangible data do managers have to measure results in these areas, and how reliable are they?
5. Which key functions and activities offer the highest potential for increasing managers' contributions to organizational goals and higher level objectives?
6. How can the maximum benefits be realized with a minimum of cost?
7. What will be the impact of improved results in these areas on other managers and organizational units?
8. Are managers' objectives and goals challenging, attainable, measurable—and also relevant?

The next step in this process involves assigning priorities to objectives that have been spelled out clearly. This step is essential because the managers now must sort out all goals and determine which ones should be achieved initially.

Priorities

Priorities involve the selection of relative weights to be assigned to each of the key functions and activities in the managers' objectives. Depending upon their nature and the relationship between them, they may be ranked in the order of descending importance (Table 11-1). Once the objectives have been ranked by priority, they should be coded at three levels according to the priorities:

Priority I

This is a "must-do" objective that is very critical to successful performance. Objectives on this level may be the result of special demands from higher management or external sources.

Priority II

This is a "should-do" objective that is necessary for improved performance. Objectives on this level generally are vital, but their achievement can be postponed if necessary.

Priority III

This is a "nice-to-do" objective that is desirable for improved performance but is not critical to survival or improved performance. Objectives at this level can be postponed or even eliminated in the quest to achieve goals of a higher priority.

Standards of Performance

These are essential in the MBO process because they are quantitative descriptions of a job well done. The whole concept of accountability in management is based upon measurable standards that involve such factors as quality, quantity, cost, and time. A standard generally is

Table 11-1 Establishing and Weighting Priorities

Objective	Relative Weight
Priority No. 1	35%
Priority No. 2	25%
Priority No. 3	15%
Priority No. 4	14%
Priority No. 5	11%
Total	100%

derived from past levels of satisfactory or acceptable performance. As long as the measurement factor remains constant, it provides the basis for setting objectives, goals, and targets for the future. Needed information includes these points:

- Standards should be defined by all individuals for their own managerial positions with the advice and counsel of the supervisor.
- Standards should specify the required results upon which satisfactory performance will be based.
- Standards should include tangible measures that determine the performance of tasks with reasonable accuracy and reliability.
- Standard measures and results should be written clearly and concisely in order to prevent ambiguity and conflict.
- Standards should provide for consistent evaluation and control of the quantity/quality, cost, and time factors of effective performance.
- Standards' format for documentation should facilitate goal setting and performance evaluation.
- Standards of performance should be determined for all jobs, at all levels, that contribute to the key result areas of the organization.
- Standards should be revised to fit the realities of changing requirements, conditions, resources, and capabilities of the organization and its individual members. (Raia, 1974)

In looking at the MBO goal dimensions, it is essential not to measure the total job but to break it down into component parts by itemizing the separate responsibilities or duties that the position entails. Important parts of the job are referred to as key result areas. They are not actually goals but are the areas of concern that ultimately are turned into goals. They will become goals when the decision is made as to how to measure them and add a precise level of accomplishment. As an example, the key result areas for a director of nursing would include: quality of care, nursing audits, budget administration, staffing patterns, patient safety, physician rotation, staff development, and personnel administration (Deegan, 1977, p. 126).

These job-related goals fall into three key result areas: routine tasks, problem-oriented tasks, and innovative tasks. The routine tasks are the normal output of a group that are measurable in units. Problem tasks are areas in which individuals are involved in problem solving. Innovative tasks are those where the people actually are attempting to be creative. It can be assumed that routine tasks are very similar to Priority I objectives, which are "must-do" critical objectives. In addition, problem-related goals to be accomplished are very similar to

Priority II tasks, which are "should-do" or necessary objectives. And finally, innovative-type goals are very similar to Priority III tasks, which are "nice to do" and desirable but not critical.

THE MBO FORM

The discussion on MBO guidelines can be put in a form that can be adopted by health care organizations committed to the process but not adept at transforming theory into practice (Exhibits 11-1, 11-2, and 11-3). They are presented in hierarchical form, with the process being initiated by the executive administrator, who develops an MBO that serves as a guide for subordinates reporting to that officer. The assistant administrator also prepares an MBO since this individual reports to the executive director and many of these objectives are intended to support this person's supervisors and areas of responsibility as well. Finally, an MBO is presented from the director of nursing, who reports to the assistant administrator. The direct linkages of the organization, reporting relationships, and macroobjectives and microobjectives to be accomplished are vivid and interdependent. The next step is to put the MBO process into operation and manage health care contingencies effectively.

Exhibit 11-1 Management by Objectives:
Bennett Medical Center—
Executive Administrator

Prepared by: John Key _____ Date: April 13, 1981 ___ Job Title: Exec. Administrator _____

Reviewed by: Rodney Morse _____ Date: April 27, 1981 ___ Job Title: Chairman of Board _____

Reviewed by: _____ Date: _____ Job Title: _____

Objective	As measured by	Priority	Present level	Desired level	Due date	Result
Continue Medical Center in existence as an acute care provider in Center City Toronto		A				
Deliver high quality health care services in a manner that assures financial viability of the hospital		A				
Continue and improve center's educational responsibilities to undergraduate students, residents, physicians, nurses, specialized technical personnel, patients, and the community		A				
Continue high quality of research activity at the center and obtain additional grant and endowment support		A				
Increase at all levels the utilization of services at center by the public we serve						
Increase patient days		A	91,000 days per year	92,000 days per year	1981	
Increase occupancy of special care units and medical-surgical beds		A	55% occupancy	75% occupancy	1981	
Increase profitability of the hospital		A	$339,000 per year	$362,000 per year	1981	
Limit increase of full-time equivalents		A	825	no greater than 858	1981	
Control days outstanding and accounts receivable		A				
Increase number of RNs through nurse recruiting program	Number of RNs recruited	B	150	200	1981	
Complete MBO project		B	N.A.		12/31/81	
Complete quality control and productivity program		B	N.A.		12/31/81	
Obtain a director of medical education and implement physician training program		B	N.A.		12/31/81	
Full operation of Medical Board under revised bylaws		A	N.A.		12/31/81	
Implement 1980 salary increase of 5% plus 1% for special adjustment		B			July 1981	

Objective	As measured by	Priority	Present level	Desired level	Due date	Result
Maintain Bennett salary level within 2nd and 3rd quartiles of Toronto hospital markets		B				
Revise all employee benefit programs to provide maximum benefit without increasing cost		B				
Negotiate two-year labor contract		A			10/12/81	
Accomplish labor realignments in nursing department		B			12/30/81	
Accomplish labor realignments in dietary department		B			12/30/81	
Continue new building project on schedule and on budget		A				
Maintain full accreditation with JCAH 7 Province of Ontario		A				
Increase volunteerism		B	135 per month	150 per month	6/30/81	

Exhibit 11-2 Management by Objectives:
Bennett Medical Center—
Assistant Administrator

Prepared by: Sylvia Lacoix   Date: May 22, 1981   Job Title: Ass't. Admin.

Reviewed by: John Key   Date: June 3, 1981   Job Title: Executive Admin.

Reviewed by: _____   Date: _____

Objective	As measured by	Priority	Present level	Desired level	Due date	Result
Goals:						
1. Maintain staffing at agreed-upon levels or below	Evaluation on FTE report.	A			6/30/81	
a. Nursing						
b. Recovery room						
c. Emergency svc.						
d. Endoscopy						
e. OR						
f. Nursing–SPU						
g. EEG						
h. Epilepsy center						
i. Anesthesia						
j. Respiratory care						
k. Audiology & speech						
l. Utilization review						
m. Medical library						
n. Cardiac cath.						
o. EKG						
p. Noninvasive lab						
q. Pharmacy						
r. Dietary						
s. Patient care administration			418.2	437.0		
t. Patient advocate						
2. Ensure the quality of health care services	a. Medical audits	A	8 audits	8 audits	6/30/81	
	b. Nursing audits	A	4 audits	4 audits	6/30/81	
	c. Patient teaching programs	A	0	2 programs	6/30/81	
	d. Orientation for all new patient care personnel	A	30%	60%	6/30/81	
	e. Formal inservice program in all patient care departments	A	30%	60%	6/30/81	
	f. Decrease in number of patient incidents	A	Look at present number	Look at present number	6/30/81	
	g. Improve discharge planning	A	Look at present number	Look at present number	6/30/81	
	h. Meet JCAH and provincial requirements	A			6/30/81	
	i. Q-PMP* for all departments	A				
	j. Patient questionnaires	A	Dietary	General	6/30/81	
	k. Departmental evaluations, as described in Q-PMP program	A	75% mostly objective	90% objective	6/30/81	
3. Obtain contracts for new approved educational programs for clinical experience in the hospital	a. Number of new contracts	C	5 programs	7 programs	6/30/81	

Objective	As measured by	Priority	Present level	Desired level	Due date	Result
4. Begin community health programs	a. Program records		0	100 community attendees/ members	6/30/81	
	b. Program schedules		0	2 programs	6/30/81	
	c. CPR program in conjunction with PHMC	C	0	500 pass the course	6/30/81	
	d. Written programs		0	3	6/30/81	
	e. Requests from community		0	1	6/30/81	
5. Develop new procedures and treatment modalities	a. Charge master	B	N/A	2	6/30/81	
	b. Monthly reports					
	c. Increase in revenue					
6. Improve holistic approach to patient care including physicians, clergy, patient advocate, patient care departments	a. Minutes of team meetings	B	0	Quarterly	6/30/81	
	b. Patient records as shown on audit					

Associated Goals:

Objective	As measured by	Priority	Present level	Desired level	Due date	Result
1. Increase utilization of special care units	a. Nursing records	B	Unknown	Difficult to assess	6/30/81	
2. Maintain operations at budget levels	FTE reports, revenue & expense printouts Capital budget	A	See FTE report	Described on FTE report See revenue & expense report	6/30/81	
3. Accomplish labor realignment in nursing	Increase number of nurses	A	150 RNs	200 RNs	6/30/81	
4. Meet needs of MBO & Q-PMP	As indicated by team	A	N/A	N/A		
5. Participate in negotiation of 2-year labor contract	New contract	A	N/A	N/A	11/1/81	
6. Participate in increasing volunteers to 150	New & interesting job descriptions	C	135	150	6/30/81	
7. Implement unit dose pharmacy		A			Total Implementation: 6/30/81	

Miscellaneous:

Objective	As measured by	Priority	Present level	Desired level	Due date	Result
1. Continue to improve risk management program	a. Number of potential suits	A	Look at present level	Look at present level	6/30/81	
	b. Decrease in number of incident reports	A	Look at present level	Look at present level	6/30/81	
	c. Insurance surveys	A	Look at present level	Look at present level	6/30/81	
	d. Insurance rates	A	Look at present level	Look at present level	6/30/81	

Exhibit 11-2 continued

Objective	As measured by	Priority	Present level	Desired level	Due date	Result
2. Begin to plan, develop, write, and implement staffing policies, procedures, & systems for care of patients in the new facility	a. Number of procedures & policies b. Written staffing plan c. Development of orientation programs	A		60%	6/30/81	
Contingencies:						
a. Patient problems b. Outside meetings c. Planning new programs d. Personnel problems e. Budgeting f. Operations of patient care areas g. Legal problems h. Equipment problems i. Surveys j. Policies & procedures k. Committee meetings l. Ambulatory services		A	N/A	N/A	6/30/81	
m. Personal educational development, continuing education		A	2 programs yearly	4 programs minimal	6/30/81	
Special Assignments:						
a. Participate in new building audiovisual program	1. List of available equipment	B	0	50% completed program	6/30/81	
1. Assist in preparing the policies & procedures part of the manual	2. Number of policies & procedures					
b. Participate in new building materials management program						
1. Do the portions that interface with the OR, ER, and nursing floors	Completion of plans for program	A		75%	6/30/81	
c. Participate in new building nursing program	Completion of written material	A		90%	6/30/81	
1. Get manual written and compile policies & procedures						
d. Participate in new building move-in & start-up manual	Completion of assignments	A		100%	6/30/81	
1. Identify specific issues regarding areas under my management						
e. Assist chaplaincy program	Completion of assignments	A			6/30/81	
1. Participate as outlined by B. Slavic						

Objective	As measured by	Priority	Present level	Desired level	Due date	Result
f. Participate in programming existing building, medical bldg. & services bldg.	As assigned	A			6/30/81	
1. Participate on programming subcom. of project mgmt. committee						
g. Assist in new medical programs						
1. Assist in coordinating executive health program	Completion of assignments			100%	6/30/81	
2. Assist in coordinating alcohol rehabilitation program	Completion of assignments			100%	6/30/81	
3. Coordinate psychiatry program	1. Written policies & procedures 2. Audits of care			75%	6/30/81	
4. Assist in coordinating dental medicine program	Completion of assignments			50%	6/30/81	
5. Coordinate health screening program	Written program and policies Marketing Ambulatory care review			50%	6/30/81	
6. Coordinate pre-admission testing program	Number of patients Number of services Physician participation			90%	6/30/81	

Exhibit 11-3 Management by Objectives Bennett Medical Center— Director of Nursing

Prepared by: Rita Berger   Date: June 28, 1981   Job Title: Director of Nursing

Reviewed by: Sylvia Lacoix   Date: July 10, 1981   Job Title: Asst. Admin.

Reviewed by: John Key   Date: July 23, 1981

Objective	As measured by	Priority		Present level	Desired level	Due date	Result
Goals:							
1. Maintain staffing at level agreed-upon or below	1. Daily staffing requirements	Turgeon	A			6/30/81	
a. Nursing service	2. Monthly staffing schedules	Wiley					
b. Emergency service	3. Evaluation of FTE reports	Coordinators					
c. OR	4. Daily evaluation of patient care hours	Supervisors					
d. Nursing SPU	5. Tool implemented in Q-PMP		A	0	Med/surg units	6/30/81	
2. Ensure the quality of health care services							
a. Nursing audit (retrospective)	Completion of 4 a year	Espinosa Committee	A	4 audits	4 audits	6/30/81	
b. Development, implementation, and participation in patient teaching	1. Documentation of programs						
	2. Evaluation through questionnaires to patients	Inservice supervisors	A	0	2 programs	6/30/81	
	3. Patient attendance records	Inservice					
c. Hold orientation for all new nursing personnel	1. 3-month evaluation of orientee	Inservice coordinators supervisors	A	100%	100%	6/30/81	
	2. Attendance record	Inservice	A	100%	100%		
	3. Evaluation by orientee or program		A	100%	100%		
	4. Exit interview		A	75%	80%		
d. Hold formal inservice programs in nursing department	1. Questionnaire regarding needs of staff		A				
	2. Number of pe people attending	Inservice	A		Increase 50%	6/30/81	
	3. Questionnaire evaluating quality of program						
	4. Availability to all shifts						
e. Decrease number of patient incidents	1. Monthly nursing audits	Inservice coordinators	A	55 falls 10 med. errors	Decrease	6/30/81	
	2. Decrease in number of incident reports	Supervisors					
f. Develop system for team approach to discharge planning (participants from other areas)	1. Participation	Inservice	A	0	System established	6/30/81	
	2. Evaluation by team	Coordinators supervisors					
	3. Benefits experienced by patient						
	4. Audit of patient records						

Objective	As measured by	Priority		Present level	Desired level	Due date	Result
g. Assist in Q-PMP for nursing department	Completed data packages	Inservice coordinators supervisors	A	100% to date	100%	6/30/81	
3. Participate in community health programs	1. Requests 2. Number of persons trained in CPR 3. Nursing participants in health care program, such as blood pressure month	Inservice	C	Participated in blood pressure month		6/30/81	
4. Participate with clergy, patient advocate, and social service to develop meaningful religious program for patients on daily basis	1. Availability of service to patients 2. Questionnaires to evaluate whether patients' needs are being met	Inservice Coordinators Supervisors	B				
5. Improve policies and procedures of patient admission to and discharge from units working through ICU committee	1. Bed utilization 2. Census 3. Patient days	Spann Lever Espinosa	B	Unknown	?	6/30/81	
6. Maintain quality care within budget levels	1. FTE report 2. Revenue and expense printouts 3. Capital budget	Coordinator	A	See FTE report	Described On FTE report See revenue and expense report	6/30/81	
7. Participate in labor realignment in nursing	Increase in number of RNs		A	150 RNs	200 RNs	6/30/81	
8. Meet needs of MBO and Q-PMP	As indicated by team		A	N/A	N/A		
9. Participate in negotiation of 2-year labor contract	New contract		A	N/A	N/A		
10. Utilize more volunteers on nursing units	1. Number of volunteers 2. New job descriptions	Coordinators Supervisors	C				
11. Participate in implementation of unit dose pharmacy			A				
12. Participate in planning, development, and writing of policies, procedures, and systems for care of patients in the new facility	1. Number of procedures and policies 2. Written staffing plan 3. Development of orientation program	Rancourt Policy and procedure					

Exhibit 11-3 continued

Objective	As measured by	Priority	Present level	Desired level	Due date	Result
13. Supervise implementation of state regulations		All supervisors				
Be responsible for new Pa. rules and regulations for nursing department		All coordinators				
14. Participate in JCAH follow-up		All supervisors				
Be responsible for JCAH rules & regulations for the nursing department		All coordinators				
Contingencies:						
1. Patient problems regarding nursing						
2. Outside meetings		A	N/A	N/A	6/30/81	
3. Planning new programs for nursing						
4. Personnel problems						
5. Budgeting						
6. Nursing care operations of patient care areas						
7. Surveys						
8. Committee meetings						
9. Policy and procedures—nursing						
10. Personal educational development continuing education		A	2 programs yearly	4 programs minimal	6/30/81	
Special Assignments:						
1. Assist in compiling equipment list for audio	Completion of equipment lists				6/30/81	
2. Participate in new building material management program	Pars for floors Exit interviews Equipment surveys					
3. See that new building—new manuals are written; nursing policies and procedures						
4. Participate and organize nursing in move-in and start-up of new facility						

BIBLIOGRAPHY

Argyris, C. Double loop learning in organizations. *Harvard Business Review,* September–October 1977, *55*(5), 115–125.

Appelbaum, S.H. An experiential case study of organizational suboptimization and problem solving. *Akron Business and Economic Review,* Fall 1975, *6*(3), 13–16.

Butteriss, M., & Albrecht, K. *New management tools.* Englewood Cliffs, N.J.: Prentice-Hall Inc., 1979, 129–130.

Carroll, S.J., & Tosi, H.L., Jr. *Management by objectives: Applications and research.* New York: The Macmillan Co., 1973,

Deegan, A.X., II. *Management by objectives for hospitals.* Germantown, Md.: Aspen Systems Corporation, 1977,

Drucker, P.F. *People and performance: The best of Peter Drucker on management.* New York: Harper Press, 1977,

————. Appraisal of what performance. *Harvard Business Review,* July–August 1976, *54*(4), 30–40, 44–46.

————. *The practice of management.* New York: Harper & Row, 1954, 128–129.

Ford, R.C., & Bell, R.R. MBO: Seven strategies for success. *S.A.M. Advanced Management Journal,* Winter 1977, 14–24.

Hand, H., & Hollingsworth, A.T. Tailoring MBO to hospitals. In A.M. Glassman (Ed.), *The challenge of management.* New York: John Wiley & Sons, 1978, 208–216.

Herzlinger, R. Can we control health care costs? *Harvard Business Review,* March–April 1978, *56*(2), 102–110.

House, R., & Mitchell, T. Path-goal theory of leadership. *Journal of Contemporary Business,* Autumn 1974, *3*(4), 81–97.

Kiev, A. A strategy for handling executive stress. Chicago: Nelson Hall Publishing, 1974,

Levinson, H. Management by objectives: A critique. *Training and Development Journal,* April 1972, *26,* 3–8.

————. Appraisal of what performance. *Harvard Business Review,* July–August 1976, *54*(4), 30–40.

————. Management by whose objectives. *Harvard Business Review,* July–August 1970, *48*(4), 125–134.

Likert, R. *The human organization.* New York: McGraw-Hill Book Co., 1967.

Locke, E.A., & Bryan, J.F. Performance goals as determinants of level of performance and boredom. *Journal of Applied Psychology,* April 1967, *51,* 120–130.

McConkey, D. *How to manage by results.* New York: American Management Association, 1965,

McConkie, M.L. A clarification of the goal setting and appraisal process in MBO. *Academy of Management Review,* April 1959, *4*(1), 29–40.

Megalino, B.M. Stress and performance: Implications for organizational policies. *Supervisory Management,* April 1977, *22,* 22–28.

Meyer, H.H., Kay, E., & French, J.R.P., Jr. Split roles in performance appraisal. *Harvard Business Review.* January–February 1965, *43,* 123–129.

Mitchell, T.R. *People in organizations: Understanding their behavior.* New York: McGraw-Hill Book Co., 1978,

Raia, A.P. *Managing by objectives.* Glenview, Ill.: Scott Foresman and Co., 1974,

Sherwood, S.W., & Varney, G.H. Group goal setting fosters employee involvement. *Hospitals, JAHA,* January 16, 1979, 125.

Sokolik, S.L. Feedback and control—The hollow in MBO practice. *Human Resources Management,* Winter 1978, 23-28.

Steiner, G. *Top management planning.* New York: MacMillan Publishing Co., 1969, 103-104.

Chapter 12

The Management of Time

CONSIDERATIONS FOR
THE HEALTH CARE MANAGER

1. The relationship between stress and managing time occurs when the manager is not able to attain or fulfill a need.
2. Time management is a two-dimensional problem. Managers clutter up their own jobs when they are ineffective. This makes it difficult for their junior managers to delegate properly to their own subordinates, since they must control their actions due to their insecurity.
3. Tension and anxiety affect managers who waste a great deal of time trying to reduce the pain. They also exercise less than accurate judgment in decision making.
4. Much time is lost by managers who do not have an agenda for dealing with time-consuming telephone calls.
5. Drop-in visitors are time wasters who must be redirected to other sources for their communications needs.
6. Meetings and conferences can occupy a great deal of nonproductive time.
7. Managers are held captive by "programmed tapes"—hidden agendas that are passed on to individuals from a host of sources and dictate how time is to be spent.

8. Managers waste time by being activity oriented and not results oriented. They also impose unrealistic time estimates on activities, which increases stress.
9. Lack of delegation creates dissatisfaction on the part of subordinates, resulting in lower organizational performance.
10. Delegation entails the setting of attainable objectives with a view of results to be determined, similar to MBO.
11. Insecurity may be a reason why managers fail to delegate to capable subordinates. These intrapsychic factors can create conflict and stress for those involved in this complex process.
12. An effective component to delegation is the process of follow-up, which may range from extremely close to laissez faire, depending upon the situation and style of the managers.
13. Time management actually means less stress for individuals, resulting in more efficient, satisfied, and healthy employees who have an impact on an effective organization.

Time is the scarcest resource, and unless it is managed nothing else can be managed.

PETER F. DRUCKER

The management of time is one of the most significant problems—and at the same time assets—of managers of health care organizations. Once objectives have been established, they must be managed, and this is where the issues of priority and timeliness become essential.

Time is most unique because its supply is inelastic (Drucker, 1966, p. 56). Managers are always being pushed to plan their assignments. This sounds realistic, but in actual practice it does not always work well. The plans tend to remain on paper as good intentions. Managers who are able to achieve do not begin with their work—they begin with their time. Managing time takes perseverance and self-discipline. However, this investment yields the greatest return-on-investment with regard to achievement, performance, and satisfaction.

Time management is one process by which managers can accomplish the tasks and goals that will enable them to be effective in their position. There are several essential phases in this process. Their purpose is to identify managers' needs and wants in terms of their relative importance and match them with the time and resources available. The goals needed to perform or achieve are prescribed by the organization, while those that managers espouse are imposed by their personal value systems or related to their long-term career objectives.

The real importance of time management lies in the fact that many people have too many tasks they need to perform but not enough time for what they want to do. The relationship between stress and time management now starts to surface. If individuals are not able to attain or fulfill a need or desire, then according to definition they are in stress. Time management is a process by which they are more likely to attain or fulfill a need or desire (Schuler, 1979, p. 852).

Preoccupations and frustrations involved with accomplishing tasks within a prescribed time slot hamper managers in enjoying the intricacies of their role and maintaining personal relationships that are supportive and satisfying and that could help resolve some of the personality conflicts inherent in the overall symptoms of stress that they experience. It is interesting to note that in North America the output per worker is increasing with mechanization and computerization, the work week is shorter, and fringe benefits are multiplying while the hours needed by the chief administrators of major organizations have increased at a rapid rate.

It is not uncommon for managers to work 60 to 70 hours a week while their employees are putting in a 35- or 40-hour week, close to half of that time. Long hours for health care administrators are not always conducive to accomplishment even though historically accomplishment and hours have been perceived as being synonymous. A major concern is that much of the managers' problems with time are tied up in nondelegation. Decision making usually is improved when tasks are delegated to subordinates since most managers would not have to be involved personally and actually might well make fewer decisions. This does not seem to be the case in administrative practice. These managers attempt to handle all the decisions that other people in the organization are capable of and equipped to cope with at a much more effective level.

The problem with managing time is two-dimensional since the direction of organizational influence is from the top down while problems for decision spiral up from the lower levels. Managers not only clutter up their own jobs when they are ineffective, they also make it very difficult for junior managers to delegate to their own subordinates as well. Such managers feel they must be in control constantly and demand that their subordinates be responsive to their every whim; this insecurity blocks their willingness to delegate. The inability or unwillingness to delegate is a problem for many health care administrators that multiplies by generating unnecessary but increasing anxieties. This unwillingness is a result, not a cause; it is a symptom, rather than a disease. One of the problems is that many individuals are not organized themselves and therefore cannot understand the need to delegate. Delegation is not the only method of managing time. However, it is an important principle that must be considered in time management and, ultimately, in stress reduction.

Some executives never attempt to analyze their jobs or break them down into components or steps so that they actually can understand the areas for which they are being held accountable. If they would look at what they perform over a one-week period, they would understand what is productive time and what is wasted time. Some do not understand their job scope and what the function really covers, what results are expected of them and what the time span perspective is. They may have little understanding of the growth potential of their position and therefore may perceive their job as a never-ending spiral with progress being tantamount to a trip through a revolving door.

They may begin by asking themselves what their work really covers. This can be done by putting their job into perspective and attempting to describe what the actual duties, responsibilities, authority, and direct supervision entail. Educational and experience qualifications should be evaluated. The basic goal here is to have a clear understanding of the executive role so that it can be managed properly and effectively.

TENSION AND TIME

Psychological studies have demonstrated that many individuals tend not to be open and honest with themselves when confronted with issues concerning their emotional health. Therefore, managers can be anxiety ridden and not be aware of it since one of the ways in which individuals maintain their equilibrium is to repress the awareness of tension without reducing its side effects. This defense of course, leads to uncertainty and inappropriate judgment.

When managers are working under stress, the quality of both their work and of their efficiency can be affected. They attempt to compensate for the quality that has been affected by increasing the energy, tension, and time they invest in work, which becomes a greater cost to themselves. When tension is excessive, it affects managers' working efficiency and may become psychologically disabling. Tension and anxiety can render managers almost helpless, so that they are working at less than half their potential efficiency. Tensions are very expensive and actually thwart managers' efforts. When these tensions are excessive, the managers do waste time by attempting to reduce the pain associated with the heightened anxiety state. Their judgment also is affected. This creates problems with decision making since the individuals now are operating at a different perception level.

When health care executives attempt to make decisions they use integration, which is the synthesis of many diverse facts, and try to focus upon an overall conceptual pattern. When they face emotional stress and the stress is above an acceptable tolerance level, the balance is lost and many of their thoughts become extremely fragmented, affecting their performance. When their ideas begin fragmenting in an uncontrolled manner, their personal security is threatened. This feeling of helplessness leads to extremely defensive behavior since the mechanism for which they have been rewarded is not functioning at an optimum level.

The stress of attempting to maintain their equilibrium at the level before they were affected by the tension forces these managers to call upon their emotional reserves and develop defensive attitudes that are not usually used in low stress situations, when they are much more efficient. A heavy burden of tension and stress wastes time because it disrupts the method of thinking by which decisions are reached so that the decisions not only take longer but are less reliable. Too much tension traps individuals into preoccupation with matters not worthy of their attention and time and creates a vicious cycle that must be broken at an early point.

Many managers underestimate their level of tension. The more they comprehend the complexity of the problems they are held responsible for solving, the more they will understand how limited their own individual resources are in coping with these situations and how much they need help from subordinates. They also develop self-doubts about their own abilities and relive and reexperience certain emotional struggles that have been problems since their origin (usually in childhood) without being resolved. When this occurs, managers are forced to undervalue their own abilities and face a great deal of added tension that must be reduced, which cuts into their time and affects their reliance upon their own judgment. Undervaluation may be caused by low self-esteem from childhood, which leads to anxiety-stress in adulthood.

The tensions also are caused by the managers' inability to trust subordinates since they have set standards so high that no normal individual can achieve them, let alone subordinates who are not even of the same caliber as the managers. These executives make the mistake of assuming that everyone should be as effective and hardworking as they are. They realize that trustworthy subordinates are not very abundant, and when they do have such assistants the managers automatically tend to underestimate their skills and feel that no one can achieve what they, personally, can achieve.

Some managers, beset by self-doubts, feel guilty about the authority that has been given to them since they believe they should not be in such positions in the first place. This guilt can create more emotional stress and tension. As individuals develop, they learn to keep these emotions under control and are taught that it is perfectly acceptable to have such feelings but not to act them out. This was explored in Chapter 2, dealing with the psychoanalytic analysis of the health care manager.

When people demonstrate how aggressive or frustrated they feel, this usually brings about retaliation by others who happen to be affected by whatever is at issue and who cannot express the feelings either. Most of executives' tensions are caused by their overly developed superegos and feelings of inadequacy or of guilt, stimulated by the temptation to use power that the managers, as noted, feel they may not deserve in the first place.

The North American culture is one in which managers have been trained to suffer in silence by repressing problems and therefore, if no one understands that they are experiencing anxiety and tension, they still can present a facade of adequacy. They must learn to distinguish between anxieties that are real and anxieties that appeal to emotional needs. One way of doing this is to use peers as sounding boards to find out whether or not some of their concerns as managers are based on reality. However, this necessitates the trusting others—a characteristic that has not been an integral part of the interpersonal climate of most organizations. It appears to be a luxury and not a necessary ingredient of an organic climate.

THE TRAPPINGS OF TIME

There are many time traps in which managers can become entangled in their quest to manage their time and juggle their responsibilities effectively. These trappings fall into five main categories.

The Telephone

The telephone, while one of the great inventions, creates a problem since it is an interrupter that forces managers to change their style of work. One system of handling the telephone is for managers to:

a. have others filter calls and handle them later whenever possible
b. encourage individuals to call other people in the organization who can handle the problem
c. reject any calls when private time is needed for thinking
d. lump together all calls and return them in one time bloc
e. cut out the chit-chat and get down to business
f. have a written agenda for each multitopic phone call
g. have all of the important information needed at hand before making the call

Drop-In Visitors

Drop-in visitors are problems because they stop by to say hello and at the same time give the manager bits and pieces of grapevine information. When the manager looks at the clock, half an hour or more has elapsed with a questionable amount of essential data transmitted and little work done. This leads to greater frustration and the feeling of lower job satisfaction. To handle this situation, managers should:

a. train their own junior managers and subordinates to respect their time and not drop in
b. close their door for a time
c. meet with subordinates on a regular basis and require them to develop an agenda to focus the discussion
d. avoid any instant discussion in recurring emergencies and crises—these will clear up
e. develop an office structure and layout that permits communicating their attitudes toward individuals who seem to want to hang around
f. stand up when an unwanted visitor comes in to say hello and remain standing until the other person leaves
g. suggest the next meeting to be held in another office
h. analyze why people drop in—it may be the managers' own need to talk to them that creates the problem

Meetings and Conferences

These create problems because their productivity is low and results tend to be questionable. Meetings seem to be popular and frequent because historically they have been part of the communication system in the organization and too many persons seem to prefer them rather than conferring one-to-one or in small project groups; therefore, meetings continue. To make meetings more productive, managers can:

1. learn something about the group process and how to deal with small units so they can minimize the number of conflicts in the meeting, leading to more productive sessions
2. keep the number of meetings to a few and explore any alternatives appearing to be valid
3. choose a time and place that will maximize attendance
4. have an agenda ready with specific objectives, times and responsibilities for each member
5. distribute the agenda prior to the meeting
6. begin and end the meeting on time and do not allow petty interruptions
7. make sure that each point is handled and settled quickly; it is important to accomplish the objectives of the meeting without tabling issues for later sessions
8. abolish committees that have no basic purpose or have achieved their purposes
9. not go to a meeting or call one unless it is essential for decision making and productivity; this is a good time to delegate responsibility to an assistant to handle aspects that the manager dealt with previously

Programmed "Tapes"

Programmed mental, not physical, "tapes" are individual psychological prerecorded hidden agendas that have been passed down by parents and others who have had an impact on individuals' lives. Some of these messages indicate how certain issues "should" be dealt with and, interestingly, individuals have accepted such "programs" communicated via clichés and statements without question. These tapes all possess subliminal messages involving the management of time:

Tape A: These messages discourage good time management by overstressing motion and activity. Some of the quotes individuals hear are: "don't waste any time," "don't just sit there, do something," "keep busy," "always work hard," "the longer and harder you work the more you get done."

Tape B: These tapes encourage overplanning, overcaution, or perfectionism and include such quotes as: "don't make any mistakes," "anything worth doing is worth doing well," and "always do it the right way."

Tape C: These tapes discourage planning and include such statements as: "all things come to those who wait," "good things are unexpected," "take care of today and let tomorrow take care of itself."

Tape D: These tapes are intended to discourage delegating by making such statements as : "if you want a thing done right, you have to do it yourself," or "never ask anybody to do something you wouldn't do yourself."

The problem with these tapes is that individuals have been conditioned by them for a long time and as a result, find that they do not have the analytical insight to make any changes.

Procrastination

One of the more popular styles of decision-making avoidance is the art of procrastination. This avoidance is associated with the fight-or-flight response, a component of anxiety and stress. Managers have a fear of mistakes and their potential punishments. They may opt to avoid making decisions because their fantasy is that the solution to the problem will be more effective if they wait a bit before making it. Individuals postpone the unpleasant by procrastinating when an effective alternative encourages avoiding whatever is unpleasant initially. Managers have a problem with priorities that affects procrastination since they do not understand what should come first—which leads to indecision. Procrastination occurs when managers have a need to be perfect and feel that everything they do must be performed in a precision effort. This creates much more of a time constraint and leads to a great deal of anxiety since apparently the only managers who are perfect have been deceased for quite a while.

OTHER TRAPPINGS

There are other "time traps" to be explored.

1. *The Breathing Paradox:* Managers complain that they do not have enough time to perform and breathe, yet everyone has all the

time they need if they allocate it properly—which is the great paradox of time.

2. *The Daily Log:* Managers rarely understand just how they spend their time since their perception may become distorted when time is compressed and when they are experiencing stressful situations. This dilemma can be examined when managers develop personal time analyses: a daily log of activities for a period of at least one week that can be measured and recorded by taking readings at 15-minute scheduled intervals. This can be important in helping managers understand how they are allocating their limited resource—time.

3. *Avoidance of Surprise:* Managers can control their time problems by avoiding surprise and by the corollary anticipatory action. This is an excellent administrative process that forces managers to plan if they are to determine result priorities before any action is undertaken unnecessarily. Effective planning results in purposeful objectives that create priorities and indicate to managers what tasks are in sequential order. These priorities do affect deadlines on which individuals must focus and lead to intense concentration on achieving essential objectives under a prioritized deadline. This can help overcome indecision, vacillation, and procrastination.

4. *The Pareto Principle:* In most areas of organized human endeavor, a critical few efforts (around 20 percent) usually produce a great bulk of the results (around 80 percent). This is known as the Pareto Principle, sometimes called the "20/80" law.

5. *Balancing Work:* Managers seek to achieve the optimum balance of efficiency and effectiveness. They may feel that effort will tend to be ineffective if expended on the wrong tasks at the wrong time or without intended consequences.

6. *Focus on Results:* Managers waste a great deal of time by becoming activity oriented and not results oriented, which impedes effectiveness.

7. *Unrealistic Estimates:* Managers may impose unrealistic time estimates on their activities, which create greater stress. They tend to forget that everything takes longer than anticipated.

8. *Urgent vs. Important:* Managers may live in a constant tension struggle between what they consider to be urgent and what they consider to be important. These issues are quite diverse.

9. *"Fire Fighting":* They are conditioned to overreact to apparent problems and become involved in "fire fighting" and "crisis management," which causes anxiety, affects their judgment, and results in improper decisions, leading to further stress. MBO can help to alleviate this dilemma.

10. *Catching Up:* When they fail to perform a problem analysis or to distinguish symptoms from causes, managers waste a great deal of effort and time, which leads to further overreaction in the attempt to catch up.

11. *Are There Alternatives?* Managers may not see any alternative solutions to a problem. This feeling of helplessness creates indecision and, ultimately, procrastination. This cycle generates more tension and stress.

12. *The Delegation Crisis:* When managers do not delegate total responsibility and authority to subordinates to complete a whole task, this creates dissatisfaction on the part of the employees, who ultimately can affect the managers by sabotaging their efforts while experiencing a heightened level of stress as well. Junior managers at lower organizational levels expect work to be delegated to them since they feel they have adequate judgment and the facts to complete a project. Managers who avoid delegating unconsciously are encouraging a dependency relationship with these subordinates, who must wait for directions from their bosses. Dependent subordinates experience feelings of invalidism. These create more conflict for the managers, who now must make decisions for an infinite number of dependent employees. This piles more accountability and stress on the managers. This management style creates turmoil for the managers, who now must balance and juggle their time and priorities.

13. *Responsibility vs. Authority:* Managers must be able to organize and utilize time effectively in their executive assignment. Benjamin Franklin addressed this situation by stating: "When your time is up, you are done." Managers who have confused the separate issues of responsibility and authority cannot clarify the programs for which they are held accountable. This spills over onto subordinates, creating ambiguous, confused situations.

14. *Saying "No:"* Troubled managers are unable to say "no" to others who are demanding their time and expertise since they may be personally unaware of the priority and importance of the issue, or they

have a great need to help others, or they want to appear to be supportive and are fearful of offending others by saying no. Some even believe that saying "yes" to everyone enhances their prospects for promotion and upward mobility in the organization.

15. *Saying "Yes:"* Other managers are so insecure and possess such low self-esteem that they feel they must always say "yes" to immediate demands. Their fallacious reasoning is that individuals in the organization who are making these instant demands will think much more highly of them for dropping everything and responding and, therefore, they ultimately will be viewed in a much more positive way. This philosophy and style leads to failure for such managers.

THE NEED TO DELEGATE OR ASSIGN TASKS

One of the major issues confronting managers is developing the linkages between time management and delegation. Delegation may be one of the most significant methods for managers to gain time and one of the most effective ways for team building. Dale McConkey in his book *No Nonsense Delegation* (1974) described delegation as

> the achievement by a manager of definite, specified results, results previously determined on the basis of a priority of needs, by empowering and motivating subordinates to accomplish all or part of the specific results for which the manager has final accountability. The specific results for which the subordinates are accountable are clearly delineated in advance in terms of output required and time allowed and the subordinate's progress is monitored continuously during the time period.

This description certainly entails the setting of objectives with a view to the results to be determined, the priorities that are necessary, and the breaking down of objectives into action plans and steps that can be delegated to subordinates. This also sets up a review system to determine progress in reaching these objectives. This process is certainly a move toward management by objectives, covered in Chapter 11.

Delegation as described is certainly different from the assigning of tasks but many managers have a difficult time in understanding this concept. When the manager *assigns* a task, the subordinate assumes the responsibility but with no authority and little accountability. When a manager *delegates*, the subordinate assumes both responsibility and authority and therefore is fully accountable. While managers worry about the risk involved in delegating, there certainly is no risk in passing down decision making until final action is to be taken, and that can be handled by the managers themselves.

Managers who worry about delegation should look at their greater concerns: the management of time. Managers who have a difficult time in delegating are easily identifiable because some of them overcontrol, take much work home at night, are under constant pressure and criticism of subordinates, lack clear policies, are slow in decision making, possess a limited span of control, and usually quote what their own supervisor wants to justify their action. As a result, their efforts appear to be quite disorganized.

When tasks are delegated for subordinates one of the key items to consider is the development of objectives and a time system for achieving results—factors that are to be determined by joint negotiation between manager and subordinate. When objectives are to be achieved by delegation, it is important to determine whether they have the highest priority value, in which the goal is essential to the organization, manager, and subordinate. These objectives and activities must be specified so that the subordinates understand what is essential and what they should accomplish in attempting to achieve the organization's goals, fulfill the supervisor's needs, and at the same time fulfill the employee's own needs.

In delegation it is important to note that the essence of an effective management system is not for the managers to do the job themselves but to delegate the work and its components to capable subordinates. Managers cannot solve all time-pressure problems by funneling everything to subordinates, abdicating their own responsibilities, and then assuming that the matter is closed. At the same time, managers cannot hope to keep tight, close control over every activity that goes on in their domain. Therefore some middle-of-the-road approach is needed to combine the ease and confidence that accrues from having a positive feeling for subordinates and the basic operation.

The delegation of an operation and its assignment to individuals has a broad-based perspective. It implies that the individuals with the responsibility are more than just extensions of someone with higher status. Therefore, they now are supervising an activity that, by its very nature, has its own implicit authority based upon professional or other value-laden standards that are not necessarily those of the managers assigning the task.

Many managers insist that in delegating work they are assigning a high degree of decision-making authority when they actually are acting as their own managers or as extensions of themselves. This confusing message and issue is an extreme problem because it gives a mixed communique to the subordinates being held responsible for the task but lacking the authority to deliver. The subordinates, are not being delegated to, but are having work assigned that leaves them quite powerless.

The ability to delegate has as its foundation block managerial skills and human resource skills. At the administrative level, the skills needed are those associated with the traditional and basic functions of management such as planning, organizing, staffing, directing, coordinating, reporting, budgeting, decision making, and controlling. The human resource area is part of the delegation process because of the selection of candidates considered capable of carrying out the assignments.

Managers who have a difficult time assuming this responsibility actually do not know either how to delegate or what to delegate. Obviously surgeons cannot delegate their unique skills during an operation to subordinates, and researchers must complete their own work and ultimately write their own reports. However, managers can delegate certain aspects of their responsibility in order to free themselves for other areas of endeavor that may have a higher priority and in which time management is essential.

If managers feel that the decision-making, judgmental aspects of the position are such that it is necessary for them to do most of the work personally, they may find it difficult to delegate portions of their work to others. Managers must ask certain questions:

1. Is there anything someone else can do better than I can?
2. Am I taking full advantage of the people on my staff who have more knowledge, background, and experience in the work?
3. Is there anything someone else can do at a lesser expense than I can?
4. Is there anything someone else can do with better timing than I can?
5. Am I trying to cover too much ground?
6. Is there a proper cutoff point for my personal decisions?

These questions are important because they indicate to managers basically what is occurring with regard to their own style and how well their time is being managed. Or, is their style affecting the effective management of their time? In the majority of cases where problems

are found and delegation does not exist, the answer is not in hiring ad
ditional persons to carry out the managers' tasks but to use individuals much more effectively so that they will be able to handle the
tasks in need of solutions.

THE FAILURE TO DELEGATE

Many managers are great offenders against the process of delegation. It doesn't matter why the managers are bogged down in their
work nor that time constraints are pressing. What does matter is that
assignments are being handled by the individual managers and they
therefore are not including subordinates in the decision-making process. The unfortunate aspect of this is that subordinates expect to be involved in decision making since they know that the upward mobility
direction leading to a managerial position has a prerequisite: the
decision-making ability that they are being denied. This leads to
frustration and ultimate stress.

If managers fail to delegate, it may be important to examine some
tangible issues to help explain this situation. The real issues may not
be intellectual or cognitive but may be psychological problems that
manifest themselves in emotional dysfunctions. If managers are cognizant of the fact that they are not performing well in their quest to
delegate, they then must examine certain aspects of their behavior so
they can discover why they are unable to handle this executive function. They may want to look into certain aspects of their own personalities, experiences, and background to see whether there are any
factors from the past still linked to current behaviors. A major problem is that managers have a great fear they will be discovered as inept.

Intellectually, managers assume that they appear to be performing
satisfactorily but internally (emotionally) their basic feelings of inadequacy and insecurity are extremely difficult to handle. They become
more immersed in details to overcompensate for assumed shortcom-
ings and therefore do not delegate because they are afraid their subordinates and peers finally will discover that they are as inept as they
really feel—or are. Other managers have an overdeveloped notion of
what perfection should be and thus set impossible standards.

The higher managers are situated in the hierarchy, the more they
tend to devote their time to planning. This is another reason for
delegating so that the managers will have the time to engage in planning, managing, and assessing events with regard to their potential for
future action.

It is not uncommon to find managers under pressure who fabricate
reasons that they may need psychologically in their attempts to avoid

making decisions while not involving subordinates either through delegation. Some managers are overwhelmed by "deadlineitis," which creates tension and a feeling that all unfinished assignments and their impending deadlines can by handled only through panic, anxiety, and stress. The managers attempt to avoid making decisions and delegating by diluting decisions and using committees to neutralize the effect of their input. They take half-measures in which they take only a partial stand when it is important to focus on a total decision. They fail to follow up on decisions so that the major impact of what they should do becomes diluted. Fatigue is a psychosomatic factor responsible for the managers' not acting on decisions and serves well for avoidance of issues.

Time is an extremely scarce resource and unless it is managed effectively and efficiently, nothing else can be managed through priorities. Managers who use their time effectively have investigated their own use of time and have been able to eliminate unproductive demands. Most managers are keenly aware that they do not have unlimited time to perform all aspects of their positions fully because the tempo and complexity of health care operations are on the increase.

The increasing pressure created by time cannot be solved by gimmicky solutions. One solid way is to examine the managers' basic working methods and style. Those methods can be improved by increasing individuals' output, which will control more of the time that is underused in lower productivity. As managerial techniques are improved and refined there should be an increase in output. When individuals feel they do not have enough time to perform their job, this may be a symptom of decreasing output and the accumulating obsolescence of their skills, expertise, and knowledge.

An interesting study examined the style of managers and the effect of this factor on the stress experienced by subordinates. While this was an experiential laboratory event, it did focus on the important issue of productivity. Sixty male undergraduates, deployed in groups of four, worked on structured and unstructured tasks under stressful or nonstressful conditions. One member of each group adopted either an authoritarian or democratic leadership style. Subjects under stress did best under authoritarian leaders but took significantly longer to complete their tasks. Unstressed subjects performed best under democratic leaders, and performed better, worked faster, and enjoyed structured tasks most. This study is most transferrable to the health care environment.

Managers in health care institutions can increase their output as they expand their capacity to gain accurate and clear perceptions of what is going on around them. To improve their "mental photography," they must increase their sensitivity and range of experiences and knowledge. This can occur only when they overcome their tendency toward being preoccupied. If they begin to change their routines and gain new skills at conserving time, these can be part of their daily standard operating procedure. They can increase their energies by eliminating personal criticism and defensive behavior involving their subordinates and peers.

Managers must remember that, at best, they can gain only a fraction of the information about what is going on. They must check and scan to find out what other individuals see in order to improve the quality of their own perceptions. This can occur through exploring ideas and being closely in touch with the individuals with whom they are involved on a daily routine. Managers can be overwhelmed by poor perception and, as a result, spend a great deal of time experiencing anxiety and stress. This intrapsychic state cuts into their productivity by demanding much of their energy in fighting the wrong forest fires.

These anxiety-ridden managers are fearful of not getting credit for a job or that someone else will know more about the work and therefore their subordinates, who are now being given this freedom to decide under delegation, will move ahead of them organizationally in extremely quick fashion. As a result, these managers fear they ultimately will be left at the starting gate. These basic fears of insecurity lead to intrinsic conflicts in which supervisors have a difficult time dealing with all of their own insecurities, which may be manifested from earlier periods of growth and development. These managers do not communicate well and have arrived at their positions in the institution as a result of being excellent technicians in their own specialized fields. However, they do have underutilized skills in imparting these data to others, particularly to subordinates.

In their own area of expertise, they are accustomed to dealing with problems from beginning to end and using their own resources and skills in isolation. They have found that solving problems intuitively is the only way they can achieve effectiveness and success. To delegate would be a problem since it would hamper their initial success pattern, which is historically rooted, and would create a new system with which they are not comfortable.

One of the basic adjustments for these managers is that they must change their basic style from being doers to being executives who get things done through other people—the classical concept of management. In this case, management does equate with delegation. Delegation multiplies efforts through the division of duties. It is the foundation for organizing, since before anyone can decide how to organize functions and at the same time direct others to perform those tasks, the managers must resolve this conflict so that these duties will be done by others and not by themselves.

Delegation means actually giving others the right to make decisions, since decision making is the core of both management and delegation. It is giving trust to others who are being held accountable for certain tasks. Lack of trust is largely to blame for not delegating in the first place and may be the source of overmanagement by executives who think they are delegating when they actually are controlling their subordinates tightly and denying them any freedom. Delegation in certain instances is similar to an investment. The second time a manager delegates to the same subordinate should require half the time that the initial delegation process took.

The ultimate accountability for subordinates' mistakes certainly rests with the managers. Rather than being in control of every function—a situation that can become overwhelming—managers can minimize the chances of errors by gradually increasing the challenge of jobs delegated to their subordinates over time. Outstanding performances by subordinates usually serve to confirm supervisors' success as managers and as delegators. Managers who are in line for promotion usually will cite the fact that they have capable and trained subordinates ready to handle the tasks for which they initially were responsible. The rewards of delegation tend to be less direct than the payoffs of doing jobs by themselves. Again, delegation really is getting work done through others. This is an essential task in the management process, particularly in the dynamic health care environment.

PROBLEMS IN DELEGATION

In some delegation problems, managers and subordinates fail to agree on the specifics of what is to be delegated. These issues include:

1. Subordinates do not have the training needed to complete the delegated tasks. This is a managerial problem that supervisors can overcome by having their subordinates fully trained in the essential aspects of the operation for which they ultimately will be held accountable.
2. Managers enjoy their work thoroughly and do not want to delegate its satisfying aspects while handing off only the tasks that are relatively meaningless, irrelevant, or redundant.
3. Managers delegate only assignments with which they are not familiar or at which they are not very proficient. This creates a problem in which the managers actually abdicate their roles as

the control force in the accountability for a task. When the task is not performed well by the subordinates, then the managers can air their frustration and wrath upon the employees. This only adds to the basic confusion created by improper delegation. This in itself becomes a problem that leads to other managerial difficulties. In actuality, when managers encounter unfamiliar or difficult tasks, they enhance their versatility by handling broader responsibilities.

4. Managers often do not explain the overall organizational mission to their subordinates, and when the employees do not understand the institution's goals they have a difficult time in dealing with the delegation of the objectives to be achieved.

5. Managers may well choose overqualified subordinates to assure that the job is being performed properly. This can be traced back to the fact that the managers may be fearful of mistakes by their employees. When overqualified individuals are used, areas of the job that are essential and in need of effective performance often are left unmanaged due to the frustration of the individual who often decides to sabotage the job by retiring early on the job as a hidden message. When managers make it clear that they really mean it when they assert that they completely support the process of delegation, then incomplete or incorrect tasks will not flow back to the managers, nor will the subordinates keep running in for continued reassurance and advice.

6. And finally, delegation is not an all-or-nothing process but it actually is a managerial process. This can be executed through the following managerial steps (these steps are arranged in a power hierarchy):

- Subordinates to take action, no further contact with managers is necessary.
- Subordinates to take action, let managers know what they did via advisory.
- Subordinates to look into problem and let managers know what they intend to do via recommendation, and perform the task unless advised not to do so.
- Subordinates to look into problem and let managers know what they intend to do: no action to be taken until managers approve.
- Subordinates to look into problem and let managers know alternative actions, include pros and cons of each, and recommend one for supervisors' approval.
- Subordinates to look into problem and report all the facts to managers, who will decide what to do.

These processes of delegation are the degrees of authority that managers are willing to grant to their subordinates. It is essential to understand how and when they work and at what level managers are in their own decision-making process when using them.

CONTROLS

One of the best ways to handle delegation and the management of time is by follow-up. While managers intend to delegate, they also must understand that the subordinates will be doing the job their own way. At such times, the managers are faced with a dilemma because they want to maintain enough control to avoid problems before they arise. At one extreme of the continuum are subordinates to whom certain programs now have been delegated and who are almost totally free to complete the assignment as they see it while making the decisions themselves. The follow-up to this increases degree by degree until the opposite extreme of the continuum is reached, with the authority to use all of the data and make the actual decisions still held completely by the managers.

The amount of control that managers exercise in a follow-up to a delegated task is determined by the personality of the executives, their style, the individuals to whom responsibilities have been delegated, and the nature of the task itself. Follow-up will be close if the managers have not delegated to the individual previously or when an unknown candidate has been selected to handle a task. When a task has clear precedence, policies, or procedures, less follow-up is needed and the manager will control carefully any decisions involving significant departures from general policy. One of the most essential functions of the manager is to determine whether *outputs* from a task have a direct, measurable linkage to the basic *inputs* that were the initial objectives of the subordinate and manager. This process ensures the necessary control mechanism.

The issues that become difficult are those that remain with the managers after they have delegated the routine decisions to others. It is important to understand that the managerial functions, leadership, policy making, goal setting, planning, disciplining, and motivating still are in the executives' arena and even if they delegate, they still are responsible for these aspects. These processes should not be delegated to subordinates, and the closer a delegated task comes to one of these prime managerial responsibilities, the closer the follow-up should be.

Managers should inform the individual to whom they are delegating an assignment that they are interested in finding out how the person is coming along through a process report but not to smother the subordinate with tight, overbearing controls. It is essential that managers encourage independence on the part of subordinates. Any time managers give subordinates their unique method by directions or short-circuiting them by dealing directly with lower level employees, they automatically undermine subordinates' authority and, as a result, are not managing either their own or their subordinates' time properly.

Managers must learn to live with variances and differences. As long as they are delegating a task to an individual, they probably will be receiving results through feedback that may be adequate but may not fit their personal style area and comfort zone. When this occurs it may be necessary for managers to continue to "let go" and allow the individual to whom they have delegated the task to complete the assignment even though they do not agree with the method. Since results are most significant, the means are not as crucial as the ends. Managers must not retract the assignment and take it out of subordinates' control because of something they may not like in a midstream progress report rather than await a final report.

Exceptional performance is difficult to measure as individuals are moving along. When managers delegate, they should follow up at an agreed upon date when all of the information is in. This is a reasonable position that has value in interpersonal relationships in the health care environment. In discussing exceptional performance, it is important for managers to determine what rewards should follow. Individuals who are successful and have performed all the delegated tasks will appreciate extrinsic rewards as well as those intrinsic rewards that they have gained from having been the recipients of a delegated project.

When managers and subordinates both understand that there is a connection between motivation, effort, performance, and intended outcomes, then they discover and even psychologically internalize the awareness of expectations. If delegation and task accomplishment on the part of subordinates is the managers' expectation, then this message will be very clear. This is one of the most efficient and effective ways of managing both responsibility and time. The management of time is connected to delegation since both are inextricably woven together.

Thus, to the extent that executives use time management practices, their overall stress level should be lower by virtue of having reduced or eliminated specific stresses, such as those related to achievement, growth, and certainty.

Time management strategies raise several important questions for executives:

1. If people use time management and actually get more done in less time, should they be rewarded?
2. Are there enough job duties to warrant an official time management program, since it does take time, effort, and money?
3. What are the advantages (and disadvantages) of knowing a job so well thanks to the self-analysis techniques?
4. Do managers really want to delegate, or will they see this as a loss of power?

There are doubtless more questions of equal importance. The crucial point is that these issues be addressed when considering the use of time management. Time management means less stress for individuals, which means more efficient, satisfied, healthy employees, which in turn means more effective organizations (Schuler, 1979, p. 854)

BIBLIOGRAPHY

Drucker, P.F. *The practice of management.* New York: Harper & Row, 1954, 128–129.

Drucker, P.F. How to manage your time. *Harper's Magazine,* December 1966, 46.

McConkey, D. *No nonsense delegation.* New York: American Management Association, 1974,

Schuler, R.S. Managing stress means managing time. *Personnel Journal,* December 1979, *58*(12), 851–854.

Part III

Cases and Incidents Involving Stress Management in Health Care Organizations

Appendix A

A Case of Departmental Custody

The Controller and Chief Financial Officer of Bennett Medical Center, Mr. Harry Boyle made a formal request to the Executive Administrator of the Hospital, Mr. John Key, that the Business Office, Data Processing and Patient Representative Functions be transferred from the Assistant Administrator for Hospital Operations, Mr. Tony Bonello to his domain. Mr. Boyle explained to his boss, John Key that these functions were financial and should not be under the supervision of Tony Bonello who was already responsible for sixteen departments. Boyle argued that local CPA firms who served other health care organizations all supported his request and found it strange for financial operations such as business office, data processing and patient representative to be under the direction of a hospital operation. The Executive Administrator, Mr. Key also spoke to Tony Bonello and was told that the system worked quite well and non-traditional managerial structures were perfectly acceptable as long as the goals were being achieved. He agreed that some conflict was being experienced but this was insignificant since all health care organizations are subjected to this event. One of the major problems in the transference was the status and disposition of two subordinates to

Tony Bonello. Ms. Naomi Pratt was the supervisor of the Patient Representative office and helped greatly in managing a major portion of the Business Office. Mr. Eric Dale was Manager of Data Processing and also helped to manage a portion of the Business Office. Both Ms. Pratt and Mr. Dale were satisfied with the organizational arrangement and felt the structure was most effective even though it was unorthodox and a deviation from other traditional health care managerial structures. Mr. John Key was uncertain as to what direction to take and recruited a consultant to study the problem and recommend a course of action. This author was given the task of interviewing all four parties who would be involved in the move which had far reaching ramifications throughout the Bennett Medical Center. A summary of interviews with each of the individuals involved is given with a summary of their perceptions of the problem and conflict in need of resolution.

Ms. Naomi Pratt

Naomi Pratt was recruited by Eric Dale, her current supervisor, and seems to enjoy her relationship with Mr. Dale. She is cognizant of the fact and relieved that John Key, the Executive Administrator of the center, is concerned about the problem involved with this reporting relationship. She enjoys her relationship with Tony Bonello, her ultimate supervisor, and has indicated that Tony is quite knowledgeable about his own area of responsibility and her area of expertise as well. He gives her direction and she feel[s] she can come to him with any problems for solutions. She enjoys the teamwork and the positive climate at Bennett. She has had minor contact with Harry Boyle and appeared to be tense and apprehensive when discussing the transference to his area. She feels that if he attempts to take on the Patient Representative system, the total system will, in fact, fail, since two basic management styles will [a]ffect the cash flow of the hospital. She feels Boyle's management style is authoritarian and he does not support his people and may, in fact, destroy some of the relationships she has developed within her department, which initially were quite problematic. She indicated that the team is definitely Eric Dale, Tony Bonello and herself. She is totally committed to the hospital, and at this time had not considered leaving the hospital if the move were to take place. She feels Tony Bonello gives her a great deal of support, but she feels she will not be given the same support from Harry Boyle if the transfer occurs.

She indicated that a great portion of the Patient Representative responsibility is interaction throughout the hospital, which is not a financial function, but one of operations, which comes under Tony's areas of responsibility. She indicated that there was a clique, historically, in the Admission's Office when she first came to the hospital, and this grouping of people were tied in with the physicians who actually controlled the Admission's Office. The function was not financially feas[i]ble at that time and only through Mr. Bonello's efforts has it been managed effectively and efficiently at this juncture.

Mr. Eric Dale

Eric Dale indicated that his decision to come to Bennet[t] was based upon the challenge of the job, the opportunity to grow, and the managerial opportunity presented by Tony Bonello, the individual with whom he would be working. He indicated that Gamma Data Systems several years ago set up the Patient Representative systems based upon a consulting agreement, and Tony Bonello made the initial study and recommended the Patient Rep system, which was, at that point, approved and supported by John Key and incorporated into the hospital.

Mr. Dale understands that the Patient Rep system can overlap into both Mr. Boyle and Mr. Bonello's areas, and one of the problems he feels is keeping it under two umbrellas with regard to leadership and function. He indicated that he was most interested in working for someone that he respected and who, in turn, respected him. He feels that dynamics and personal chemistry are significant in any relationship within the hospital. He feels in working with Tony he has this chemistry. He indicated that he works approximately 10 hours a day, primarily for Tony and the current needs. He is part of Tony's team and is concerned that a commitment may have been made by John Key to Harry Boyle to switch the functions over to Financial. He indicated that, to him, traditionally these three functions, Business Office, Data Processing, and Patient Rep, have not always fallen under the Financial Director, and all three must be linked together within one department. He indicated that he feels a great deal of risk will be illuminated if this area is switched to the Controller's Department, and could be harmful to the hospital. He also indicated that he does not feel secure with Harry Boyle's leadership style, and when problems occur, he cannot depend on Mr. Boyle the way he has with Mr. Bonello.

One of the problems is that for the last several years Eric Dale has been put in the position of defending his position to Harry Boyle, and appears to be caught in the middle of two divergent forces. He also indicated that Boyle has never demonstrated any confidence in Dale's ability, and this is most upsetting to him personally and professionally. He must always sell his effectiveness to Harry Boyle, and finds that this is quite counterproductive to a relationship and to the hospital itself.

Eric Dale also indicated that his career will be somewhat limited if he swings over to the Financial area, since one of the main motivations for staying with Tony Bonello is that he can succeed Mr. Bonello's position in total or in part if certain changes occur, when his present supervisor moves into other domains. Mr. Dale is also concerned with the staff in the Financial Department and he feels that he has never really had a positive working relationship with them at all. He indicated that the current organizational structure is a good one, and he feels it creates a positive check and balance system. He feels that hospital operations is a necessary control for the Business Office, Data Processing, and Patient Rep functions at this time. He indicated that he feels that he is successful in his job and wants to continue assuming responsibility, but wants things to stay as they are.

Mr. Tony Bonello

Tony Bonello came to Bennett Medical Center in January of 1976, and was given the responsibility for eight departments. He was given an additional three departments shortly afterwards, as a result of current emergency and ineffective operation at that time. He was considered to be quite competent at that time in handling Patient Representation, Admittance, and Data Processing. But, at that time he was not thoroughly immersed in the Business Office operation. Tony Bonello shortly thereafter hired Eric Dale, who was acting as a consultant for Gamma Data Systems, and, at that point, suggested a financial control committee to implement a plan of action intended to reduce Accounts Receivable, back billing, and other problems. As a result of all of the problems, Tony Bonello built a team consisting of Mr. Dale and Ms. Naomi Pratt to achieve all the goals that had not been accomplished previously, and appeared to be successful. He indicated that cohesiveness and dedication were components of his team.

Approximately in January 1978, Tony was made aware that Harry Boyle indicated to Mr. John Key that he wanted these three areas, which were originally and historically under the umbrella of the Financial Department. These departments were transferred to Tony due to the previous controller's inept performance. He was ineffective, and these functions had to be given at that point in time to Tony for management and not technical expertise.

Mr. Bonello informed me that the hospital literature varies with regard to unity of command. He indicated that traditionally, the controller has the Accounting, the Business Office and Data Processing functions. However, contemporary health care literature indicates that there has been a separation of Business Office and Data Processing with the intention of developing a check and balance system. One of the major problems that Tony Bonello indicated is that if Naomi Pratt and Eric Dale are transferred to Harry Boyle, and both have indicated that they don't want to be, then one will probably leave. This will set off a chain reaction, with both leaving, since both are dedicated and loyal and have worked with each other for approximately 15 years, a period of time which came prior to their employment with Bennett. Tony is responsible for operations and is not totally immersed in the financial aspects of health care management. It is quite questionable at this point as to where the clear division begins and ends.

In discussing this problem with Tony, it is quite clear that he has maintained an extremely tight control over both Eric Dale and Naomi Pratt. Tight, in that, their interpersonal relationships are totally involved with the job and their social attraction for each other. Tony appears to have a difficult time in letting go of both Eric Dale and Naomi Pratt and can easily create guilt feelings within both, which could be self-destructive to Mr. Dale and Ms. Pratt if they are to be transferred. It is inevitable that both would ultimately quit according to Mr. Bonello.

It is also clear that Eric Dale is ultra-sensitive and uses a rigid, tough posture as a defense mechanism, which is difficult to read. Harry Boyle is apparently picking up a great deal of Dale's rigidness, which leads to more conflict between the two and is not being resolved by Tony at this juncture.

Tony Bonello possesses the ability to resolve conflicts, which seems to be a major part of patient counseling and physician interaction. This is not a piece of the financial job which Harry Boyle handles, but one which Tony is responsible for and appears to be quite adept at doing.

Mr. Harry Boyle

Harry Boyle feels Bennett Medical Center is the only installation in which the Business Office, Patient Representative function, and Data Processing are not part of the Financial function of the organization.

He claims that he has spoken with several CPA firms and indicated that in every case, these three functions are under the control of the Chief Financial Officer. He feels that this is a problem which [a]ffects him personally, since these three departments are financial and he is not being held accountable but responsible for them. All financial policies are set by the board, and he is personally being held accountable at board meetings for the reporting of these functions, which he is not managing.

His basic responsibility is profitability, which is measured by cash flow and bad debts. However, these functions are now under Tony Bonello and Mr. Boyle is not in control of these functions. Mr. Boyle feels his visibility at the board level is significant and an area in which Tony Bonello is absent from. He feels that he is being asked by the Board to assess and report on these functions but is unable to give a valid, accurate report because he is not managing these as well. He further indicated that Eric Dale, according to Boyle, does not have a great deal of expertise with regard to Admissions, Data Processing, and the Business function, but has been given a great deal of power by Tony Bonello and is "over his head" with regard to this responsibility. There appears to be a constant problem with Accounts Receivable and this is another reason why Mr. Boyle feels he should be in control of this function. He agreed that he will treat Eric Dale quite positively if the transfer takes place.

This is an interesting point to consider, since a great deal of the covert fighting is between Harry Boyle and Tony Bonello, which actually never surfaces. Tony however, appears to be willing to have Eric Dale take on Harry Boyle in financial meetings and other sessions, and, within this domain, Harry usually controls the situation and ventilates his hostilities for Tony onto Eric Dale, who ultimately serves as "whipping boy" under this arrangement.

Mr. Boyle does not feel that Tony Bonello's style and philosophy is congruent with Bennett's financial needs. He indicates that he personally likes Eric Dale and Naomi Pratt and feels both need direction and support in their decisions. He also indicated that Tony Bonello is not involved in the major management decision-making in which Harry Boyle and Mr. John Key are both involved, and this significant financial situation is another factor supporting his position for a switch.

He claims he has been encouraging John Key to settle this situation for a year and a half, and to date, no decision has been made, which has been a negative motive for Harry Boyle to continue seeking this change. He does not see any other alternatives and feels that Naomi Pratt and Eric Dale will have to be moved to the Financial Department or stay with Tony Bonello in Operations, since apparently both do not want to be separated at this reading.

Harry Boyle appears to have a great deal more regard for Naomi Pratt than he does for Eric Dale, and feels Dale is being rewarded not for his performance, but for his ability to take direction from Tony Bonello and to be controlled by Tony as well. He promised that his own management style will be one of delegation to all new people coming within his department, and he will be able to decentralize his functions through them and give them a great deal more autonomy.

Observations of Organizational Problems

A brief summary is indicated to put this situation into perspective. Harry Boyle wanted to absorb these three functions in mid 1976, but Tony Bonello continued to assume these functions, which he originally acquired on a temporary basis, and was never actually encouraged to turn them over to the Financial Department by John Key. As time went on, Tony's operational departments were quite effective, and the basic decision was kept intact since the tampering with something positive and effective was not indicated. Historically, the move should have been made, because it does appear that these functions are financial, but seem to be effective within the current operations of the hospital.

As of Fall 1978, Tony had increased from 8 to 16 departments, for which he is held responsible. He is also quite concerned with the human factor within all departments, while Harry Boyle is much more concerned with bottom line data. Both Harry Boyle and Tony Bonello agreed that the situation should have been resolved by John Key and both indicated that they felt they were manipulated into this adversary position several years ago.

The relationship between Boyle and Bonello had certainly [a]ffected Eric Dale and Naomi Pratt in their reluctance to change. Boyle was equally frustrated, since he felt he had to answer to the board for Tony Bonello's responsibility, but had not been given the authority, and this led to conflict. Boyle was constantly going to Eric Dale for data and business office tasks to be performed, and this created more of a conflict situation, since it actually avoided the hierarchy and equal relationships between Boyle and Bonello. Tony, on the other hand, had indicated that he would certainly fulfill all of Boyle's needs if Harry would inform him prior to any intervention within the operations department and concerning his need to get Dale to complete a project. Tony had further asked Harry Boyle to set priorities and objectives that he felt Eric Dale and Naomi Pratt should achieve and Bonello would incorporate them into the MBO's which were to be developed by both Dale and Pratt for Tony Bonello. The ongoing conflict had created negative relationships in these departments and all of the employees in both financial and operations who happened to interact throughout the day for various reasons also were cognizant of the conflict and reported some hostilities as a spill-over.

Eric Dale appeared to be quite insecure in his position and had been attacked by Harry Boyle historically, and had been supported by Tony historically, and presently. Boyle felt that Dale was not significant, but that Naomi was, and Eric can be reprogrammed to function as a significant resource with the proper management and leadership. This, of course, necessitates no negative punishment on the part of Boyle towards Dale, which would have to be agreed upon prior to any moves.

Recommended Action

After examining all of the data and spending a great deal of time talking to the four participants in the study, the consultant basically recommend[ed] at that point in time that both Naomi Pratt and Eric Dale remain with Tony Bonello since both were reluctant to leave the department, and Bennett, as a humanistic institution tried to respect the wishes of productive employees who were considered to be effective and efficient in their performance. Unless there were glowing negative reports concerning either or both parties involved from other areas within the hospital organizaton, it appeared to be an unwise move at that time to make any transference to the financial department. A move in that direction should be considered if it is decided that a further organizational analysis be conducted with the purpose of restructuring the reporting relationships and power distribution within the hospital. It was clear at that juncture that Mr. John Key was not willing to take the chance in disrupting an operation that subjectively appeared to be functioning. In addition, Tony Bonello has greater influence than Harry Boyle which created an additional blockage for change. The dynamics of Bonello, Pratt and Dale were so intense that a recommended change to shift operations to Harry Boyle would have created unresolved conflict and stress.

It is difficult to discount history and it is also unfeas[i]ble to alter a situation which appears to be productive and satisfying. It was recommended however, that Harry Boyle develop a demand list of expectations for Eric Dale and Naomi Pratt and present these to Tony Bonello, so that they can, in fact, be incorporated in both individual's

MBO's and within Mr. Bonello's objectives to John Key as well. It was further recommended that Eric Dale not be directly confronted with Harry Boyle on any special assignments, but that Mr. Boyle go directly to Tony Bonello to clear any projects or programs and Tony, in fact, would then contact Eric Dale to inform him of changes in his objectives and further accountabilities.

An added recommendation would be that the consultants report be duplicated and given to both Harry Boyle and Tony Bonello so that the findings can be discussed, in order to qualify the position which was taken, and to resolve the conflict that existed between both individuals. It was clear that hostility and a great deal of local infighting had been the rule for the last three years, and there was no indication that this covert arena would be reduced because of this change and recommendation.

It was important that the process of the change and not the authority for change be worked out between Bonello, Boyle, and John Key. This report, of course, was a recommendation, and certainly, should be discussed prior to this last recommendation. The Executive Administrator, Mr. John Key decided to keep the situation intact and did not accept the input from Harry Boyle with regard to a functional, managerial system which was needed for the long run and one which should be reinforced for the purpose of satisfying a "team" reluctant to make functional changes and reporting relationships.

Concluding Note

In January of 1980 Mr. Harry Boyle left the Bennett Medical Center to join a Public Accounting Firm and was replaced by Donald Mc-Craw. The Board of Trustees, upon the suggestion of Harry Boyle and several CPA consultants requested Mr. John Key to consider formally placing the Business Office, Data Processing, and Patient Representative under the direction of Mr. Donald McCraw the new Controller and Chief Financial Officer. As the pressure mounted to have this change realized, John Key reconsidered his earlier position and switched the accountability from Tony Bonello, the Assistant Administrator for Hospital Operations to McCraw.

As a result of this, Bonello's domain and workload were reduced to a more manageable level and Don McCraw immediately restructured these functions within his area of responsibility where policies and procedures were developed to help reduce some ambiguity and conflict. Bonello became focused in other directions and was unavailable to assist the "team" of Eric Dale and Naomi Pratt who were experiencing confusion and anxiety. Naomi Pratt quickly decided to become involved in her new reporting arrangement and adjusted relatively quickly while Eric Dale experienced greater anxiety and stress. This intrapsychic situation affected his supervision of subordinates as well. Other departments [began] to complain to Don McCraw about the poor services they were receiving and a new decision had to be made by Mr. McCraw regarding managerial, organizational and personal factors affecting the operation of his newly acquired department.

Appendix B

Boston City Hospital:
A House Divided Still Stands

On February 2, 1973, as part of an "austerity budget" for the city of Boston, Mayor Kevin White announced that the budget for the Department of Health and Hospitals would be reduced by about $13 million from the previous year, to $56 million. About 80 percent of the Health and Hospitals budget was spent at the 580-bed Boston City Hospital, which was the only public acute care hospital in the city.

Boston City Hospital (BCH) has held a unique place among the Boston-area hospitals. In 1968, it treated 27.4 percent of all Boston residents treated at Boston hospitals; it was the major emergency hospital for gunshot and stab wound victims and other traumatic injuries; and it was the main center for mass hospitalizations from serious fires or auto accidents. Located in Boston's South End, it had long served a community of poor people; the majority of its patients were the medically indigent. BCH was the only hospital in the area where three medical schools—Harvard, Tufts, and Boston University—had coexisted for half a century, allowing the hospital to maintain the large staff needed to care for the city's poor.

The Mayor's announcement sparked a furor. About 60 protesters led by two BCH doctors met the Mayor in his office after the announcement. "Questioned about the cuts in the hospital's budget, White at

Authors Karen S. Heller and Duncan Neuhauser, *Changing Health Services. Teaching Cases.* Ford Foundation Seminar on the Delivery of Urban Health Services. Boston, Mass.: Harvard School of Public Health and the Center for Community Health and Medical Care, 1975, Copyright © Harvard University.

one point told one of the physicians: 'I know what I'm doing more than you do.' "[1]

> A black woman told her story, the story of thousands of people—her child has a congenital disease, she cannot afford to go to Children's Hospital, BCH has saved her child's life for years. Mayor White listened and then actually said to her: "Some of you people may have to die." Then he went on to talk about the tight straits the City is in, especially with the cutbacks in federal spending, the need to provide relief for taxpayers and the need for all of us to pull in our belts. He didn't mention, as he looked out over Boston harbor from his office, that some people's belts were already past the last hole.[2]

On February 9, the Department of Health and Hospitals' Board of Trustees voted not to accept the $56 million budget. According to *Globe* reporter Carl M. Cobb, the emerging issue was not so much the drastic cuts, but whether the budget would allow enough money for rational planning.[3] The next day, the Board met with the Mayor at a meeting described as "tough, exhausting, angry." Most felt that it was an impossible task to reduce hospital expenditure by $13 million and retain three medical schools without closing the hospital. There was debate on all sides: some felt a reduction in services would mean a reduction in revenue, since 80 percent of the hospital costs were borne by third party payers, including Medicare, Medicaid, and welfare. Others contended that real reductions in costs were only possible by eliminating services that provided little revenue: i.e. outpatient community health centers, obstetrics and gynecology, and pediatric services. "However, it was politically unwise or impossible to eliminate these."[4]

It was concluded that among the actions needed to be taken were a major reduction in beds from 850 to 500, a ceiling accomplished by cancelling all elective admissions; elimination of all duplication of services resulting from the presence of three medical schools in the hospital; closure of specialty services also available at Boston University's University Hospital, located 400 yards away; a freeze on overtime and hiring; a 10-20 percent cut in house officers; and a considerable reduction in other employee positions.

> . . . other institutions have successfully responded to financial crises without subjecting themselves to such a bloodletting. What made the BCH different and was, in my opin-

ion, the underlying problem, was the administrative monstrosity with which it was saddled: three independent medical and surgical services and a dozen or so semiautonomous fiefdoms, accountable to three deans of three medical schools. The BCH consisted for all practical purposes of three competing hospitals under one roof.[5]

According to Dr. William V. McDermott, Harvard's Cheever Professor of Surgery and Director of the BCH Sears Surgical Laboratory, pointing out the inefficiency of three medical schools in the same hospital "had always been a favorite political diversionary tactic when any crisis arose."[6]

Although BCH had survived this way for many years, the hospital was under heavy pressure to demonstrate that it was doing everything possible to reorganize to save money. Dr. Richard Ryan, at that time Special Assistant to the Dean of Harvard Medical School, recalled that in communications between the three medical school faculties it became apparent that the perceptions of each were so "parochial" (in terms of their own teaching needs) that they were unable to agree on what reforms were necessary or feasible.[7] Ultimately, unification of the medical services was called for to eliminate unnecessary duplication.

> In actual fact, cost benefit analyses indicating the economies of a unified system in contrast with the three school systems was never provided. It is possible that the additional expenses that derived from the triple medical and surgical services were more than counterbalanced by the additional faculty, services, and overhead income to the hospital provided by Harvard, and to a lesser extent, by Tufts.[8]

The three medical schools were asked to submit plans which had to be formulated and reviewed in two weeks. On February 21, 1973, the Board of Trustees voted to replace the BCH "managerial madness" by turning over responsibility for staffing all medical services to the Boston University School of Medicine. It was a foregone conclusion that no individual general medical or surgical unit would be permitted to either Harvard or Tufts after the end of that fiscal year. Harvard and Tufts were encouraged to stay at BCH and to contribute to teaching and research, but despite public statements of reassurance, it rapidly became apparent that this would not be possible, at least in the traditional sense.

> Most agree that the Board's action was probably more important than any other taken in the Hospital's 109-year

history. The interschool competition that preceded the
decision was one of the fiercest ever in any institution, that
has brought academic politics to the level of a fine art.[9]

In recent years, Boston University had begun to assume increasing
academic responsibilities for services at the hospital and a close
working relationship developed between the Dean of the Boston
University School of Medicine and the Director of BCH. According to
Dr. Ryan,

> Harvard and Tufts faculty members were unwilling to accept
> the ascendancy of Boston University and what developed on
> the part of Harvard and Tufts was a sense that Boston Uni-
> versity had the inside track and that they were being put in
> jeopardy. Rumors that Boston University intended to
> assume control were in circulation a year before that actual
> change took place. In about 1968, for example, when an
> administrator at BCH was recruited as Assistant Dean
> at Boston University School of Medicine, this was inter-
> preted by the faculty of the other schools as an intention to
> consolidate under Boston University control. After the
> budget announcement (in 1973) a number of Harvard faculty
> came to the BCH director Francis Guiney and said that they
> had been told that it was a fait accompli that Boston Uni-
> versity would take over the hospital. Guiney denied this
> and said the Board would hold hearings on proposals from
> each school. From Harvard's point of view, the Tufts pro-
> posal was the most viable. Harvard felt if Tufts got control,
> that would be acceptable to them, and vice versa.[10]

Dr. Ryan, who participated in the negotiations between the hospital
and the three schools, recalled that Herbert Gleason, counsel for the
City of Boston and a Harvard alumnus, felt so strongly that Harvard
behaved arrogantly and was highhanded during the negotiations
about the transfer that he wrote a letter of protest to Harvard's
President Derek Bok. "Gleason denied bitterly that there was any prior
decision with respect to BU," said Dr. Ryan. However,

> The Harvard and Tufts faculty felt the rumors were very
> real: people were suspicious [and Ryan says he is still
> suspicious] that even if it was *not* contrived to give BU con-
> trol and to reduce BCH eventually to a 300–400 bed

infirmary-type operation, there is every suggestion that that is what's going to happen.

Harvard's Reaction

> Though the decision had been foreseen and feared by many in the Harvard Services of the Boston City Hospital for years, it still came as a stunning shock and a grievous disappointment to members of the Harvard Medical Unit and the Thorndike Memorial Laboratory.[11]

The Harvard house staff was to be dissolved; intern applicants to the Harvard medical service for 1973-74 were immediately scratched from the BCH matching plan list and BCH interns were selected from applications to the BU service, with a few applications to the Tufts service.[12] Assurances initially were given that Harvard medical students could continue to have their Core Clinical Clerkship taught at BCH by Harvard faculty, but such instruction could not be localized on the same wards during the year, lest they continue to be identified as Harvard wards. Nurses on the former "Harvard wards," used to working together as a unit, were scattered throughout the hospital.

Dr. Franklin Epstein, director of the Thorndike Laboratory, observed:[13]

> The decision to eliminate the vestige of a Harvard house staff, so critically important in the undergraduate teaching of medicine, and the maintenance of continued growth within a medical department . . . forced the decision for the gradual departure of the Harvard department of medicine from the Boston City Hospital . . . with the loss of the house staff, Harvard had lost its raison d'etre at the Boston City Hospital. It had lost its growing tip, its flood of renewal, which for so long had permeated all of its activities.

Dr. McDermott commented:[14]

> I think the whole hospital is going down the drain anyway — that's the real tragedy. Almost 25 percent of the medical school deans in the country trained at the Boston City Hospital on the Harvard Service, an immense proportion of the medical professors did. It's sad to see this history disappear. It's worse than a crime, it's a blunder.

Dr. McDermott pointed out that Harvard had brought BCH about $8.2 million in endowment funds and over $3 million from other sources annually.

> . . since all of these monies are linked to the existence of a Harvard Service at the BCH, they will ultimately be used to support patient care, teaching, training, and research elsewhere, a result neither willed nor desired by the University or its faculty.[15]

Dr. Epstein accepted the position of chief of medicine at the Beth Israel, another Harvard teaching hospital. The Thorndike Laboratory and some of his staff relocated with him, while the old Thorndike Building remained under BCH direction with different personnel.[16] Dr. McDermott remarked about the change:[17]

> It will be difficult, if not impossible, for the past and present staff to accept emotionally the forced separation of the previously inseparable Thorndike and BCH. It is always hard to grasp the fact that institutions, no matter how ancient and venerable, are not immortal, were created by man, and can be destroyed by man.

The Harvard Clinical Center, funded by the USPHS grant, was also transferred to the Beth Israel, where new facilities were prepared for it. Some Harvard staff remained at the BCH to provide supervision for house staff "who had little or no choice but to remain for another year in an amalgamated program."[18]

Harvard's Fifth Surgical Service and the Sears Surgical Lab were already committed to a broad base of activities involving five other hospitals besides BCH (Cambridge Hospital, which also treated many poor patients, Faulkner Hospital, Manchester Hospital, the V.A. Hospital, Mt. Auburn Hospital, and the New England Deaconess Hospital). The entire structure could be continued outside the BCH, therefore, with little sense of dislocation. The Cheever Professorship of Surgery, held by Dr. McDermott, was moved out of BCH and the department offices and personnel were relocated in the Cancer Research Institute of the New England Deaconess Hospital. The Channing Laboratory has remained at BCH for the time being, although there has been some discussion about moving it to Harvard Medical School.[19]

Tufts' Reaction

Tufts University, which like Harvard had been associated with BCH from its earliest days, reacted to the decision to place administrative responsibility for medical services with Boston University by announcing a total withdrawal from the hospital. Tufts did not have Harvard's financial resources with which to attract large numbers of researchers, who bring both prestige and federal money. Over the years, their commitment at BCH had diminished. Thus, according to one observer, "when Tufts got the chance this past winter (1973) finally to rid itself of this albatross, it did so quite willingly although it went through the motions of submitting a proposal for taking over BCH on its own."[20]

Reaction from Staff and Employees

The cutbacks in budget, beds, and staff were opposed, without much effect, by various groups. The House Officers Association (HOA; with 300 dues-paying members) expressed its concern about the elimination of 70 house officer positions. Although the HOA sought an alliance with the South Boston community to oppose the cutbacks, "the gap between young white, male, professional, suburban-dwelling members and the real hospital community was so great that it did not go anywhere."[21]

The attending physicians at the hospital were reticent in public about opposing the changes, since their allegiance was to their respective medical schools.

The Massachusetts Nursing Association held several meetings to discuss the BCH nurses' plight, but since most of their leadership was non-hospital based, they had little empathy with the BCH nurses.

The Better Breaks Group (BBG), an activist hospital workers group, were mostly white, transient, educated employees in their first year at BCH. They organized an Ad Hoc Committee to Save the Hospital, and though they lacked solid political unity, organizational structure, and real connections with most of the hospital workers, they managed to produce more than 50 people on 12 hours notice for a demonstration at the Mayor's office on the day of his budget announcement. This was followed by a mass meeting of 200 people, who planned another demonstration, a petition drive, and efforts to reach out to the community for support. According to some BBG members, these plans failed because the only people willing to work actively were affiliated with the Progressive Labor Party (PLP), whom many people found to be too exclusive and sectarian. A second mass meeting of 150 people broke up within a half-hour, after factional bickering began among members of the National Caucus of Labor Committees, the Communist Party, and the PLP. Efforts to organize the diverse community living near BCH were unsuccessful. According to Jeff Blum, a member of the BBG:[22]

> Linking consumers and workers would have been difficult at best, given the divisions of race and class that existed. The Hospital's political groups and leaders were mostly White, in contrast to the mostly Black and Third World community . . . the hospital hierarchy was topped by those who [saw] themselves primarily as professionals, unwilling to grant others the ability to make intelligent decisions in a field as "specialized" as health.

Non-professional BCH employees were represented by two major unions: about 1,800 blue collar workers belonged to Local 1489 of the American Federation of State, City, and Municipal Employees, and another 1,200 white collar workers belonged to Local 285 of the Service Employees International Union. Neither union seemed to show much interest in preserving the jobs of their members at BCH; Local 285 had not held a meeting in the hospital for over a year.

> In fact, the leadership of both unions seemed to be protecting both the Mayor and the older, long-term workers, a vast majority of them white. Despite great talk of militancy on the part of the leaders of Local 1489, they never once took a stand against the cuts even though hundreds of their member jobs were at stake.[23]

Blum and his co-authors summarized the efforts of those opposed to the cutbacks by saying:[24]

> Those who actively organized against the cuts were afflicted with the same lack of contact with most workers and patients that affected the sectarian groups. Also, things happened too fast, far too fast for them to act intelligently. The overriding sense was that of being overwhelmed by the Mayor, the Trustees, the administration, and the medical empires at play.

BCH Before the Cutbacks: A Brief History

None of the problems facing the hospital were new, but there was a confluence of problems that had reached a critical stage requiring some action. The following brief history of BCH will provide a context for evaluating events of February 1973, which came, according to one observer, "with startling suddenness in an atmosphere of crisis and confusion."

Boston City Hospital opened in the South End of Boston on June 1, 1864, with 200 beds for medical, surgical, and ophthalmic patients, staffed by six visiting physicians, six visiting surgeons, six senior physicians (who formed a Board of Consultation) and five residents (two in medicine, two in surgery, and one in ophthalmology).[25] From its first years, the hospital was devoted to providing care for the working poor. The January 1865 Report of the Trustees articulated the BCH philosophy at that time:[26]

> It may not be unnecessary to repeat what has been so often stated, that this is not in the strict sense of the word, a free hospital. It is free to those industrious persons, who from sickness or misfortune, have been temporarily disabled and who can, on recovery, maintain themselves. Neither is it intended for the reception of paupers, for whom ample accommodations are provided elsewhere. It is designed to do the greatest good to the greatest possible number, and for this reason, chronic and incurable cases which would speedily and permanently fill the wards are not received.

In 1865, the budget request was for $65,000. In the first full year of operations, 1,066 patients were admitted and 1,143 outpatients were treated. The cost of maintaining the hospital in its first year of operations was $54,276.57.[27]

In the Fall of 1864-65, Harvard undergraduate teaching began under four instructors and by 1892, clinical teaching required a four-year curriculum. There was an early separation of medical specialties: contagious diseases (1866); dermatology (1869); diseases of women (1874); neurology (1876); tropical diseases (1921); and pediatrics (1922).[28]

The First and Third Medical Services date to 1864 and 1866, respectively. By the early 1900s, there were 12 house officers for all services. From February 1, 1904 to January 31, 1905, the First Medical Service admitted 1,150 patients and the Third admitted 1,208.[29] Many of the patients were immigrants from Italy, Russia, England, Germany,

Sweden, and Ireland. For a while, this population, dependent on municipal hospitals, represented a sizable voting block and influenced financial and political support for municipal institutions.

> All shared the sense of the time that hospitals were no longer pesthouses to which people came to die, but were new institutions of healing and hope from which would emanate the means for curing disease. The Hospital became the focus of the social service system of the time, and no political figure considered any act that would suggest less than full support for the hospital.[30]

Those diseases most prevalent among the poor, who settled near the hospital, were listed among the admissions in 1904-05.[31]

There was no formal affiliation between the First and Third medical services and any medical school until 1915, when it was decided that the heads of these services would be appointed by the Trustees only after conference with the Tufts and Harvard University corporations, respectively. The Fourth Medical Service (Harvard) was created that same year. Eventually, Tufts became responsible for both the First and Third services; Harvard, for the Second and Fourth.

> The Fifth Medical Service was established in 1930, after nearly a decade of persistent knocking at the door by the then Dean of Boston University's School of Medicine, Dr. Alexander Begg.[32]

Ten years later, the creation of the Sixth Medical Service brought BU into balance with Tufts and Harvard regarding ward area and patient responsibility at BCH.

From 1868, the hospital assumed a leading role in the development of medical care, research, and teaching. In 1918, 2,300 influenza patients swamped the hospital, taxing its capacity. A special service was formed to meet this crisis and another specialty service for blood diseases was started the same year. In 1923, the Thorndike Memorial Laboratory was opened, headed by Harvard's Dr. Francis Peabody, who became a BCH folk hero.[33]

> The world renown of the Harvard Services during the 50 years that followed the establishment of the Thorndike Memorial Laboratory engendered a keen sense of competition that was often friendly and usually intense. Because of

Harvard's preeminent role in research and national prestige stress was created among the faculty of the three schools at the hospital. Harvard's assumption that it deserved the leadership role in medicine and surgery at City Hospital engendered bitter talk of "Harvard arrogance" in the hospital administration, the trustees, and the Boston University faculty, that had deep roots and would surface later.[34]

The hospital pioneered in the use and development of many medical innovations and the physical facilities were expanded to meet the needs of more patients. In 1964, one hundred years after its founding, BCH had 26 buildings, more than 30,000 annual inpatient admissions, about 300,000 outpatient visits, and about 135,000 emergency patients were treated. The number of beds had grown to 1,243, plus 91 bassinets; there were 500 visiting doctors, 351 house officers (interns, residents, and fellows), and the total cost of operations in 1964 was $17,241,207, with an expected revenue from paying patients of about $5 million. (For trends in hospital growth see Tables 1, 2, and 3.) [At end of Appendix B.]

Steven Miller described the hospital in 1970 as follows:[35]

> The City is, by the nature of its patient population, a medical facility for the acutely ill alcoholic, a geriatric facility for the chronically ill, and a social welfare agency. The alcoholic, according to an intern on the Second Medical Service, "comes to the Accident Floor by police ambulance, or is dragged in by friends, or just comes walking in acutely ill." Patients who are sixty years old or older also come in off the street or are brought from rooming houses by the police. Others come every Friday afternoon, sent by nursing homes, in the belief that some medical problem will erupt over the weekend. These patients may stay in the hospital for weeks before returning to the original nursing home or getting located at another one. . . . Most of these patients are seriously ill and require a great deal of care. For the intern, this situation is fortunate, because it affords him exceptional opportunities for studying diseases and obtaining clinical experience.

Each medical service consisted of a male and female ward with about 30 beds each. During a usual year, about 1,500 patients were admitted to the wards, with their care entrusted to interns assisted by medical students.

The informal hierarchi[c]al rule runs this way: a medical service belongs to the senior resident; a ward, to the assistant resident; and the patient, to the intern.[36]

In 1964, for example, the house staff of the Second and Fourth medical services had four senior residents, 16 assistant residents, and 16 interns.

By the 1960s, each of the three medical schools at BCH were responsible for training and research units, staffing and supervising the medical care of the acutely ill, operating outpatient and follow-up clinics, and in rotation, supplying interns and residents for the examination and emergency treatment of patients on the Accident Floor. Each school supported programs of teaching and research of particular interest; all such programs were more or less associated with one or more specialty outpatient clinics: e.g., cardiology, dermatology, diabetes, endocrynology, and gastroenterology. According to Dr. Ryan, in order to sort out teaching responsibilities each school had its own chiefs and associate chiefs of services, and different hospital floors were assigned by school and teaching services; e.g., Harvard, BU and Tufts each had their own Admitting Service, which admitted their own patients. Among the problems with this type of arrangement were difficulties in accountability and a "built-in feeling of frustration" that each school was at the mercy of the other. Steven Miller summarized the administrative set-up as follows:[37]

Although operating under public auspices, the three private medical schools staff and manage their own medical, surgical, and specialty services. Not only are all hospital departments affiliated with one or more of the schools, but the medical schools share the cost of teaching, research, and patient care. During 1964 and 1965, Harvard University, for example, budgeted approximately a million and a half dollars for the cost of maintaining and operating its unit. Hospital administrators are appointed by the City of Boston. Each medical and surgical service, as well as most departments, however, has an administrative head who is selected from the physicians on the staff of the particular school with which the service or department is affiliated, or is selected from physicians throughout the country. Thus, the director of the Thorndike Laboratory and the Harvard Medical Services is appointed by the trustees of BCH, but only on the recommendation of the Dean and Faculty of the Harvard Medical School.

The administrative head of a service or department was technically a member of the hospital's administrative staff, but his appointment and the policy that guided him were based on decisions of physicians responsive to their colleagues' expectations in one of the three medical schools, to their shared understanding of medicine and the medical profession and of the proper behavior of a physician. Each medical school also selected its own interns, residents, and visiting physicians, who were appointed by the Board of Trustees to the BCH staff only on the recommendation of the administrative head of a service or department. Steven Miller observed:[38]

> The most obvious consequence of these circumstances is a conflict between the medical schools and the administration appointed by the City. "Much of the stress and tension occurring in hospitals," writes [Sydney H.] Croog, "can be traced to varying types of clashes between the (administrative and medical) systems of authority." These clashes result in large part from the differences of opinion regarding the problems and purposes of a hospital. One line of authority is the hospital administration, appointed by the Board of Trustees and responsible for the day-to-day maintenance and operation of the hospital. The other line, the medical staff, is divided among groups of physicians from three medical schools. Because the three schools jointly occupy the hospital, Boston City has more than the two commonly noted lines of authority. . . . Needless to say, the more occasions for conflict, the more discord. . . . The shared medical setting heightens the friction between the hospital's administration and its multiple medical staff.

According to Dr. Ryan, the three schools differed in their interests in and methods of dealing with the BCH administration. He said that BCH director Francis Guiney had found Harvard to be highhanded in its dealings with the hospital, and that in general there was less involvement from the Harvard Dean's office than from the deans of the other schools. The seed of later problems was planted by Harvard's Associate Dean for Hospital Programs, Dr. Sidney Lee, who was "not really that committed to BCH—he felt it was a liability," according to Ryan, in contrast to the "real sense of identification and dedication to BCH shared by Dr. McDermott and others on the Harvard faculty." Although Dean Robert Ebert, who had been associated with the Thorndike Lab, was personally committed to BCH, Ryan felt "he could not transcend his responsibilities at that time" sufficiently to foster greater rapport with the hospital administration.

In contrast, BU was quite involved in the administrative details of their teaching hospitals; because they were more vocal and more visible than Harvard, the BCH administration interpreted them to be more involved and more concerned. Director Guiney felt the BU Dean's office was more accessible and that BU contributed more responsibly to the ongoing needs of running the hospital.[39] Another source of possible conflict stemmed from different values placed by each of the three schools on their three functions in the hospital: training of physicians, scientific investigation, and treatment of patients.

> Although the schools attempt to perform each of the tasks creditably, they have somewhat different purposes for being in the hospital. All physicians would agree that the proper concerns of the medical profession are the study and treatment of human diseases. But opinion regarding the relative importance of study and treatment varies greatly, and the opinions of physicians at Boston City Hospital are as varied as those entertained by the medical profession in general.

> * * * * *

> Each group of physicians at the hospital cherishes a view of medicine not quite like that of the other two. Each group's understanding of medicine unites in varying combination, the following elements: (1) academic medicine—medicine as the scientific study of human diseases, their nature, causes, and management in the individual patient; (2) traditional medicine—medicine as a private practice with a clientele; and (3) contemporary medicine—medicine as the treatment of patients as members of a community. One group is only slightly less academic but more contemporary than the Harvard physicians [BU] and the other inclines to a more traditional understanding of medicine [Tufts]. Each of the medical subcultures is a particular version of the general medical culture, emphasizing a somewhat different understanding of the purposes of medicine.

> Physicians may be on the hospital staff, but they pride themselves on their faculty appointments at the different medical schools. Also, the physicians of any one group are,

by implicit understanding, excluded from participating in the administrative affairs of either of the others. . . . Medical matters, therefore, are not a general concern of a medical staff, but the particular concern of separate groups. . . . Conditions at the hospital permit each medical school to assume responsibility for its own affairs, . . . and to maintain and implement its own understanding of medicine. [40]

The differences of opinion with regard to medical practice went back 100 years, when following a notorious two-year trial, the Massachusetts Medical Society expelled seven Boston physicians for practicing homeopathy. [41] The leader of these doctors, Dr. Israel Tisdale Talbot, negotiated an alliance between the New England Female Medical College and Boston University, under the auspices of the Massachusetts Homeopathic Medical Society, to establish the Boston University School of Medicine in 1873. Talbot became its first dean and held that position for 24 years. Boston University School of Medicine (BUSM) was in close physical proximity to BCH and in 1886 both women medical students and BUSM students were allowed to receive clinical instruction on BCH wards.

The Board (of the hospital) apparently reasoned that since the BCH was a public institution, it could not deny places to students of any institution chartered by the Commonwealth . . . there could have been no quarrel with the quality of the BUSM students, for its standards for admission and graduation were unusually high, in contrast to the disgraceful laxity in this regard of most schools at that time [i.e. as revealed in the Flexner Report of 1910]. [42]

The BUSM faculty, however, could not teach BU students at BCH, since the Massachusetts Medical Society required in its bylaws that "regular" physicians who had professional associations or even consultations with "irregulars" must be disciplined. BU became "regular" in 1918, dropping its association with homeopathy, although some of its faculty continued to practice homeopathic medicine. Dr. Ephraim Friedman of the BUSM speculated that this taint interfered for a long time with a formal BUSM-BCH affiliation and contributed to the irony we perceived in BUSM's assumption of full responsibilities for medicine and surgery at the hospital. [43]

Since its formal affiliation with BCH in 1930, BUSM has funnelled much of its resources into the hospital, and its geographic proximity suggested to many BUSM faculty that the natural direction of BUSM expansion was to incorporate the clinical BCH services into a unified administrative structure. Dr. Ryan observed that as Harvard "made concessions" to BU, giving up certain services to accommodate BU's "real academic needs for growth in terms of teaching beds," the balance of power at BCH shifted. BUSM faculty successively assumed administrative leadership of the BCH departments of pediatrics, urology and thoracic surgery in the 1950s and the departments of radiology, OB-Gyn., rehabilitative medicine, op[h]thalmology, and pediatric surgery in the 1960s.[44] In the process, BUSM came to control about half the beds at BCH. A close working relationship developed between the dean of BUSM and the BCH administrator.[45]

In addition, BUSM was associated with the 350-bed University Hospital. Originally chartered as Massachusetts Homeopathic Hospital in 1855, the hospital became the Massachusetts Memorial Hospital in 1918 and took its present name in 1965. In many cases, the same BUSM professional staff provided duplicate services at both UH and BCH, with "needless inefficiency, and excess cost to both institutions."[46]

In 1965, BU launched an expansion program and subsequently built or bought four new buildings for research, teaching space, and private doctor offices, going $14 million into debt in the process. In what some observers felt was part of a "strategy" to take over BCH, University Hospital closed down maternal and pediatric facilities a few years ago and BUSM renovated these services at BCH. In December 1972, BU abandoned a plan to construct a new hospital next door to BCH to replace University Hospital and a newspaper report quoted an anonymous "highly placed" BU official who suggested a new UH would be unnecessary because of possible expansion of the BUSM role at BCH. Although outpatient services at University Hospital were the oldest and most crowded part of the hospital, BU's new hospital plan had not included an outpatient building. The City of Boston, meanwhile, was constructing an outpatient facility at BCH as part of a plan developed in the late 1960s for a $91 million hospital with 1,000 acute and 300 chronic care beds. As of October 1973, only the ancillary facilities were built—a 28-story, 112-unit apartment building for doctors, a new nursing school, and rooms for 300 nurses. Some members of the BCH Better Breaks Group commented:[47]

> With the cut in BCH's beds and a concomitant 20 percent cut in house officers this year, the apartment building is larger than needed by BCH, but presumably will come in handy for the house staff at University Hospital.

According to Dr. Edward Kass, director of the BCH Channing Laboratory, Harvard's responsibility for over 2/3 of the medical functions at BCH declined over the past 20 years to less than 1/3, as "time began to decimate Harvard's leaders" and the University did not always show a commitment to replacing them with comparable people or to maintaining the departments as Harvard units. The decline of Harvard's position at BCH accompanied a general decline in the hospital's system of operation. There were several reasons for this: [48]

> Among these were the increasing attention to the ambulatory patient, to integrating preventive and social concepts with clinical practice at the bedside, the changing population base, increasingly difficult financial problems of the city, the decaying physical plant, and the severe administrative problems. These and other considerations were looming larger and larger in the total medical care problems of the hospital and of the city.

Dr. Ryan noted that in recent years, the hospital began to amass major deficits, which he attributed in part to an inequitable policy on the part of the state in remunerating welfare costs at a lower rate than for patients at voluntary hospitals. [49]

> In 1972 and 1973, BCH ran deficits which were, I feel, only partially identified and were more significant than what was ever published—in the area of about $9 or $10 million. The Mayor felt he couldn't raise the tax rate again and the additional funds needed to keep the hospital together were really beyond him, politically.

In addition, recently the hospital has had difficulty meeting the accreditation requirements of the Joint Commission on Accreditation of Hospitals. In 1964, for example, the JCAH was sharply critical in its recommendations to the hospital, and considerable adverse publicity appeared in the press; however, following an inspection in June 1965, BCH was granted full approval for another three years. In 1971, the hospital received only a one-year accreditation, followed by a two-year accreditation granted in 1973. Some problem areas noted by the JCAH in 1964 remained troublesome in 1971 (e.g. medical record-keeping and housekeeping), but these were subject to only minimal or no criticism by 1973.

There has been a steady decline over the years in inpatient population of the hospital, to one-half its former peak levels, in contrast to a well-maintained outpatient population, increasingly scattered among the neighborhood health centers. In the 1970s, daily inpatient population hovered between 550 and 650. The medical services of Harvard, BU and Tufts were reduced to three wards apiece, averaging not more than 60 patients. Surgical services required external rotations to provide adequate training for surgery residents.[50]

Among the factors contributing to the declining bed census was the availability of more nursing home and chronic disease convalescent facilities. In addition, there was a decline in the incidence of certain communicable diseases so that the average age of patients has steadily increased. The disease spectrum reflected more and more the effects of chronic disease and its acute complications rather than acute disease. There has been a change in the constituency of the hospital: only the elderly remain from the original poor European immigrant population. Now the community is predominantly Black, Puerto Rican, and Haitian.

> The new constituency is younger, less hospital-oriented, not yet fully politically articulate and is not enthusiastic over the fact that much of the power structure of the city and of the Hospital still resides in the older political forces.[51]

BUSM Takes Over Medical and Surgical Services at a 500-bed BCH

In April 1973, the new BUSM administration of BCH announced their plan to make BCH "a community . . . hospital focused on provision of high quality family care." The plan excluded all but the most basic services: medical, surgical, child and maternal health. BUSM's Dr. Ephraim Friedman explained that the BU plan was in keeping with a trend begun by Medicare and Medicaid to shift responsibility for health care delivery from the municipal to the state and federal levels.

> If the trend started by Medicare and Medicaid continues, it will speed the return of BCH from its present role as a municipal general hospital for the medically indigent to a role that it had a generation ago as a community hospital for all of Boston's residents. Although it should provide excellent medical care to needy citizens of Boston as a whole, it should particularly serve those who live a short distance from the BCH and look to it as their local community hospital.[52]

Friedman saw the BCH as part of a continu[u]m of community care, via a network of neighborhood health centers, ambulatory and emergency services, and backup inpatient care. Viewed in these terms, "it may be neither appropriate nor necessary" for BCH to house inordinate numbers of "often underutilized" special inpatient services, said Friedman, such as radiotherapy, cardiac catheterization, cardiac surgery, renal dialysis and transplantation, and psychiatry. These services could be available from pooled resources and cooperative arrangements with University Hospital and other components of the BU Medical Center, the School of Graduate Dentistry, and the BU-Commonwealth of Massachusetts Treatment, Training, and Research Center in Mental Health.

Dr. Kass commented on this plan:[53]

> From the point of view of simple efficiency and of regional planning, there is little doubt that University Hospital and Boston City Hospital can integrate certain services and realize some economies and efficiencies. The degree to which these economies are realized, however, is not yet certain, and the cost in terms of quality of patient care are by no means clearly charted.

Kass was pessimistic about any major budgetary solutions coming from the unification of services under BUSM "because I see no way that the working poor will be dealt with more effectively in the new framework." Kass said these were the people primarily responsible for the BCH deficit and in this regard, BCH has served as a safety valve for other hospitals in the area, freeing them somewhat from service to this population and allowing them to come closer to efficient and profitable operation. He noted:[54]

> Some have tended to regard the inefficiencies of the municipal hospital systems, not as an important feature of the present system of medical care, but as a regrettable but understandable consequence of the political inadequacies of city machines.

> . . . most of the financial problems of the BCH center around who is going to take care of the working poor, and will not be solved by the most cost-conscious of administrative efforts, desirable as these may be.

The cutback in beds was also an inadequate solution, according to Dr. Kass.[55]

> It will not do to argue that the BCH may slowly be lowering its census anyway, through market forces. Those patients who are voluntarily going elsewhere are the ones with third party coverage, and not the working poor, so the BCH may be lowering its bed capacity, but is not likely to be reducing its deficit in proportion. This may take a while to be tested, but it seems unlikely to me that the recent events will in fact reduce the budgetary deficit by as much as the public has been led to expect.

During the Winter months, the normal BCH census was 600 patients; Jeff Blum pointed out that the cut in BCH beds from 850 to 500 would leave the hospital 100 beds short. When the cutback was announced in July 1973, it was couched in terms of a bed surplus presumed to exist in private hospitals. The newly appointed Commissioner of Health and Hospitals, Leon White, had spoken of an "untapped reservoir of goodwill" among the local hospitals and solicited their cooperation in absorbing any excess BCH patients. Dr. Kass felt that the plan to send patients to other hospitals would work "up to a point, because the numbers to be accommodated . . . will be small and because an empty bed costs about 75 percent as much as a full bed, so the excess cost of the patient to the recipient hospital is small."[56] Others pointed out, however, that private hospitals tended to regard poor patients as a burden, because they had diseases which included complications from alcoholism, heart disease, results of an inadequate diet, poor housing, unsafe working conditions, and almost no preventive care. These patients would take up beds for longer than the elective surgery patients the hospitals made money on and they came in sicker than patients with a private doctor who could afford convalescence and who were taken care of in old age.[57] Blum and his co-authors pointed out that "a majority of BCH admissions are on the danger list and cannot be transferred out. What is more, if other patients are transferred and the number of danger-list patients at BCH rises, greater burdens will be put on its already overburdened staff and the result will be inferior care."[58]

University Hospital agreed to take the first three non-danger list admissions every morning, but four months after making this agreement, Blum noted that UH often did not take three patients and sometimes took none.[59]

After all, as an unnamed University Hospital administrator put in, "As a private, non-profit voluntary hospital, we cannot just swing open the doors like a drop-in health center, treating anyone who comes in. We already have a deficit of one million dollars." At the same time, University Hospital's chief administrator John Betjeman was complaining they couldn't fill their new beds! It seems they are only willing to fill them with certain patients.

Blum also cited evidence from the State Senate's social welfare committee which suggested that private hospitals were starting to resist the influx of the poor:[60]

"We have documented cases," says a legislative aide, "in which the private hospitals have taken people into their emergency wards and then sent them after the initial workup to Boston City if they can't pay."

As of September 1973, the BCH 500-bed capacity was full on several occasions during the summer, traditionally its slackest period, and Blum et al. predicted a bitter winter.

On January 8, 1974, the situation Blum had anticipated was reported by Richard Knox in the *Boston Globe* under the headline "Patients Wait Hours for Admission to Filled-to-Capacity BCH." In what hospital personnel called the most severe admitting crisis since the 500-bed limit was effected, Knox said:[61]

At least six patients, some elderly and severely ill, were forced to wait as long as four hours on Boston City Hospital's congested accident floor last night because hospital officials could not find them beds and every other major hospital in the city told BCH it was full.

The BCH attributed the crisis to an unusually high number of emergency service admissions and the coincidental and unprecedented inability of any major facility to accept transfers. A 93-year-old woman with congestive heart failure and digitoxicity was admitted finally to University Hospital. A 97-year-old man with pneumonia and severe dehydration and a 60-year-old man with congestive heart failure and pneumonia were accommodated ultimately at BCH by transferring less sick medical patients from the medical wards to the surgery service. Some patients also were bedded in the Intensive Care Unit, although they did not need such expensive care, because that was where the beds were. The medical staff at BCH concurred that "boarding patients on other services was a clear detriment to the quality of their care." As of mid-evening, there were only three medical beds available in case any danger-list patients had to be admitted during the night; it was hospital policy to hold 12 such beds under normal circumstances.

The president of the BCH House Officers Association, Dr. Steven Salzman, said: "I thought things would get bad sooner. I've been impressed at how smoothly it has gone—probably due to the good weather and the absence of a flu epidemic and any major fires or natural disasters." The director of the emergency service, Dr. Jeremy Ramp, remarked: "Five hundred beds is tough to operate under."[62]

The following day, it was reported that at least three major hospitals claimed that they had had medical beds available to accept the BCH overflow. The Peter Bent Brigham, the Beth Israel, and the New England Medical Center all said they had no record of being contacted by BCH. Five of six hospitals contacted said they could find no record of having been contacted. The Peter Bent Brigham and the Beth Israel reported that each had six empty medical beds and the New England Medical Center said it had 16 empty beds. In an article on January 31, 1974, Richard Knox commented:[63]

> The truth about the calls—and thus the blame—will probably never be known. But at this point that doesn't matter too much. What does matter is what kind of a system engendered the snafu in the first place and the undignified squabbling that followed it.

Not one administrator other than BCH's Francis Guiney stated publicly that the system of communication should be tightened up, since it was not a routine practice at other hospitals to log in-coming BCH calls. Dr. Mitchell T. Rabkin, the Beth Israel director, wrote to his hospital staff claiming the transfer system worked well and that the incident had amounted to a "newspaper brouhaha." Health Commissioner Leon White made no public statement, but complained privately to the hospitals concerned. According to Knox, the incident sensitized the hospitals to the fact that "a communications slip-up can appear like an attempt to evade responsibility for a BCH patient who is more likely to be a nonpaying patient and possibly a 'dispositional' or behavioral problem as well."[64] From that time on, all Boston-area hospitals would log bed-available calls from BCH and would know how to verify such calls.

Among the questions Knox raised about the incident were whether or not BCH had the appropriate mix of medical and surgical beds and whether or not BCH staff members unconsciously or consciously were restricting hospital admissions because they knew space was tight, thereby excluding some patients they might have admitted before the cutbacks were made. Knox concluded:[65]

> It is still too early to answer any of the questions definitively. Theoretically, of course, there are enough hospital beds in Boston to serve the City's needs with BCH at its current size. But this is only if the old barriers between hospitals are vigorously attacked.

* * * * *

In summarizing what had been the strengths and weaknesses of Boston City Hospital Dr. Ryan said:[66]

> BCH interfaced outstanding academic clinicians with people who suffered the consequences of incremental neglect in health care; it focused significant research acumen on those problems, bringing world-renowned people to Boston. It provided the attention and diligence of three schools, competing in a constructive way in terms of high quality of care to indigent patients. The destructiveness of the competition came in terms of the administrative quagmire.

> The hospital had grown too large and did not have an overall focus in providing comprehensive health services to people of Boston: this was an artifact of neglect on the part of administrators and executives of the city and was conceivably indicative of an inability on the part of the professionals to get it all together and to identify the parameters of the citizen's needs.

Table B-1 Statistical Summary:
Boston City Hospital 1962–1974

Year	Admissions	Aver. Beds	Aver. Daily Census	A.L.O.S.*	Aver. Daily Adm.	Inpatient Days	Occupancy Rate
1962	29,320	1,235	896	11.2	80.3	327,040	72.5
1963	29,326	1,249	878	10.9	80.3	320,470	70.3
1964	30,022	1,243	869	10.6	82.3	317,185	69.9
1965	29,383	1,243	844	10.5	80.5	308,060	67.9
1966	29,501	1,257	855	10.6	80.8	312,075	68.0
1967	27,936	1,180	847	11.1	76.5	309,155	71.7
1968	27,115	1,132	806	10.8	74.3	294,190	71.2
1969	28,047	1,132	766	10.0	76.8	279,590	67.7
1970	23,732	1,022	702	10.7	65.0	256,230	68.7
1971	23,789	859	658	10.1	65.2	240,170	76.6
1972	21,812	809	603	10.1	59.6	220,095	74.5
1973	21,380	829	577	9.8	58.5	210,605	69.6
1974	21,598	500	540	9.1	59.2	197,100	100.0

* Average length of stay.

Source: American Hospital Association, *Hospitals*, Guide Issue, respective years. (Some figures computed on the basis of figures reported in the Guide Issues.)

Table B-2 Boston City Hospital Payroll and
Numbers of Employees 1962–1974

Year	Payroll	No. of Employees
1962	$10,964,000.	2,886
1963	10,913,000.	3,228
1964	11,315,000.	2,902
1965	13,279,000.	2,977
1966	13,927,000.	3,058
1967	15,334,000.	3,561
1968	17,952,000.	3,531
1969	19,835,000.	3,325
1970	22,918,000.	4,069
1971	27,218,000.	4,398
1972	31,372,000.	3,669
1973	34,703,000.	4,003
1974	35,442,000.	3,010

Source: American Hospital Association, *Hospitals*, Guide Issue, respective years.

Table B-3 Boston City Hospital Budget Figures—1968-1973

	1968	1969	1970	1971	1972	1973
Total Expenditures[1]	$29,981,427	$32,848,822	$40,493,379	$44,247,966	$50,318,329	$74,182,493[2]
Income (all sources)	16,997,900	22,453,914	31,880,414	35,950,215	32,413,341	55,623,000[2]
Cash Receipts	16,745,415	22,201,172	21,737,295	35,229,681	31,792,539	39,238,622
Total Charges[3]	26,786,342	33,711,868	36,403,567	43,841,015	43,818,306	42,542,058
Cost per Patient Day	90.69	112.03	135.78	154.66	188.63	221.36

Notes: 1. Expended against regular hospital appropriations and income from all sources.
2. 18-month period (January 1973–June 1974).
3. Includes Adult and children, Newborn, and Ambulatory charges, as follows:

	1968	1969	1970	1971	1972	1973
Adults/ Children	$25,653,470	$31,156,316	$32,275,990	$36,650,742	$34,752,330	$32,495,985
Newborn	295,450	343,808	588,489	547,342	627,917	874,922
Ambulatory	837,422	2,211,744	3,539,088	6,642,931	8,438,059	9,171,151
Total Charges	$26,786,342	$33,711,868	$36,403,567	$43,818,306	$43,818,306	$42,542,058

Sources: Personal Communications from Helen Gaffey, Assistant Deputy Commissioner, Budget and Control, Boston City Hospital (Total Expenditures and Income, all sources), and Edwin Katzman, Assistant Deputy Commissioner Comptroller, Boston City Hospital (Cash Receipts, Total Charges, Cost per Patient Day).

NOTES

1. Peter Lucas, *Boston Globe,* February 4, 1973.

2. Jeff Blum, Jerry Feuer, Kate Mulhern, and Joan Tighe, "As the Nation Goes, So Goes Boston," *Health/Pac Bulletin,* No. 54, October 1973, p. 18.

3. Carl M. Cobb, "City Hospital Demands Meeting with White," *Boston Globe,* February 8, 1973.

4. Franklin H. Epstein, M.D., "Boston City Hospital: Part I," *Harvard Medical Alumni Bulletin,* January/February 1974, p. 6.

5. Ephraim Friedman, M.D., "Annual Discourse—The Boston City Hospital: A Tale of Three 'Cities,'" *NEJM,* Vol. 289, No. 10, September 6, 1973, p. 504.

6. William V. McDermott, Jr., M.D., "Boston City Hospital: Part II," *Harvard Medical Alumni Bulletin,* January/February 1974, p. 9.

7. Dr. Richard Ryan, Interview, December 31, 1974.

8. Epstein, op. cit., p. 7.

9. Friedman, op. cit., p. 503.

10. Dr. R. Ryan, Interview.

11. Epstein, op. cit., p. 6.

12. The elimination of the Harvard interns was the source of considerable bad feeling between Harvard and BU. Dr. Franklin Epstein was anxious to continue his Department of Medicine at BCH for another year, since the interns had already been interviewed for the Harvard Service. He felt that the interns should be apprised of the fact that they would no longer be serving on a "Harvard" service, and sent them telegrams to that effect. BU took this action to be an insult, and in turn, wrote letters to each formerly "Harvard" intern inviting him to be a part of the BU service and pointing out that it would still be a *BCH* internship. This, so far as Harvard was concerned, eliminated any possibility of their remaining at BCH for another year.

13. Epstein, op. cit., p. 6.

14. McDermott, quoted in the *Harvard Gazette,* March 16, 1973.

15. Ibid.

16. The use of the name "Thorndike," which remains on the building it occupied at BCH, as well as in BCH parlance in referring to the laboratory now housed there, is subject to possible legal dispute. People at Harvard are adamant that there can be only one "real" Thorndike Laboratory, but the terms of the original endowment were unclear. Money was left in trust to the City of Boston and to Harvard for the laboratory. If Harvard left, the will specified that the money would go to Tufts; since both schools left the hospital, whether the name of the lab and the entire trust belongs to Harvard remains in question. The Sears Surgical Lab and the Channing Lab endowments were never at risk because the wills clearly specified that these were designated to Harvard. (Interview, Dr. R. Ryan, op. cit.).

17. Dr. McDermott, op. cit., p. 10.

18. Ibid.

19. What will happen to the Channing Building, built in 1968 at a cost of $1.6 million, remains in question.

20. Blum, et al., p. 19.

21. Ibid., p. 22.

22. Ibid., p. 23.

23. Ibid., p. 22.

24. Ibid., p. 23.

25. John Bryne, *A History of Boston City Hospital, 1905–1964* (Boston: Sheldon Press, 1964), p. 15. NOTE: since the Civil War had enlisted all available doctors, the five young men who could be found for the resident positions had not yet received their degrees from Harvard Medical School at the time of their appointments, but they were granted degrees before they began actual services at the hospital.

26. Ibid., p. 392.

27. Ibid., p. 387.

28. Ibid., p. 57.

29. Ibid.

30. Edward H. Kass, M.D., "Boston City Hospital: Part III," *Harvard Medical Alumni Bulletin,* January/February 1974, p. 12.

31. Byrne, op. cit., p. 42. NOTE: These included 477 cases of pneumonia (166 deaths), 402 cases of typhoid (156 deaths), 203 cases of erysipelas, 104 cases of lung TB, 207 chronic endocarditis cases, 252 rheumatic arthritis cases, and 147 cases of poisoning, including from alcohol.

32. Ibid., p. 93.

33. Steven Miller, *Prescription for Leadership* (Chicago: Aldine Publishing Co., 1970). NOTE: The Thorndike Lab was the first clinical research facility in a U.S. municipal hospital. It consisted of a ward for the study of patients with particular problems, usually transferred from the wards of the medical services, as well as labs occupied by members of the several research divisions within the hospital. At its dedication, Mayor Curley called the Thorndike Laboratory, "without any exaggeration, the most important event in the latter day history of Boston: its discoveries and achievements will interest all earth and add to the righteous pride and real glory of Boston." (McDermott, op. cit., p. 8).

34. Epstein, op. cit., p. 6.

35. Miller, op. cit., p. 40.

36. Ibid., p. 42.

37. Ibid., p. 43.

38. Ibid., p. 44.

39. Interview with Dr. Richard Ryan, op. cit.

40. Ibid., pp. 44–46.

41. Homeopathy is a system of therapy developed on the theory that large doses of a certain drug given to a healthy person will produce certain conditions which, when occurring spontaneously as symptoms of a disease, are relieved by the same drug in small doses. This was called "the law of similia" from the aphorism *similia similibus curantur*—a "fighting fire with fire" theory (Stedman's Medical Dictionary).

42. Friedman, op. cit., p. 504.

43. Ibid.

44. Harvard agreed to transfer radiology, obstetrics and pathology services to BUSM to help strengthen their teaching program, and the psychiatric inpatient treatment in the Dorchester-Roxbury area was declared to be within the BU catchment area.

45. Friedman, op. cit.

46. Ibid.

47. Blum et al., p. 20.

48. Kass, op. cit., p. 13.

49. Interview with Dr. R. Ryan, op. cit.

50. Epstein, op. cit.

51. Kass, op. cit., p. 12.

52. Friedman, op. cit., p. 505

53. Kass, op. cit., p. 13.

54. Kass, op. cit., p. 11.

55. Ibid., p. 12.

56. Kass, loc. cit.

57. Blum et al., op. cit., p. 18.

58. Ibid., p. 21.

59. Ibid.

60. Ibid., p. 22. NOTE: Blum et al. also reported that shortly after the announcement of the BCH cutback, the Peter Bent Brigham Hospital came out with a new outpatient form "by which the patient signed away all rights and agreed to pay his bill by any means necessary. The form, which was probably illegal, was withdrawn after worker and community pressure was exerted."

61. *The Boston Globe,* January 8, 1974.

62. Ibid.

63. R. Knox, "Transfer of Patients at City Hospital Sparks Questions," *Boston Globe,* January 31, 1974.

64. Ibid.

65. Ibid.

66. Interview with Dr. Richard Ryan, op. cit.

Appendix C

From Disequilibrium to Disequilibrium

At the close of the Jackson Regional Medical Center's (JRMC) monthly board meeting, Bibbins, the hospital administrator, brought out what he felt was the most important issue on the meeting's agenda:

"I have given a great deal of thought recently to our upcoming facility expansion. As you know, this move into our new facility is going to take a tremendous amount of coordination and cooperation on the part of our entire organization. The staff has mentioned to me on several occasions that the employees and supervisors are becoming increasingly restless and apprehensive as a result of the anticipated move. After some preliminary investigation and considerable thought, we have decided to recommend to the board that JRMC contact a consultant to assist us in adapting to this ongoing expansion program."

The board was aware of the hospital's past instability and the need for outside management assistance was acknowledged. After a brief discussion, the members unanimously recommended to Bibbins that he contact the local university for assistance. Members of the university management department had provided consulting assistance earlier.

Authors: Daniel S. Cochran, Donald R. Latham, and Donald D. White of the University of Arkansas.

History of JRMC

JRMC was a 160-bed general hospital in northeastern Arkansas. The American Hospital Association classified it as a short-term ambulatory hospital. In 1975, the hospital officially became a regional facility and adopted the name of Jackson Regional Medical Center. The community in which JRMC operated was expanding, primarily due to the influx of retired individuals and a growing university community. Due to this expansion in the immediate area, demand for medical services had increased significantly. A major physical facility expansion program had been adopted in 1972, and a projected completion date of June, 1977, was set. Construction began and progressed on schedule. The project was scheduled for completion in 18 months.

The Medical Center employed approximately 500 persons. This figure was planned to be increased 22 percent when the expansion program was completed. The expanded facility will have 240 beds. The structure of JRMC management also has changed. Prior to the initiation of the physical expansion program, there was only one assistant administrator. When the program is completed, there are to be three assistant administrators. All functional departments anticipate expanding employment rosters, with the need for additional nurses to be particularly critical.

JRMC has had four administrators in the past eight years. The present administrator, Bibbins, has been with JRMC for less than one year. The previous three administrators were asked to resign for various reasons. Bibbins seemed to have established his credibility with department heads and general employees. However, an aura of uncertainty continued to surround the administrator's position. This uncertainty has been a contributing factor to one present departmental dilemma—that of departmental autonomy. Various departments throughout the Medical Center tended to segregate themselves into autonomous groups rather than working closely with one another. Many persons familiar with internal conditions at JRMC believed that permanent leadership emanated from department heads, rather than from the administrator's office.

Consultants' Meeting with JRMC

Two weeks after the monthly board meeting Dr. Harold and Dr. Black, from the University's management department, met with Bibbins; his assistant administrator, James; and the director of personnel and training, Arnold. The men discussed their organizations' problem of trying to adapt to the institution's facility change. Bibbins and his staff quickly briefed the two management professors on their facility's expansion situation and stressed the "disequilibrium" that existed in the hospital as a result of this organizational change.

"Dr. Harold and Dr. Black, I feel that I must warn you before we go any further that our employees, including our supervisors, are extremely suspicious when it comes to 'outsiders,'" Bibbins said. "They are even suspicious of anyone outside of their particular department, and especially the administration. In fact, I'm confident that by this afternoon, rumor will have it that 'the administration' has just hired two New York psychologists to analyze our organization."

After additional discussion, Dr. Black concluded the meeting by suggesting that after the consultants' intervention, the administrator provide some feedback to the hospital employees about the nature, purpose, and worth of the consultants' assistance. Bibbins and his staff agreed to this suggestion.

Intervention Strategy

As a result of the first meeting, it was concluded that obtaining inputs from employees in the form of either ideas or suggestions might clarify the real and imagined problems that they believed were related to a major building program. This was thought to have the advantages of enumerating real problems and also would allow top management to obtain an awareness of the perceived problems at various employee levels. It was hoped that a free flow of uninhibited responses could be generated.

Group meetings rather than the questioning of individuals through opinion surveys was decided upon as the information-gathering approach to be used. It was agreed that "group think" would probably yield better results than isolated individual reactions to printed questions and would be more efficient, time-wise, than face-to-face interviews. Harold and Black informed Bibbins that they were involved in the study of a number of such group decision-making processes. They were convinced that any of the group processes they had been working with would be beneficial to the Medical Center. However, they saw in the hospital's situation an opportunity to study the performance of three specific group techniques in a field setting. Consequently, they requested that Bibbins allow them to conduct a series of group meetings using these three information-gathering processes.

Harold explained to Bibbins, "We are agreed that the group approach to gathering this information will no doubt be superior to obtaining employee inputs on an individual basis. I think that Dr. Black and I can safely say that the information we will gather from your employees will be beneficial to JRMC no matter what group technique we use. However, this will afford us an excellent opportunity to determine for future use which technique might be best in this type of setting and/or situation." After a brief discussion, the administrator gave his consent to the joint consulting-research effort.

The three group decision-making processes utilized in the project were: nominal group technique (NGT), brainstorming, and interacting group. The employee groups were administered all three technologies, while the supervisors were administered the NGT and brainstorming technologies. Each technique utilized the same beginning question, "What significant personal and/or organizational factors (or changes) must be taken into account in connection with a hospital expansion program?" It was felt that this question would generate relevant ideas that would help the hospital better adapt to changes resulting from its expansion program. The actual ideas generated from these techniques are listed in Exhibits C-1 through C-5.

Methodology

A separate systematic random sample was drawn from a computer printout of pay records for daytime employees and supervisors. Five groups of six individuals each (three employee and two supervisor groups) made up the sample; however, additional individuals were selected and used as alternates. The names selected were examined by departments to ensure that the sample was representative.

A brief orientation meeting for the participants was conducted a week prior to the actual experiment. The purpose of this introductory meeting was to help ensure that the employees could participate at the scheduled time and to generate favorable interest in the project.

To minimize interviewer bias, one consultant conducted both NGT sessions, and one consultant conducted both brainstorming sessions and the interacting group session. Each group meeting was conducted at approximately the same time of day in the same surroundings (JRMC library).

Anonymity was a prime concern, and each group interviewed was told the importance of keeping the session private until all groups had met.

Exhibit C-1 Group #1—Nominal Group Technique (NGT): Supervisor

1. Need more personnel
2. Priorities on purchasing equipment
3. Priorities on equipment requirements prior to even planning
4. Adequate expansion for meeting public needs
5. Communication coordination among departments
6. Creation of new status among present personnel
7. How to perform effectively while in the midst of moving
8. Communication with employees to make them feel they are a part of the program (expansion)
9. Inadequate preplanning—resulting in inadequate facilities
10. Versatile and open-minded staff
11. Satisfying personnel remaining in old building
12. Different functions as a result of moving
13. New facilities may not be adequate
14. Coping with financial increases—all internal cost increases
15. Only one walkway between old and new building—problem of
16. Concern with physical movement of patients to new facility
17. Uncertainty of move for some departments
18. Insufficient number of elevators for number of supplies, visitors, patients
19. Salary increases
20. Scattered centers of attention due to layout
21. Mental adjustment from small to large operation
22. Through improvement of serious nursing services, the quality of care given will be improved
23. Dealing with hostilities in departments that have been overlooked during expansion

Exhibit C-2 Group #2—Brainstorming: Supervisor

1. Well planned (exceptionally)
2. Temporary confusion
3. Leadership changes
4. Decision-making process (changes)
5. Lacking continuity of concepts
6. Communications
7. Employees' understanding
8. How will it be financed?
9. Priorities of financing
10. Priorities in planning total project
11. Changes in staff?
12. Informal power structure changes
13. Coping with the change (people)
14. Quality control changes
15. Lines (levels) of communications will change
16. Responsibility will change (institution)
17. Internal responsibilities will change
18. Employee auto
19. Need to be more competitive (patients, personnel, service, and wages)
20. Change of community image
21. Expectations of hospital by community will change
22. Depersonalization among employees and community
23. Maple trees cut down!
24. Parking?
25. Security of facility (internal and external)
26. Promoting urbanization!
27. Outpatient facilities
28. Longer hours for employees
29. Escort services
30. No salary increases as result of expansion (money drained away)
31. Physical layout problems (directional)
32. Competition for expansional space (internal—departmental)
33. Handling of disappointment due to poor planning (i.e., not getting what wanted or needed)
34. Work flow problems
35. Recruitment of personnel

36. Training and retraining (inservice education)
37. Regulatory standards change
38. Safety problems
39. Public orientations of availability of services
40. Better facilities for specific diseases
41. Public reactions to health care changes (cost)
42. Present inconvenience
43. Need tolerance until more complete
44. Present fatigue of staff (mental and physical)
45. Disbelief of eventuality of results
46. Insecurity about jobs, personal space, job description, and loss of familiar surroundings (community included)
47. Increased opportunity for employment (positive)
48. Need of bad debts (patients) to decrease to help finance new building
49. Inflation problems
50. More job satisfaction (positive)
51. Prestige of working in a medical center (positive)
52. Disillusionment
53. Now have a greater teaching capacity (positive)
54. Can now draw more from University due to size (inservice education, etc.)
55. Expansion is a good idea! Necessary
56. Expansion is a continual process
57. Lack of consultation with personnel involved prior to decision making
58. Employee turnover
59. Cost of high turnover
60. Hidden cost of education (financial resources not available for needed training)
61. Hidden cost of donation
62. Administrative continuity
63. Need for internal socialization and recreation
64. Lack of support from administration and medical staff

Exhibit C-3 Group #1—Interacting: Employee

1. Probably bother nursing more
2. Major problems with switchboard!
3. Dietary—only one lab
4. Very little known about expansion program
5. Purchasing problems (when order, kind of service, maintenance contracts)
6. New personnel techniques
7. Size of departments will increase
8. Will have to learn more
9. Training new personnel
10. Recruiting new personnel
11. Changed telephone system (but we don't know about the new system Centrex!)
12. Need training on new system (telephone)
13. Apprehensive about new telephone system
14. Personnel, supply, and new equipment problems
15. Parking problems
16. Moving supplies a problem
17. Reorder points (supply) will change
18. New dietary facilities will be better (more room)
19. Haven't been told anything about the move!

Exhibit C-4 Group #2—NGT: Employee

1. We are here for the good of the patient and the public and all personnel should work toward that end
2. Personnel shortages now and in the future more obvious
3. Reevaluate what we are doing—jobs
4. Need for more administrative people
5. Building safety
6. Need for additional parking places for employees
7. Need for additional personnel after expansion
8. Needs for additional compensation to "live" needed additional personnel

9. Financial responsibility to the public
10. Need for employees to see what is going on
11. New employees need a job description
12. Need for more doctors
13. Employees' training--present
14. Communication between administration and employees
15. Need for new and better equipment for patients
16. Need for new and better equipment for employees
17. Need for more efficient food processing
18. Need for food that patients would like
19. Need for larger cafeteria
20. Need for free parking for employees
21. Need nursery for visitors (keep them out of lobby)
22. Mandatory insurance needs to be done away with
23. Present care is good
24. Priority system for employee duties
25. Need for isolation floor (only)
26. Need for psychiatric facilities
27. Need for separation of patients due to illness
28. Employee safety—diseases in hospital
29. Need more patient accessories—linen, etc.
30. Need additional day care facilities
31. Need for better laundry
32. Need for specialized training for employees
33. Employees need better understanding with supervisors
34. Need for employees to know what's being built
35. Need for new facility to be more efficiently designed than old
36. Need recreation facilities for patients
37. Lounge for patients
38. Need prayer room
39. Present prayer room is inadequate
40. Need new administrative system
41. Need more work clerks
42. Need employee pool (all departments)
43. Need additional security

Exhibit C-5 Group #3—Brainstorming: Employee

1. Orientation to new facility
2. Parking problems
3. Need for more space
4. Noise!
5. More elevators
6. Work flow (uniform) from old to new hospital
7. Traffic flow
8. Visitor control
9. Security control
10. Proper staffing for new facility
11. Lack of equipment
12. Dining room space!
13. Education of personnel
14. Immediate community concern
15. Automobile traffic control around hospital (narrow street and congestion)
16. Financing of new facility
17. Bigger waiting room for visitors
18. Separate surgical waiting area (with hostess)
19. Bathrooms (more)!
20. Overnight facilities for family of seriously ill
21. Orientation (tours!) for child patients
22. Playroom facilities for pediatric patients
23. Separate pediatric patients by age (room—teenagers and children)
24. Communications between departments
25. Telephone system (Is it adequate?)
26. How will departments work while moving to new building?
27. Time allot[t]ed for moving
28. Control of utilities while moving
29. Personal relationships during move (tempers!)
30. Are architects familiar with hospital design needs?
31. Never consulted with employees concerning expansion!
32. Concerned about emergency room facilities (enough?)
33. Separate emergency room entrance (not lobby)
34. Better emergency transportation (helicopter and pad)
35. Faster emergency care (so patients don't have to wait so long)
36. Need signs to direct people to hospital

37. Special facilities for prisoner patients
38. Fire prevention (regulations, etc.)
39. Adequate storage facilities
40. Need to anticipate future needs (expansion!—buy land)
41. Heating and air conditioning control (separate or master control)
42. Linens (more)
43. All supplies (more)
44. More adequate control supply
45. Is pharmacy going to be adequate?
46. Security of drugs!
47. Servicing of facility
48. Need oxygen and suction in new surgical holding area
49. Lounges for employees (locker space, eat lunch, and secure personal gear, and resting area beds)
50. Attitudes of patients during move
51. Remodeling of old hospital
52. Concern for phasing out old jobs and entrance of new
53. Enforcing smoking regulations (positive!)
54. Control of safety regulations
55. Fire drills (actual)
56. Need a full-time safety director
57. Necessary emergency power?
58. Disaster drills (actual!)
59. Enforce ID regulations (especially doctors)
60. Is there an alarm system to alert security personnel?

Final Report and Follow-up

After all of the group meetings were held, the results were analyzed by the consultants and submitted to Bibbins. The report was accompanied by a request that a subsequent meeting of the three men be held to discuss its content after the findings were reviewed by Bibbins. However, unexpected problems with the building program occurred during the same week in which the report was transmitted. Bibbins became involved in extensive negotiations with the contractor and failed to get to Harold and Black. Six months later Bibbins still had not acted on the consultants' report.

Discussion

The findings can be analyzed in terms of a number of ideas generated by supervisors and employees separately. The results then can be combined to give an overview of the salient characteristics of each technique as well as response characteristics. (This approach to analyzing the data is by no means the only acceptable method. The purpose is to cause the student to analyze the data logically.)

Overall, the two supervisor groups generated 88 ideas: 23 NGT and 65 brainstorming. The three employee groups generated 122 ideas: 43 NGT, 60 brainstorming, and 19 interacting group.

All groups showed a desire to participate under the premise that management would be given a copy of this report. This acceptance of external consulting, coupled with the desire on the part of most to contribute, suggested a desire by members of the organization to become more involved in hospital affairs.

The problems identified by the participants can be grouped for purposes of analysis. The following represents one such categorization scheme: (1) patient care (inpatients only), (2) public relations/community relations needs, (3) supplies/equipment, (4) physical facility conditions, (5) management (employee relations), (6) financial/legal constraints, (7) organizational problems, (8) individual worker problems, and (9) staffing (training, number). This classification system, or a similar one, should help the administrator to better pinpoint possible problem areas resulting from the expansion program and relate those areas to the employee groups to which they are most significant (see Table C-1.*

---

* This table, and subsequent analysis, is based on ideas generated from numerous hospitals and *does not* correspond directly to the number of ideas included in this case. Its purpose is to give the instructor an example of how the data can be analysed.

Table C-1 Supervisory + Nonsupervisory Responses According to Response Category (Less I.G.)

	1) Patient care		2) Public rel./community rel.		3) Supplies & equipment		4) Facility conditions		5) Mgmt.-empl. relations		6) Financial/legal constraints		7) Organ. problem		8) Individual worker problem		9) Staffing	
	r	%	r	%	r	%	r	%	r	%	r	%	r	%	r	%	r	%
Employees	39*	.15	13*	.05	27*	.10	63	.24	24	.09	5*	.02	40	.15	22	.08	29	.11
Supervisors	14%	.06	24*	.10	10*	.04	49	.20	22	.09	27*	.11	50	.21	17	.07	30	.12
Total	43	.09	37	.07	37	.07	112	.22	46	.09	32	.06	90	.18	39	.08	59	.12

*P < .05

r — number of responses
% — percent of responses for organizational level
Employees = 262
Supervisors = 243
505

The greatest number of items generated appeared under facility conditions (4), and organizational problems (7). Areas that apparently were of least concern to participants were public relations/community relations (2) and supplies and equipment (3). A statistically significant difference occurred between the response of supervisors and nonsupervisory personnel in certain categories. Items concerning patient care (1) and supplies and equipment (3) were mentioned a significantly greater number of times by general employees than supervisors. On the other hand, supervisory personnel generated a significantly greater number of items in the categories of public relations/community relations (2) and financial/legal constraints (6). Thus, the classification scheme developed allowed not only for the categorization of items generated, but also enhanced the client system's awareness of concerns of employees relative to their status as supervisory or nonsupervisory persons.

The theme that recurred most often revolved around better communications between the administration and employee groups. Another major concern was that the community must be made aware of the quality services offered by JRMC.

The following recommendations could be submitted to the administration of JRMC for its consideration:

1. All ideas presented should be reviewed and actions taken based on the judgment of the administrator.
2. Department heads and employees should be encouraged to correct those difficulties over which they have control.

3. Any and all actions, including the review of the report, should be communicated (written and/or orally) through appropriate channels to all employee levels—for example, through the use of bulletin boards or the formal chain of command. Possibly a section of the JRMC newsletter could be designated to relate information pertaining to the new expansion program.
4. The administration should consider methods of improving two-way communication between the various levels of the organization (for example, employee councils, or use of participative group decision-making techniques—such as NGT or brainstorming).
5. A follow-up study should be implemented to evaluate the effectiveness of this action research project.

In order to help the organization build a climate of trust rather than suspicion, the consultants were interested in letting the employees know that the administration was indeed interested in what the employees thought and felt. By explaining to the employees the nature of the consulting engagement, its results, and appropriate follow-up by the administration, the desired organizational climate might better be achieved

Appendix D

How High the Doc?

Ms Barret was head nurse of the operating room at Mountain View Hospital. She was experiencing some difficulties in scheduling scrub technicians and circulating RNs to certain surgery rooms. People who had been doing fine during one surgery had come to the nursing station during clearance of the operating room to ask to be relieved of their next surgery. They complained of feeling dizzy or just in need of a break. This often put the RN at the desk on the spot as she had difficulty in replacing personnel in the middle of the day. Requests were always granted and the employees would break for 15 minutes to an hour, and then ask to be reassigned.

After about two weeks of this, the problem was brought to Ms Barret's attention and she told the nurses to send all relief requests to her personally. Gary, a Certified OR Technician who had been with the hospital for two years, was the first to come to her with a request.

Barret: Gary, what seems to be the problem?

Gary: Well, Ms Barret, I just don't feel very good and I'd just like to lie down for a while.

Barret: If you don't feel good you'd better take the rest of the day off.

Gary: I don't think I need to do that.

Barret: Gary, can you tell me what's going on around here?

Author: Dr. Richard B. Chase, University of Arizona.

Gary: Well, most people just don't like to work for Dr. Collins. He's pretty slow and seems to be out of it most of the time.

Barret: Have you talked to Ms Johnston, the circulating RN about this?

Gary: I've talked to her and Dr. Martin. Ms Johnston gave me a hard time as usual. She says I am getting too big for my britches and if I don't like the situation I can ask for a transfer. Dr. Martin says that he's with Dr. Collins most of the time and he looks fine to him.

Barret: Thank you, Gary, this will be kept confidential.

Ms Barret went to ask Ms Johnston to come in to see her. After four days without seeing her, Ms Barret went to find her.

Barret: Ms Johnston I'd like to ask you some questions. I asked to see you four days ago.

Johnston: I have been trying to find time to see you.

Barret: I have some questions to ask you about Dr. Collins. Do you feel he's competent in surgery?

Johnston: As far as I know.

Barret: Have you ever seen him overly tired or not feeling well?

Johnston: Well, he did come in last week hung over but that was an emergency. He was on call and had just been to a cocktail party the night before. That's what those techs are complaining about, isn't it?

Barret: How many times has this happened?

Johnston: Well, I don't know. But if Dr. Collins has any problems, Dr. Martin is always there to take over. I always circulate for him and I know my business. The techs are complaining because they don't like to be told what to do. They just can't take orders and Dr. Collins gives it to them when they don't. They think just because they have been through a few cholesectomies they can start questioning the doctors and RNs' orders.

Barret: Thank you, Ms Johnston, that is all the questions I have.

Two days later Gary gave his notice and quit working three weeks later. Relief requests stopped coming in but two other OR techs gave their notice. Absenteeism rose.

Ms Barret scheduled Ms Johnston to work under another doctor and assigned Ms McEvers to circulate for Dr. Collins. Later that day Ms Barret went to visit the OR room where Dr. Collins was working.

There she found Dr. Collins, as well as the head anesthesiologist, with Dr. Martin assisting and Ms Johnston circulating as usual. She inquired into where Ms McEvers was as she was scheduled for this surgery. She was informed by Dr. Martin that this operation could involve complications and they needed an experienced circulator.

Barret:	Dr. Martin, you have every right to request certain circulators. I would appreciate some notice before you tamper with room scheduling.
Martin:	I am giving you notice that I would like to have Ms Johnston circulate for me and Dr. Collins.
Barret:	Due to some difficulties in scheduling, Ms McEvers will circulate for you for the rest of the week. After that if I have your request in writing I will have no choice but to assign Ms Johnston to you, scheduling problems or not.

Ms McEvers worked out the week under the two doctors and at the end of the week Ms Barret asked to see her in her office to inquire into Dr. Collins' competence.

McEvers:	I refuse to make waves here so I want this confidential. Dr. Collins often looks hung over in the morning when he does his patients pre-op. I wouldn't stand up in court and swear he had been drinking but he sometimes smells of alcohol.
Barret:	Have you ever inquired into his behavior?
McEvers:	I asked Dr. Martin about it. He always has some story of Dr. Collins just being called in or not feeling up to par.

Later that week, Ms Barret confronted Dr. Martin with this information.

Martin:	Those are pretty serious charges you're leveling at Dr Collins.
Barret:	No one is accusing anybody of anything at this point.
Martin:	What you're saying could have serious repercussions around here. If anyone got wind of this it could look very bad, not only for us but for the profession and the hospital.
Barret:	I am concerned here with the patient's safety.
Martin:	No one is in danger. Ms Johnston and I are always with him.
Barret:	That isn't the point.

Martin: Take it to the Chief of Staff, then, but let me give you
            some advice. You need some hard facts to make anything
            stick. You need the testimony of at least four nurses and
            under the circumstances that might be hard to get. You
            might like to know Dr. Collins is retiring next year.

Exhibit D-1 Partial Organization Chart of
                 Mountain View Hospital (185 activated beds)

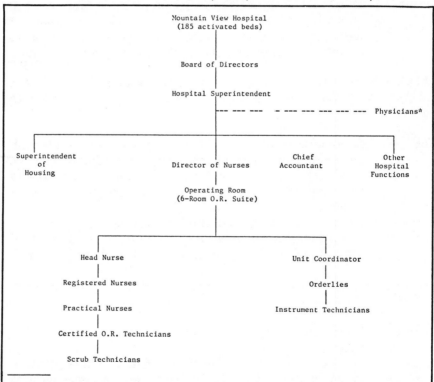

*Physicians are at this hospital to use the facilities and often are considered more
in staff than line positions. They are answerable to themselves and the chief of staff.

Exhibit D-2 Organization Chart of Physicians at
Mountain View Hospital

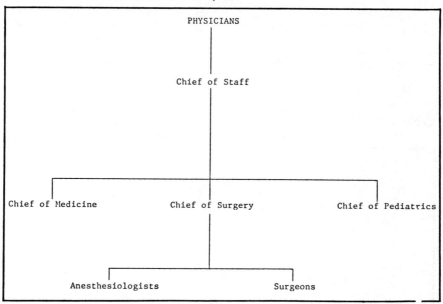

Appendix E

Davidson Psychiatric Hospital

Pre-1965 Treatment at Davidson

Until 1965, the Davidson Psychiatric Hospital operated in much the same fashion as its sister institutions. It catered to the mentally ill in a manner centered on the diadic relationship between the physician and patient. Psychiatrists prescribed treatment, usually in the form of drugs, shock therapy, and so forth. The nursing and technical support staff in the hospital assumed very limited therapeutic roles and were occupied primarily in providing the variety of maintenance functions necessary to keep the institution in good running order.

New Developments in the Field

Interesting trends had been developing in the way of new psychiatric regimens since the early 1950s. In England, Maxwell Jones was conducting fascinating and successful experiments with mental patients. Jones was troubled with the types of therapy that allowed patients to sit idly in their rooms for the greatest part of their stay in an institution. He began to consider the negative effects of isolation upon mental patients, and concluded that increased social interaction amongst patients and their environment would help give them a more stable and concrete perception of reality. Interaction between all forms of support staff and patients and amongst the patients

Author: Danny Miller under supervision of Sidney S. Lee, M.D., McGill University.

themselves was thus encouraged. Treatments that required private sessions between doctor and patient were still to be maintained where necessary but this was to be supplemented and to some extent supplanted by interaction between the individual and all potentially helpful members of the environment. This afforded a more or less constant form of therapy and the patient's time in the hospital could be more effectively spent.

The benefits of interactive or "milieu" therapy are not confined to the medical or psychiatric realm. The classical doctor-patient treatment requires large numbers of psychiatrists and as a result is quite costly. Interactive therapy, on the other hand, was found to be more economical since fewer doctors could deal with more patients. For example, even in the absence of psychiatrists, patients would be able to interact with nursing and technical staff and with their peers. According to Jones, such interaction could, to a certain extent at least, take the place of direct patient-psychiatrist contact.

Organization Structure and Administrative Climate

Davidson Psychiatric is run by a staff committee of doctors who are responsible to a board of governors. The latter are charged with approving major allocations of funds and key changes in medical policy. However, since the board is made up mainly of lay personnel, it tends as a rule to go along with the recommendations of the staff committee. Proposals from the committee are usually of such a complex or technical nature that it is difficult for the board to deal with them with any degree of rigour. Relationships between the two bodies are characterized by a minimum of conflict.

The staff committee is made up of 12 attending physicians, the director of nursing, and the director of technical and support staff. It is chaired by the current director of the hospital, Dr. Stephenson. The committee is the effective governing body. Issues are decided upon by vote (each member of the committee has one vote). For the most part, the decision-making climate is as democratic as can be, with all proposals being subject to the "push and haul of debate." Dr. Stephenson considers this type of structure to be vital to psychiatric hospitals attempting to keep up to date. He claims this is true:

> . . . not only because of the technical nature of the matters being discussed but more importantly because of considerations of philosophy and morality which are intertwined with many decisions. In addition, the uncertainty and

changeableness inherent in the field make it impossible for one man to play God.

Another member of the committee asserted that in psychiatry, "it is impossible to reduce things down to solely hard facts and rigid rules; this is not an exact science."

Dr. Stephenson pointed out that the people who sit on the committee are a very diverse lot of individuals. They are not "organization men" but professionals, each with his own set of interests and competences. The dispositions of these men are nourished not only by the hospital setting but also by their past jobs, educational experiences, professional affiliations, and a host of other factors that make for diversity in professional philosophies.

A polarization amongst proponents of two schools of psychiatric thought has developed at Davidson. The first group consists of psychiatrists who adhere to the traditional approach to therapy. Psychosis is viewed as a disease that must be fought by the physician. The doctor is the principal warrior in the battle and he will use drugs and other techniques at his disposal to combat the illness. The other group is made up of doctors who adopt the Jonesian "milieu" approach to psychiatry, believing that the entire environment of the patient, including his peers, should be enlisted in helping with therapy. These men prefer group-oriented forms of treatment that maximize the patient's exposure to interpersonal interaction.

Dr. Stephenson claims that far from reducing the disagreement amongst these groups, the forum provided by the monthly staff committee meetings actually intensifies antagonisms. What started as a difference of opinion has become a cause celebre that has resulted in increasingly frequent vituperative outbursts at the committee meetings. According to Dr. Stephenson, the morale in the hospital is as low as he has ever seen it and he wasn't very optimistic about the future. "We just can't seem to get a meeting of minds any more."

In order to gain an appreciation of how this situation developed, it is important to look at a sequence of past events that stem as far back as the early days of the hospital.

The Early Days: 1949–1960

Davidson Psychiatric was founded in 1949 as a private institution. Since inception, it enjoyed a fine reputation. Its success record, using medical (nonmilieu) forms of therapy, was very favourable compared to other institutions in its class. The director, Dr. Richards, who had chaired the hospital committee for many years, was widely respected for his extensive and innovative publications in the medical area of mental health. He was one of the few individuals in the medical community whose pioneering ideas and theories had successfully been put into practice. The hospital was well-staffed with a full complement of excellent psychiatrists. During the 1950s, the institution was known for the unusual amount of individual attention patients received from the medical staff. All patients were private—there were no public wards.

A Dynamic Environment: 1960-1965

During the late 1950s, society became increasingly aware of mental health problems. As a result, cases that would not previously have come to the attention of a psychiatric hospital were being increasingly referred to such institutions by other hospitals, social agencies, or schools. Davidson became flooded with private patients, and there was pressure on the hospital to also open its doors to public patients. It did this first in 1961 by opening a day clinic, and, soon thereafter, by allocating one ward to resident public patients. The hospital used only medical types of treatment, hence the professional psychiatric staff became hopelessly overburdened. A meeting of the committee was held to discuss the problem and, with only a very few exceptions, everyone agreed that technicians and nurses should begin to play a greater role in administering treatments. By 1963, such staff had taken over a good deal of the work hitherto performed only by psychiatrists.

Because there were inadequate resources available to train technical and nursing personnel for their responsibilities, all parties interviewed agreed that the quality of treatment declined very substantially during this period. Two staff members recruited in 1963 had enjoyed extensive experience in "more progressive" institutions in England and the United States and began to complain bitterly about the quality of treatment. They were well aware of the restricted financial resources available to the hospital but felt this was no excuse for the situation. Drs. Theoret and Gosselin, the new recruits, felt that Davidson could make much better use of its resources by commencing milieu therapy, at least in certain wards. Dr. Gosselin claimed that:

> ... the staff shortage and the belligerence of the old guard to new forms of treatment resulted in the type of environment where for at least 90 per cent of the day, the patient sits

> around and vegetates. The other 10 per cent of the time he is
> more often than not subject to treatment by amateurs.
> These people try hard—its just that they aren't sufficiently
> trained to work in a field that is 30 per cent a science and 70
> per cent an art

The suggestion was defeated after a very emotional discussion between Dr. Richards and his eminent colleagues, who were members of the conservative school of medical therapists, and Drs. Theoret and Gosselin. The former claimed that the staff shortage was insufficient cause to adopt an unproven mode of therapy and asserted that before this shortage they had enjoyed an excellent reputation using "more acceptable, tried-and-true" techniques. They agreed, however, that something had to be done to improve patient care and decided to look into a fund-raising campaign that would afford them the resources to hire more staff. Drs. Theoret and Gosselin claimed that the committee took a reactionary approach and thought that the "vested psychological interests on the part of the conservative staff to treatments which they themselves helped to develop" were responsible for the "stopgap" approach (fund raising) to solving the problem. They claimed that clinical-experimental evidence had proven beyond a doubt the superiority of milieu therapy.

By the end of 1964, it became clear that raising additional funds was indeed only a very short-term solution. The number of public patients had increased substantially, and two wards had to be devoted to them. The more economically lucrative private patients began to stabilize in number as older members of the staff retired. Funds gathered during 1964 were insufficient to substantially improve treatment.

A Change in Personnel: 1965–1968

In March 1965, Dr. Richards, aged 70, retired as director. He was replaced by Dr. Stephenson, 42, who was noted for his dynamism and progressiveness at a medium-sized British psychiatric hospital. The latter had worked on applying milieu therapy in England and had witnessed its success in a fairly broad variety of clinical situations. In July 1965 Dr. Stephenson hired three new staff members—each familiar with and a proponent of milieu therapy. Two of the new staff members served as replacements for two members of the retiring personnel. One came to fill a new position created as a result of increased demand and made possible by the fund-raising campaign initiated the year before.

During the committee meeting in September 1965, a real schism between pre-Stephenson staff and the "young turks" became apparent. At that meeting, Dr. Stephenson expressed the desire to "bolster the reputation of the Davidson to what it once was." Only one device to accomplish this was proposed: the implementation on a trial basis of milieu therapy.

Immediately, Dr. Silverton, a former close associate of Dr. Richards and an eminent member of the psychiatric community, took objection to Dr. Stephenson's approach. He claimed that:

1. the past "medically" oriented therapy was by no means outmoded and was still the most reliable approach;
2. the new unproven types of treatment were employed mainly by "faddist" institutions—usually located in Southern California, and
3. the new director had best turn his attention to getting more "medically competent" personnel.

Dr. Silverton's stance was heartily endorsed by six of his "pre-Stephenson" colleagues who believed that it was time to "put an end to this milieu nonsense once and for all."

Drs. Stephenson, Gosselin, and Theoret, as well as the three recently recruited staff members, were "visibly shaken" by the reaction of their colleagues and by the defeat of the motion to introduce milieu therapy. So were the directors of the nursing and technical staff who sat on the committee ex officio on matters directly relevant to the types of medical treatment employed. These individuals had been receiving an increasing number of complaints from their staffs who claimed they were party to a suboptimal effort. In fact, the interviewers learned that the nurses had all along been performing a simplified form of milieu therapy. They "cared for the patients throughout the day and coaxed them into performing some activity—any activity." They were distressed by patients who were "always alone, as though committed to solitary confinement as a form of punishment."

The meeting was adjourned by Dr. Stephenson, who asked all committee members to come to another gathering three weeks hence with concrete proposals regarding the improvement of treatment. At that meeting, Miss Verdone, the director of nursing, asked for a very small amount of money to begin conferences and classes to educate the nursing staff about better methods of patient care. When asked to explain the types of courses she had in mind, she mentioned that a number of them would be oriented to imparting methods of communicating better with patients in order to be more responsive to their needs. The committee agreed (almost unanimously) that this was a good idea and recommended that it be implemented as soon as possible.

Dr. Stephenson then directed the attention of the committee members to a recent statement from a well-respected American body of psychiatrists. It asserted that the refusal to implement milieu therapy is tantamount to malpractice. To bolster his arguments further, Dr. Stephenson and the milieu therapy advocates had prepared a report that outlined a gradual and voluntary scheme for the introduction of the new therapy in the public wards (most of the patients of the conventional treatment advocates were private). He mentioned that this was the only possible solution. Meetings with the board of governors, the government, and some professional fund raisers had disclosed that there was no way to obtain enough money to procure the personnel required to effectively pursue old methods of therapy. The suggestion that more psychiatrists be hired was thus shown to be inoperative. In closing, Dr. Stephenson mentioned that it should be the right of any doctor who so desires it to prevent his private patients from participating in group therapy.

After a good deal of debate, the proponents of conventional treatment approved, on a trial basis, the implementation of milieu therapy in the "outpatient" day hospital only. Because of the physical layout of the hospital, it was not possible to practice milieu therapy in certain specified areas and conventional treatment in others. The traditionalists insisted on retaining the right to withhold such therapy from their patients in cases where they should deem such action advisable. After the meeting Dr. Stephenson was satisfied that some ("but not nearly enough") progress had been made. The medical therapy advocates, still in the majority, believed and hoped that this would at last "get the adventurers off our backs."

More Trouble: 1970+

For more than three years, the hospital was run with milieu therapy being administered solely to outpatients. In February 1970, the technical and nursing staff went on strike. As a result, public patients in one ward were sent home. The nursing director summarized the reasons for the strike as follows:

> We (my staff) were doing all we could for the patients. Still, they were confined to restricted areas, usually their rooms, where they whiled away the time staring into space. What a pathetic waste of humanity. We're fully aware of the pro-

grams going on at this and other institutions where this type of thing is minimized. It's really begun to grate on our nerves. Something had to be done.

Dr. Stephenson called a committee meeting three days prior to the strike. He asked the nursing director to summarize the reasons for the strike. It was resolved that committee members should have a week to mull things over and return with some creative suggestions in time for the next meeting. This they did. Dr. Gosselin proposed that since the conventional treatment proponents had little concern for the public ward, they should allow the introduction of milieu therapy to take place at least in this area of the hospital. The vote was close, and Dr. Gosselin's recommendation was passed. Not, however, before the traditional therapy psychiatrists had had a chance to stipulate precisely their much anticipated proviso that:

> private doctors maintain the right to restrict their patients'
> group activities and deny them the chance to take part in
> milieu therapy.

The nurses and the technical staff returned to work. All the while, however, animosity was building between the opposite sides of what was becoming an ongoing dispute. The problems were far from over.

The Last Straw: 1970+

In May 1971, Dr. Berg joined the staff. He was another firm believer in milieu therapy. Drs. Theoret, Gosselin, Berg and the balance of the post-Stephenson staff were becoming increasingly incensed at the difficulty they encountered in employing milieu therapy in the public wards. Since they had to share wards with psychiatrists employing conventional therapy, their efforts at organizing patients into milieu groups or interaction cells were hindered. Individuals within groups tended to be scattered throughout the hospital's three wards.

During a September 1971 committee meeting, Dr. Silverton commented on the confused and "chaotic" nature of the wards. He mentioned that his patients were being bothered by the milieu therapy staff and that there was far too much activity going on around them. The milieu therapy staff retorted that the confused nature of the wards was due to the patients of "reactionaries" who, scattered throughout the wards, prevented the effective organization of interactive cells. Dr. Theoret claimed that this factor was the main obstacle to the effectiveness of the new treatment.

Two weeks after the meeting, Drs. Gosselin and Theoret, who had become very well-respected members of the psychiatric community, threatened to resign unless milieu therapy was instituted on a compulsory basis throughout the hospital. The old-school physicians responded to the joint letter of intended resignation (which was circulated to all staff members on the committee and to the board of governors) with: "It will be good to get things back to normal again after those guys leave." Dr. Stephenson was at a loss as to what to do.

Appendix F

Federal Medical Center

Dr. John Whitaker, administrator of the Federal Medical Center (FMC), got up from his desk and started for the door after reviewing the consultant's report (Exhibit F-1) on his management by objectives system. As he approached the door he noticed his wall chart displaying the medical center's overall objectives and he could not help but wonder if the MBO system was effective, if it served to integrate the organization, if it provided a mechanism for improved resource utilization, and if it improved motivation and morale. Foremost in his mind was the question: Is the system really worth all the effort and expense involved?

For example, specifically was it worthwhile for an institution such as Federal Medical Center. By way of background, FMC is located in Major City, Texas, which is a large metropolitan area. Within a twenty-five mile radius are many other health facilities, including three other government hospitals. The center itself consists of two major hospitals, a psychiatric facility, and some 60 additional buildings that house related health activities and supportive services. The center's capacity is approximately 750 beds and it provides a myriad of comprehensive health services to a population of 98,640. It also serves as a major referral center for many other federal health facilities and offers teaching programs in a wide variety of medical specialties and subspecialties.

The original hospital was dedicated in 1937. As the mission and eligible population of the hospital expanded, another major facility

---

Author: Bob M. Inge, DBA, Baylor University Medical Center, Dallas, Texas evolved. It was housed in a building originally constructed for other purposes. The physical limitations of these two structures and their separation necessitated a duplication of many of the major support services, i.e., laboratory and radiology. This physical separation and the necessary gerrymandering of clinics and offices coupled with the high degree of professional specialization has caused FMC to become a highly differentiated organization.

There is no anticipated building project that would eliminate the problems caused or accentuated by the facilities.

Dr. Whitaker reflected on how carefully he and the staff had weighed the potential advantages and disadvantages prior to implementing the MBO system. At that time, he recalled, the potential advantages had been: (1) improved communication, cooperation, and coordination; (2) better planning; (3) better resource management; (4) improved motivation and morale; (5) a method of objective performance evaluation; and, (6) a method of providing feedback to improve both individual and organizational performance.

The major potential disadvantages had been: (1) quality being sacrificed for quantity due to an emphasis on measurability; (2) short-range objectives adversely affecting long-range objectives; (3) objectives set too high or too low, resulting in frustration or a lack of challenge; and, (4) the activity of an MBO system becoming more important than what it was designed to accomplish. Dr. Whitaker now realized that the advice he had received had been logical and rational: (1) appoint a project coordinator; (2) attend a two-week university course on MBO so that they would be fully knowledgeable of its underlying philosophy as well as its technical aspects; and (3) conduct an MBO orientation for the key FMC staff members so they could be familiarized with the basic concepts and thus provide observations and opinions about its potential advantages or disadvantages in the center.

The one-day orientation for 26 key staff members had been challenging and his decision to announce his intent to implement MBO at the center at that time had been appropriate. He recalled that the vital decisions at this point had been to allow a period for the idea to germinate, and to contract the services of Dr. Becker, who had an extensive background as an MBO consultant to hospitals. Dr. Becker's interaction with the key staff members had satisfied many of their questions and had set the climate for a successful start.

Several members of the staff, including the medical director, voiced strong reservations about the practicality of implementing such a system at the center. Many others indicated either a favorable attitude or at least one of "it may be worth trying." Nevertheless, Dr.

Whitaker realized that the consultant's services during implementation had been valuable and had served to: (1) provide the necessary technical expertise, (2) facilitate the MBO process with the center's staff that consisted of many members who tend to evaluate individuals based upon credentials and recognized expertise, and (3) provide the catalyst for change necessary to overcome organizational inertia that frequently blocks the acceptance of new ideas and methods.

Dr. Whitaker smiled as he recalled the first implementation meeting. It had been an eye-opener. The objectives of the meeting had been to define the purposes and roles of FMC and its respective organizational elements. All present had been surprised at how difficult it was to agree upon the center's major purposes and the misconceptions on the part of individual staff members concerning the roles of the various departments. Dr. Whitaker remembered how several times one staff member would turn to another and say ..."I thought you were doing that" or ..."Are you doing that? We are doing that too."

The discussions on FMC's objectives for the coming year had been stormy, with several persons challenging the importance of certain suggested key result areas and the staff's ability to adequately establish measures for evaluating the objectives. The consultant, Dr. Becker, had served as a facilitator and challenged the staff with his own series of questions, thus causing them to rethink some of their initial statements. Dr. Whitaker had made it clear to the staff that while their input concerning center objectives was important—he would make the final decisions. He remembered Dr. Becker's explanation that..."the term 'democratic management' implies that issues are settled by a vote; whereas, 'participative management' implies that input is encouraged, but the final decision remains with the individual responsible for making such decisions."

There was never a question in his mind that FMC would endorse participative management. There was also no question in Dr. Whitaker's mind that the most difficult aspect of the previous year had been establishing the departmental objectives. Dr. Becker had worked long and hard with the department chiefs on the drafting and writing of objectives. These sessions had been argumentative at times— particularly the exchanges between the chief of the department of surgery and Dr. Becker. Dr. Whitaker recalled that the chief of surgery had said: "You know, Dr. Becker this is all a waste of time. I don't need to spend time trying to decide what my objectives are; my objective is simply to provide the best possible surgical services." Further conversation between the two had been as follows:

Dr. Becker: Do you provide the best possible surgical services?

C, D of S: What do you mean by that? You're damn right we do!

Dr. Becker: How do you know you provide the best possible services?

C, D of S: Oh, I see, here we go again—the old argument about measuring the quality of care.

Dr. Becker: It may be an old argument, but it is one that accrediting bodies and government agencies are demanding. Also, I thought you had a teaching program within your department; don't you have some objectives with regard to that program? I am not saying that initially we are going to be able to sit down and design objectives that, if accomplished, will guarantee that you achieve your broadly stated goal with regard to providing the best possible care or objectives that will ensure that you have the best possible teaching program. In addition, I am not saying that you are not accomplishing those goals, but I am asking: how do you know you are? For example, I notice here that one of your objectives is..."to reduce patient appointment waiting time." As a goal, it is consistent with the center's objectives, but what should appointment time be reduced to? What is the present appointment waiting time? Although you and your superior will negotiate the range of the reduction, you should develop a realistic draft objective prior to your negotiations. Let's assume that the average waiting time at present is 15 days. Would you say that perhaps the minimum acceptable time would be 14 days? And that, perhaps, the maximum you could expect would be 12 days with an average of 13 days? This is merely an example. I do not know what your objective should be. However, you should write an objective that provides a focus for action. It should be measurable, and it should be verifiable. For example, your objective might be to reach an average appointment waiting time of 12 to 14 days.

As he thought about all these events of the past year, Dr. Whitaker recalled that there had been many similar interactions with Dr. Becker and other members of the staff pertaining to the principles and technical aspects of MBO. Yet the underlying question was still unanswered: Does MBO help the manager in day-to-day operations, or merely impose a greater workload?

Exhibit F-1 Consultant Report on MBO

MEMORANDUM

TO: Dr. John Whitaker
Administrator, Federal Medical Center
Major City, Texas 78205

FROM: I. Associates
475 North Central Road
Major City, Texas 78205

RE: Report on Attitudinal Survey for the Management by
Objectives System in Federal Medical Center

The attached report is divided into the following sections for your
convenience:

I trust this report is in accordance with instructions and that it provides the desired information.

I. INTRODUCTION

Since the late 1960s, a plethora of literature has been published
regarding the implementation of a Management by Objectives (MBO)
program as a results-oriented technique for enhancing both organizational efficiency and effectiveness. The process of MBO necessitates
the identification of top-level organizational objectives (or goals)
followed by the formulation of supportive subordinate objectives, the
identification of areas of responsibility, and the delineation of expected
results. This process enhances the integration of subordinate effort
toward the attainment of the overall missions of the organization.

In light of the MBO program's emphasis on results, objectives are utilized by both the superior and the subordinate as operational guidelines and also as a mechanism for evaluating subordinate performance. Thus, information in the literature on MBO program evaluation is limited to measuring the user's progress toward attainment of the stated objectives. In fact, there is an abundance of information on evaluating the participant's contributions to the program and the program's contributions to the overall organization, but little, however, on evaluating the contributions of MBO to the individual manager. In other words, is MBO helping the manager in day-to-day operations or merely imposing a greater workload? Thus, the opportunity to evaluate the "MBO system" at the Federal Medical Center (FMC or the "center") permitted the consultants to evaluate such program contributions through a survey poll of the individual participants. Although most authorities discourage *formal* program appraisal until after several years of operation, the FMC-MBO system was evaluated after approximately one year.

To enhance the evaluation of the FMC-MBO system, the consultants developed a step-by-step model of the planned survey method (see Exhibit F-1). In step three of this model, an attitude survey was developed consisting of fifty scalar questions with available responses ranging from "strongly agree" to "strongly disagree," and nine narrative questions. The consultant's decision to retain participant anonymity was strongly endorsed by the administrator of the Federal Medical Center; however, this decision negated any follow-up or response clarification, and is now perceived to be a shortcoming of the survey.

Several assumptions were defined by the consultants with the concurrence of the administrator: (1) all survey participants had been involved with the MBO program at the department level since its inception in January 1976; (2) all participants were thoroughly instructed and involved in the implementation and application of the FMC-MBO system; (3) the "negotiation process" was conducted uniformly with each department chief; (4) the entire FMC population presently utilizing MBO could be surveyed; and (5) anonymity would encourage candor. Thus, those department chiefs assuming their positions after September 1976 were not polled by the survey. The survey distribution was controlled by the administrator and may have in fact included a few department chiefs arriving after the system's implementation.

It should be further noted that the positive support of the administrator fostered a unique 100 percent return of the questionnaire distributed throughout FMC. Therefore, the following evaluation was based on the total population, but due to the desire for anonymity, no

Exhibit F-1 MBO Evaluation Model

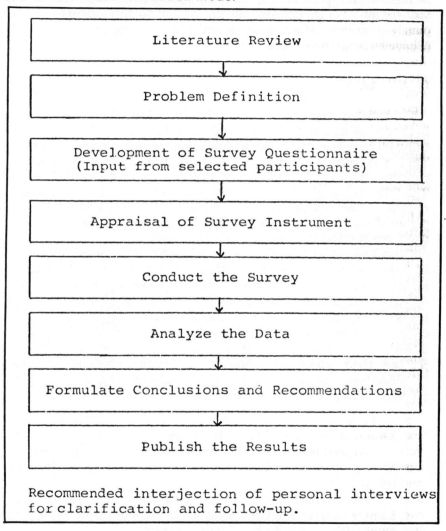

demographic breakout was included. Although the administrator completed the relevant portions of the survey, by his request, his responses were not included in this evaluation to prevent bias.

The responses were evaluated and tallied in an attempt to analyze the FMC-MBO system. Again, due to the small population size and time constraints, no demographic nor statistical breakouts were attempted. Although the consultants have drawn some conclusions and recommendations regarding the MBO system, it is important to note that the intent of the consultants' project was to investigate the participant's attitudes and perceptions, and *not* to judge the program or its implementation procedure.

II. EVALUATION

The MBO system at FMC was implemented to actuate improvement in the following areas: (1) communication, both vertically and horizontally; (2) resource utilization; and (3) employee morale and motivation. Thus, the consultants directed their attention toward these areas of concern, utilizing the participant's perception as an evaluation tool. The following evaluation also incorporated a general appraisal of the objectives themselves and the desirability of utilizing MBO results in personal performance appraisal. By design, many of the scalar questions are applicable to several areas of interest.

Communications. The first area analyzed by the consultants is that of improved communications within the organization. Theoretically, an MBO system should increase participant awareness, not only of the departmental and organizational objectives, but also of his specific areas of responsibility; such an increased awareness is indicative of enhanced communications. Thus, the consultants designed several questions to evaluate the respondents' knowledge of the center's objectives, their subordinates' knowledge of both center and departmental objectives, and the general, overall understanding of departmental responsibilities. These questions were:

1 I know the Center's MBO objectives.

      Agreed 94%   No opinion 3%   Disagreed 3%

2 Most persons in my Department know the Center's MBO objectives.

      Agreed 58%   No opinion 9%   Disagreed 33%

3 I know exactly what performance is expected from my Department with respect to the Center's objectives.

      Agreed 85%   No opinion 9%   Disagreed 6%

4 I am aware of the impact of my Department's objectives upon other elements of FMC and elsewhere.

      Agreed 82%   No opinion 6%   Disagreed 12%

5 My subordinates assisted me in developing my Department's objectives.

      Agreed 64%   No opinion 3%   Disagreed 33%

6 MBO results in greater understanding of the Department's efforts and objectives by most persons within my Department.
Agreed 70%   No opinion 9%   Disagreed 21%
7 MBO results in greater understanding of the Center's efforts and objectives by most persons within my Department.
Agreed 64%   No opinion 18%   Disagreed 18%

Although 94 percent of the department chiefs are knowledgeable of the center's objectives and 82 percent are cognizant of the relationship and impact of their departmental objectives on other organizational units, it is somewhat contradictory that over 15 percent indicated that they did not know exactly what was expected of their respective departments. Perhaps such a misunderstanding can be somewhat explained by the fact that 24 percent of the respondents indicated they had not received sufficient guidance in formulating their departmental objectives. Furthermore, despite the systematic explanation and introduction of the system at numerous staff meetings, it is considered relevant that 6 percent of the respondents do not know the center objectives and that 15 percent are unaware of center expectations. Evidently, communication problems still exist since those respondents claimed to have been present at the introductory meetings.

Another survey objective was to determine the respondents' perception of their subordinates' level of knowledge regarding center and departmental objectives. It must be reiterated that the MBO system at FMC has thus far been implemented only to the department chief level. Although the theory of MBO implementation requires negotiation with and input from lower organizational levels, a significant one-third of the respondents indicated that the center's objectives were *not* known to those at the departmental level. Moreover, on question six, 21 percent indicated subordinate lack of knowledge of departmental objectives. This is probably correlated to the fact that one-third of the department chiefs were not assisted by their subordinates in developing objectives.

A greater insight into the area of communication enhancement through MBO was extracted from the narrative portion of the questionnaire. A particular question on the survey asked what the respondents liked about the present MBO system, to which several respondents addressed the following items: (1) it enhances the definition of mission objectives; (2) it assists in both short- and long-range planning of activities; (3) it assists in decision making; (4) it focuses attention on problem areas; and (5) it facilitates communication with superiors. Although these responses do indicate improvement in overall communications, it is believed that there is still considerable room for progress by incorporating subordinate personnel in the planning and development process.

Resource Optimization. A second important objective of the FMC MBO system was to encourage the optimal utilization of resources. Theoretically, MBO should enhance resource utilization through: (1) mission clarification; (2) focused direction and effort; (3) reduced duplication of effort; (4) forced long-range planning; and (5) increased availability and use of feedback. The consultants utilized the following scalar questions to specifically address this area of concern:

1 My Department's objectives are congruent with the Center's objectives.

      Agreed 94%   No opinion 6%   Disagreed 0%

2 I can attain my Department's objectives with my present resources.

      Agreed 63%   No opinion 6%   Disagreed 31%

3 It is extremely difficult to get the additional resources required to accomplish my Department's objectives.

      Agreed 36%   No opinion 15%   Disagreed 49%

4 Attainment of my Department's MBO objectives is detrimental to the attainment of other aspects of the Department's mission.

      Agreed 21%   No opinion 3%   Disagreed 76%

5 The costs involved in implementing MBO (i.e., planning, reviewing, and evaluating management activities) far outweigh the benefits of attaining those objectives.

      Agreed 15%   No opinion 15%   Disagreed 70%

Although the consensus of respondents agreed that their departmental objectives were supportive of the center objectives and attainable with present resource allocation, it is significant that 39 percent either disagreed or indicated no opinion regarding the attainment of their objectives with present resources. Although only 15 percent of the respondents indicated that the costs involved in implementing MBO at FMC far outweigh the derived benefits, 24 percent indicated that the quality within their department would suffer by emphasizing the attainment of objectives. Further, 21 percent agreed that attainment of some departmental objectives would be detrimental to the attainment of other aspects of the department's mission.

A comment contained within the narrative sections noted that a lack of additional resources fostered the development of less ambitious objectives than would otherwise have occurred. Since 61 percent of the respondents agreed that departmental objectives could be obtained with present resources, this may be indicative of less than optimal objectives regarding allocation of resources. This was also endorsed by another comment noting that some objectives did not key-in on problem areas due to limited resources.

Therefore, it is concluded that while MBO may increase the present awareness of resource utilization, it has yet to enhance the *optimal* utilization of *all* resources available. MBO may, in fact, focus so intently on present resources that long-range optimal utilization is impaired.

Motivation and Morale. The third area appraised by the consultants was the effect of the FMC-MBO system on motivation and morale within the organization. Since MBO has been heralded to be an effective motivation tool, the consultants tried to obtain the participants' appraisal of their motivation to work towards the department and center objectives. The consultants were also interested in assessing the overall attitude of the participants toward the FMC-MBO system as an indicator of morale. The following questions approached this subject area:

1 MBO theory can be realistically applied to a medical center.
    Agreed 85%   No opinion 9%   Disagreed 6%
2 MBO is an effective method of managing my Department.
    Agreed 64%   No opinion 15%   Disagreed 21%
3 There is a lack of direction from above regarding the MBO system at FMC.
    Agreed 9%   No opinion 12%   Disagreed 79%
4 MBO is not an appropriate measure of the Center's effectiveness because of the diversification of specialties throughout the center.
    Agreed 33%   No opinion 9%   Disagreed 58%
5 MBO should be implemented within the middle and lower levels of an organization.
    Agreed 70%   No opinion 6%   Disagreed 24%
6 My superiors are sincerely committed to MBO.
    Agreed 72%   No opinion 19%   Disagreed 9%
7 The overall attitude towards MBO in my Department is good.
    Agreed 64%   No opinion 18%   Disagreed 18%
8 Morale within my Department has been improved by the implementation of MBO.
    Agreed 18%   No opinion 33%   Disagreed 49%

Although there was general agreement (85 percent) that MBO can be realistically applied to a medical center, question four inexplicably elicited a response of 33 percent indicating that MBO is *not* an appropriate measure of the center's effectiveness. Nevertheless, all the respondents noted that attainment of their own department's objectives was important, which is indicative of participant support and generally positive attitudes.

While 64 percent stated that overall attitude toward MBO within the department is good, it did not appreciably improve morale as evidenced by question eight in which 49 percent disagreed that departmental morale had improved. In the narrative portion, several additional comments were offered concerning motivation and morale, such as: (1) MBO motivates individual initiative; (2) it affords flexibility not normally found in the federal hospital setting; (3) it provides realistic feedback; and (4) it permits departmental input into center operations.

Although 83 percent of the narrative responses specifically recommend extending the MBO system down to the service and branch levels at FMC, 24 percent indicated on question five that the system should *not* be extended to the middle or lower levels of the organization. Perhaps such a discrepancy can be explained by one narrative response which recommended that the extension of the system should be contingent upon the results of the second year of use of MBO at FMC. Thus, many respondents held a "wait and see" attitude regarding system expansion.

Interestingly, 21 percent either agreed or held no opinion concerning question three; moreover, 28 percent either disagreed or did not indicate an opinion concerning the sincerity of superior commitment to the MBO system. Such responses are significant indicators of uncertainty and somewhat less than optimum morale.

Perceived Effectiveness of the MBO System. Since MBO systems are designed to facilitate the development of specific objectives, and to promote the direction of effort towards attaining them, several questions were included in the questionnaire to evaluate the usefulness and effectiveness of FMC's MBO system. These questions were:

1 I was instrumental in the formulation of my Department's objectives.

    Agreed 91%   No opinion 3%   Disagreed 6%

2 Some previously set objectives now appear unlikely to be achieved for reasons beyond my control.

    Agreed 42%   No opinion 16%   Disagreed 42%

3 MBO is not an appropriate measure of the Center's effectiveness because of the diversification of specialties throughout the center.

    Agreed 33%   No opinion 9%   Disagreed 58%

4 Narrative Question. Once the MBO objectives had been negotiated for your department, was implementing action to attain the objectives simple or difficult? What did you have to do?
Simple 59%   Difficult 41%
Some reasons cited for difficulty:
   a. Minimum commitment by departmental staff
   b. Monitoring is necessary
   c. Lack of control over personnel turnover
   d. Additional resources required
   e. Difficulty in developing reporting system within a department
   f. Orientation/involvement of departmental personnel was difficult
   g. No supportive attitude on part of departmental staff

The majority of participants (91 percent) stated that they were instrumental in developing their departmental objectives, and that the objectives are generally measurable and meaningful. One-third of the respondents also stated that MBO is *not* an appropriate measure of the center's effectiveness. Twenty-four percent of the respondents agreed that they cannot attain some of the departmental objectives within the specified time frame. Most notable is the equal difference of opinion (42 percent agreed and disagreed) on the unlikelihood of achieving their objectives for reasons beyond their control.

The consultants believe that the high number of negative responses to these questions indicate the need for careful reexamination of the individual center and the departmental objectives, policies, procedure, and allocation of resources. The department chiefs should also evaluate their priorities and commitment to the objectives. In the future, routine review and evaluation by the superior and the subordinate will better ensure the achievement of the organization's objectives.

A General Appraisal of the Objectives. Although the first set of objectives and performance goals developed under an MBO system are generally based on guesswork and are often inaccurate, the consultants were nonetheless interested in assessing the effectiveness of the 1976 FMC departmental objectives. Another consultant, Dr. Becker, was employed as FMC's MBO consultant and advisor during the implementation process. Four of his criteria were applied to this evaluation. Dr. Becker stressed that the objectives should be: (1) measurable, (2) challenging (to enhance motivation), (3) recorded in writing and frequently consulted, and (4) attainable (within the manager's control).

Only one question specifically addressed the quantification of the established objectives:

1 The negotiating sessions with my superior(s) resulted in measurable objectives.
      Agreed 88%   No opinion 12%   Disagreed 0%

Interestingly, one respondent complained of having to divert significant resources in order to measure progress toward departmental objectives; unfortunately, however, the opportunity for clarification was not afforded by this survey.

Three questions addressed the second criterion—the challenge presented to the participants by the departmental objectives:

2 The MBO format at FMC discourages initiative of new management ideas.
      Agreed 6%   No opinion 12%   Disagreed 82%
3 My Department's MBO objectives are easily attainable.
      Agreed 15%   No opinion 6%   Disagreed 79%
4 My Department's MBO objectives are challenging.
      Agreed 85%   No opinion 9%   Disagreed 6%

Additionally, it was commented in the narrative that MBO is a good "brainstorming and planning exercise."

The third criterion noted was partly met by the published center and departmental objectives distributed to the department chiefs Response to a narrative question indicated that the participants consulted the published objectives on a widely ranging basis; such a range varied from daily to quarterly, but the majority (61 percent) indicated monthly references and evaluations to be sufficient. Approximately one-half of the respondents further indicated that the department chief should review interim progress with his superior on a quarterly basis.

The fourth criterion, that of affording the responsible manager reasonable control over the attainment of his own objectives, was indirectly evaluated through several questions:

5 I was instrumental in the formulation of my Department's objectives.
      Agreed 91%   No opinion 3%   Disagreed 6%
6 I can attain my Department's objectives with my present resources.
      Agreed 63%   No opinion 6%   Disagreed 31%
7 I have the authority to renegotiate my Department's objectives at any time.
      Agreed 76%   No opinion 9%   Disagreed 15%

8 Some previously set objectives now appear unlikely to be achieved for reasons beyond my control.

    Agreed 42%   No opinion 14%   Disagreed 42%

9 Attainment of some of my Department's objectives within the specified time frame is not realistic.

    Agreed 24%   No opinion 3%   Disagreed 73%

Consideration of the responses to questions 5 and 7 indicates that participants do not have reasonable control over the formulation of their objectives. However, it is significant that only 63 percent believed that those objectives were attainable with present resources. Thus, it is not surprising that the respondents were equally divided on question 8. It is, therefore, apparent that while managers are afforded the predominant input into the formulation of departmental objectives, they have relatively little control over the resources necessary to attain them.

Performance Appraisals and Progress Evaluations. The final areas of interest to the consultants were the frequency of interim progress evaluations and the use of such evaluations in performance appraisals. A requirement of any MBO system is the need to periodically and routinely evaluate the organizational objectives and subordinate progress toward their attainment. Thus, MBO lends itself to evaluating each individual member of the organization through the assessment of his progress toward attaining his specific objectives. The consultants were, therefore, interested in the frequency of interim progress evaluations between the respondents and their supervisor, and the respondents' attitudes toward this method of performance appraisal. The following questions were utilized:

1 Interim progress towards the attainment of my Department's MBO objectives is evaluated with my superior on a regularly scheduled basis.

    Agreed 58%   No opinion 3%   Disagreed 39%

2 My performance rating *should be* influenced by my performance towards attainment of my Department's objectives.

    Agreed 64%   No opinion 12%   Disagreed 24%

3 My performance rating *will be* influenced by my performance towards attainment of my Department's objectives.

    Agreed 39%   No opinion 39%   Disagreed 22%

4 Attainment of the MBO objectives is primarily the responsibility of the operating activity chief and not his/her superior with whom the objectives were negotiated.

    Agreed 61%   No opinion 6%   Disagreed 33%

Narrative Questions:

5 How often did you expect your Department's MBO objectives to be reviewed and evaluated with your superior?

Monthly	19%
Quarterly	47%
Semi-annually	16%
Annually	3%
As needed	6%
Unknown	9%

6 How frequently do you think that your Department's MBO objectives should be reviewed and evaluated with your superior?

Daily	3%
Monthly	12%
Quarterly	55%
Four Months	6%
Semi-annually	21%
Never	3%

Although the objectives themselves were previously noted to be challenging and the attainment of these objectives important to *all* respondents, it is noteworthy that only 64 percent indicated that progress toward objective attainment should influence performance ratings. Such a response is not surprising, in light of the previously discussed uncertainties and resource limitations. Perhaps, as one respondent noted, MBO should be only one of many factors incorporated into the performance appraisal and progress report.

Digressing into the area of routing and periodic interim progress review, the consultants noted that only 58 percent of the respondents indicated that such evaluations are accomplished on a regularly scheduled basis. Such a differing opinion is further noted in questions five and six in which participants indicated a wide range of frequencies, both expected and recommended, for interim progress review with their superiors.

Since periodic evaluations keep managers informed of their department's progress, and may indicate the need for the redirection of effort or reallocation of resources, it is important to formalize a policy of routine and periodic interim progress review. Furthermore, such a periodic evaluation would facilitate the addition, modification, or elimination of objectives within the framework of a changing institution or environment.

Although the MBO system at FMC is in its late stages of formative development, it has apparently not yet scheduled regular, routine evaluation policies. Such policies should be established as soon as feasible to facilitate and precipitate the formal review and analysis so important to sustain a viable MBO system. Each department chief should then know when and what is expected regarding objectives review and whether or not the system would influence performance ratings.

III. CONCLUSIONS AND RECOMMENDATIONS

Based on the general nature of the survey and the methodology utilized, it would be presumptuous of the consultants to expound definitive findings and conclusions. It should be noted, however, that the overall attitude toward the FMC MBO system is remarkably good. Such a finding is especially important since most authorities refer to this period in the system's life as "the depression stage." Usually, early enthusiasm and support decline after the first year of operations; thus, it is highly significant that participants' attitudes were generally quite positive. Moreover, a majority of the respondents indicated that the MBO system should be extended to lower levels in the organization. Such a response, however, was predicated on "successful" operations at the present levels during the second year.

Probably the most frequently voiced criticism of the FMC MBO system concerns the lengthy time requirements and the difficulty of quantifying quality of patient care. However, such criticisms were strongly countered by the indicated positive aspects of the system: (1) improved communications; (2) delineation of individual responsibilities; (3) focused direction; (4) forced long-term planning; (5) enhanced flexibility and feedback mechanisms; and, (6) mission clarification.

The MBO system at FMC appears to be generally well accepted and supported by the principal center staff. Most of those favorable respondents further indicated that the administrator has been the strong, guiding force of the system, without whom the MBO system would probably not have progressed and succeeded.

It should again be emphasized that the consultants have evaluated only the perceived contributions and problem areas of the FMC MBO system, as interpreted and expressed by the participants. Based on these perceptions, the consultants have evaluated the responses and recommendations and found that although the department chiefs are generally knowledgeable of both the center's objectives and their departmental responsibilities, the elements which support the department itself are generally unfamiliar with the system. Because of this it is recommended that both service and branch levels be exposed to the program to enhance support of departmental objectives and to facilitate the eventual use of MBO in the lower levels of the organization.

A second proposed recommendation would rectify the uncertainty of some respondents regarding "center level" support and sincerity. This recommendation is that more open and positive support is needed to deter static or regressive progress by the departments. Additionally, such support may rectify another problem area—the divergency of responses and expectations regarding the interim progress evaluation. The format and frequency of such review sessions should be established. Additionally, as several respondents suggested, the participants could be afforded the opportunity, on a quarterly basis, to brief the administrator on departmental progress toward objective attainment.

A third recommendation is offered in light of those respondents who, due to limited resources, downgraded the quality of their objectives. Although a majority of the respondents claimed to have established quality objectives, it may be of benefit to reevaluate or renegotiate the present departmental objectives. Such a process should attempt to establish not only realistic and attainable objectives, but also objectives to which resources, efforts, and spirits can be earnestly committed.

The preceding recommendations can be combined to incorporate the consultants' fourth suggestion, that of "selling" the concept to the participants. As one respondent indicated, there is presently an overemphasis on internalizing the *process* rather than the *concept* of MBO at FMC; this often results in frustration when attempts are made to develop "top level" support, open communication channels, regularly reviewed objectives, and the reevaluation of present objectives will possibly "win over" the minority of respondents who indicated that the MBO system was not effective or useful.

Index

About the Author

Dr. Steven H. Appelbaum is Associate Professor of Management, Faculty of Commerce and Administration, Concordia University, Montreal, Canada. His research and teaching focus on human resource management, organizational development, and stress management.

He is an active management-organizational consultant who develops and conducts varied research studies and programs dealing with leadership-power-conflict, management by objectives, team building, and organizational development. Clients in the last eight years include The Graduate Hospital, Children's Hospital of Philadelphia, Union Carbide Inc., Rhone-Poulenc Inc., Government of Delaware County, Pa., and others.

He has written more than 50 publications that have appeared in *The University of Michigan Business Review, Business and Society, Academy of Management Proceedings, The Personnel Administrator, Group Process, Akron Business and Economic Review, American Management Association,* and *Health Care Management Review.* He is currently coauthoring two books—*Effective Time Management for Health Care Professionals* and *Hospital Survival: Strategies for Success*—both for Aspen Systems Corporation. He is an active member of the American Psychological Association, the Academy of Management, and the American Society for Personnel Administration. He also is a reviewer for *The Personnel Administrator.*

Dr. Appelbaum previously served as Manager of Personnel Services for TRW Inc., Manager of Organizational Development for Union Carbide Inc., and Assistant Professor of Behavioral Sciences at the Graduate School of Pace University in New York City. He also served as Director of the Master of Business Administration program in the Graduate School.

He received his B.S. in business administration from Temple University and his M.A. in social sciences from St. Joseph's University, both in Philadelphia. He was awarded the Ph.D. by the University of Ottawa (Canada) in 1972. Dr. Appelbaum currently resides in Ottawa, Canada.